Foundations of PEAR

Rapid PHP Development

Nathan A. Good and Allan Kent

Foundations of PEAR: Rapid PHP Development

Copyright © 2006 by Nathan A. Good and Allan Kent

ISBN-13 (pbk): 978-1-59059-739-2

ISBN-10 (pbk): 1-59059-739-7

Printed and bound in the United States of America 9 8 7 6 5 4 3 2 1

Lead Editor: Matt Wade
Technical Reviewer: Ligaya Turmelle
Editorial Board: Steve Anglin, Ewan Buckingham, Gary Cornell, Jason Gilmore, Jonathan Gennick,
    Jonathan Hassell, James Huddleston, Chris Mills, Matthew Moodie, Dominic Shakeshaft, Jim Sumser,
    Keir Thomas, Matt Wade
Project Manager: Denise Santoro Lincoln
Copy Edit Manager: Nicole Flores
Copy Editor: Susannah Davidson Pfalzer
Assistant Production Director: Kari Brooks-Copony
Production Editor: Kelly Winquist
Compositor: Susan Glinert
Proofreader: Lori Bring
Indexer: John Collin
Cover Designer: Kurt Krames
Manufacturing Director: Tom Debolski

Distributed to the book trade worldwide by Springer-Verlag New York, Inc., 233 Spring Street, 6th Floor, New York, NY 10013. Phone 1-800-SPRINGER, fax 201-348-4505, e-mail orders-ny@springer-sbm.com, or visit http://www.springeronline.com.

For information on translations, please contact Apress directly at 2560 Ninth Street, Suite 219, Berkeley, CA 94710. Phone 510-549-5930, fax 510-549-5939, e-mail info@apress.com, or visit http://www.apress.com.

The source code for this book is available to readers at http://www.apress.com in the Source Code/Download section.

Nathan would like to dedicate this book to his grandfather, Luther Munsinger, who passed away while the book was being written. Luther's amazing work ethic, tenderness, and character will inspire Nathan and his family for lifetimes to come. I love you, Grandpa, so much.

Contents

Introduction

Authentication

Utilities and Tools

HTML

Images and Text

Database

Files and Formats

HTTP

XML

Mail

About the Authors

■**NATHAN A. GOOD** lives in the Twin Cities area in Minnesota. Professionally, he does software development, software architecture, and systems administration for a variety of companies and clients. When he's not writing software, Nathan enjoys building PCs and servers, reading about and working with new technologies, and trying to get all his friends to make the move to open-source software. When he's not at a computer, he spends time with his family, with his church, at the movies, and tries to spend the three weeks of summer in Minnesota kayaking and biking. In June 2006 he biked the MS 150 from near Duluth, Minnesota to the Twin Cities area and has promised he'll do it again.

He's written or cowritten five books, including *Professional Red Hat Enterprise Linux 3* (Wrox, 2004), *Regular Expression Recipes: A Problem-Solution Approach* (Apress, 2005), *Regular Expressions for Windows Developers: A Problem-Solution Approach* (Apress, 2005), and *PHP 5 Recipes: A Problem-Solution Approach* (Apress, 2005).

Nathan can be reached by e-mail at mail@nathanagood.com.

■**ALLAN KENT** is a born and bred South African and still lives and works in Cape Town. He has been programming in various languages and on diverse platforms for more than 20 years. He's currently the head of technology at Saatchi & Saatchi Cape Town.

About the Technical Reviewer

 **LIGAYA TURMELLE** is a full-time goddess, occasional PHP programmer, and obsessive world traveler. She lives in Guam with her husband and daughter and their two Belgian Malinois. Actively involved with the PHP community as a founding principal of phpwomen.org, administrator at codewalkers.com, roving reporter for the Developer Zone on Zend.com, PHP blogger, and long-time busy body of #phpc on freenode, she hopes one day to actually meet the people she talks to. Ligaya Turmelle is a Zend Certified Engineer and MySQL Core certified. When not sitting at her computer staring at the screen, Ligaya can usually be found playing golf, scuba diving, snorkeling, kayaking, hiking, or just out playing with the dogs all over Guam.

Acknowledgments

I'd first like to thank God for giving me the passion for learning, writing, and teaching others. I'd also like to thank my wonderful and supportive wife and kids for being patient and sacrificing while I was working on his book.

I'd also like to thank the team at Apress that worked so hard to keep this book on schedule, despite my tardiness and underestimation of timelines (I am a developer, after all). Lastly, I'd like to thank my coauthor, Allan Kent, for helping with this project.

Nathan A. Good

Preface

This book is about PEAR. It's not about the fruit, although it's pronounced the same, so you don't have to say "P-E-A-R" like you would spell out "C-A-K-E" or "P-I-E" in front of a small child with whom you don't intend on sharing. Like anything else in computer languages and computers, PEAR is an acronym that stands for something, which in this case is "PHP Extension and Application Repository."

PEAR is a collection of packages written in PHP. Each package has specific functionality that can be incorporated into your existing code, a benefit that makes it much less time consuming to build a site or application from scratch. If you've done web application development in other languages, such as ASP.NET or Perl CGI, think of PEAR packages as being similar to "application blocks" or Perl modules.

Who This Book Is For

It probably goes without saying that if you're reading a book on extensions and applications built in the PHP programming language that you should already be a PHP developer.

Perhaps if you're curious about PEAR and just glancing at this to see if it's something you'd have an interest in, but you don't know a lick of PHP, feel free to pick up a copy of this book. However, also look nearby for a copy of *Beginning PHP and MySQL 5: From Novice to Professional, Second Edition* by W. Jason Gilmore (Apress, 2006) to start out with, and maybe a copy of *PHP 5 Recipes: A Problem-Solution Approach* by Lee Babin, et al (Apress, 2005).

You'll benefit most from this book, though, if you already have a solid foundation in PHP 5, because this book will assume that you're already familiar with the syntax, variables, and behaviors of the language. Explanations in this book will be focused on the packages and not on general characteristics of PHP 5.

Note Most of the PEAR repository is written in code that will work fine with PHP 4. Some of the packages in this book, such as PHPUnit2, require PHP 5, leaving the previous package PHPUnit still intact for use with PHP 4.

How This Book Is Structured

Because the purpose of this book is to serve as a reference on several PEAR packages, the book is split up into sections that contain similar packages. Each package is introduced and described in the introductory section. The "Common Uses" and "Related Packages" sections discuss where you can best fit the package in your application and where you can find similar packages.

The "Dependencies" and "API" sections detail what you need to install and use the package. Finally, each package contains a few short but complete examples that show you the package in action.

In the first section of this book, you'll see packages that deal with authentication.

In the second section, you'll read about utilities and tools. The third section of this book covers numbers and dates.

The fourth section gets into HTML forms. The fifth section covers images and text.

The sixth section goes into databases. The seventh section discusses files and formats. The eighth section talks about using HTTP packages.

The ninth section talks about XML. The tenth section goes into mail.

Finally, the last three sections of this book cover code projects that put various packages together. We hope these projects are exciting for you as you see how the packages can be used to build "real" applications. We've modeled these projects after ones that we've either built personally or helped other people build in the recent past.

Conventions Used in This Book

PHP works on many platforms: Unix, Linux, *BSD, Mac OS X, and Microsoft Windows. To avoid being redundant, the command line samples you'll see in this book have the customary bash-style $ prompt, like this:

```
$ echo "Hello"
```

We won't list both Unix and Windows commands unless they're vastly different for some reason. If you're a Windows user, you'll simply replace $ with C:\>.

PEAR package names are in normal text; for example, MyPackage. Names of classes included in the packages are printed like this: MyClass. Method (or function) names are listed in the same font as classes, but have trailing () to set them off, such as myMethod(). Code listings, such as the contents of sample PHP, configuration, or XML files are printed like this:

```
<?php echo "Code Sample"; ?>
```

Instead of showing screenshots of how your browser will render the HTML, in cases where the HTML is relevant we include it, or any other results of running a script, like this:

```
Script results here
```

Important notes and hints are printed like this:

■**Note** PEAR is cool.

Prerequisites

To be able to apply what you're reading in this book right away, you need to have PHP 5 installed on a system, and you need access to a web server that serves the pages you'll build in the examples. If you're not sure what version of PHP your web server supports, put the following line into a file called info.php:

```php
<?php phpinfo(); ?>
```

Put the info.php file into a folder accessible by your web server, and open a browser to the appropriate URL. When you hit this page, PHP will print tables out that give you various information about the version of PHP that's installed, including support for MySQL, XML, the PHP variables, and a plethora of other information. If PHP isn't even installed, or there's something wrong with the installation, you'll see nothing but the code that you typed into the file.

You'll probably need a good text editor or an IDE to edit the code quickly. Although features such as syntax highlighting aren't exactly required for working with PHP, these features often help to make the files more understandable.

One of the author's favorite editors for writing any code is Vim, which he used to write nearly all the code samples for this and previous books. However, there are many different editors available with which you can create and edit PHP files, such as Macromedia's (now Adobe) Dreamweaver. PHPEclipse, a plug-in for Eclipse that allows you to edit and view PHP files, is a good choice if you want more than a simple text editor but don't have the need to install Dreamweaver.

Downloading the Code

The code that you see in this book is available for free in the Source Code/Download area of the Apress website at http://www.apress.com. Just look for this book on the site. The code is packed in a ZIP file, so you'll need an application to extract it properly. If you're using Microsoft Windows XP Home or Professional, that capability is already built into the OS. If you're using a combination of Linux and Mac OS X like one of the authors, you can use the unzip command or the built-in Archive utility, respectively.

Using the Examples in This Book

Many of the examples in this book can be put into a script and executed using the PHP 5 command line interpreter, php. If you've downloaded the code from the Apress site, you'll notice that the PHP files are organized by the section name, then by the package name in lowercase, followed by _exN, where N is the number of the example for that package. For instance, in the 03_Utilities_and_Tools directory, config_ex01.php is the first example shown in the book for the Config package. You can run that sample on the command line by typing the following:

```
$ cd path/to/03_Utilities_and_Tools
$ php config_ex01.php
```

The other examples in this book are files that should be accessed from your web browser just like any static HTML page. To run those examples, you have to place them in a directory that's accessible by your web server, and ensure that your web server is set up to execute PHP files.

Support

If you run into problems using PEAR, there are places you can go for help. One is the general mailing list, which is an e-mail distribution list for asking questions regarding the installation of PEAR or using one of the PEAR packages. You can reach this list at pear-general@lists. php.net. Please take care not to send generic PHP questions to this list, as its purpose is to support PEAR.

   If you're interested in becoming a part of PEAR, by either developing or maintaining a package, doing QA, or writing documentation, you can volunteer at pear-dev@lists.php.net, pear-qa@lists.php.net, or pear-doc@lists.php.net, respectively.

Introduction

This first chapter of the book discusses how to install PEAR and how to use the PEAR package manager. It also discusses how to configure PEAR. If you've already been using the PEAR package manager and some PEAR packages, feel free to skip the first part of this chapter or lightly skim it for review. The second part of this chapter discusses PEAR_Error, a package that you'll run into and use when you're adding exception handling to your application using PEAR packages.

Installing PEAR

Fortunately, if you're using PHP 5 in a Unix or Linux environment, the PEAR package manager is automatically installed as part of PHP—that is, unless you've specifically compiled PHP with the --without-pear option. If you compiled PHP one night at three in the morning while writing your own port of Scorched Earth in assembler in a different window, and can't remember what configuration options you used, check the info.php file that's mentioned in the "Prerequisites" section.

As long as the PHP bin directory is part of your path, you can access the package manager in a Unix or Linux environment by typing pear at the command line.

Installing the PEAR package manager on Windows requires a few more manual steps. First, you must have installed PHP from the ZIP package and *not* from the installer package (a Windows MSI). The Windows installer doesn't include the go-pear.bat script referenced here to begin the installation of PEAR.

After extracting the PHP from the ZIP archive, the first step is to execute the go-pear.bat file that's located in the directory PHP is installed in. Once you have the PATH variable set correctly, you can access the package manager from the command line by typing pear.

```
> cd \PHP
> go-pear.bat
```

When you initiate the go-pear.bat script from the command line, it will start by prompting you:

```
Are you installing a system-wide PEAR or a local copy?
(system|local) [system] :
```

At this prompt, just hit Enter to continue, unless you need to change system to local. You'll then be confronted with the following:

Below is a suggested file layout for your new PEAR installation. To
change individual locations, type the number in front of the
directory. Type 'all' to change all of them or simply press Enter to
accept these locations.

```
1. Installation base ($prefix)    : C:\php
2. Binaries directory             : C:\php
3. PHP code directory ($php_dir) : C:\php\pear
4. Documentation directory        : C:\php\pear\docs
5. Data directory                 : C:\php\pear\data
6. Tests directory                : C:\php\pear\tests
7. Name of configuration file     : C:\WINNT\pear.ini
8. Path to CLI php.exe             : C:\php\.
```

1-8, 'all' or Enter to continue:

At this point, you can change one or more of the directories to make sure they're correct. You might consider leaving everything as the default, as long as the PHP directory is set up correctly. Once you're finished, the PEAR setup will continue.

You might be asked to modify the include_path setting in your php.ini file—make sure that the include_path directive includes the directory where PEAR is installed. After you've made this change, the go-pear.bat script will finish and you can access the package manager by typing pear at the Windows command prompt.

Configuring PEAR

You can use configuration commands with the pear command to set up channels, directories, and proxy settings, to name a few options. To view your current configuration settings, type the following:

```
$ pear config-show
```

The first few lines of the results will look something like this:

```
Configuration (channel pear.php.net):
=====================================
Auto-discover new Channels    auto_discover    <not set>
Default Channel               default_channel  pear.php.net
HTTP Proxy Server Address     http_proxy       <not set>
...
```

The first column contains the description of the configuration key, the second column is the key itself, and the last column contains the value. If you'd like more information about any of the keys, just pass the name of the key along with the config-help command, like this:

```
$ pear config-help http_proxy
```

The output of this command will look something like this:

```
Config help for http_proxy
===========================
Name        Type    Description
http_proxy  string  HTTP proxy (host:port) to use when
                    downloading packages
```

To display and set a single configuration value, use the config-get and config-set commands, respectively. The next few examples show you how to display, set, and redisplay a setting that could be useful for you if you begin to do advanced work with the pear command:

```
$ pear config-help verbose
```

This displays the help for the verbose key, which is used to set the level of debugging output:

```
Config help for verbose
========================
Name     Type     Description
verbose  integer  verbosity level
                  0: really quiet
                  1: somewhat quiet
                  2: verbose
                  3: debug
```

Using the config-get command, you can display the current value of the verbose setting by typing the following at the command prompt:

```
$ pear config-get verbose
```

The current level will be displayed:

```
1
```

Now, set the verbose configuration setting by using the config-set command, passing the value as the last parameter. The command will look like this, bumping up the verbose setting to "debug":

```
$ pear config-set verbose 3
```

```
config-set succeeded
```

Just to show that you aren't being ignored, use the config-get command again to see how the verbose configuration setting has been updated:

```
$ pear config-get verbose
```

3

The location of the configuration file used by PEAR is listed at the end of the output of the config-show command. Be forewarned—the file is pretty obscure to be editing by hand and we don't recommend it. If your configuration file becomes corrupt for some reason, you can create a new default one by using the config-create command:

```
$ pear config-create /usr/local/php5 pear.conf
```

You can use the -w option for Windows installations. As mentioned in the help for this command, it's also useful when creating configuration files for remote PEAR installations.

For the most part, after installation you won't need to adjust the PEAR configuration often.

Using the PEAR Package Manager

The PEAR package manager allows you to install packages without having to worry about installing dependencies, placing files in particular locations, or tracking them down. You can use a number of commands, although if you're not building your own packages you won't use many of them.

In the table here we've listed the commands that will be covered in this book to install packages. We've also listed a couple of the commands that can be used to list available packages and update your currently installed ones.

Pear commands

Command	Description
download	This command allows you to download a package without installing it. You might have used similar commands when banished to a dial-up when the download might take a long time.
info	This command prints information about the specified package.
install	This command downloads the package and puts it onto your system.
list	This command lists all the installed packages on your system.
list-all	This command lists all the available packages. You can specify a channel with the --channel= option.
package-dependencies	This command lists all the dependencies that the given package has.
run-scripts	Some packages include scripts that can be run after they've been installed; this command executes those scripts.
search	This command allows you to search for a particular package given keywords.

Pear commands

Command	Description
uninstall	This command allows you to remove a package from the system once it's installed.
upgrade	This command allows you to bring a specific package up to the latest version of the package.
upgrade-all	This command allows you to bring all your installed packages up to the latest version of the packages.

Finding a Package

If you're looking for a PEAR package to install, you have a couple different ways to find it. You can use the list-all command to get a comprehensive list of packages and scan through the list, or you can pipe the output to another command such as grep, or you can use the search command to find matching packages. The example here shows how to search for services:

```
$ pear search "Services"
```

```
========================================
Package            Stable/(Latest)        Local
Services_Amazon    -n/a-/(0.4.0 beta)             Provides access to ➥
                                                  Amazon's retail and associate➥
                                                  web services

Services_Delicious -n/a-/(0.2.0beta beta)         Client for the del.icio.us ➥
                                                  web service.

Services_DynDNS    -n/a-/(0.3.1 alpha)            Provides access to the ➥
                                                  DynDNS web service

Services_Ebay      -n/a-/(0.12.0 alpha)           Interface to eBay's XML-API.
Services_ExchangeRates -n/a-/(0.5.3 beta)         Performs currency conversion
Services_Google    -n/a-/(0.1.1 alpha)            Provides access to the ➥
                                                  Google Web APIs

Services_Pingback  -n/a-/(0.2.0dev2 devel)        A Pingback User-Agent class.
Services_Technorati -n/a-/(0.6.6beta beta)        A class for interacting ➥
                                                  with the Technorati API

Services_Trackback -n/a-/(0.5.1 alpha)            Trackback - A generic ➥
                                                  class for sending and ➥
                                                  receiving trackbacks.

Services_Weather   1.3.2/(1.3.2 stable)           This class acts as an ➥
                                                  interface to various online➥
                                                  weather-services.

Services_Webservice -n/a-/(0.4.0 alpha)           Create webservices
Services_Yahoo     -n/a-/(0.1.1 alpha)            Provides access to the ➥
                                                  Yahoo! Web Services
```

Installing a Package

Once you've found a package that you want to use, use the install command and pass it the package name that you found using search.

Here's an example of installing an interface for weather services called Services_Weather. Of course, you'll want to make sure that PEAR handles the dependencies for you—that's one of the benefits of using a package manager—so make sure to specify the --alldeps option.

```
$ pear install --alldeps Services_Weather
```

```
Failed to download pear/SOAP, version "0.7.5", latest release is version 0.9.3, ➥
stability "beta", use "channel://pear.php.net/SOAP-0.9.3" to install
Failed to download pear/XML_Serializer, version "0.8", latest release is ➥
version 0.18.0, stability "beta", use ➥
"channel://pear.php.net/XML_Serializer-0.18.0" to install
pear/Services_Weather can optionally use package "pear/SOAP" (version >= 0.7.5)
pear/Services_Weather can optionally use package "pear/XML_Serializer" ➥
(version >= 0.8)
downloading Services_Weather-1.3.2.tgz ...
Starting to download Services_Weather-1.3.2.tgz (44,849 bytes)
............done: 44,849 bytes
downloading Cache-1.5.4.tgz ...
Starting to download Cache-1.5.4.tgz (30,690 bytes)
...done: 30,690 bytes
downloading DB-1.7.6.tgz ...
Starting to download DB-1.7.6.tgz (124,807 bytes)
...done: 124,807 bytes
downloading HTTP_Request-1.3.0.tgz ...
Starting to download HTTP_Request-1.3.0.tgz (13,808 bytes)
...done: 13,808 bytes
downloading Net_URL-1.0.14.tgz ...
Starting to download Net_URL-1.0.14.tgz (5,173 bytes)
...done: 5,173 bytes
downloading Net_Socket-1.0.6.tgz ...
Starting to download Net_Socket-1.0.6.tgz (4,623 bytes)
...done: 4,623 bytes
install ok: channel://pear.php.net/Net_URL-1.0.14
install ok: channel://pear.php.net/Net_Socket-1.0.6
install ok: channel://pear.php.net/HTTP_Request-1.3.0
install ok: channel://pear.php.net/DB-1.7.6
install ok: channel://pear.php.net/Cache-1.5.4
install ok: channel://pear.php.net/Services_Weather-1.3.2
```

As you can see, the PEAR package manager downloads the dependencies and installs them in the correct order for you so you don't have to worry about them. Another option that you can use is --onlyreqdeps, which unlike --alldeps only downloads the dependencies that are absolutely required for the package to be installed. If the --onlyreqdeps option would have been used to install the Services_Weather package, no other packages would have been installed because all of them are optional dependencies.

Upgrading a Package

If you want to upgrade any package that you already have installed, use the update command and specify the package:

```
$ pear update Services_Weather
```

The update-all command updates all the packages you have installed:

```
$ pear update-all
```

Working with Channels

A new feature as of PEAR 1.4.0, channels are ways of organizing packages. Using channels, you can subscribe to locations other than the main PEAR repository and still have dependencies managed for you.

The following commands allow you to discover, add, list the contents of, and remove channels using the pear command.

Channel commands

Command	Description
list-channel	Lists the available channels that you already have in your subscription list.
channel-add	Adds a channel from a channel server to your list.
channel-delete	Deletes a channel from your list of channels.
channel-discover	Discovers (and adds) any channel found at the given URL to your list of channels.
channel-info	Displays information about the given channel.

All the packages covered in this book are from the default PEAR channel at pear.php.net.

Installing the Packages in this Book

After this Introduction, each section's heading is the full name of the package documented in the section. To install the packages, just use PEAR. So, for the Auth package, which is the first package documented in this book after the Introduction, just type:

```
$ pear install auth
```

The case of the package is not important.

Some of the packages in this book were in alpha or beta when this book was written, and still might be. We've avoided calling them out because the package status could change quickly, thus making the book out of date. If a package is in alpha or beta, you'll get an error if you attempt to install the package with the pear command with the default configuration of PEAR. If the package was called PACKAGENAME, you would get the error shown here:

```
Failed to download pear/PACKAGENAME within preferred state "stable", latest ➡
release is version 0.5.0, stability "beta", use ➡
"channel://pear.php.net/PACKAGENAME-0.5.0" to install
Cannot initialize 'PACKAGENAME', invalid or missing package file
Package "PACKAGENAME" is not valid
install failed
```

We suggest that, rather than modify your configuration to install alpha or beta packages by default, explicitly install alpha or beta packages if prompted to do so. You can install the package simply by appending -alpha or -beta to the package name, like this:

```
$ pear install PackageName-alpha
```

PEAR_Error

It's useful when working with PEAR packages to be familiar with the PEAR_Error class, which is used for error handling. Many of the functions that you'll see throughout this book will return PEAR_Error if an error occurs in them. Others will throw PEAR_Error, as the PEAR_ERROR_EXCEPTION mode throws Exception.

PEAR_Error()

The constructor for the PEAR_Error class.

```
PEAR_Error PEAR_Error([string $message = 'unknown error'] [, integer $code = null]
                      [, integer $mode = null] [, mixed $options = null]
                      [, string $userinfo = null])
```

Parameters	Type	Description
$message	string	The error message.
$code	integer	An error code.
$mode	integer	The mode to use to process the error. See the "Error Modes" table for more information about available modes.
$options	mixed	The options to use for the error.
$userinfo	string	Additional information about the error.

addUserInfo()

Adds more information about the error.

```
void addUserInfo($info)
```

Parameters	Type	Description
mixed	$info	Additional information about the error.

getBacktrace()

Returns the call trace where the error occurred.

```
array getBacktrace([integer $frame = null])
```

Parameters	Type	Description
$frame	integer	The index of the frame to fetch. This is the index of the array returned by the function debug_backtrace(), which is used to populate the backtrace variable.

getCallback()

Returns the callback, if any.

```
mixed getCallback()
```

getCode()

Returns the error code for the current PEAR_Error.

```
integer getCode()
```

getDebugInfo()

Returns the same result as getUserInfo().

```
string getDebugInfo()
```

getMessage()

Returns the message associated with the current PFAR_Error.

```
string getMessage()
```

getMode()

Returns the mode of the current PEAR_Error. See the "Error Modes" table for more information about the available modes.

```
integer getMode()
```

getType()

Returns the name of the exception as a string.

```
string getType()
```

getUserInfo()

Returns the user information that was added with `addUserInfo()` or set in the constructor.

```
string getUserInfo()
```

toString()

Prints the `PEAR_Error` as a string.

```
string toString()
```

Error modes

Mode	Description
PEAR_ERROR_CALLBACK	Tells `PEAR_Error` to call the function provided in the options when an error occurs.
PEAR_ERROR_DIE	Dies, or quits, when an error occurs.
PEAR_ERROR_EXCEPTION	An PHP 5 exception is created when an error occurs.
PEAR_ERROR_PRINT	The error message is printed when an error occurs.
PEAR_ERROR_RETURN	The error just returns and does no more action.
PEAR_ERROR_TRIGGER	Calls the `trigger_error()` method, which creates a user-level error message.

Creating a Simple PEAR_Error Object

This example demonstrates how to create an instance of `PEAR_Error` and how it looks when printed as `toString()`.

```php
<?php

require_once 'PEAR.php';

$error = new PEAR_Error('An error has occurred!', 100, PEAR_ERROR_RETURN);

print $error->toString() . "\n";

?>
```

When you run the script, it will print out the following message:

```
[pear_error: message="An error has occurred!" code=100 mode=return level=notice ➡
prefix="" info=""]
```

Using a Callback with PEAR_Error

This example shows how to use a callback with PEAR_Error. The name of the function is passed in as an option.

```php
<?php

require_once 'PEAR.php';

function printError() {
    print "Running printError now!\n";
}

$error = new PEAR_Error('An error has occurred!', 3000, PEAR_ERROR_CALLBACK, ➡
'printError');

?>
```

When the script runs, the output looks like this:

```
Running printError now!
```

Dying with an Error

This example shows how to use the PEAR_ERROR_DIE mode to exit the script when the error occurs. The script won't get to the last line because it will exit when the PEAR_Error object is created.

```php
<?php

require_once 'PEAR.php';

$error = new PEAR_Error('An error has occurred!', 3000,
    PEAR_ERROR_DIE, "Additional information\n");

print "You won't get here!\n";

?>
```

The output looks like this:

Additional information

Looking Ahead

Armed with the commands that you'll be using to manage packages, now it's time to start installing and using some of the PEAR packages. In the following section, you'll see packages that are used for authentication.

Authentication

Many Internet sites have at least some form of authentication, requiring a username and password that allows a user to be able to view content on the site or to post comments and edit content.

The authentication packages in this section provide a way of adding authentication and basic preference management to a site without you having to spend the time writing your own. After all, nearly all authentication is identical in its basic functionality, and there's usually no good reason to spin off your own code if it's already written for you.

The Auth package provides the base for authentication and allows you to store user information in a variety of different locations. The Auth package can use a database, a Simple Object Access Protocol (SOAP) call, or the traditional Unix-style passwd file.

The Auth_HTTP package provides a way for you to use HTTP standard challenges for authentication. Your web browser interprets the challenge from the server and shows an input box for the username and password. You might like this option if you don't want to worry about writing your own HTML form to request the information.

The third and final package that's discussed in this section is the Auth_PrefManager package. You can use this package to allow users to customize their experience with the site by storing user preferences. The examples of this behavior in this section are basic, but the projects at the end of this book dig deeper into using the Auth_PrefManager package.

Auth

You use the Auth package to authenticate users in your site. Out of the box, it supports many different ways of authenticating users, including storage in a database, in files, or even by using SOAP calls. You can even write a custom container object that allows you to write your own method to authenticate users.

Common Uses

The common uses of the Auth package include the following:

- Quickly adding authentication to a database
- Adding authentication to Lightweight Directory Access Protocol (LDAP)
- Authenticating against password files

Related Packages

- Auth_HTTP
- Auth_PrefManager

Dependencies

The Auth package depends on the packages listed here.

Required Packages

None

Optional Packages

- File_Passwd
- Net_POP3
- DB
- MDB

- MDB2 2.0.0.RC1

- Auth_Radius

- Crypt_CHAP

- File_SMBPasswd

API

Auth() Constructor

The constructor creates an instance of an Auth object.

```
void Auth(mixed $storageDriver [, mixed $options] [, string $loginFunction]
    [, boolean $showLogin = true])
```

Parameter	Type	Description
$storageDriver	mixed	This parameter can either be the name of the driver to use or it can be a custom Auth_Container object.
$options	mixed	The options that are given for the provided storage driver.
$loginFunction	string	The name of the function that can be called to log in.
$showLogin	boolean	Determines whether or not to display the login page. Default value is true.

addUser()

Adds a new user and returns true if the addition is successful. If the addition fails, the function will return AUTH_METHOD_NOT_SUPPORTED.

```
mixed addUser(string $username, string $password [mixed $additional - ""])
```

Parameter	Type	Description
$username	string	The name of the user that will be added to the storage container. The storage container is the repository of user information, such as a database or passwd file.
$password	string	The user's password that will be added.
$additional	mixed	Additional options used by the storage container.

changePassword()

Changes the password for the given user and returns true if the change is successful. If the change fails, it will return AUTH_METHOD_NOT_SUPPORTED.

```
mixed changePassword(string $username, string $password)
```

Parameter	Type	Description
$username	string	The name of the user that is getting the password changed.

checkAuth()

Returns true if there is a session with valid authentication.

```
boolean checkAuth()
```

getAuth()

Returns true if the current user is logged in.

```
boolean getAuth()
```

getAuthData()

Returns the authentication data for the given field. If nothing is passed to the function, it will return everything that it knows about the current session.

```
mixed getAuthData([string $name = null])
```

Parameter	Type	Description
$name	string	The name of the field that contains the authentication data.

getPostPasswordField()

Returns the name of the field used for the password.

```
string getPostPasswordField()
```

getPostUsernameField()

Returns the name of the field used for the username.

```
string getPostUsernameField()
```

getStatus()

Returns the status of the current user.

```
string getStatus()
```

getUsername()

Returns the name of the current user.

```
string getUscrname()
```

listUsers()

Returns an array containing the names of all the users in the current storage container.

```
array listUsers()
```

logout()

First calls the logout callback method, if one is defined, then sets the username and password to empty strings and sets the session to null.

```
void logout()
```

removeUser()

Deletes the given user from the storage container and returns true if the function is successful. If the user wasn't deleted, the function returns AUTH METHOD NOT SUPPORTED,

```
mixed removeUser(string $username)
```

Parameter	Type	Description
$username	string	The login name of the user to be removed.

sessionValidThru()

Returns the time in seconds until the session expires.

```
integer sessionValidThru()
```

setAdvancedSecurity()

If passed true, Auth begins to perform more advanced security checks, such as detecting IP address and user agent changes.

```
void setAdvancedSecurity([boolean $flag = true])
```

Parameter	Type	Description
$flag	boolean	If `true`, the Auth package will do more advanced checking. Default value is `true`.

setAllowLogin()

Determines if the login form should be shown.

```
void setAllowLogin([boolean $allowLogin = true])
```

Parameter	Type	Description
$allowLogin	boolean	If `true`, the Auth package will display the login form if the user isn't authenticated (that is, the login expires). Default value is `true`.

setAuth()

Sets the authentication of the user in the session.

```
void setAuth(string $username)
```

Parameter	Type	Description
$username	string	The name of the user for which to set the authentication in the session.

setAuthData()

Sets the authentication data, by field, for a particular user.

```
void setAuthData($string name, mixed $value [, boolean $override])
```

Parameter	Type	Description
$name	string	The name of the field to set that's stored in the session.
$value	mixed	The value that will be put in the field.
$override	boolean	If `true`, any existing data will be overridden.

setExpire()

Sets the time at which the session will expire.

```
void setExpire(integer $time [boolean $add = false])
```

Parameter	Type	Description
$time	integer	Time in seconds when the session will expire.
$add	boolean	If true, the given time will be added to the current expire time. Default is false.

setFailedLoginCallback()

Sets the name of a function that can be used to handle a failed login.

```
void setFailedLoginCallback(string $failedLoginCallback)
```

Parameter	Type	Description
$failedLoginCall-back	string	The name of the function that's called when a login fails. The function receives as a parameter the name of the user as a string, along with a reference to the Auth object.

setIdle()

Sets the maximum allowable idle time for the session.

```
void setIdle(integer $time [, boolean $add = false])
```

Parameter	Type	Description
$time	integer	The amount of time in seconds allowed for the session to be idle.
$add	boolean	If true, the provided time is added to the current idle time. The default value is false.

setLoginCallback()

Sets the name of the callback function that can be used to handle the login.

```
void setLoginCallback(string $loginCallback)
```

Parameter	Type	Description
$loginCallback	string	The name of the function that will be called when a user logs in successfully. Two parameters are passed to the given function— the user's name and a reference to the Auth object.

setLogoutCallback()

Sets the name of the callback function that can be used to handle logging out.

```
void setLogoutCallback(string $logoutCallback)
```

Parameter	Type	Description
$logoutCallback	string	The name of the function that's used to log the user out. The function is passed the name of the user and a reference to the Auth object.

setSessionName()

Sets the name of the session. Setting the name of the session is useful if a single website (domain) has areas that require different levels of authentication, such as a normal and administration area.

```
void setSessionName([string $name = 'session'])
```

Parameter	Type	Description
$name	string	The name of the session. Sessions can be given a name to make them unique so more than one Auth object can be created at the same time.

setShowLogin()

Sets whether or not the login form should be shown if the user's session is no longer authenticated.

```
void setShowLogin([boolean $showLogin = true])
```

Parameter	Type	Description
$showLogin	boolean	If true, the user will be shown a login form if the session has expired or is otherwise not valid.

start()

This method is used to begin the Auth session.

```
void start()
```

staticCheckAuth()

Looks for a session with valid authentication information. This method checks to make sure the user has been authenticated, and is especially useful for calling at the beginning of web pages that require you to verify that the user has been authenticated by a login page.

```
boolean staticCheckAuth([mixed $options = null])
```

Parameter	Type	Description
$options	mixed	Options for statically checking authentication. An example of an option used here is the name of the session by setting the option sessionName.

Examples

Basic Authentication Using a Database

This first example shows how to connect to a database and authenticate a user (see Listing 1). If the user needs to be authenticated, the callback function is called. The callback function here, showLogin(), simply displays the input fields and submit button that the user will use to enter the login information. When the page is redisplayed, the checkAuth() function will skip calling the showLogin() callback because the user has been authenticated.

Listing 1. *auth ex01.php*

```php
<!-- Put standard HTML here for the page, like the
    DOCTYPE declaration, head, title, etc. -->
<?php

/* Auth Example 2 */
require_once "Auth.php";

/* This function will be called if the user needs to
 * be authenticated.
 */
function showLogin() {
    /* This HTML can be anything you want to show for a
     * login.
     */
    print "<form method=\"post\" action=\"auth_ex01.php\">";
    print "Username:  ";
    print "<input type=\"text\" name=\"username\"/><br/>";
    print "Password:  ";
    print "<input type=\"password\" name=\"password\"/><br/>";
    print "<input type=\"submit\"/>";
    print "</form>";
}
```

```
/* DSN is in form of driver://user:password@server/database
 * See the DB package for more information.
 */
$dsn = 'mysql://web:secret@localhost/auth';
$a = new Auth("DB", $dsn, "showLogin");

$a->start();

if ($a->checkAuth()) {
    /* Put some action here that is appropriate for logging in */
    echo "You're in!";
} else {
    echo "You are not logged in!";
}
?>
<!-- Put HTML footer stuff here -->
```

Authentication Using SOAP

This SOAP example is a bit more advanced because the SOAP storage container takes a couple different options, such as the endpoint Uniform Resource Identifier (URI) and SOAP namespace (see Listing 2). An example Web Service Description Language (WSDL) is shown here so you can see what the SOAP web service expects as inputs and returns as a result. The WSDL here shows the web service returning a simple boolean, but as explained in depth later, an option passed to the Auth package makes this return value somewhat unnecessary.

Listing 2. *auth.wsdl*

```
<?xml version ="1.0" encoding ="UTF-8" ?>
<definitions name="AuthWebService"
  targetNamespace="urn:AuthWebService"
  xmlns:tns="urn:AuthWebService"
  xmlns:soap="http://schemas.xmlsoap.org/wsdl/soap/"
  xmlns:xsd="http://www.w3.org/2001/XMLSchema"
  xmlns:soapenc="http://schemas.xmlsoap.org/soap/encoding/"
  xmlns:wsdl="http://schemas.xmlsoap.org/wsdl/"
  xmlns="http://schemas.xmlsoap.org/wsdl/">

<message name="authenticateRequest">
  <part name="username" type="xsd:string"/>
  <part name="password" type="xsd:string"/>
</message>

<message name="authenticateResponse">
  <part name="result" type="xsd:boolean"/>
</message>
```

```xml
<portType name="AuthPortType">
  <operation name="authenticate">
    <input message="tns:authenticateRequest"/>
    <output message="tns:authenticateResponse"/>
  </operation>
</portType>

<binding name="AuthBinding" type="tns:AuthPortType">
  <soap:binding style="rpc"
    transport="http://schemas.xmlsoap.org/soap/http"/>
  <operation name="authenticate">
    <soap:operation soapAction="urn:AuthWebService#authenticate"/>
    <input>
      <soap:body use="encoded" namespace="urn:AuthWebService"
        encodingStyle="http://schemas.xmlsoap.org/soap/encoding/"/>
    </input>
    <output>
      <soap:body use="encoded" namespace="urn:AuthWebService"
        encodingStyle="http://schemas.xmlsoap.org/soap/encoding/"/>
    </output>
  </operation>
</binding>
<service name="AuthService">
  <port name="AuthPort" binding="AuthBinding">
    <soap:address location="http://servername.example.com/path/to/authws.php"/>
  </port>
</service>
</definitions>
```

After you've cut and pasted an example WSDL and made it your own, create a simple SOAP server like the one shown in authws.php (see Listing 3). This example uses the PHP 5 SOAP extensions to make a web service quickly that complies to the definition specified in auth.wsdl.

Listing 3. *authws.php*

```php
<?php

/* This example provides the barest of examples of
 * generating a quick SOAP server. I wrote the WSDL first, then
 * wrote this simple server to provide basic authentication
 * functionality. It uses PHP 5 SOAP extensions, which must
 * be compiled into PHP 5 as an option. You can also use
 * the SOAP PEAR package.
 */
```

```php
function authenticate($username, $password) {
    /* This is just hard-coded to get the point across.
     * Ideally, you would have a database call or some other kind
     * of authentication mechanism inside this function.
     */
    if ($username == "myuser" && $password == "secret")
    {
        return $password;
    }
    else
    {
        /* The matchpasswords feature is off, so Auth is expecting
         * a SOAP error if the login is invalid.
         */
        return new SoapFault("Server", "Error logging in!");
    }
}
/* Shut caching off, otherwise you might be wondering why your
 * changes aren't getting picked up.
 */
ini_set("soap.wsdl_cache_enabled", "0");
$server = new SoapServer("auth.wsdl");
$server->addFunction("authenticate");
$server->handle();
?>
```

Now for the example that shows the authentication against the authws.php web service (see Listing 4).

Listing 4. *auth_ex02.php*

```php
<?php
/* Auth Example 2 */
require_once "Auth.php";

function showLogin() {
    /* This HTML can be anything you want to show for a
     * login.
     */

    /* You can use the same code as in example 1... */
}
```

```
/* Build the options used by the SOAP storage
 * container.
 */
$soapOptions = array(
    'endpoint'=>'http://servername.example.com/path/to/authws.php',
    'namespace'=>'urn:AuthWebService',
    'method'=>'authenticate',
    'encoding'=>'utf8',
    'usernamefield'=>'username',
    'passwordfield'=>'password',
    'matchpasswords'-> false
);
$a = new Auth("SOAP", $soapOptions, 'showLogin');
$a->start();

if ($a->checkAuth()) {
    /* Put some action here that is appropriate for logging in */
    echo "You're in!";
} else {
    echo "You are not logged in!";
}
?>
```

Note a couple things in these examples. The first is the matchpasswords option that's sent to the SOAP container. This option tells the container to look for a SOAP fault if the login is invalid. If you don't pass the matchpasswords option, you'll need to return the username and password back in a structure. The SOAP container checks to make sure the password that's coming back matches the one sent, and if the passwords match, the SOAP container will consider the user authenticated.

Authentication Against a passwd File

The example in Listing 5 demonstrates using a Unix-style passwd file that contains the login information.

Listing 5. *auth_ex03.php*

```
<?php
/* Auth Example 2 */
require_once "Auth.php";

function showLogin() {
    /* This HTML can be anything you want to show for a
     * login.
     */
    /* Snipped.  Same code as in Example 1... */
}
```

```
/* Once the user has been authenticated on this page, you
 * can use the staticCheckAuth() method on other pages to
 * make sure the user's login is still valid.
 *
 * Example:
 *
        if (Auth::staticCheckAuth($options)) {
            print "Logged in!";
        } else {
            print "Not logged in!";
        }
 */


$passwdFile = "/path/to/mypasswd";

$a = new Auth("File", $passwdFile, 'showLogin');
$a->start();

if ($a->checkAuth()) {
    /* Put some action here that is appropriate for logging in */
    echo "You're in!";
} else {
    echo "You are not logged in!";
}
?>
```

The file found at /path/to/mypasswd is in the standard Unix passwd file format. To create the file, I used the File_Passwd package because it's what Auth is using to read the file. I thought it easiest to use the same package to write the file.

Auth_HTTP

The Auth_HTTP package provides authentication in the form of header commands to the clients. These commands prompt the client to display an authentication dialog instead of using an authentication web form.

Common Uses

This package may be a good choice for you if you don't want to show the user a custom login form, but instead would prefer to use the standard HTTP authentication system. Using the standard HTTP authentication system means the browser displays a dialog box prompting the user for a username and password.

Related Packages

- Auth
- Auth_PrefManager

Dependencies

The Auth_HTTP package depends upon the following other packages.

Required Packages

Auth

Optional Packages

None

API

Note The Auth_HTTP class extends Auth, so the Auth_HTTP class has functions in its API that Auth has. For brevity, we don't repeat them here.

Auth_HTTP()

The class constructor.

```
void Auth_HTTP(string $storageDriver [, mixed $options = ''])
```

Parameter	Type	Description
$storageDriver	string	The name of the driver that's used to access the store of user information.
$options	mixed	Options for the given storage driver. Default is an empty string.

Options

The options shown in the following table are set to their default values first, and are overridden by options passed into the constructor or set using the setOption() method. The names of the options are used in the getOption() method to get the value. A few of the options map directly to parts of the WWW-Authenticate response header as defined in RFC 2617. To read more about it, go to http://www.ietf.org/rfc/rfc2617.txt.

Option name	Description	Default Value
algorithm	Specifies which algorithm to use to produce the digest and checksum, used in the algorithm directive in the header.	MD5
cryptType	The type of encryption to use.	md5
digestRealm	The name of the digest realm, assigned to the realm directive in the header.	"protected area"
forceDigestOnly	If true, basic authentication isn't used—only digest is used.	false
nonceLife	Specifies the amount of time that should be passed before the nonce section of the header is regenerated.	300
noncekey	A unique key not visible to the client that's encrypted and sent with each authentication header.	moo
opaquekey	A key that's used in authentication between the client and server in each request in the same authentication area.	moo
qop	The qop (*quality of protection*) portion of the header.	auth-integer, auth
sessionSharing	If true, the session ID will be set using the PHP function session_id().	true

assignData()

Assigns session variables to the values stored in $PHP_AUTH_USER and $PHP_AUTH_PW.

```
void assignData()
```

getOption()

Returns the value of the authentication option specified by the given name.

```
mixed getOption(string $name)
```

Parameter	Type	Description
$name	string	The name of the authentication option for which to return a value.

selfURI()

Returns the URI of the current site.

```
string selfURI()
```

setCancelText()

Sets the text that will be sent if the user clicks the cancel button. The cancel text is sent to the browser and displayed as if it were a web page.

```
void setCancelText(string $text)
```

Parameter	Type	Description
$text	string	The text sent if the user decides to cancel authentication.

setOption()

Sets the value of the given option.

```
void setOption(string $name [, mixed $value = null])
```

Parameter	Type	Description
$name	string	The name of the option to set.
$value	mixed	The option's value.

setRealm()

Sets the name of the current authentication realm. The name of the realm is used to identify the secure area, and is displayed to the users. It can help the users be aware of where they're logging in, so it should be unique and descriptive. An example is "Example.com Secure Area."

```
void setRealm(string $realm [, string $digestRealm = ''])
```

Parameter	Type	Description
$realm	string	The name of the authentication realm.
$digestRealm	string	The name of the realm for digest authentication.

Examples

Basic HTTP Authentication Using a Database

Shown in Listing 6 is an example of using the Auth_HTTP package to authenticate against a database. In this case, the database is the same one that's used in Listing 1. Using the options, you can identify your own table to use for the login information, as well as the encryption mechanism. Here the name of the table is auth, and the encryption type is MD5, to be compatible with the default Auth DB storage container options.

Listing 6. *auth_http_ex01.php*

```php
<?php
/* Auth_HTTP Example 1 */
require_once "Auth/HTTP.php";

$options = array('dsn'=>'mysql://web:secret@localhost/auth',
'table'=>'auth',
'usernamecol'=>'username',
'passwordcol'=>'password',
'cryptType'=>'MD5');

$a = new Auth_HTTP("DB", $options);
$a->setRealm("Secret zone!");
$a->setCancelText("<h1>Access is forbidden!</h1>");
$a->start();

if ($a->getAuth())
{
    echo "Open, sesame!";
}
```

```php
else
{
    echo "Not logged in!";
}

?>
```

HTTP Authentication Against a passwd File

This example of the Auth_HTTP package demonstrates using Auth_HTTP to authenticate against a Unix-style passwd file (see Listing 7). The significant differences between this example and Example 1 are the options. The options for database connectivity are replaced with the file option and authType options. The file option specifies the location of the passwd-formatted file (remember, this file must be readable by the web server user or you'll never be authenticated). The authType can be either basic or digest. If it's set to basic, the class will attempt to get the authentication information from the Internet Information Services (IIS) variable HTTP_AUTHENTICATION.

Listing 7. *auth_http_ex02.php*

```php
<?php
/* Auth_HTTP Example 2 */
require_once "Auth/HTTP.php";

$options = array(
    'file'=> '/your/path/to/passwd',
    'authType'=>'basic'
    );

$a = new Auth_HTTP("File", $options);
$a->setRealm("Secret zone!");
$a->setCancelText("<h1>Access is forbidden!</h1>");
$a->start();

if ($a->getAuth())
{
    echo "Open, sesame!";
}
else
{
    echo "Not logged in!";
}

?>
```

Auth_PrefManager

This package is used to store and retrieve user preferences from a database. A related package—Auth_PrefManager2—seeks to make the storage mechanism flexible so the data can be stored in a database, LDAP, or some other container. However, as of this writing, the Auth_PrefManager2 package was in alpha with no available user documentation.

Common Uses

The common use of this package is to store settings for a user. This package doesn't care about how a user is authenticated or if a user is authenticated—that's up to the related packages in this chapter, Auth and Auth_HTTP. Along with the requirement of the DB PEAR package, this package also requires a DB-compatible database.

Related Packages

- Auth
- Auth_HTTP

Dependencies

The Auth_PrefManager package depends on the following package.

Required Packages

DB

Optional Packages

None

API

Auth_PrefManager

Constructor for the Auth_PrefManager class.

```
boolean Auth_PrefManager(string $dsn [, array $properties = null])
```

Parameter	Type	Description
$dsn	string	The data source name of the DB connection where the table containing user preferences is located.
$properties	array	An array containing properties that are relevant to the data source.

clearCache()

Clears the cache of user preferences.

```
void clearCache()
```

deleteDefaultPref()

Deletes the preference for the default user and returns true if the function completed successfully.

```
boolean deleteDefaultPref(string $pref_id)
```

Parameter	Type	Description
$pref_id	string	The name of the preference to remove for the default user.

deletePref()

Deletes a preference setting for a specific user and returns true if the function completed successfully.

```
boolean deletePref(string $user_id, string $pref_id)
```

Parameter	Type	Description
$user_id	string	The name of the user for which to delete the preference.
$pref_id	string	The name of the preference that will be deleted for the given user.

getDefaultPref()

A convenience function for getting a given preference for the default user, even if a different user is currently logged in.

```
mixed getDefaultPref(string $pref_id)
```

Parameter	Type	Description
$pref_id	string	The name of the setting to get for the default user.

getPref()

Returns the value of the given preference for a specific user.

```
mixed getPref(string $user_id, string $pref_id [, boolean $showDefaults = true])
```

Parameter	Type	Description
$user_id	string	The name of the user.
$pref_id	string	The name of the preference to get for the user.
$showDefaults	boolean	If true, the function will also search the default user's preferences. Default value is true.

setDefaultPref()

Sets a preference for the default user and returns true if the function was successful.

```
boolean setDefaultPref(string $pref_id, mixed $value)
```

Parameter	Type	Description
$pref_id	string	The name of the preference that will be saved for the default user.
$value	mixed	The value stored in the preference.

setPref()

Sets a preference value for a specific user and returns true if the function was successful.

```
boolean setPref(string $user_id, string $pref_id, mixed $value)
```

Parameter	Type	Description
$user_id	string	The name of the user for which to store the preference.
$pref_id	string	The name of the preference that's getting stored.
$value	mixed	The value of the preference stored for this user.

setReturnDefaults()

If this is `true`, the `getPref()` function will return defaults if asked. If this is `false`, the `getPref()` function won't return defaults, even if the `$showDefaults` parameter is set to `true`.

```
void setReturnDefaults([boolean $returnDefaults = true])
```

Parameter	Type	Description
$returnDefaults	boolean	Defaulted to `true`, this value specifies if default values will be returned in the `getPref()` function.

useCache()

If set to `true`, the class will use caching to store the preferences for a user instead of going to the database for each trip. Unless you have specific reasons for shutting caching off, you should consider leaving it on.

```
void userCache([boolean $use = true])
```

Parameter	Type	Description
$use	boolean	Is `true` if the cache should be used to store preferences (default is `true`).

Examples

A Simple Preference Set and Retrieve

To show off a simple preference setting, the example in Listing 8 loads the logged-in user's nickname and displays it to the user in a friendly message.

■**Note** Before using the Auth_PrefManager package, you need to set up a database table for storing the preferences. The SQL for setting up the table is listed in the comments of this first example for your convenience, but make sure to check the latest documentation on the `http://pear.php.net` site to make sure it's up to date.

Listing 8. *auth_prefmanager_ex01.php*

```php
<?php

/* Auth_PrefManager Example 1 */
require_once 'Auth/PrefManager.php';
```

```
/* SQL that must be run to create the preference table in
 * the database.
 * CREATE TABLE preferences (
   user_id varchar( 255 ) NOT NULL default '',
   pref_id varchar( 32 ) NOT NULL default '',
   pref_value longtext NOT NULL ,
    PRIMARY KEY ( user_id , pref_id ));
 */
$dsn = 'mysql://web:secret@localhost/auth';
$options = array('serialize' => true);
$prefManager = new Auth_PrefManager($dsn, $options);
$username = 'myuser1';
/* Use these just to set some values */
$prefManager->setPref($username, 'nickname', 'Really cool user guy');
$prefManager->setDefaultPref('city', 'Deshler');
?>
<h1>Welcome,
<?php echo $prefManager->getPref($username, 'nickname');?>
of <?php echo $prefManager->getPref($username, 'city', true);?></h1>
```

Notice that the city preference wasn't set up for the user myuser1, but thanks to the ability to search for default values, the getPref() method includes the default city preference in the result. The output HTML of the preceding PHP is as follows:

```
<h1>Welcome,
Really cool user guy
of Deshler</h1>
```

User-Modifiable Preferences

The example in Listing 9 demonstrates how users can set their own preferences by providing a web form and then printing the example back out to them.

Listing 9. *auth_prefmanager_ex02.php*

```
<?php
/* Auth_PrefManager Example 2 */
require_once 'Auth/PrefManager.php';

/* SQL that must be run to create the preference table in
 * the database.
 * CREATE TABLE preferences (
   user_id varchar( 255 ) NOT NULL default '',
   pref_id varchar( 32 ) NOT NULL default '',
   pref_value longtext NOT NULL ,
    PRIMARY KEY ( user_id , pref_id ));
 */
```

```php
$dsn = 'mysql://web:secret@localhost/auth';
$options = array ('serialize' => true);
$prefManager = new Auth_PrefManager($dsn, $options);
$username = 'myuser1';
?>

<form action="<?= htmlspecialchars($_SERVER['PHP_SELF'])?>" method="post">
What is your favorite color?  
<input type="text" name="favcolor"
value="<?= htmlspecialchars($_POST['favcolor'])?>"/><br/>
<input type="submit"/>
</form>

<?php
if ($_SERVER['REQUEST_METHOD'] == 'POST')
{
    $prefManager->setPref($username, 'color', $_POST['favcolor']);
    echo "Successfully saved preference: " .
        $prefManager->getPref($username, 'color');
}
?>
```

This example still uses a hard-coded username. An example of how to use Auth_HTTP with the Auth_PrefManager package is shown in Listing 10.

Usage with Auth_HTTP

The example in Listing 10 includes examples of using the Auth_PrefManager package along with the Auth_HTTP package. When the page is first drawn, it will prompt the user with the standard username and password dialog box that the web browser uses for authentication. When the user is authenticated, this example will look up the user's nickname preference in the data store and welcome the user.

If you haven't run the first example of the Auth_PrefManager, you'll have to set the nickname preference before you can display it here.

Listing 10. *auth_prefmanager_ex03.php*

```php
<?php
/* Auth_PrefManager Example 3 */
require_once 'Auth/HTTP.php';
require_once 'Auth/PrefManager.php';

$dsn = 'mysql://web:secret@localhost/auth';
/* Set up the options for the Auth_PrefManager */
$prefOptions = array ('serialize' => true);
/* Set up the options for Auth_HTTP */
$authOptions = array('dsn'=>$dsn,
    'table'=>'auth',
```

```php
            'usernamecol'=>'username',
            'passwordcol'=>'password',
            'cryptType'=>'MD5');

$prefManager = new Auth_PrefManager($dsn, $prefOptions);
$auth = new Auth_HTTP('DB', $authOptions);

$auth->setRealm('Site with Preferences');
$auth->setCancelText('<h1>Access is forbidden!</h1>');
$auth->start();

if ($auth->getAuth())
{
    /* The 'nickname' option is still in the database from
     * running Example 1.  If you haven't run Example 1 you
     * will need to populate this preference first!
     * The PHP_AUTH_USER variable has the name of the currently
     * logged in user. */
    echo '<h1>Welcome, ' .
        $prefManager->getPref($_SERVER['PHP_AUTH_USER'], 'nickname') .
        '!</h1>';
}
else
{
    echo 'Not logged in!';
}
?>
```

Utilities and Tools

The utilities and tools in this section help you write code that can execute faster, give you better messaging during runtime, and execute with fewer errors. A common theme you'll see in the packages in this section is their flexibility. Most of them allow you to quickly switch the type of container or handler that's used either to persist or retrieve data.

- Cache_Lite is a package that allows you to store data on the local file system that you might otherwise have to get somewhere on the Internet, such as from a web service.

- The Config package helps you store values such as database server names and database names in configuration files instead of hard coding them into your PHP code.

- The Event_Dispatcher package allows you to register callback functions on objects.

- Log allows you to prioritize messages and send them to a variety of different containers, including those that log to the console, files, and databases.

- PHPUnit2 and phpDocumentor are different from the other packages in this section because most of your interaction with these will be running their command-line interfaces. PHPUnit2 allows you to do unit and regression testing on classes that you've written. PhpDocumentor allows you to generate documentation for the code you've written.

Cache_Lite

You use the Cache_Lite package to store information to the local file system. The data you store is up to you, but consider putting in data you'd normally have to get by going out to the Internet or by going to a different server. Because the data is cached locally, in theory reading from the local file system should be much faster than making a connection to a remote host and transporting data.

Common Uses

Cache_Lite has the following common uses:

- Locally caching data from a remote database
- Locally caching data from a web service
- Locally caching data from an RSS feed

Related Packages

None

Dependencies

Cache_Lite has the following dependencies.

Required Packages

None

Optional Packages

None

API

Cache_Lite() Constructor

The constructor creates the `Cache_Lite` object.

`void Cache_Lite([array $options = array(null)])`

Parameter	Type	Description
$options	array	Array that contains options for the Cache_Lite constructor.

Constructor Options

Option	Description	Default Value
cacheDir	The directory where the cache files are stored.	/tmp/
caching	boolean value that enables or disables caching.	true
lifeTime	Integer value for cache time in seconds.	3600
fileLocking	boolean value that enables or disables caching.	true
writeControl	boolean value that enables or disables write control.	true
readControl	boolean value that enables or disables read control.	true
readControlType	Type of read control (crc32, md5, strlen).	crc32
pearErrorMode	PEAR error mode.	CACHE_LITE_ERROR_RETURN
memoryCaching	boolean value that enables or disables memory caching.	false
onlyMemoryCaching	boolean value that enables or disables memory-only caching.	false
memoryCachingLimit	Integer that sets the maximum number of cache records.	1000
fileNameProtection	boolean value that enables or disables filename protection.	true
automaticSerialization	boolean value that enables or disables automatic serialization.	false

Constructor Options (Continued)

Option	Description	Default Value
automaticCleaningFactor	Integer that allows automatic tuning settings to be set. A value of 0 means no automatic cleaning is done, a value of 1 means systematic cache cleaning is done, a value greater than 1 means the cache is cleaned every *n* cache write.	0
hashedDirectoryLevel	Integer that sets the level of the caching directory.	0
hashedDirectoryUmask	Umask for caching directory.	0700
errorHandlingAPIBreak	boolean value that enables or disables API breaks for error handling.	false

clean()

Cleans out all the cache files.

```
boolean clean([string $group = false] [, string $mode = 'ingroup'])
```

Parameter	Type	Description
$group	string	The name of the cache group that will be cleaned.
$mode	string	The flush mode. Valid values are old, ingroup, notingroup, or function_callback.

extendLife()

Extends the life of a cache file. The cache file must be valid—that is, it hasn't already expired.

```
void extendLife()
```

▓**Note** This method was added in 1.7.0 beta 2 to accommodate request 6681 (see http://pear. php.net/bugs/bug.php?id=6681).

get()

Returns the cache specified by the given ID, or `false` if the cache specified by the ID is unavailable.

```
string get(string $id [, string $group = 'default']
                        [, boolean $doNotTestCacheValidity = false])
```

Parameter	Type	Description
$id	string	Used to identify the cache.
$group	string	The name of the cache group.
$doNotTestCacheValidity	boolean	If set to true, the function won't test to see if the cache is valid first. By default, the cache will be tested before the values are returned.

getMemoryCachingState()

Loads the state of the caching memory array from a given cache file cache.

```
void getMemoryCachingState(string $id [, string $group = 'default']
                        [, boolean $doNotTestCacheValidity = false])
```

Parameter	Type	Description
$id	string	The id of the cache.
$group	string	The name of the cache group.
$doNotTestCacheValidity	boolean	If this is set to true, the validity of the cache won't be validated first.

lastModified()

Returns the last modification time of the cache.

```
integer lastModified()
```

■Caution The `lastModified()` method is included "FOR HACKING ONLY," as the comments in the code explain. You shouldn't use this function for most application development.

raiseError()

Throws a PEAR error. Note that the method includes PEAR.php dynamically, which can improve performance by not including the file when an error doesn't occur.

```
void raiseError(string $msg, integer $code)
```

Parameter	Type	Description
$msg	string	The message that's included in the error.
$code	integer	The message's error code.

remove()

Removes the cache file.

```
boolean remove(string $id [, string $group = 'default'])
```

Parameter	Type	Description
$id	string	A string that identifies the cache.
$group	string	The name of the cache group.

save()

Saves the supplied data in a cache file.

```
boolean save(string $data [, string $id = null] [, string $group = 'default'])
```

Parameter	Type	Description
$data	string	The data to put into the cache.
$id	string	The cache ID.
$group	string	The name of the cache group.

saveMemoryCachingState()

Saves the state of the caching memory array into a file.

```
void saveMemoryCachingState(string $id [, string $group = 'default'])
```

setLifeTime()

Sets the new lifetime of the cache.

Parameter	Type	Description
$id	string	The cache ID.
$group	string	The name of the cache group.

```
void setLifeTime(integer $newLifeTime)
```

Parameter	Type	Description
$newLifeTime	integer	The new lifetime of the cache in seconds.

setOption()

Provides a way to set Cache_Lite options.

```
void setOption(mixed $name, mixed $value)
```

Parameter	Type	Description
$name	mixed	The name of the option. If the name isn't included in the list of available options, it's ignored (see the constructor documentation for the available options and their default values).
$value	mixed	The new value of the option.

setToDebug()

Calling this function turns debugging on. When debugging is turned on, any error that occurs in the Cache_Lite class stops the script and displays an error. Calling this method is a shortcut for running setOption('pearErrorMode', CACHE_LITE_ERROR_DIE).

```
void setToDebug()
```

Examples

Caching a Simple String

This example shows how to store a simple string using the Cache_Lite class to a local directory. The first time this page loads, you'll see a message that says "No data!" However, the second time the page loads it finds data in the cache, and you'll see "Hello, World!" in the browser.

Tip The /tmp directory is being written to by Cache_Lite in these examples. Make sure to change this value to a directory to which your web server account has access to write.

```php
<?php
/* Caching a simple string */

require_once 'Cache/Lite.php';

$cacheOptions = array(
    'cacheDir' => '/tmp/',
    'lifeTime' => '7200',
    'pearErrorMode' => CACHE_LITE_ERROR_DIE
    );

$cache = new Cache_Lite($cacheOptions);

if ($data = $cache->get('cache_lite_ex01.php'))
{
    echo $data;
}
else
{
    echo '<html><head></head><body>No data!</body><html>';
    /* Stuff some data in the cache so it'll be there the
     * next time the page is loaded.
     */
    $data = '<html><head></head><body>Hello, World!</body><html>';
    $cache->save($data);
}

?>
```

Caching Data from a Web Service

This example shows another use of Cache_Lite, this time to cache data locally from a web service with a pretty tight cache life (60 seconds). There's an expected performance advantage of accessing the data from the local file system instead of going out to get it from the Internet.

```php
<?php

require_once 'Cache/Lite.php';

/* Setting a couple options.  The cache files
 * will be written to the /tmp directory, and
 * the data inside the files will be good for
 * 60 seconds.  Obviously, you'll want a longer
 * amount of time, but the short increment helps testing.
 */
$cacheOptions = array(
    'cacheDir' => '/tmp/',
    'lifeTime' => '60',
    'pearErrorMode' => CACHE_LITE_ERROR_DIE
    );

$cache = new Cache_Lite($cacheOptions);

if (! ($data = $cache->get('cache_lite_ex02.php')))
{
    /* The data is not cached, so we have to go get it
     * from the source.  For this example, the source
     * is a web service somewhere.  For right now the details
     * are unimportant. See the SOAP chapter for details.
     */
    $client = new SoapClient("http://www.example.com/echo.wsdl");

    try
    {
        $data = $client->echoMessage("Hello from Mars!");
        $cache->save($data);
    } catch (SoapFault $fault) {
        print $fault;
    }
}

echo $data;

?>
```

Config

Config is a handy package to install if you're doing any sort of website that connects to a data source. At the least, it's a handy way to externalize your *data source name* (DSN). You'll see the DSN assigned to the variable $dsn in most code samples in this book, and you can read more about it in the DB package documentation. Because the DSN can possibly change if you change database servers or even databases, putting the DSN in a configuration file that can be loaded without changing a single line of code is a good idea because you'll only have to change the value once in the configuration file, instead of many times throughout your PHP files.

Common Uses

The Config package has the following common uses:

- Storing DSNs in config files

- Storing filenames and paths in config files

- Storing web service URLs in config files

Dependencies

The Config package has a couple optional dependencies, but you only need them if you're reading and saving Extensible Markup Language (XML) configuration files.

Required Packages

None

Optional Packages

- XML_Parser

- XML_Utils

API

Config() Constructor

The constructor creates an instance of the `Config` object.

```
Config()
```

getRoot()

Returns the root container for the `Config` object.

```
Config getRoot()
```

isConfigTypeRegistered()

Returns `true` if the specified container is a registered Config container.

```
boolean isConfigTypeRegistered(string $configType)
```

Parameter	Type	Description
$configType	string	The type name you're testing.

parseConfig()

Parses the given configuration with the specified container and returns a pointer to the `Config_Container` object. If an error occurs while attempting to create the container, a `PEAR_Error` will be returned.

```
mixed parseConfig(mixed $datasrc, string $configType [, array $options = null])
```

Parameter	Type	Description
$datasrc	mixed	The source for the configuration data.
$configType	string	The type of configuration container to use when parsing and holding the data.
$options	array	An array of options for the configuration container.

registerConfigType()

Registers the specified configuration container and returns true if the container was properly registered. The method will return a PEAR_Error object if an error occurred while trying to register the config type.

```
mixed registerConfigType(string $configType [array|boolean $configInfo = false])
```

Config Types

$configType Value	Container Class That Handles Configuration
apache	Config_Container_Apache
genericconf	Config_Container_GenericConf
inifile	Config_Container_IniFile
inicommented	Config_Container_IniCommented
phparray	Config_Container_PHPArray
xml	Config_Container_XML

Parameter	Type	Description
$configType	string	The type of configuration container to register.
$configInfo	array or boolean	If false, the $configType is assumed to be a standard container added in at runtime, which would allow for new configuration containers to be added that didn't come with the Config package in the package's Container directory. If $configInfo is an array, the first element will be the location of the container, and the second element will be the name of the class. If you developed a custom configuration container, the values could look like registerConfigTypes('custom', new array('Lib/MyClass', 'Lib_MyClass')), where a class called MyClass is located in a directory in your application called Lib.

* These configuration containers come with the Config package, located in the Container directory.

setRoot()

Sets the root container for the configuration. The root container holds the configuration settings.

```
mixed setRoot(object &$rootContainer)
```

Parameter	Type	Description
$rootContainer	object	A reference to the object that contains the configuration setting and that will be set as the new configuration root object.

writeConfig()

Writes the configuration data out to a data source, which can be a database, XML, or INI file. If an error occurs in the method, it returns a PEAR_Error object. If successful, it returns true.

```
mixed writeConfig([mixed $datasource = null] [, string $configType = null]
                         [, array $options = array()])
```

Parameter	Type	Description
$datasource	mixed	The location where the data will be written. With the XML and INI configuration containers, this is the name of the file.
$configType	string	The type of configuration container that's being used to store the configuration data.
$options	array	An array of options that the configuration container will interpret.

Examples

Reading INI Configuration Files

This example demonstrates reading an INI configuration file with the IniFile configuration container. The root configuration object contains elements that map to the INI file sections MyConfig and MyDatabase. The settings under each of these sections are available by accessing the names of the INI keys (for example, value and dsn, as follows).

```php
<?php
/* Reading an INI configuration file. */

/* INI file looks like this:
[MyConfig]
value=Hello
[MyDatabase]
dsn=mysql://user:password@servername/dbname
 */

require_once 'Config.php';

$config = new Config();

$configRoot = $config->parseConfig('/tmp/myconfig.ini', 'IniFile');
$settings = $configRoot->toArray();
```

```
/* 'root' is always the root configuration.  The 'MyConfig'
 * element is the section heading.
 */
echo $settings['root']['MyConfig']['value'];
echo $settings['root']['MyDatabase']['dsn'];

?>
```

Reading XML Configuration Files

No modern programming book would be complete without copious examples of dealing with XML, and this one is no exception. The example here shows similar values to the INI file example, but with the values nested safely inside XML elements.

Note This example requires the PEAR packages XML_Parser and XML_Utils, which are optional dependencies.

The root configuration object contains values that can be accessed by using the names of the XML elements. In the sample XML file, dsn is nested inside database, and is accessed that way in the $settings object.

```
<?php
/* Reading an XML configuration file */

/* XML file looks like this:
<?xml version="1.0"?>
<database>
    <dsn>mysql://user:password@servername/dbname</dsn>
</database>
 */

require_once 'Config.php';

$config = new Config();
/* This part looks the same as the INI example,
 * with the difference of the filename and 'XML'
 * as the container type.
 */
$configRoot = $config->parseConfig('/tmp/myconfig.xml', 'XML');
$settings = $configRoot->toArray();

echo $settings['root']['database']['dsn'];

?>
```

Writing XML Configuration Files

This example demonstrates how to build a Config_Container from scratch and fill it with values. The writeConfig() method uses the XML configuration container to write the settings out to XML. Just by changing the container to IniFile and changing the extension of the file-name to .ini, you can just as easily write the configuration to an INI file.

```php
<?php
/* Writing to a new XML file */

require_once 'Config.php';

$settings =& new Config_Container('section', 'MyConfig');
$settings_WebServices =& $settings->createSection('WebServices');
$settings_WebServices->createDirective('url', 'http://www.example.com/ws');
$settings_WebServices->createDirective('user', 'myuser');
$settings_WebServices->createDirective('password', 'secret');

$config = new Config();
$config->setRoot($settings);

$config->writeConfig('/tmp/newconfig.xml', 'XML');

/* The written file looks like this:
<?xml version="1.0" encoding="ISO 8859-1"?>
<MyConfig>
  <WebServices>
    <url>http://www.example.com/ws</url>
    <user>myuser</user>
    <password>secret</password>
  </WebServices>
</MyConfig>

 */

?>
```

Event_Dispatcher

The Event_Dispatcher package allows you to register methods as callbacks and later use those to handle events that occur in your application. For more information about callbacks, see the PHP documentation at http://www.php.net/manual/en/language.pseudo-types.php.

Common Uses

The Event_Dispatcher class has the following common uses:

- Handling button clicks on your web pages with event handlers
- Allowing events to bubble from one object to another
- Adding events that handle errors and other conditions

Related Packages

None

Dependencies

Event_Dispatcher requires the following other PEAR packages.

Required Packages

None

Optional Packages

None

API

addNestedDispatcher()

Allows you to add a second dispatcher where events will also be sent. This allows you to chain dispatchers together to run more than one callback function whenever events occur.

```
void addNestedDispatcher(Event_Dispatcher &$dispatcher)
```

Parameter	Type	Description
&$dispatcher	Event_Dispatcher	An Event_Dispatcher object that's also notified of events.

addObserver()

Adds a callback function that's called when an event occurs. You can provide the addObserver() method with optional criteria: the name of the notification and the name of the class, both of which can be used as filters.

```
void addObserver(mixed $callback [, string $nName = EVENT_DISPATCHER_GLOBAL]
                                 [, string $class = null])
```

Parameter	Type	Description
$callback	mixed	The name of the function or an array containing the name of the object and the name of the callback.
$nName	string	The name of the event, used for filtering. Default is EVENT_DISPATCHER_GLOBAL, which is an empty string
$class	string	The expected contained object class, also used for filtering. Default is null.

getInstance()

Returns the instance of Event_Dispatcher specified by the name. If no name is specified, "__default" is used.

```
Event_Dispatcher &getInstance([string $name = '__default'])
```

Parameter	Type	Description
$name	string	The name of the Event_Dispatcher.

getName()

Returns the name of the Event_Dispatcher object.

```
string getName()
```

getObservers()

Returns an array containing the observers specified by $nName.

```
array getObservers([string $nName = EVENT_DISPATCHER_GLOBAL]
                            [, string $class = null])
```

Parameter	Type	Description
$nName	string	The name of the observer stored in the Event_Dispatcher object.
$class	string	The contained object class.

observerRegistered()

Returns true if the specified observer is already registered in the current instance of the Event_Dispatcher.

```
boolean observerRegistered(mixed $callback,
                           [string $nName = EVENT_DISPATCHER_GLOBAL],
                           [string $class = null])
```

Parameter	Type	Description
$callback	mixed	A PHP callback.
$name	string	The name of the observer.
$class	string	The class of the contained object.

post()

Creates, posts, and returns a notification object.

```
&post (object Notification &$object, string $nName [, array $info = array()]
                           [, boolean $pending = true]
                           [, boolean $bubble = true])
```

Parameter	Type	Description
&$object	object	The notification object. In the example for this package, the object is sending the notification, or $this.
$nName	string	A name for the notification.
$info	array	An array that contains information, or parameters to send to the callback.
$pending	boolean	If true, the notification will be posted immediately.
$bubble	boolean	If true, the notification will also be sent along to nested Event_Dispatcher objects.

postNotification()

Posts and returns a notification object.

```
&postNotification (object The &$notification [,boolean $pending = true]
                          [, boolean $bubble = true])
```

Parameter	Type	Description
&$notification	object	The notification object. In the example for this package, the object is sending the notification, or $this.
$pending	boolean	If true, the notification will be posted immediately.
$bubble	boolean	If true, the notification will also be sent along to nested Event_Dispatcher objects.

removeNestedDispatcher()

Removes the specified Event_Dispatcher from the collection of nested Event_Dispatcher objects. It returns true if the dispatcher was removed successfully, and false if it wasn't registered.

```
bool removeNestedDispatcher (Event_Dispatcher $dispatcher)
```

Parameter	Type	Description
$dispatcher	Event_Dispatcher	The Event_Dispatcher to remove.

removeObserver()

Removes the specified observer and returns true if it was successfully removed. false is returned if it wasn't removed, or wasn't registered in the first place.

```
boolean removeObserver (mixed $callback
                          [, string $nName = EVENT_DISPATCHER GLOBAL]
                          [, string $class = null])
```

Parameter	Type	Description
$callback	mixed	A PHP callback.
$nName	string	The name associated with the observer.
$class	string	The class associated with the observer.

setNotificationClass()

Changes the class used for notifications.

```
boolean setNotificationClass (string $class)
```

Parameter	Type	Description
$class	string	The class used for notification.

Examples

Dispatching Button Click Events

The example in Listings 1 and 2 shows how to add callback methods to handle notifications when a button is clicked on a web form. It could be a little overkill just to print out echo statements, but if the Form1Handler class was going out to a database or doing something significant in response to the button clicks, you can imagine how splitting the code up this way would help keep the UI code relatively clean, and keep the "real work" in the class that has the callbacks in it.

Note For more examples of the Event_Dispatcher, see the online content for this book in the Source Code/ Download area of http://www.apress.com.

Listing 1. *The form1handler class, which is the receiver*

```php
<?php
require_once 'Event/Dispatcher.php';
class Form1Handler
{
    var $someData = "";

    function btnClick_OnClick(&$notification)
    {
        echo 'Handling event for btnClick!';
        $notification->someData = "Data1";
    }

    function btnClick2_OnClick(&$notification)
    {
        echo 'Handling event for btnClick2!';
        $notification->someData = "Data2";
    }
}
?>
```

Listing 2. *The web form*

```
<!DOCTYPE html PUBLIC "-//W3C//DTD XHTML 1.0 Strict//EN"
    "http://www.w3.org/TR/xhtml1/DTD/xhtml1-strict.dtd">
<html xmlns="http://www.w3.org/1999/xhtml">
<!-- Handling a click event on a web page -->
<head>
<title>Event_Dispatcher Example</title>
<script type="text/javascript" language="javascript">
function __handlePost(s) {
    document.form1.submitSource.value = s;
    document.form1.submit();
}
</script>
</head>
<body>
<form name="form1"
action="<?php echo htmlspecialchars($_SERVER['PHP_SELF']);?>"
method="post">
<input type="hidden" name="submitSource"
    value="<?php
echo issel ($_POST['submitSource']) ? $_POST['submitSource'] : '';
?>" />
<?php

require_once 'FormiHandler.php';
require_once 'Event/Dispatcher.php';

class Form1
{
    var $_dispatcher = null;

    function Form1(&$dispatcher)
    {
        $this->_dispatcher = &$dispatcher;
    }

    function buttonClick()
    {
        $notification = &$this->_dispatcher->post($this, 'onButtonClick', '...');
        echo "<br/><b>Finished handling event!</b>";
        /* This property is set now by the callback that was
         * fired by the notification.
         */
        echo $notification->someData;
    }
}
```

```php
$dispatcher = &Event_Dispatcher::getInstance();
$sender = &new Form1($dispatcher);
$receiver = new Form1Handler();

if ($_SERVER['REQUEST_METHOD'] == 'POST') {
    /* The callback name is dynamically generated, so you
     * can quickly add buttons and event handlers to
     * handle them in the Form1Handler class.
     */
    $dispatcher->addObserver(array(&$receiver,
        sprintf('%s_OnClick', $_POST['submitSource'])));
    /* Handle the event for that button */
    $sender->buttonClick();
}
?>
<p>Click this button to test me.</p>
    <input type="button" name="btnClick" value="Click Here!"
        onclick="javascript:__handlePost('btnClick');"/>
    <input type="button" name="btnClick2" value="Or click Here!"
        onclick="javascript:__handlePost('btnClick2');"/>
</form>
</body>
</html>
```

Log

Log is a package that allows you to add logging functionality to your PHP application with minimal effort, especially considering all the features that Log supports.

Log supports different priorities for the log messages—eight of them—and different logging *handlers*. The handlers allow the Log package to send messages transparently to a variety of different output devices. One example is the file handler, which simply allows you to log messages to a file. Another handler allows you to log messages to a Unix-style syslog, and yet another allows you to log messages to a database.

Common Uses

The Log package has the following common uses:

- Logging messages to a file

- Logging messages to a database table

- Logging messages to the syslog

Related Packages

None

Dependencies

Log has the following dependencies.

Required Packages

None

Optional Packages

None

API

attach()

Attaches an instance of a log observer to listen for messages. It returns `true` if the operation was successful; otherwise it returns `false`.

```
void attach(object &$observer)
```

Parameter	Type	Description
&$observer	object	The Log object that picks up messages with one of the logging functions.

close()

Closes the log observer. The actual implementation varies for each observer because it's an abstract method. For instance, when logging to the console, the `close()` method simply flushes any open buffers. When logging to a database, the `close()` method disconnects from the database and frees resources.

```
void close()
```

detach()

Removes the specified observer from the registered observers. `detach()` returns `true` if the operation was successful, and `false` if an error occurred.

```
void detach(object $observer)
```

Parameter	Type	Description
$observer	object	The observer to remove from the Log object.

factory()

Returns a concrete instance of the Log handler, or observer.

```
object Log &factory (string $handler [, string $name = ''] [, string $ident = '']
                     [, array $conf = array()]
                     [integer $level = PEAR_LOG_DEBUG])
```

Parameter	Type	Description
$handler	string	The type of Log subclass to return. Can be one of console, syslog, sql, file, and mcal.
$name	string	The name of the log file, table, or store to use.
$ident	string	The identity that's given to the Log instance.
$conf	array	An array of configuration values that are used to configure the logging handler.
$level	integer	Tells the logging handler to log messages up to and including this level.

flush()

Flushes the messages in the handler out to whatever container is being used.

```
void flush()
```

getIdent()

Returns the identity string of the current logging handler.

```
string getIdent()
```

getMask()

Returns the level mask. The level mask tells the logging handler which messages to log, so anything with lower priority than the level mask gets dropped and not logged out to the container.

```
integer getMask()
```

getPriority()

Returns the current default priority.

```
integer getPriority()
```

isComposite()

Returns true if the current handler is a composite class.

```
boolean isComposite()
```

MASK()

Calculates the logging mask given the priority and returns the newly calculated mask. MASK() doesn't modify the mask setting on the object; use the setMask() method to modify the mask setting on the object. Only messages that match the mask are printed, as shown in the section "Logging Messages to syslog."

```
integer MASK(integer $priority)
```

Parameter	Type	Description
$priority	integer	The priority that will be used as a mask.

MIN()

A method that calculates the mask for setting a threshold of the highest priority to be logged. Remember, it's calculating a mask so the minimum priority in the mask will be the maximum priority shown in the output. See the "Logging Messages to the Console" example for this package to see how MIN() works. It may be called statically.

```
integer MIN(integer $priority)
```

Parameter	Type	Description
$priority	integer	The logging priority.

MAX()

A method that calculates the mask for setting the lowest priority that will be included in the output. This is a little confusing, because the name of the method would imply that it sets the maximum, or highest priority to be logged. See the first example for this package to see how it works. It may be called statically.

```
integer MAX(integer $priority)
```

Parameter	Type	Description
$priority	integer	The logging priority.

open()

Opens the logging handler.

```
void open()
```

priorityToString()

Returns the string representation of the logging priority.

```
string priorityToString(integer $priority)
```

Parameter	Type	Description
$priority	integer	The priority that will be converted to a string.

setIdent()

Sets the current logger's identification string.

```
string setIdent(string $ident)
```

Parameter	Type	Description
$ident	string	The name to use to identify the logger.

setMask()

Sets and returns the message priority mask for the current logging handler.

```
integer setMask(integer $mask)
```

Parameter	Type	Description
$mask	integer	The bitwise mask to use for determining which messages are logged. Because the mask is a bitwise mask, you set the mask to allow more than one logging level.

setPriority()

Sets the default message priority.

```
void setPriority(integer $priority)
```

Parameter	Type	Description
$priority	integer	The logging priority. See the "Logging Levels" table in the section "Logging Methods for Convenience" for available values.

singleton()

The singleton() method does the same thing as the factory() method, except it checks to see if an instance is already created of the logging handler that you're attempting to create. Because it's a singleton, if an instance is already created, this method will simply return that existing instance. If an instance isn't already created, this method will create a new instance and return a reference to it.

See factory() for the documentation on the parameters.

stringToPriority()

This is the anti-priorityToString() method. It accepts a string representation of a priority and returns the appropriate integer constant. This method is particularly useful when put into a configuration file, where the "nice" names are more self-documenting and easier to work with than integer values.

```
integer stringToPriority(string $name)
```

Parameter	Type	Description
$name	string	A word that's converted to the priority constant. Possible values are emergency, alert, critical, error, warning, notice, info, and debug.

UPTO()

Calculates the mask for all the priorities up to the given priority. This method has been deprecated as of version 1.9.4; use the MAX() method instead. This method may be called statically.

```
integer UPTO(integer $priority)
```

Parameter	Type	Description
$priority	integer	See the "MAX()" section

Logging Methods for Convenience

A number of logging methods are exposed in the Log class that allow you to log messages of a particular level quickly and easily. All these require the same parameter, $message, of type mixed. Yes, that means that finally with the Log class you can send mixed messages without complications. All these methods return true if they've successfully logged the message. The methods are listed in this table from highest priority to lowest priority.

Logging Levels

Method name	Method Logs Messages at This Level
emerg()	PEAR_LOG_EMERG
alert()	PEAR_LOG_ALERT
crit()	PEAR_LOG_CRIT
err()	PEAR_LOG_ERR
warning()	PEAR_LOG_WARNING
notice()	PEAR_LOG_NOTICE
info()	PEAR_LOG_INFO
debug()	PEAR_LOG_DEBUG

The methods listed in the previous table have the same signature, shown in the following table.

Parameter	Type	Description
$message	mixed	The message to log.

Examples

Logging Messages to the Console

This example demonstrates how to use the Log package to write messages out to the console, and shows a couple of the convenience methods that log messages of certain priorities.

```php
<?php
/* Logging to the console. */

require_once 'Log.php';

$logger = &Log::factory('console', '', 'MyLogger');
```

```php
/* Here is the list of possible logging levels:
 *
 * PEAR_LOG_EMERG
 * PEAR_LOG_ALERT
 * PEAR_LOG_CRIT
 * PEAR_LOG_ERR
 * PEAR_LOG_WARNING
 * PEAR_LOG_NOTICE
 * PEAR_LOG_INFO
 * PEAR_LOG_DEBUG
 * PEAR_LOG_ALL
 * PEAR_LOG_NONE
 */

/* Now set a mask using MIN and see what happens */

$min = Log::MIN(PEAR_LOG_WARNING);
$logger->setMask($min);
$logger->debug('Debug message');
$logger->info('Info message');
$logger->notice('Notice message');
$logger->warning('Warning message');
$logger->err('Error message');
$logger->crit('Critical message');
$logger->alert('Alert message');
$logger->emerg('Emergency message');

/* Now set a mask using MAX and see what happens */

$max = Log::MAX(PEAR_LOG_NOTICE);
$logger->setMask($max);
$logger->debug('Debug message');
$logger->info('Info message');
$logger->notice('Notice message');
$logger->warning('Warning message');
$logger->err('Error message');
$logger->crit('Critical message');
$logger->alert('Alert message');
$logger->emerg('Emergency message');


?>
```

When the preceding script is executed, the output looks like this:

```
Aug 28 20:21:49 MyLogger [debug] Debug message
Aug 28 20:21:49 MyLogger [info] Info message
Aug 28 20:21:49 MyLogger [notice] Notice message
Aug 28 20:21:49 MyLogger [warning] Warning message
Aug 28 20:21:49 MyLogger [notice] Notice message
Aug 28 20:21:49 MyLogger [warning] Warning message
Aug 28 20:21:49 MyLogger [error] Error message
Aug 28 20:21:49 MyLogger [critical] Critical message
Aug 28 20:21:49 MyLogger [alert] Alert message
Aug 28 20:21:49 MyLogger [emergency] Emergency message
```

Logging Messages to a File

This example is a simple one that demonstrates both logging to a file and using a mask to limit the types of messages that are persisted. In this example, the mask is set to PEAR_LOG_WARNING, which means any message with lower priority than PEAR_LOG_WARNING won't be written to the log file. This type of masking is useful because you can set the mask to a high priority in production environments, for example, thus limiting the size of your log by only capturing important messages.

```php
<?php
/* logging messages to a file. */

require_once 'Log.php';

$logger = &Log::factory('file', '/tmp/myfile.log', 'MyLogger');

$mask = Log::MAX(PEAR_LOG_WARNING);

$logger->setMask($mask);

$logger->debug('This is a debug message.');
$logger->info('This is an info message.');
$logger->warning('This is a warning message.');
$logger->err('This one is logged, too!');

?>
```

The contents of the /tmp/myfile.log after running the preceding script look like this:

```
Apr 01 22:34:50 MyLogger [warning] This is a warning message.
Apr 01 22:34:50 MyLogger [error] This one is logged, too!
```

Logging Messages to syslog

This example demonstrates two different features of the Log package. The first is using the syslog handler to log the messages, and the second is using a bitwise operator to include more than one logging priority in the priority mask. The mask prints only messages of type PEAR_LOG_NOTICE and PEAR_LOG_ERR, but even the PEAR_LOG_ALERT message is ignored.

```php
<?php
/*  Logging to syslog */
require_once 'Log.php';

$logger = &Log::factory('syslog', 'LOG_LOCAL0', 'MyLogger');
$mask = Log::MASK(PEAR_LOG_NOTICE) | Log::MASK(PEAR_LOG_ERR);
$logger->setMask($mask);
$logger->notice('My notice message!');
$logger->err('My error message!');
$logger->warning('My warning message!');
$logger->alert('My alert message!');
?>
```

The last lines in the syslog look like this:

```
Apr 09 22:42:44 myserver MyLogger[2497] <Notice>: My notice message!
Apr 09 22:42:44 myserver MyLogger[2497] <Error>: My error message!
```

If you're unfamiliar with how bit masking works, you might be a little confused about the | notation. It's the bitwise operator for OR, which tells the mask to show either PEAR_LOG_NOTICE or PEAR_LOG_ERR messages. For more information about bitwise operators, see the PHP documentation at http://www.php.net/manual/en/language.operators.bitwise.php.

PHPUnit2

PHPUnit2 is an important package when it comes to writing testable code (instead of *de*testable code). PHPUnit2 was built for PHP5; you should use PHPUnit for older versions of PHP. Both packages have methods that allow you to make *assertions* for values that you expect to see when you call the methods you're testing with certain parameters. Assertions are methods that allow you to see easily if two values are the same, if objects aren't null, or if certain conditions are false. If you've written a class in PHP with a method that adds two numbers together, you can use the PHPUnit2 tests to make sure the result of the function is equal to the actual result of adding the numbers together. With your tests in place, you can now make changes to your class and be sure that your changes don't accidentally break its functionality.

PHPUnit2, when installed, comes with a useful command-line utility called phpunit that allows you to run tests and view the results. Also, one useful feature is the ability to *generate* the test class. As I mentioned this to a colleague of mine, he reminded me that this breaks *test-first methodology* (thanks, Chris!), so make sure you follow the methodology of your team. But if your development process allows you to benefit from automatically creating tests on code that's already at least partially generated, it's worth the time savings.

Tip *Test-first methodology* is a key component to some development methodologies, such as Agile and XP (eXtreme Programming). In test-first methodology, you write tests for your code before you write any of your code. The idea is to build complete tests, ensure they all fail because no implementation has been done, then begin writing code to pass the tests, and stop once they all pass.

Common Uses

PHPUnit2 has the following common uses:

- Developer unit testing
- Regression testing

Related Packages

None

Dependencies

PHPUnit2 has the following dependencies.

Required Packages

PEAR_Benchmark (not covered in this book)

Optional Packages

None

More Information

- For more information about PHPUnit2, see the Wiki page at `http://phpunit.de/wiki`.

- Unit testing is a huge subject on which entire books have been written. For more information about unit and regression testing, start with the following:

  - `http://en.wikipedia.org/wiki/Unit_testing`

  - `http://www.extremeprogramming.org/rules/unittests.html`

API

■**Note** PHPUnit2 has several classes available with several methods, but in everyday testing you'll mostly use the `PHPUnit2_Framework_TestCase` class. The API for the `PHPUnit2_Framework_TestCase` class is listed here, as the examples make use of classes that extend `PHPUnit2_Framework_TestCase`. The other class documented here is the `PHPUnit2_Framework_Assert` class, which contains the methods you call to do the actual assertions.

PHPUnit2_Framework_TestCase() Constructor

The constructor creates the `PHPUnit2_Framework_TestCase` object with the name provided.

`void __construct([string $name = null])`

Parameter	Type	Description
$name	string	Sets the name of the test case.

countTestCases()

Counts the number of test cases executed during `run()`.

```
integer countTestCases()
```

createResult()

Creates and returns a `PHPUnit2_Framework_TestResult` object. Protected.

```
PHPUnit2_Framework_TestResult createResult()
```

getName()

Returns the name of the test case.

```
string getName()
```

run()

Runs the test case and returns a `PHPUnit2_Framework_TestResult` object that contains the test results. An exception will be thrown if the object passed into `run()` isn't of type `PHPUnit2_Framework_TestResult`.

```
PHPUnit2_Framework_TestResult run([PHPUnit2_Framework_TestResult $result = null])
```

Parameter	Type	Description
$result	PHPUnit2_Framework_TestResult	A result that's appended to the results from the run() method. A new object will be created if this one is blank.

runBare()

Runs the bare test sequence.

```
void runBare()
```

runTest()

Runs the test and asserts its state. If the name of the test is `null`, it throws `PHPUnit2_Framework_Error`. Protected.

```
void runTest()
```

setName()

Sets the name of the test object.

```
void setName(string $name)
```

Parameter	Type	Description
$name	string	The name that's given to the test case.

setUp()

Sets up the test fixture. A good candidate for code inside a setUp() is to open a database connection or to initialize an object to a predetermined state. Protected.

```
void setUp()
```

tearDown()

Tears down the tests. Good candidates for code inside tearDown() include closing any connections created in setUp, disposing of any other resources (such as files), or destroying objects. Protected.

```
void tearDown()
```

toString()

Returns a string representation of the object.

```
string toString()
```

Assert Functions

The functions listed here are used to assert, or check, the results of a test.

assertContains() and assertNotContains()

Use the assertContains() method to make sure that a given object is found in an array of objects. Use assertNotContains() to make sure that an object isn't found in an array of objects.

```
void assertContains (mixed $needle, mixed $haystack [, string $message = ''])
void assertNotContains (mixed $needle, mixed $haystack [, string $message = ''])
```

Parameter	Type	Description
$needle	mixed	The object to look for.
$haystack	mixed	The object to look inside of to find the $needle.
$message	string	The message that gets printed if this test fails.

assertEquals() and assertNotEquals()

Use assertEquals() to make sure that the expected value is equal to the actual value. Use assertNotEquals() to verify that two values—the expected and actual—are *not* equal to each other.

```
void assertEquals (mixed $expected, mixed $actual [, string $message = ''],
                                mixed $delta = 0)
void assertNotEquals (mixed $expected, mixed $actual [, string $message = ''],
                                mixed $delta = 0)
```

Parameter	Type	Description
$expected	mixed	The value that's the "correct" value.
$actual	mixed	The result of the method or a variable that you're testing.
$message	string	The message printed if this test fails.
$delta	mixed	The delta is the difference that's allowed between the two values. If the values are all numbers, the delta is the maximum allowed for the absolute value of the difference between $actual and $expected. For example, if the expected value is 3 and the actual value is 4, the test will pass if the delta is 1 or more.

assertNull() and assertNotNull()

Use assertNull() to make sure that the given object is null. Use assertNotNull() to verify that the given value is *not* null.

```
void assertNull (mixed $actual [, string $message = ''])
void assertNotNull (mixed $actual [, string $message = ''])
```

Parameter	Type	Description
$actual	mixed	The value that will be tested to see if it's null.
$message	string	The message that's printed if the test fails.

assertRegExp() and assertNotRegExp()

Use assertRegExp() to verify that a regular expression finds a match in a given string. Use assertNotRegExp() to verify that a regular expression doesn't find a match in a given string.

```
void assertRegExp (string $pattern, string $string [, string $message = ''])
void assertNotRegExp (string $pattern, string $string [, string $message = ''])
```

Parameter	Type	Description
$pattern	string	The regular expression to test.
$string	string	The string that the regular expression is tested against.
$message	string	The message that's printed if the test fails.

assertSame() and assertNotSame()

Use assertSame() to make sure that two variables are of the same value and the same type, and that they refer to the same object. Use assertNotSame() to verify that the two values aren't the same value and same type, and that they aren't referring to the same object.

```
void assertSame (mixed $expected, mixed $actual [, string $message = ''])
void assertNotSame (mixed $expected, mixed $actual [, string $message = ''])
```

Parameter	Type	Description
$expected	mixed	The value that $actual should be equal to, and of the same type.
$actual	mixed	The actual value from the method or variable to test.
$message	string	The message that's printed if the test fails.

assertTrue() and assertFalse()

Use assertTrue() to verify that a given condition is true. Use assertFalse() to make sure that $condition is false. If the condition isn't a boolean, the methods will throw an exception.

```
void assertTrue (boolean $condition [, string $message = ''])
void assertFalse (boolean $condition [, string $message = ''])
```

Parameter	Type	Description
$condition	boolean	A true or false condition that will be evaluated.
$message	string	The message that will be written if the test fails.

assertType() and assertNotType()

Use assertType() to verify that a given object is of a specific type. Use assertNotType() to make sure that the given object is *not* of the given type.

```
void assertType (string $expected, mixed $actual [, string $message = ''])
void assertNotType (string $expected, mixed $actual [, string $message = ''])
```

Parameter	Type	Description
$expected	string	The type of the object.
$actual	mixed	The actual type to test.
$message	string	The message that's written if the test fails.

fail()

Use this method to fail a test explicitly. You can use this method when the other assertions aren't adequate to cover a particular test condition. This method throws PHPUnit2_Framework_AssertionFailedError.

```
void fail ([string $message = ''])
```

Parameter	Type	Description
$message	string	The message that's written if the test fails.

format()

Returns a string in the format of: $message *expected:* $expected *but was:* $actual.

```
void format (mixed $expected, mixed $actual, string $message)
```

Parameter	Type	Description
$expected	mixed	The expected value.
$actual	mixed	The actual value.
$message	string	The message that's printed when the expected and actual values don't match.

setLooselyTyped()

If this value is set to true, the assertion methods will compare the values by their string representations and not their types. It could be handy if you wanted a comparison of the integer 3 and the string "3" to return true.

```
void setLooselyTyped (boolean $looselyTyped)
```

Parameter	Type	Description
$looselyTyped	boolean	true if the types of the actual and expected values in assertEquals should be ignored.

Examples

Writing a Simple Test

This example shows how to test a simple class with a single method.

```php
<?php
/* VERY simple class, created just to have something
 * to test.
 */
class Greeter
{
    public function sayHello($myname)
    {
        return sprintf('Hello, %s!', $myname);
    }
}
?>
```

The test was automagically generated using the --skeleton option with PHPUnit. After the test was generated, code was added into the testSayHello method. The code creates a new Greeter, then calls sayHello(), passing a hard-coded name. The output of sayHello() is compared to a hard-coded value that represents what the value should be that's returned from the sayHello() method.

```php
<?php
// Call GreeterTest::main() if this source file is executed directly.
if (!defined("PHPUnit2_MAIN_METHOD")) {
    define("PHPUnit2_MAIN_METHOD", "GreeterTest::main");
}

require_once "PHPUnit2/Framework/TestCase.php";
require_once "PHPUnit2/Framework/TestSuite.php";

require_once "phpunit2_ex01.php";

/**
 * Test class for Greeter.
 * Generated by PHPUnit2_Util_Skeleton
 */
class GreeterTest extends PHPUnit2_Framework_TestCase {
    /**
     * Runs the test methods of this class.
     *
     * @access public
     * @static
     */
```

```php
    public static function main() {
        require_once "PHPUnit2/TextUI/TestRunner.php";

        $suite  = new PHPUnit2_Framework_TestSuite("GreeterTest");
        $result = PHPUnit2_TextUI_TestRunner::run($suite);
    }

    /**
     * Sets up the fixture, for example, open a network connection.
     * This method is called before a test is executed.
     *
     * @access protected
     */
    protected function setUp() {
        /* Put setup code here... */
    }

    /**
     * Tears down the fixture, for example, close a network connection.
     * This method is called after a test is executed.
     *
     * @access protected
     */
    protected function tearDown() {
        /* Put code to tear down tests here... */
    }

    /**
     * @todo Implement testSayHello().
     */
    public function testSayHello() {
        // Remove the following line when you implement this test.
        $greeter = new Greeter();
        $this->assertEquals('Hello, User!', $greeter->sayHello('User'));
    }
}

// Call GreeterTest::main() if this source file is executed directly.
if (PHPUnit2_MAIN_METHOD == "GreeterTest::main") {
    GreeterTest::main();
}
?>
```

Here's the output of running this command:

```
PHPUnit 2.3.5 by Sebastian Bergmann.

.


Time: 0.018597

OK (1 test)
```

Testing a Config file

This example shows how to test a configuration file to make sure that it's properly being parsed by the Config class (see the Config package reference within this book for more details on how to use that class). It's a practical example of using the assertContains() method.

```php
<?php
// Call ConfigTest::main() if this source file is executed directly.
if (!defined("PHPUnit2_MAIN_METHOD")) {
    define("PHPUnit2_MAIN_METHOD", "ConfigTest::main");
}

require_once "PHPUnit2/Framework/TestCase.php";
require_once "PHPUnit2/Framework/TestSuite.php";
require_once "Config.php";

class ConfigTest extends PHPUnit2_Framework_TestCase
{

    public static function main()
    {
        require_once "PHPUnit2/TextUI/TestRunner.php";

        $suite  = new PHPUnit2_Framework_TestSuite("ConfigTest");
        $result = PHPUnit2_TextUI_TestRunner::run($suite);
    }
```

```php
    public function testConfig()
    {
        /* Take a look at the INI configuration example in the Config
         * chapter for more about using Config.
         */
        $config = new Config();
        $configRoot = $config->parseConfig('/tmp/myconfig.ini', 'IniFile');
        $settings = $configRoot->toArray();
        /* INI file looks like this:
            [MyConfig]
            value=Hello
            [MyDatabase]
            dsn=mysql://user:password@servername/dbname
         */
        $this->assertContains(array('value'=>'Hello'), $settings['root'],
            'Expected \'value\' in settings.');
    }
}

if (PHPUnit2_MAIN_METHOD == "ConfigTest::main") {
    ConfigTest::main();
}
?>
```

Testing for Nulls

This example shows how to test for null values. The output of running the script is listed after the example.

```php
<?php
/* Testing for nulls */

// Call ConfigTest::main() if this source file is executed directly.
if (!defined("PHPUnit2_MAIN_METHOD")) {
    define("PHPUnit2_MAIN_METHOD", "NullTest::main");
}

require_once "PHPUnit2/Framework/TestCase.php";
require_once "PHPUnit2/Framework/TestSuite.php";
```

```php
class NullTest extends PHPUnit2_Framework_TestCase
{

    public static function main()
    {
        require_once "PHPUnit2/TextUI/TestRunner.php";

        $suite  = new PHPUnit2_Framework_TestSuite("NullTest");
        $result = PHPUnit2_TextUI_TestRunner::run($suite);
    }

    public function testNulls()
    {
        $myval = null;
        $this->assertNull($myval, 'Expected value to be null.');
        $myval = 'something';
        $this->assertNotNull($myval, 'Expected value to be not null.');
    }
}

if (PHPUnit2_MAIN_METHOD == "NullTest::main") {
    NullTest::main();
}
?>
```

PHPUnit 2.3.5 by Sebastian Bergmann.

.

Time: 0.001893

OK (1 test)

PhpDocumentor

PhpDocumentor is an invaluable addition to the tools of writing and documenting PHP code. It allows you to have up-to-date documentation that's easy to read and navigate, provided that you add *DocBlocks* to your code. DocBlocks are similar to block comments, but they start with /** instead of just /* and include *tags* inside them. The tags are specially formatted identifiers that phpDocumentor parses and turns into useful documentation.

Without phpDocumentor, writing this book would have been a lot more difficult, as I used the generated documentation as a basis for the API documentation. Some of the PEAR packages in this book even had complete examples in their DocBlocks.

However, because the DocBlocks have to be kept up to date, the fact that phpDocumentor parses the source code file doesn't guarantee the accuracy of the documentation. I found a few discrepancies here and there when I was putting together the API documentation for packages throughout this book, but for the most part the documentation was right on. I expect the documentation to get better as more people use PEAR.

Common Uses

PhpDocumentor has the following common use:

Automatically generating HTML or PDF documentation

Related Packages

None

Dependencies

PhpDocumentor has the following dependencies.

Required Packages

None

Optional Packages

XML_Beautifier

API

It's not that you can't call phpDocumentor from PHP code—for most uses there's no reason to do so. Instead, listing the class API here, I've detailed the command-line parameters to phpDocumentor.

Parameter	Description
--filename (-f)	The name of the file to parse. You can specify more than one file by separating them with commas.
--directory (-d)	The name of the directory to parse. You can specify more than one file by separating them with commas.
--examplesdir (-ed)	The full path that contains files specified by the @example tags.
--templatebase (-tb)	The base location of all the templates to parse.
--target (-t)	The output directory, where the generated files are stored.
--ignore (-i)	Files that are ignored. You can specify more than one file by separating the names with commas.
--ignore-tags (-it)	Tags to ignore while generating the documentation. The @package, @subpackage, @access, and @ignore tags may not be ignored.
--hidden (-dh)	Turn this on to parse hidden directories.
--quiet (-q)	This feature is useful for scripts because it turns messages printed to the console off.
--title (-ti)	Sets the title of the generated documentation.
--help (-h)	Displays the help message.
--useconfig (-c)	Uses a configuration file in the user's subdirectory for all command-line options.
--parseprivate (-pp)	Tells phpDocumentor to parse @internal and elements marked private with @access.
--packageoutput (-po)	Specifies a comma-delimited list of packages to parse.
--defaultpackagename (-dn)	Sets the name of the default package.
--defaultcategoryname (-dc)	Sets the name of the default category.
--output (-o)	Specifies a comma-delimited list of the output types for the generated documentation.
--converterparams (-cp)	Parameters used for the output converter (such as HTML and PDF converters).
--customtags (-ct)	A list of custom tags.
--sourcecode (-s)	Generates a syntax-highlighted version of the source code file.
--javadocdesc (-j)	Turns on JavaDoc-compatible parsing.

Parameter	Description
--pear (-p)	Tells phpDocumentor to parse a PEAR-style repository.
--readmeinstallchangelog (-ric)	Specifies custom filenames to parse, such as README, INSTALL, or CHANGELOG files.

Tags

PhpDocumentor uses tags to identify what parts of the DocBlocks to include in the documentation.

Tag	Purpose
@access	Sets the visibility of the function. Valid values are private, protected, or public.
@author	Allows you to identify the author of the given PHP code.
@category	Identifies the category into which the PHP package should be sorted.
@copyright	Allows you to specify the code's copyright.
@deprecated	Tells other users that this code has been replaced by newer code, and that this shouldn't be used anymore.
@example	With this tag, you can specify a location where a sample shows the usage of the code.
@filesource	Tells phpDocumentor to create a syntax-highlighted version of the current page.
@global	Identifies global variables.
@ignore	Tells phpDocumentor to ignore the code marked with this tag.
@internal	Allows you to reserve certain comments for advanced developers.
@license	Specifies a URL for the license under which the code is released.
@link	Specifies a URL that's used inside the documentation.
@name	Provides the name for a global variable. Use it in conjunction with @global.
@package	Specifies the name of the package.
@param	Allows you to describe the parameters passed to a function.
@return	Allows you to describe what's returned when a function is called.
@see	Displays a link that allows users to jump to other related topics.
@since	Specifies when particular code was added to the class or package.
@static	Documents methods that can be called without instantiating the class.
@staticvar	Documents static variables in a class.
@subpackage	The name of the subpackage inside the package.
@todo	Identifies tasks that still need to be done.

Tag	Purpose
@tutorial	Allows you to specify a link where more documentation can be found.
@uses	Displays a link in the documentation to a related method or class.
@var	Documents class variables.
@version	Allows you to specify a version string for the file. Note that if you're using CVS or Subversion to manage your source, you can put the Id tag here.

Examples

Example of Class Documentation

This is an example of a DocBlock that should be used to document a class. At the bare minimum, you should include the name of the package and category, as well as the version of the class and the name of the author and e-mail address.

```
/**
 * Brief description of the class goes here.
 *
 * A much longer description of the class goes here.  It might
 * talk about the history of the class, why it was written, how
 * it is intended to be used, etc.
 *
 * @package  Cow
 * @category FarmAnimals
 * @version  CVS:  $Id$
 * @author   Example Author <example.author@example.com>
 */
class Cow

    /* parts of the class here */
}
```

Example of Method Documentation

This is an example of a DocBlock for a function. The variables are described with the @var tag, which contains their data type, name, and a short description of the variable. The @access tag tells you that the function is public.

```
/**
* Short description of the function
*
* @var string $var1 Some variable descriptoin
* @var mixed $var2 Another variable description
* @access public
*/
function setOption($var1, $var2)
{
    /* Implementation goes here... */
}
```

Example of Variable Documentation

Here's an example of variable documentation. The @var tag is used to identify the variable type and name.

```
/**
 * A short description of the variable goes here.
 *
 * @var string $ myVar
 */
var $_myVar = 'initialValue';
```

Dates and Numbers

As you might be able to guess from the name, the packages in this section allow you to deal with dates and numbers. The Date package has an extensive API that allows you to compare dates, add and subtract time spans, convert time zones, and perform just about every other date-related function you can imagine. The Date_Holidays package allows you to see if a given date is a holiday, to list all holidays between two dates, and to find out what the date is for a given holiday. It works with a variety of different holiday *drivers*, including those for Christian, Jewish, US, and United Nations Organization (UNO) holidays, to name a few. Numbers_Roman has a small API, but has the useful purpose of converting given numbers into Roman numerals and converting Roman numerals into numbers. Finally, Numbers_Words is capable of printing the text representation of numbers.

Date

The Date package provides a `Date` class that offers many methods for dealing with dates. The `Date` constructor accepts a string representation of a `Date` and builds an object that can be formatted, added to, subtracted from, and compared to other dates. The Date package includes two other useful classes, `Date_Span` and `Date_TimeZone`, which are also detailed in the API documentation in this chapter. The `Date_Span` class allows you to build time spans easily that can be added or subtracted to and from `Date` values. The `Date_TimeZone` class allows you to get the information about a time zone, including its offset from Coordinated Universal Time (UTC), and to get daylight saving time information using a short name for the time zone.

Common Uses

The Date package is used for the following purposes:

- Formatting dates
- Adding and subtracting dates
- Comparing dates

Related Packages

The following package is related because it depends on this one:

Date_Holidays

Dependencies

The Date package has the following dependencies.

Required Packages

None

Optional Packages

None

Date API

Date Constructor

Creates a new instance of a Date object, with the current date and time if no parameter is passed. You can provide a date to the constructor in a couple different formats, including ISO 8601 (for example, 1997-08-29 02:14:00), timestamp (for example, 19970829021400), or Unix time (for example, 872820840) formats. You may also pass in another Date object.

```
Date Date ([mixed $date = null])
```

Parameter	Type	Description
$date	mixed	A string representation of a date.

addSeconds()

Adds the given number of seconds to the current date and time, changing the value.

```
void addSeconds(integer $sec)
```

Parameter	Type	Description
$sec	integer	The number of seconds to add to the Date.

addSpan()

Adds the given Date_Span object (the API of which is detailed later in this chapter) to the current date.

```
void addSpan(Date_Span $span)
```

Parameter	Type	Description
$span	Date_Span	A Date_Span object that contains the specification for a unit of time that can be added to the Date.

after()

Returns true if the Date object is chronologically after the given date.

```
boolean after(Date $when)
```

Parameter	Type	Description
$when	Date	Another Date object to compare to the Date.

before()

Returns true if the Date object is chronologically before the given date.

boolean before(Date $when)

Parameter	Type	Description
$when	Date	Another Date object to compare to the Date.

compare()

Returns a signed integer that indicates the relationship between the two dates. If $d1 is greater than $d2, the method will return 1. If $d1 is less than $d2, the method will return -1. compare() returns 0 if the Date objects are equal. This is a good method to use for sorting dates.

integer compare(Date $d1, Date $d2)

Parameter	Type	Description
$d1	Date	One Date object in the comparison.
$d2	Date	The other Date object in the comparison.

convertTZ()

Converts the Date's time zone to the time zone represented by the Date_TimeZone.

void convertTZ(Date_TimeZone $tz)

Parameter	Type	Description
$tz	Date_TimeZone	An object that represents a time zone.

■**Caution** This method uses a function called putenv() to obtain the time zone information, especially when getting information about whether or not the current time zone is in daylight saving time. This method might not work on all operating systems (such as Microsoft Windows) because it relies on underlying calls for the information.

convertTZbyID()

Converts the Date's time zone to the time zone represented by the given string identifier.

```
void convertTZbyID(string $id)
```

Parameter	Type	Description
$id	string	An identifier for a time zone: CST, DST, MST.

■Caution The same limitations with convertTZ() apply to convertTZbyID().

copy()

Copies the value of $date into the Date object.

```
void copy(Date $date)
```

Parameter	Type	Description
$date	Date	Another Date from which to copy the values into the Date object.

equals()

Returns true if the provided Date is equal to the instantiated Date object.

```
boolean equals(Date $when)
```

Parameter	Type	Description
$when	Date	Another Date to compare for determining if the two Date objects are equal.

format()

Formats the Date into a string that can include many different date parts.

```
string format(string $format)
```

Parameter	Type	Description
$format	string	The format in which the Date will be printed.

The following table lists the format string objects, along with what they represent.

Format Strings for Formatting Date Objects

Format	Description	Example
%a	Short weekday name.	Sun, Mon, Tue, Wed
%A	Long weekday name.	Sunday, Monday, Tuesday, Wednesday
%b	Short month name.	Jan, Feb, Mar, Apr
%B	Long month name.	January, February, March, April
%C	Century	18, 19, 20 *(1800s, 1900s, and 2000s, respectively)*.
%d	Day of month.	00, 01, 02, 03 . . . 31
%D	Short date format.	03/04/05 (shortcut for %m/%d/%y)
%e	Single digit day of month.	0, 1, 2, 3 . . . 31
%E	Number of days since epoch.	3223, 23333, 34333
%H	Hour as number.	00, 01, 02, 03 . . . 23
%I	Hour as number (12-hour).	01, 02, 03 . . . 12
%j	Day of year.	001, 002, 003 . . . 366
%m	Month as number.	01, 02, 03 . . . 12
%M	Minute as number.	00, 02, 03 . . . 59
%n	Newline character.	\n
%o	Time zone offset.	-06:00, -05:00, -04:00
%O	Time zone offset, corrected for daylight saving time.	-06:00, +05:00
%p	p.m. or a.m. on a 12-hour clock.	pm, am
%P	AM or PM on a 12-hour clock.	PM, AM
%r	Time for 12-hour clock.	12:00 PM (shortcut for %I:%M:%S %P)
%R	Time for 24-hour clock.	23:30 (shortcut for %H:%M)
%s	Seconds, including tenths.	30.10, 59.99
%S	Seconds as a number.	00, 01, 02, 03 . . . 59
%t	Tab character.	\t
%T	Time.	12:00:01, 21:32:00 (same as %H:%M:%S)
%w	Weekday as a number.	0, 1, 2, 3 . . . 6
%U	Number of the week in the year.	0, 1, 2, 3 . . . 51
%y	Year.	00, 01, 02 . . . 99
%Y	Year, including century.	1999, 2000, 2001
%%	Literal.	%

getDate()

Returns the date in one of a couple predetermined formats. When passed the DATE_FORMAT_ISO constant, the date returns in a string that looks like 2006-04-10 13:00:00.

```
string getDate([integer $format = DATE_FORMAT_ISO])
```

Parameter	Type	Description
$format	integer	A value that specifies the format in which to return the date.

Date Formats

Constant	Date Format	Example
DATE_FORMAT_ISO	YYYY-MM-DD HH:MM:SS	1997-08-29 02:14:00
DATE_FORMAT_ ISO_BASIC	YYYYMMDD➡ THHMMSS (Z|(+/-)HHMM)?	19970829T02:10:00Z-0400
DATE_FORMAT_ ISO_EXTENDED	YYYY-MM-DDTHH:MM: SS(Z|(+/-)HH:MM)?	1997-08-29T02:14:00Z-04:00
DATE_FORMAT_ISO_ EXTENDED_MICROTIME	YYYY-MM-SSTHH:MM: SS(.S*)?(Z|(+/-)HH:MM)?	1997-08-29T02:14:00.0000000Z-04:00
DATE_FORMAT_TIMESTAMP	YYYYMMDDHHMMSS	19970829021400
DATE_FORMAT_UNIXTIME	long integer	072020040

getDay()

Returns an integer that represents the number of the day in the month.

```
integer getDay()
```

getDayName()

Returns the name of the day in the week, such as Monday, Tuesday, Wednesday.

```
string getDayName([boolean $abbr = false] [, mixed $length = 3])
```

Parameter	Type	Description
$abbr	boolean	true if the day's name should be shortened.
$length	mixed	If specified, determines the maximum length of the day name returned.

getDayOfWeek()

Returns the number of the day in the week, starting with 0 on Sunday.

```
integer getDayOfWeek()
```

getDaysInMonth()

Returns the number of total days in the current month.

```
integer getDaysInMonth()
```

getHour()

Returns the Date's hour as an integer from 00 to 23.

```
integer getHour()
```

getJulianDate()

Returns the Julian date as an integer, which is the number of days since Monday, January 1, 4713 BC. You can find more information about Julian dates at http://en.wikipedia.org/wiki/Julian_date.

```
integer getJulianDate()
```

getMinute()

Returns the minute as an integer between 00 and 59.

```
integer getMinute()
```

getMonth()

Returns the month as an integer between 01 and 12.

```
integer getMonth()
```

getMonthName()

Returns the name of the month in the Date.

```
string getMonthName([boolean $abbr = false])
```

Parameter	Type	Description
$abbr	boolean	If true, the name of the month is abbreviated. An example is Jan instead of January.

getNextDay()

Returns a Date object that represents the day immediately following this one chronologically. The time portion of the new Date object is the same as the original object's time.

```
Date getNextDay()
```

getNextWeekday()

Returns a Date object that represents the weekday that follows this one chronologically. If the current Date object is a Friday, this method will return the following Monday represented as a Date object. The time portion of the new Date object is the same as the original object's time.

```
Date getNextWeekday()
```

getPrevDay()

Returns a Date object that represents the date immediately preceding this one chronologically. The time portion of the new Date object is the same as the original object's time.

```
Date getPrevDay()
```

getPrevWeekday()

Returns a Date object that represents the weekday (Monday through Friday) that immediately precedes this one. The time portion of the new Date object is the same as the original object's time.

```
Date getPrevWeekday()
```

getQuarterOfYear

Returns the Date's quarter of the year as an integer, 1 through 4.

```
integer getQuarterOfYear()
```

getSecond()

Returns the second in the Date's time as an integer between 00 and 59.

```
integer getSecond()
```

getTime()

Returns the time as an integer expressing the number of seconds since January 1, 1970.

```
integer getTime()
```

getWeekOfYear()

Returns the number of the current week in the year. The numbering starts at 1 with the first Sunday in the year.

```
integer getWeekOfYear()
```

getWeeksInMonth()

Returns the number of weeks in the current month.

```
integer getWeeksInMonth()
```

getYear()

Returns the current year as an integer. For April 1, 2007, the returned value is 2007.

```
integer getYear()
```

inDaylightTime()

Returns true if the Date is in daylight saving time, taking time zone into account.

```
boolean inDaylightTime()
```

■**Caution** See the sections "convertTZ()" and "convertTZbyID()" for limitations on time zones with different operating systems. Because this method takes time zone into account, it's subject to the same limitations.

---

isFuture()

Returns true if the Date represents a date and time that are in the future.

```
boolean isFuture()
```

isLeapYear()

Returns true if the Date represents a leap year.

```
boolean isLeapYear()
```

isPast()

Returns true if the Date represents a date and time that are in the past.

```
boolean isPast()
```

setDate()

Sets the value of the Date given the string, and optionally the format of the string.

```
void setDate(string $date [, integer $format = DATE_FORMAT_ISO])
```

Parameter	Type	Description
$date	string	A string representation of a date, such as 2005-04-11 12:00:00.
$format	integer	A constant that describes the format of the given string. See the section "getDate()" for a list of these constants.

setDay()

Sets the day of the Date, expecting an integer 0 through 31. If you specify a number outside this range, the value is set to 1.

```
void setDay(integer $d)
```

Parameter	Type	Description
$d	integer	The number of the day in the month.

setHour()

Sets the hour of the Date, expecting an integer value 00 through 23. If you specify a number out of that range, the hour is set to 00.

```
void setHour(integer $h)
```

Parameter	Type	Description
$h	integer	The number of the hour in a 24-hour day.

setMinute()

Sets the minutes portion of the Date, expecting an integer with the value 0 through 59. If you specify out of that range, the minute is set to 00.

```
void setMinute(integer $m)
```

Parameter	Type	Description
$m	integer	The minute in the hour.

setMonth()

Sets the month of the Date, expressed as an integer between 0 and 12. If you specify a number out of this range, the value is set to 1.

```
void setMonth(integer $m)
```

Parameter	Type	Description
$m	integer	The month of the Date object.

setSecond()

Sets the second portion of the Date, expressed as an integer 0 through 59. If you specify a number that's out of this range, the value is set to 0.

```
void setSecond(integer $s)
```

Parameter	Type	Description
$s	integer	The second in the minute.

setTZ()

Sets the time zone of the Date. The date and time are both left unmodified. See the section "convertTZ()" to change the date and time to a different value. This method will call setTZbyID() if the parameter specified isn't a Date_TimeZone object.

```
void setTZ(Date_TimeZone $tz)
```

Parameter	Type	Description
$tz	Date_TimeZone	A Date_TimeZone object that contains all the time zone information.

setTZbyID()

Sets the time zone using a string identifier that indicates which time zone to set. Values might be CST, PST, EST, or EDT. If you specify a value that isn't valid, the system's default time zone is used.

```
void setTZbyID(string $id)
```

Parameter	Type	Description
$id	string	An identifier that indicates which time zone to set on the Date.

setYear()

Sets the year part of the Date.

```
void setYear(integer $y)
```

Parameter	Type	Description
$y	integer	The year to set on the Date.

subtractSeconds()

Subtracts the given number of seconds from the Date, modifying it and setting the Date's value to the result.

```
void subtractSeconds(integer $sec)
```

Parameter	Type	Description
$sec	integer	The number of seconds to subtract from the Date.

subtractSpan()

Subtracts the given Date_Span from the Date and sets the Date to the new value. Date_Span objects can be easier to use than subtracting seconds when subtracting large amounts of time, such as days, weeks, and so on.

```
void subtractSpan(Date_Span $span)
```

Parameter	Type	Description
$span	Date_Span	The Date_Span object to subtract from the Date.

toUTC()

Sets the Date to UTC time and sets the time zone to "UTC."

```
void toUTC()
```

toUTCbyOffset()

Sets the UTC time by using an offset, such as -06:00, +04:00, +0800, and -1200.

```
void toUTCbyOffset(mixed $offset)
```

Parameter	Type	Description
$offset	mixed	A string that indicates the time to offset first, then set the Date's time zone to UTC.

Date_Span API

Date_Span Constructor

Creates a new instance of a Date_Span object, and initializes the value to the time given as an argument.

```
Date_Span(mixed $time [, mixed $format = null])
```

Parameter	Type	Description
$time	mixed	A value representing a time. Most commonly, this is a string formatted in either the default input format or the one specified by $format.
$format	mixed	The format used by $time.

add()

Adds the provided Date_Span object to the current Date_Span.

```
void add(Date_Span $time)
```

Parameter	Type	Description
$time	Date_Span	The Date_Span to add.

compare()

Compares two Date_Span objects. If $time1 is longer than $time2, the result is 1. If $time2 is longer than $time1, the result is -1. The result is 0 if they're equal, which makes this method ideal for sorting algorithms.

```
integer compare(Date_Span $time1, Date_Span $time2)
```

Parameter	Type	Description
$time1	Date_Span	The first Date_Span to compare.
$time2	Date_Span	The second Date_Span to compare.

copy()

Copies the value of the Date_Span into the given Date_Span object and returns true if the operation was successful.

```
boolean copy(Date_Span $time)
```

Parameter	Type	Description
$time	Date_Span	The Date_Span that the current Date_Span will be copied into.

equal()

Returns true if the Date_Span is equal to the provided Date_Span.

```
boolean equal(Date_Span $time)
```

Parameter	Type	Description
$time	Date_Span	The Date_Span to compare.

format()

Formats the Date_Span as a string.

```
string format([string $format = null])
```

Parameter	Type	Description
$format	string	The format to use when representing the Date_Span as a string.

Format strings for Date_Span

Format	Description	Example
%C	Days with time, same as %D, %H:%M:%S.	2, 02:15:30
%d	Total days as a float number.	1.25 (1 day, 6 hours)
%D	Days as a decimal number.	2 (2 days)
%e	Total hours as a float number.	23.25
%f	Total minutes as a float number.	2.5 (2 minutes, 30 seconds)
%g	Total seconds as a decimal number.	75 (1 minute, 15 seconds)
%h	Hours as a decimal number.	3
%H	Hours as a decimal number limited to two digits.	03s
%m	Minutes as a decimal number.	5
%M	Minutes as a decimal number limited to two digits.	05
%n	Newline character (\n).	\n
%p	Either "am" or "pm"—case insensitive—depending on the time. If "pm" is detected, it adds 12 hours to the resulting time span without any checks.	pm
%r	Time in am/pm notation, same as %H:%M:%S %p.	02:15:30 pm
%R	Time in 24-hour notation, same as %H:%M.	14:15
%s	Seconds as a decimal number.	50
%S	Seconds as a decimal number limited to two digits.	03
%t	Tab character (\t).	\t
%T	Current time equivalent, same as %H:%M:%S.	04:22:00
%%	Literal "%."	%

getDefaultFormat()

Returns the default format of the Date_Span.

```
mixed getDefaultFormat()
```

getDefaultInputFormat()

Returns the default input format of the Date_Span.

```
mixed getDefaultInputFormat()
```

greater()

Returns true if this Date_Span is greater than the provided Date_Span.

```
boolean greater(Date_Span $time)
```

Parameter	Type	Description
$time	Date_Span	The Date_Span to compare.

greaterEqual()

Returns true if this Date_Span is either greater than or equal to the provided Date_Span.

```
boolean greaterEqual(object Date_Span $time)
```

Parameter	Type	Description
$time	Date_Span	The Date_Span to compare.

isEmpty()

Returns true if the Date_Span is empty.

```
boolean isEmpty()
```

lower()

Returns true if this Date_Span represents a shorter amount of time than the provided Date_Span.

```
boolean lower(object Date_Span $time)
```

Parameter	Type	Description
$time	Date_Span	The Date_Span to compare.

lowerEqual()

Returns true if this Date_Span contains a shorter or equal time span than the Date_Span provided.

```
boolean lowerEqual(object Date_Span $time)
```

Parameter	Type	Description
$time	Date_Span	The Date_Span to compare.

set()

Sets the Date_Span using the given time and optional format.

```
boolean set(mixed $time [, mixed $format = null])
```

Parameter	Type	Description
$time	mixed	A value representing the time for the Date_Span.
$format	mixed	The format to use when parsing $time into the Date_Span value. See the format() method for available formats. Optional.

setDefaultFormat()

Sets the default format to use when returning the value of the Date_Span as a formatted string. It returns the last used format.

```
mixed setDefaultFormat(mixed $format)
```

Parameter	Type	Description
$format	mixed	The format to use as the new default. The default is %C. For more information about the formats, see the format() method.

setDefaultInputFormat()

Sets the default input format to use when providing strings to set the value of the Date_Span.

```
mixed setDefaultInputFormat(mixed $format)
```

Parameter	Type	Description
$format	mixed	The default input format to use.

setFromArray()

Sets the value of the Date_Span using the items in the provided array. The first element in the array holds seconds, the second minutes, the third hours, and the fourth days. Zeros are used for any elements that are missing.

```
boolean setFromArray(array $time)
```

Parameter	Type	Description
$time	array	The new Date_Span value to set as an array.

setFromDateDiff()

Sets the value of the Date_Span to be equal to the difference between the two Date objects provided. true is returned if the method is successful.

```
boolean setFromDateDiff(object Date $date1, object Date $date2)
```

Parameter	Type	Description
$date1	Date	The first Date to use in the difference.
$date2	Date	The Date to subtract from the first date to get a time span value to set the Date_Span.

setFromDays()

Sets the value of the Date_Span to the number of days provided. Returns true on success.

```
boolean setFromDays(float $days)
```

Parameter	Type	Description
$days	float	The number of days to use for the value of the Date_Span.

setFromHours()

Sets the value of the Date_Span to the number of hours provided. Returns true on success.

```
boolean setFromHours(float $hours)
```

Parameter	Type	Description
$hours	float	The number of hours to use for value of the Date_Span.

setFromMinutes()

Sets the value of the Date_Span to the number of minutes provided. Returns true on success.

```
boolean setFromMinutes(float $minutes)
```

Parameter	Type	Description
$minutes	float	The number of hours to use for the value of the Date_Span.

setFromSeconds()

Sets the value of the Date_Span to the number of seconds provided. Returns true on success.

```
boolean setFromSeconds(integer $seconds)
```

Parameter	Type	Description
$seconds	integer	The number of seconds to use for the value of the Date_Span.

setFromString()

Sets the value of the Date_Span given a formatted string. The format is optional, and if it's not provided, the Date_Span will use the default input string format.

```
boolean setFromString(string $time [, string $format = null])
```

Parameter	Type	Description
$time	string	The time duration for the Date_Span expressed as a string.
$format	string	A string that describes the format of the $time string.

■**Note** The setFromString() method always uses the last provided values. This is important when providing times that might override each other, such as setFromString('06, 1', '%M %m'). In this case, the time span is one minute. The method doesn't add time to the existing values.

subtract()

Subtracts the value of the Date_Span provided from the current Date_Span. If the time span to subtract is larger than the original, the result is zero.

```
void subtract(Date_Span $time)
```

Parameter	Type	Description
$time	Date_Span	The value to subtract from the current Date_Span.

toDays()

Returns the Date_Span as a value in days.

```
float toDays()
```

toHours()

Returns the Date_Span as a value in hours.

```
float toHours()
```

toMinutes()

Returns the Date_Span as a value in minutes.

```
float toMinutes()
```

toSeconds()

Returns the Date_Span as a value in seconds.

```
integer toSeconds()
```

Date_TimeZone API

Date_TimeZone Constructor

Creates a new Date_TimeZone object using the given identifier. The identifier is a name that uniquely identifies the time zone. You can obtain the list of IDs using the getAvailableIDs() method.

```
Date_TimeZone Date_TimeZone(string $id)
```

Parameter	Type	Description
$id	string	An identifier for the time zone. See the getAvailableIDs() method to get a list of the available IDs.

getAvailableIDs()

Returns a list of the available identifier strings that you can use to create new Date_TimeZone objects.

```
mixed getAvailableIDs()
```

getDefault()

Returns a Date_TimeZone with the same time zone as the system's default time zone.

```
Date_TimeZone getDefault()
```

getDSTLongName()

Returns the long name of the of the time zone, including the daylight saving time information, such as Mountain Daylight Time.

```
string getDSTLongName()
```

getDSTSavings()

Returns the number of milliseconds of time offset for daylight saving time. It's always 3600000.

```
integer getDSTSavings()
```

getDSTShortName()

Returns the short name of the time zone, including the daylight saving time information; for example, PDT for Pacific Daylight Time.

```
string getDSTShortName()
```

getID()

Returns the string identifier of the Date_TimeZone object.

```
string getID()
```

getLongName()

Returns the long name of the Date_TimeZone object.

```
string getLongName()
```

getOffset()

Returns the offset from UTC for the time zone, taking into account the offset for daylight saving time, if applicable.

```
integer getOffset(Date $date)
```

Parameter	Type	Description
$date	Date	The Date from which to get the offset.

getRawOffset()

Returns the offset from UTC for the time zone, without taking into account daylight saving time.

```
integer getRawOffset()
```

getShortName()

Returns the short name of the `Date_TimeZone` object. Example: CST, DST, GMT-12:00, WST.

```
string getShortName()
```

hasDaylightTime()

Returns `true` if the time zone observes daylight saving time.

```
boolean hasDaylightTime()
```

inDaylightTime()

Returns `true` if the date is in daylight saving time. This method isn't necessarily reliable on Windows systems because it uses OS calls to get the result.

```
boolean inDaylightTime(Date $date)
```

Parameter	Type	Description
$date	Date	The `Date` to test to see if it's observing daylight saving time.

isEqual()

Returns `true` if the `Date_TimeZone` object is equal to the provided `Date_TimeZone`.

```
boolean isEqual(Date_TimeZone $tz)
```

Parameter	Type	Description
$tz	Date_TimeZone	The `Date_TimeZone` to test.

isEquivalent()

Returns `true` if the `Date_TimeZone` has an offset that's equal and offset of the provided `Date_TimeZone`. For them to be equivalent, both must have the same observation of daylight saving time (either they both do, or both don't observe it).

```
boolean isEquivalent(Date_TimeZone $tz)
```

Parameter	Type	Description
$tz	Date_TimeZone	The `Date_TimeZone` to test.

isValidID()

Returns true if the provided string is a valid identifier for one of the time zones stored in the Date_TimeZone data.

```
boolean isValidID(string $id)
```

Parameter	Type	Description
$id	string	The identifier to look for in the list of available identifiers.

setDefault()

Sets the default time zone.

```
void setDefault(string $id)
```

Parameter	Type	Description
$id	string	The identifier of the time zone to set as default.

Examples

Converting UTC to a Different Time Zone

This example shows how to create a new Date object given a formatted string that represents a date and time, then use a Date_TimeZone object to convert the time zone on the Date. The format() method shown at the end of the example demonstrates how to show the Date in a somewhat user-friendly output string.

```php
<?php
/* Converting a UTC date to a time zone */

require_once 'Date.php';

$date = new Date('2006-04-10 13:00:00');
$date->toUTC();
/* This will print the date out, which is now a UTC date */
echo $date->getDate(DATE_FORMAT_ISO) . "\n";

$cst = new Date_TimeZone('CST');

/* Now convert the date to the new time zone. */
$date->convertTZ($cst);
/* This will print that date again, this time in CST (UTC -6) */
echo $date->getDate(DATE_FORMAT_ISO) . "\n";
```

```
/* This will print the same date, but in a more friendly
 * format. The date will look like: Monday, April 4 2006 at 07:00 am.
 */
echo $date->format("%A, %B %e %Y at %I:%M %p%n");

?>
```

When you run the preceding example, the output will look like this:

```
2006-04-10 13:00:00
2006-04-10 07:00:00
Monday, April 10 2006 at 07:00 am
```

Adding Dates and Times

This example demonstrates how to do a little bit more than simply add a few days to a given date. In this example, a Date_Span object is used to add a certain number of days, but then the getNextWeekday() method is called to get the weekday that falls on the next weekday (Monday through Friday) after the dates have been added. Why go to all this trouble? It's handy if you're calculating times, such as for payroll processing, which might be done on the third business day after month closing.

```php
<?php
/* Adding Dates and Times. */

require_once 'Date.php';
require_once 'Date/Span.php';

$date = new Date('2006-04-05');
$date->setTZbyID('CST');
echo $date->format("Original date:  %A, %B %e %Y %n");

/* Now add three days to the current day */
$span = new Date_Span();
$span->setFromDays(3);

$date->addSpan($span);
echo $date->format("Three days later:  %A, %B %e %Y %n");

/* Now find the next business day */
$nextBusinessDate = $date->getNextWeekday();
echo $nextBusinessDate->format("The next weekday:  %A, %B %e %Y %n");
?>
```

You'll see the following output when you run the preceding example:

```
Original date:  Wednesday, April 5 2006
Three days later:  Saturday, April 8 2006
The next weekday:  Monday, April 10 2006
```

Comparing Dates

This example contains a potpourri of different date comparison methods. First, the isPast()
method is used to compare the date to today's date. Then, the Date::compare() method is used
to show the integer value of comparing two dates.

```php
<?php

/* Comparing dates */

require_once 'Date.php';

$date = new Date('2006-02-10');
echo $date >format("Date is:  %D%n");
echo sprintf("The date is %s today.\n",
    $date->isPast() ? "before" : "after");

/* Set the year to something in the future */
$date->setYear(2015);
echo $date->format("Date is:  %D%n");
echo sprintf("The date is %s today.\n",
    $date->isPast() ? "before" : "after");

$now = new Date();

/* Compare the future date with now. */
$result = Date::compare($now, $date);
echo sprintf('Comparing $now with $date:  %s', $result) . "\n";

$result = Date::compare($date, $now);
echo sprintf('Comparing $date with $now:  %s', $result) . "\n";
?>
```

The output of running the preceding example looks like this:

```
Date is:  02/10/2006
The date is before today.
Date is:  02/10/2015
The date is after today.
Comparing $now with $date:  -1
Comparing $date with $now:  1
```

Date_Holidays

The Date_Holidays package contains classes that allow you to get information about holidays during the course of a year. The Date_Holidays class includes a factory() method that returns a Date_Holidays_Driver. This driver class contains methods you can use to see if a particular date is a holiday, grab the holidays that fall within date ranges, and more.

Common Uses

Following are common uses of the Date_Holidays package:

- Printing out the dates of holidays throughout the year
- Checking to see if a given date falls on a holiday

Related Packages

The following related package is found in this book:

Date

Dependencies

Following are the dependencies for the Date_Holidays package.

Required Packages

XML_Serializer

Optional Packages

Console_Getargs

Date_Holidays API

Date_Holidays Constructor

Creates a new instance of a Date_Holidays object. Instead of using the constructor to create a new instance of the object, use the factory() method.

Date_Holidays Date_Holidays()

errorsOccurred()

Returns true if errors have occurred while attempting to create the Date_Holidays_Driver class.

boolean errorsOccurred()

factory()

Builds and returns an instance of an object that inherits the Date_Holidays_Driver class with the specified driver ID.

Date_Holidays_Driver factory(string $driverId [, string $year = null]
                                    [, string $locale = null] [, mixed $external = false])

Parameter	Type	Description
$driverId	string	A string that identifies the driver to load. See the getInstalledDrivers() method to get a list of the drivers you can use.
$year	string	The year you'd like to use for the holidays.
$locale	string	The locale to use, such as en_US.
$external	mixed	true if the specified driver ID is for a driver that isn't loaded with the base installation of the package.

factoryISO3166()

Builds and returns an instance of an object that inherits from the Date_Holiday_Driver class that conforms to the given International Standards Organization (ISO) code. The ISO codes are documented at http://www.iso.org/iso/en/prods-services/iso3166ma/02iso-3166-code-lists/list-en1.html.

Date_Holidays factoryISO3166(string $isoCode [, string $year = null]
                                    [, string $locale = null] [, mixed $external = false])

Parameter	Type	Description
$isoCode	string	The ISO 3166 code to use for loading the driver. Examples are FR, GB, and US for France, the United Kingdom, and the United States, respectively.
$year	string	The year for the holidays that are found by the driver.
$locale	string	The language locale to use, such as en_US.
$external	mixed	true if the specified locale is not in the standard package.

getErrors()

Returns an array of errors.

```
array getErrors([boolean $purge = false])
```

Parameter	Type	Description
$purge	boolean	If true, the existing errors are purged after they're returned.

getErrorStack()

Returns the error stack.

```
PEAR_ErrorStack &getErrorStack()
```

getInstalledDrivers()

Returns an array of the available driver names. The getInstalledDrivers() method does this by looking into its Driver directory and returning the files found, minus the .php extension.

```
array getInstalledDrivers([string $directory = null])
```

Parameter	Type	Description
$directory	string	The directory to look in for the drivers.

getInstalledFilters()

Similar to the getInstalledDrivers() method, this one parses through the Filters directory and returns the filters contained in it. Both these methods are handy if you don't have access to the file system, and therefore can't determine the names of the drivers and files.

```
array getInstalledFilters([string $directory = null])
```

Parameter	Type	Description
$directory	string	The directory to look in for the filters.

isError()

Returns true if the object passed in is an error object.

```
boolean isError(mixed $data [, integer $code = null])
```

Parameter	Type	Description
$data	mixed	The object to inspect to see if it is an error.
$code	integer	The error code to look for in the object.

raiseError()

Raises an error with the specified code and optional message.

```
PEAR_Error raiseError(integer $code [, string $msg = null])
```

Parameter	Type	Description
$code	integer	The code to use for the error.
$msg	string	The message that will be included in the new error.

staticGetProperty()

Returns the value of the given property without having an instance created of the Date_Holidays class.

```
mixed staticGetProperty(string $prop)
```

Parameter	Type	Description
$prop	string	The name of the property to return.

staticSetProperty()

Assigns the value of the given property without having an instance of the Date_Holidays class created.

```
void staticSetProperty(string $prop, string $value)
```

Parameter	Type	Description
$prop	string	The name of the property to set.
$value	string	The value that the property should be set to.

Date_Holidays_Driver API

Date_Holidays_Driver Constructor

Don't use the constructor to create an instance of the driver—instead use the factory() method on the Date_Holidays class.

```
Date_Holidays_Driver Date_Holidays_Driver()
```

addCompiledTranslationFile()

Makes the contents of the given file available to the driver.

```
boolean addCompiledTranslationFile(string $file, string $locale)
```

Parameter	Type	Description
$file	string	The name of the translation file.
$locale	string	The name of the locale for the translation.

addDriver()

Adds a driver.

```
void addDriver(object Date_Holidays_Driver $driver)
```

Parameter	Type	Description
$driver	Date_Holidays_Driver	A driver object that's added to load holidays.

Note The Date_Holidays package is in alpha status, so some of the methods are only partially implemented. As of the time of this writing, the addDriver() method is blank.

addTranslationFile()

Adds a file's content. The information in the file is available for the specified locale.

```
boolean addTranslationFile(string $file, string $locale)
```

Parameter	Type	Description
$file	string	The name of the file to load.
$locale	string	The locale contained in the file.

getHoliday()

Returns a Date_Holidays_Holiday object that's identified by the internal name.

```
Date_Holidays_Holiday getHoliday(string $internalName [, string $locale = null])
```

Parameter	Type	Description
$internalName	string	The internal designation for a holiday.
$locale	string	The locale to use when loading holiday information.

getHolidayDate()

Returns a Date that represents the given holiday name. The Date includes the month, day, and year of the holiday. If an error occurs, the method returns PEAR_Error.

```
Date getHolidayDate(string $internalName)
```

Parameter	Type	Description
$internalName	string	An internal designation for the holiday.

getHolidayDates()

Returns an array of Date objects using the specified filter.

```
array getHolidayDates([Date_Holidays_Filter $filter = null])
```

Parameter	Type	Description
$filter	Date_Holidays_Filter	A Date_Holidays_Filter object to use when retrieving the holidays.

getHolidayForDate()

Returns a Date_Holidays_Holiday object for the given date.

```
object getHolidayForDate(mixed $date [, string $locale = null]
                              [, boolean $multiple = false])
```

Parameter	Type	Description
$date	mixed	A string or object that contains a date.
$locale	string	The locale to use when loading the holiday information.
$multiple	boolean	If true, the method will load more than one holiday.

getHolidayProperties()

Returns an array of properties for the holiday identified by $internalName, or an empty array if properties are found.

```
array getHolidayProperties(string $internalName [, string $locale = null])
```

Parameter	Type	Description
$internalName	string	The internal name for the holiday.
$locale	string	The locale to use when loading information about the holiday.

getHolidays()

Returns an array of Date_Holidays_Holiday objects that match the specified filter, or a PEAR_Error object if an error occurred.

```
array getHolidays([Date_Holidays_Filter $filter = null] [, string $locale = null])
```

Parameter	Type	Description
$filter	Date_Holidays_Filter	The filter to use when retrieving holiday information.
$locale	string	The name of the locale to use when loading information about the holidays.

getHolidaysForDatespan()

Returns an array of Date_Holidays_Holiday objects for the holidays that occur between the two specified dates. If no holidays are found, then an empty array will be returned.

```
array getHolidaysForDatespan(mixed $start, mixed $end
                            [, Date_Holidays_Filter $filter = null]
                            [, string $locale = null])
```

Parameter	Type	Description
$start	mixed	The starting date of the time span.
$end	mixed	The end date of the time span.
$filter	Date_Holidays_Filter	The filter to use for loading holidays.
$locale	string	The locale to use when loading holiday information.

getHolidayTitle()

Returns the title of the holiday.

```
string getHolidayTitle(string $internalName [, string $locale = null])
```

Parameter	Type	Description
$internalName	string	An internal designation for the holiday.
$locale	string	The name of the locale to use for holiday information.

getHolidayTitles()

Returns an array of holiday titles that match the specified filter.

```
array getHolidayTitles([Date_Holidays_Filter $filter = null]
                       [, string $locale = null])
```

Parameter	Type	Description
$filter	Date_Holidays_Filter	The filter to use when retrieving holiday titles.
$locale	string	The locale to use for holiday information.

getInternalHolidayNames()

Returns an array of internal holiday names for the driver that's loaded.

```
array getInternalHolidayNames()
```

getISO3166Codes()

Returns an array of ISO 3166 codes for the holidays known by the driver that's loaded.

```
array getISO3166Codes()
```

Note The Date_Holidays package is in alpha status, so some of the methods are only partially implemented. As of the time of this writing, the `getISO3166Codes()` method simply returns an empty array.

---

getYear()

Returns the year for the current driver. When the factory loads the driver, you can specify a year. The driver loads the holidays that occur during that year.

```
integer getYear()
```

isHoliday()

Returns true if the given date is a holiday, or PEAR_Error if an error occurs.

```
boolean isHoliday(mixed $date [, Date_Holidays_Filter $filter = null])
```

Parameter	Type	Description
$date	mixed	The date that's being checked for holidays
$filter	Date_Holidays_Filter	The filter to apply when checking the date.

removeDriver()

Removes the specified driver from the list of loaded drivers.

```
boolean removeDriver(Date_Holidays_Driver $driver)
```

Parameter	Type	Description
$driver	Date_Holidays_Driver	The driver to remove from the list of holiday drivers.

Note As of the time of this writing, the `removeDriver()` method is blank.

---

setLocale()

Allows you to set the locale for which the driver will find and name holidays.

```
void setLocale(string $locale)
```

Parameter	Type	Description
$locale	string	The name of the locale to use for holiday information.

setYear()

Sets the year for holidays that are found by the driver, rebuilding the holidays for the given year.

```
boolean setYear(integer $year)
```

Parameter	Type	Description
$year	Integer	The year during which the holidays will occur. If 2003 is specified, the methods for the driver will return holidays that are specific to the year 2003.

Examples

Determining the Date of a US Holiday

This example demonstrates how to determine the dates for two US holidays in a particular year. The first holiday is formatted to display the long month name and the date. The second holiday is formatted to display the weekday on which the holiday falls.

```php
<?php
/* Determining the date of a US holiday */

require_once 'Date/Holidays.php';

$holidays = &Date_Holidays::factory('USA', 2007, 'en_EN');
if (Date_Holidays::isError($holidays)) {
    die('Factory was unable to produce driver-object');
}

$mlkDay = &$holidays->getHoliday('mlkDay', 'en_EN');
$date = $mlkDay->getDate();

echo $date->format("In %Y, Martin Luther King Day is on %B %d.%n");
```

```php
$independenceDay = &$holidays->getHoliday('independenceDay', 'en_EN');
$idDate = $independenceDay->getDate();
echo $idDate->format("In %Y, Independance Day is on a %A.%n");

?>
```

The output of this example is as follows:

```
In 2007, Martin Luther King Day is on January 15.
In 2007, Independance Day is on a Wednesday.
```

Determining If a Day Is a Holiday

Using a specific date, this example checks to see if the date is a holiday.

```php
<?php
/* Determining if a day is a holiday */

require_once 'Date/Holidays.php';

$holidays = &Date_Holidays::factory('Christian', 2008, 'en_EN');
if (Date_Holidays::isError($holidays)) {
    die('Factory was unable to produce driver-object');
}

$date = new Date('2008-12 25');

if ($holidays->isHoliday($date)) {
    echo $date->format('%D is a holiday!%n');
} else {
    echo $date->format('%D is NOT a holiday!%n');
}

?>
```

The output is as follows:

```
12/25/2008 is a holiday!
```

Getting the Holidays Between Two Dates

This example uses a range of dates to find out which holidays are within the date range. The getTitle() method displays the title of the holiday, and the format() method displays the day the holiday occurs.

```php
<?php

/* Getting the holidays between two dates. */

require_once 'Date/Holidays.php';

$holidays = &Date_Holidays::factory('USA');
if (Date_Holidays::isError($holidays)) {
    die('Factory was unable to produce driver-object');
}
$holidays->setLocale('en_EN');

$dates = $holidays->getHolidaysForDatespan('2006-04-01', '2006-08-01');
$limit = count($dates);

echo "Looking for holidays between '2006-04-01' and '2006-08-01':\n";

for ($i = 0; $i < $limit; $i++) {

    $date = $dates[$i]->getDate();

    printf("\t\"%s\" is on %s\n",
        $dates[$i]->getTitle(),
        $date->format("%B %d"));
}

?>
```

The output of this example is as follows:

```
Looking for holidays between '2006-04-01' and '2006-08-01':
    "Memorial Day" is on May 29
    "Independence Day" is on July 04
```

Numbers_Roman

The Numbers_Roman package, although smaller in API, is handy for making the translation between Roman numerals and decimal numbers.

Common Uses

The Numbers_Roman package is useful for the following purposes:

- Interesting display of copyright dates
- Using Roman numerals in titles and text
- Parsing Roman numerals into decimal numbers

Related Packages

The following package found in this book is related to Numbers_Roman:

Numbers_Words

Dependencies

Numbers_Roman depends on the following packages.

Required Packages

None

Optional Packages

None

API

toNumber()

Converts a given string, expressed as a Roman numeral such as IV or XII, into a decimal number such as 4 or 12.

```
integer toNumber(string $roman)
```

Parameter	Type	Description
$roman	string	A Roman numeral as a string.

toNumeral()

Converts a decimal number into a string that represents a Roman numeral; for example, 6 is converted to VI.

```
string toNumeral(integer $num, [boolean $uppercase = true], [boolean $html = true])
```

Parameter	Type	Description
$num	integer	A decimal number, such as 10, 100, or 1211.
$uppercase	boolean	If true, the Roman numeral string that's returned will be in uppercase.
$html	boolean	If true, the string that is returned will use HyperText Markup Language (HTML) formatting to place the bars above and below the numbers.

Examples

Converting to Roman Numerals

This example shows how you can convert decimal numbers into Roman numerals, in this case allowing you to be fancy with displaying a copyright notice by converting the year into a Roman numeral.

```
<?php
/* Converting to Roman Numbers */

require_once 'Numbers/Roman.php';
/* Getting fancy with turning years into Roman numerals. */
printf("Copyright (c) %s\n",
    Numbers_Roman::toNumeral(2006, true, false));

?>
```

Following is the output of the example:

```
Copyright (c) MMVI
```

Converting Roman Numerals to Decimal Numbers

One of the authors of this book is not known for being a sports fanatic. This example shows how to convert the Roman numerals, as used in the name of some famous sporting event in the US, into a decimal number.

```
<?php
/* Convert Roman Numerals to numbers */

require_once 'Numbers/Roman.php';

/* What was that Super Bowl, anyway? */

printf("Super Bowl XXXIV is number %s\n",
    Numbers_Roman::toNumber('XXXIV'));

?>
```

Here's the output of the preceding example:

```
Super Bowl XXXIV is number 34
```

Numbers_Words

The Numbers_Words package converts decimal numbers into words.

Common Uses

You can use Numbers_Words for the following purposes:

- Converting a number such as 100 into its text equivalent: one hundred
- Converting currency into text

Related Packages

The following package in this book is similar to Numbers_Words:

Numbers_Roman

Dependencies

Numbers_Words depends on the following other packages.

Required Packages

None

Optional Packages

None

API

raiseError()

Raises a PEAR error with the specified message. For performance reasons, the PEAR.php file is dynamically included in this method.

```
void raiseError(string $msg)
```

toCurrency()

Returns a string that represents the currency that's passed as an argument to the method, given the locale.

```
string toCurrency(float $num [, string $locale = 'en_US']
                         [, string $integer_curr = ''])
```

Parameter	Type	Description
$num	float	The currency expressed as a number, such as 1.50, 1,200.50, or 1,000.
$locale	string	The locale to use when interpreting the currency.
$integer_curr	string	A three-digit international currency code to use, as defined by the ISO 4217 standard.

toWords()

Returns a string that represents the number in words.

```
string toWords(integer $num [, string $locale = 'en_US'])
```

Parameter	Type	Description
$num	integer	The number to convert to words.
$locale	string	The name of the locale to use when assembling the words.

Examples

Converting Numbers into Words

This example demonstrates how to turn numbers into words.

```php
<?php
/* Converting numbers to words */
require_once 'Numbers/Words.php';

/* Print a bunch of different numbers out to see what they
 * say...
 */
printf("%s\n", Numbers_Words::toWords(1));
printf("%s\n", Numbers_Words::toWords(10));
printf("%s\n", Numbers_Words::toWords(100));
printf("%s\n", Numbers_Words::toWords(1000));
```

```
printf("%s\n", Numbers_Words::toWords(1002));
printf("%s\n", Numbers_Words::toWords(1357));

?>
```

The output of the example is as follows:

```
one
ten
one hundred
one thousand
one thousand two
one thousand three hundred fifty-seven
```

Converting Currency into Words

The example here shows how to turn numbers into words, using the toCurrency() method.

```php
<?php
/* Converts currency to words */
require_once 'Numbers/Words.php';

printf("%s\n", Numbers_Words::toCurrency(1.50));
printf("%s\n", Numbers_Words::toCurrency(10.99));
printf("%s\n", Numbers_Words::toCurrency(100.20));
printf("%s\n", Numbers_Words::toCurrency(17999.99));

?>
```

Here's the output:

```
one dollar fifty cents
ten dollars ninety-nine cents
one hundred dollars twenty cents
seventeen thousand nine hundred ninety-nine dollars ninety-nine cents
```

HTML

The PEAR packages in this section present ways in which you can quickly and easily work with HTML.

- The HTML_Crypt package provides a way for you to encrypt text in such a way that it can be decrypted on the client side using JavaScript.

- The HTML_Form package enables you to build HTML forms.

- The HTML_JavaScript package provides a set of PHP methods for writing out JavaScript code into the page.

- The HTML_Menu package builds a navigation structure from the data provided, in one of five possible formats.

- The HTML_Progress2_Lite package builds a JavaScript loading bar for your page.

- The HTML_QuickForm package provides an additional way of building and managing forms in your page, as well as validating their contents.

- The HTML_Safe package strips unsafe HTML tags from your page.

- The HTML_Table package lets you work with HTML tables just as you would with a spreadsheet table.

HTML_Crypt

The HTML_Crypt package contains methods for encrypting text in the page. Client-side JavaScript can then decrypt this text.

Common Uses

Common uses of the HTML_Crypt package are as follows:

Encrypting e-mail addresses in your web pages

Related Packages

None

Dependencies

HTML_Crypt has the following dependencies.

Required Packages

None

Optional Packages

None

API

HTML_Crypt

The HTML_Crypt constructor function creates the new HTML_Crypt object, optionally with the values provided. If you don't provide the text to encrypt, you can set it after you've created the object by using the setText method.

```
HTML_Crypt HTML_Crypt([string $text = ''] [, integer $offset = 3]
                                   [, boolean $JS = true])
```

Parameter	Type	Description
$text	string	The string to encrypt.
$offset	integer	The offset used when encrypting and decrypting the text.
$JS	boolean	Sets whether to use JavaScript to encrypt the text or not. Setting this to `false` does a simple obfuscation of the e-mail address.

addMailTo

Turns the encrypted text into a mailto: link. When a browser clicks on this link, the mail client will open with the correct To: field filled in.

```
void addMailTo()
```

getScript

Returns the HTML source for the JavaScript function to decrypt the encrypted text.

```
string getScript()
```

obEnd

Ends the output buffering previously enabled with `obStart`. The buffered contents are output to the browser.

```
obEnd()
```

obStart

Turns on PHP output buffering within the object.

```
void obStart()
```

output

Outputs the full JavaScript to the browser.

```
void output()
```

setText

Sets the text to be encrypted. For a mailto: link, you only have to provide the actual e-mail address, not the full link.

```
void setText(string $text)
```

Parameter	Type	Description
$text	string	The text string that you want to encrypt.

Examples

Doing Simple Encryption of an E-Mail Address

The HTML_Crypt package includes two styles of encrypting text and e-mail addresses. The first method we'll look at uses simple obfuscation of the elements that typically signify a piece of text as an e-mail address. By doing this, scripts that search through web pages for e-mail addresses miss the telltale @ signs, and your e-mail address is safe. Of course, this doesn't stop someone from manually converting the e-mail address into something usable.

Let's take a look at how this works:

```php
<?php
require_once('HTML/Crypt.php');
$crypt = new HTML_Crypt('allan@mediafrenzy.co.za',3,false);
$crypt->output();
?>
```

After requiring the class file, build the new HTML_Crypt object, passing it the third optional parameter as false, specifying that the encryption shouldn't be JavaScript-based.

The output looks like this:

```
allan ^at^ mediafrenzy-dot-co-dot-za
```

Encrypting a mailto: Link with JavaScript

In this example, you'll use the JavaScript encryption of the address in the page, as well as making it a mailto: link:

```php
<?php
require_once('HTML/Crypt.php');
$crypt = new HTML_Crypt('allan@mediafrenzy.co.za');
$crypt->addMailTo();
$crypt->output();
?>
```

When initializing the object this time, we've left off the optional attributes, because by default it will use JavaScript encryption of the text. The addMailto method converts the encrypted text into a mailto: link:

allan@mediafrenzy.co.za

Although the results in the browser look as if they include a standard e-mail address in a link, the source for that isn't what you would expect:

```
<script language="JavaScript" type="text/JavaScript">var a,s,n;function
da55f86951df8d8fe3fba99abfc65bcb1(s){r='';for(i=0;i<s.length;i++)
{n=s.charCodeAt(i);if(n>=8364){n=128;}r+=String.fromCharCode(n-3);}
Return r;}a='?d#kuhi@%pdlowr=doodqCphgldiuhq}
|1fr1}d%AdoodqCphgldiuhq}|1fr1}d?2dA';document.write
(da55f86951df8d8fe3fba99abfc65bcb1(a));</script>
```

HTML_Form

Even though the HTML_Form package has a large number of methods, the package is simply used to build an HTML form. The form object is built by calling methods to add individual form elements, and the resulting form is then displayed.

Common Uses

Common uses of the HTML_Form package are as follows:

Building forms for your web pages

Related Packages

None

Dependencies

HTML_Form has the following dependencies.

Optional Packages

None

Required Packages

None

API

HTML_Form

The HTML_Form constructor function builds a new HTML_Form object. This is the base object to which you'll add all your HTML form elements.

```
void HTML_Form(string $action [, string $method = 'GET']
                           [, string $name =''] [, string $target= '']
                           [, string $enctype = ''] [, string $attr = ''])
```

Parameter	Type	Description
$action	string	The filename or URI to which the form contents will be submitted.
$method	string	The form submission method—either GET or POST.
$name	string	The name attribute to give the form.
$target	string	The target window for the form submission.
$enctype	string	The encoding to use when submitting the form.
$attr	string	A string of any additional attributes that you wish to add to the form tag.

addBlank

Adds a blank row to the list of form fields.

```
void addBlank(integer $rows [, string $title = '']
                     [string $thattr = HTML_FORM_TH_ATTR]
                     [, string $tdattr = HTML_FORM_TD_ATTR])
```

Parameter	Type	Description
$rows	integer	The number of rows to create. If $title is specified, then this will be ignored.
$title	string	The label to be used for this row.
$thattr	string	A string of additional attributes to be included in the <th> element.
$tdattr	string	A string of additional attributes to be included in the <td> element.

addCheckbox

Adds a checkbox input type to the list of fields.

```
void addCheckbox(string $name, string $title [, boolean $default = false]
                       [, string $attr = '']
                       [, string $thattr = HTML_FORM_TH_ATTR]
                       [, string $tdattr = HTML_FORM_TD_ATTR])
```

Parameter	Type	Description
$name	string	The value to be used for the checkbox name.
$title	string	The string to be used as the label for the checkbox.
$default	boolean	If this is set to true, then the checkbox will be checked.
$attr	string	A string of any additional attributes to be included in the checkbox tag.
$thattr	string	A string of additional attributes to be included in the <th> element.
$tdattr	string	A string of additional attributes to be included in the <td> element.

addFile

Adds a file-upload form input to the list of fields in the form object.

```
void addFile(string $name, string $title
                [, integer $maxsize = HTML_FORM_MAX_FILE_SIZE]
                [, integer $size = HTML_FORM_TEXT_SIZE] [, string $accept = '']
                [, string $attr = ''] [, string $thattr = HTML_FORM_TH_ATTR]
                [, string $tdattr = HTML_FORM_TD_ATTR])
```

Parameter	Type	Description
$name	string	The name to give the form element.
$title	string	A string to be used as the label.
$maxsize	integer	How large the submitted file can be, in bytes.
$size	integer	The value to be used in the size attribute of the element.
$accept	string	A string that determines which MIME types are allowed.
$attr	string	A string of any additional attributes to be included in the file tag.
$thattr	string	A string of additional attributes to be included in the <th> element.
$tdattr	string	A string of additional attributes to be included in the <td> element.

addHidden

Adds a hidden input type to the list of fields.

```
void addHidden(string $name, string $value [, string $attr = ''])
```

Parameter	Type	Description
$name	string	The name of the form element.
$value	string	The value of the hidden form element.
$attr	string	Any additional attributes you want to give the form element.

addImage

Adds an image input type to the list of fields.

```
void addImage(string $name, string $title, string $src
                [, string $attr = ''] [, string $thattr = HTML_FORM_TH_ATTR]
                [, string $tdattr = HTML_FORM_TD_ATTR])
```

Parameter	Type	Description
$name	string	The name of the form field.
$title	string	The label to give the form field.
$src	string	The path to the image that should be displayed.
$attr	string	A string of any additional attributes to be included in the input image tag.
$thattr	string	A string of additional attributes to be included in the <th> element.
$tdattr	string	A string of additional attributes to be included in the <td> element.

addPassword

Adds two fields to the field list—a password entry box and a second box to confirm the new password.

```
void addPassword(string $name, string $title [, mixed $default = null]
                [, integer $size = HTML_FORM_PASSWD_SIZE]
                [, integer $maxlength = 0] [, string $attr = '']
                [, string $thattr = HTML_FORM_TH_ATTR]
                [, string $tdattr = HTML_FORM_TD_ATTR])
```

Parameter	Type	Description
$name	string	The name of the form field.
$title	string	The label to give the form field.
$default	mixed	A default value to use for the password field.
$size	integer	A value to use in the field's size attribute.
$maxlength	integer	The maximum number of characters that the field can contain.
$attr	string	A string of any additional attributes to be included in the password input tag.
$thattr	string	A string of additional attributes to be included in the <th> element.
$tdattr	string	A string of additional attributes to be included in the <td> element.

addPasswordOne

Adds a single password field to the list of form fields.

```
void addPasswordOne(string $name, string $title [, mixed $default = null]
                            [, integer $size = HTML_FORM_PASSWD_SIZE]
                            [, integer $maxlength = 0] [, string $attr = '']
                            [, string $thattr = HTML_FORM_TH_ATTR]
                            [, string $tdattr = HTML_FORM_TD_ATTR])
```

Parameter	Type	Description
$name	string	The name of the form field.
$title	string	The label to give the form field.
$default	mixed	A default value to use for the password field.
$size	integer	A value to use in the field's size attribute.
$maxlength	integer	The maximum number of characters that the field can contain.
$attr	string	A string of any additional attributes to be included in the password input tag.
$thattr	string	A string of additional attributes to be included in the <th> element.
$tdattr	string	A string of additional attributes to be included in the <td> element.

addPlaintext

Adds a row of text to be inserted at this point in the form.

```
void addPlaintext(string $title [, string $text = '']
                          [, string $thattr = HTML_FORM_TH_ATTR]
                          [, string $tdattr = HTML_FORM_TD_ATTR])
```

Parameter	Type	Description
$title	string	The label to give the form field.
$text	string	The text to include.
$thattr	string	A string of additional attributes to be included in the <th> element.
$tdattr	string	A string of additional attributes to be included in the <td> element.

addRadio

Adds a radio button type of input to the list of fields.

```
void addRadio(string $name, string $title , string $value
                [, boolean $default = false] [, string $attr = '']
                [, string $thattr = HTML_FORM_TH_ATTR]
                [, string $tdattr = HTML_FORM_TD_ATTR])
```

Parameter	Type	Description
$name	string	The name of the form field.
$title	string	The label to give the form field.
$value	string	The value that this radio element has.
$default	boolean	If set to true, then this radio button will be checked.
$attr	string	A string of any additional attributes to be included in the radio tag.
$thattr	string	A string of additional attributes to be included in the <th> element.
$tdattr	string	A string of additional attributes to be included in the <td> element.

addReset

Adds a reset button to the form.

```
void addReset([string $title = 'Discard Changes'] [, string $attr = '']
                [, string $thattr = HTML_FORM_TH_ATTR]
                [, string $tdattr = HTML_FORM_TD_ATTR])
```

Parameter	Type	Description
$title	string	The caption to include on the reset button.
$attr	string	A string of any additional attributes to be included in the reset input tag.
$thattr	string	A string of additional attributes to be included in the <th> element.
$tdattr	string	A string of additional attributes to be included in the <td> element.

addSelect

Adds a drop-down selection list to the list of fields. The individual options that are displayed are passed through as an associative array.

```
void addSelect(string $name, string $title, array $entries[, mixed $default = null]
                    [, integer $size = 1] [, string $blank ='']
                    [, boolean $multiple = false] [, string $attr = '']
                    [, string $thattr = HTML_FORM_TH_ATTR]
                    [, string $tdattr = HTML_FORM_TD_ATTR])
```

Parameter	Type	Description
$name	string	The name of the form field.
$title	string	The label to give the form field.
$entries	array	An associative array of the entries, where the key is used as the option value and the value of the array is used as the displayed text.
$default	mixed	A default value for the element.
$size	integer	The number of rows in the select element to display. A value of 1 shows a drop-down list; any other value shows that many rows of data.
$blank	string	If this is set to anything, it will be used as the text of the first option, and will have a blank value.
$multiple	boolean	If this is set to true, then multiple options can be selected simultaneously.
$attr	string	A string of any additional attributes to be included in the select tag.
$thattr	string	A string of additional attributes to be included in the <th> element.
$tdattr	string	A string of additional attributes to be included in the <td> element.

addSubmit

Adds a submit button to the list of fields.

```
void addSubmit([string $name = 'submit'] [, string $title = ''Submit Changes]
                    [, string $attr = '']
                    [, string $thattr = HTML_FORM_TH_ATTR]
                    [, string $tdattr = HTML_FORM_TD_ATTR])
```

Parameter	Type	Description
$name	string	The name to give the submit button.
$title	string	The caption to include on the submit button.
$attr	string	A string of any additional attributes for the element.
$thattr	string	A string of additional attributes to be included in the `<th>` element.
$tdattr	string	A string of additional attributes to be included in the `<td>` element.

addText

Adds a text input to the list of fields.

```
void addText(string $name, string $title [, mixed $default = '']
                [, integer $size = HTML_FORM_TEXT_SIZE]
                [, integer $maxlength = 0] [, string $attr = '']
                [, string $thattr = HTML_FORM_TH_ATTR]
                [, string $tdattr = HTML_FORM_TD_ATTR])
```

Parameter	Type	Description
$name	string	The name of the form field.
$title	string	The label to give the form field.
$default	mixed	A default value to use for the text field.
$size	integer	A value to use in the field's size attribute
$maxlength	integer	The maximum number of characters that the field can contain.
$attr	string	A string of any additional attributes to be included in the text input tag.
$thattr	string	A string of additional attributes to be included in the `<th>` element.
$tdattr	string	A string of additional attributes to be included in the `<td>` element.

addTextarea

Adds a text area to the list of fields.

```
void addTextarea(string $name, string $title [, mixed $default = null]
                    [, integer $width = HTML_FORM_TEXTAREA_WT]
                    [, integer $height = HTML_FORM_TEXTAREA_hT]
                    [, integer $maxlength = 0] [, string $attr = '']
                    [, string $thattr = HTML_FORM_TH_ATTR]
                    [, string $tdattr = HTML_FORM_TD_ATTR])
```

Parameter	Type	Description
$name	string	The name of the form field.
$title	string	The label to give the form field.
$default	mixed	A default value to use for the textarea field.
$width	integer	A value to specify how wide the textarea should be.
$height	integer	A value to specify how many rows high the textarea should be.
$maxlength	integer	The maximum number of characters that the field can contain.
$attr	string	A string of any additional attributes to be included in the textarea tag.
$thattr	string	A string of additional attributes to be included in the <th> element.
$tdattr	string	A string of additional attributes to be included in the <td> element.

display

Processes the list of fields that you've added using the add* methods, and outputs them all in a complete form. The form is output to the browser and not returned to you as a string. If default values for the form input elements haven't been provided, the method looks for values passed in the $_GET and $_POST arrays. You can disable this behavior with the setDefaultFromInput() method.

```
void display([string $attr = ''] [, string $caption = ''] [, string $capattr = ''])
```

Parameter	Type	Description
$attr	string	A string of additional attributes to be included in the table tag.
$caption	string	If present, the table caption is set to this.
$capattr	string	A string of additional attributes to be included with the caption tag.

displayBlank

Outputs an   character.

```
void displayBlank()
```

displayBlankRow

Displays a blank row in the table.

```
void displayBlankRow(integer $i [, string $title = '']
                            [, string $thattr = HTML_FORM_TH_ATTR]
                            [, string $tdattr = HTML_FORM_TD_ATTR])
```

Parameter	Type	Description
$i	integer	The number of blank rows to display. If $title is set, then this will be ignored and only one row will be displayed.
$title	string	A string to be used as the label for the table row.
$thattr	string	A string of additional attributes to be used in the `<th>` element of the row.
$tdattr	string	A string of additional attributes to be used in the `<td>` element of the row.

displayCheckbox

Prints out a checkbox input.

```
void displayCheckbox(string $name [, boolean $default = false]
                                  [, string $attr = ''])
```

Parameter	Type	Description
$name	string	The name to give the checkbox.
$default	boolean	If this is set to true, then the checkbox will be checked when displayed.
$attr	string	A string of any additional attributes to be included in the input tag.

displayCheckboxRow

Prints out a checkbox form element in a table row.

```
void displayCheckboxRow(string $name, string $title [, boolean $default = false]
                                   [, string $attr = '']
                                   [, string $thattr = HTML_FORM_TH_ATTR]
                                   [, string $tdattr = HTML_FORM_TD_ATTR])
```

Parameter	Type	Description
$name	string	The name to give the checkbox.
$title	string	A string to be used as the label for the table row.
$default	boolean	If this is set to true, then the checkbox will be checked when displayed.
$attr	string	A string of any additional attributes to be included in the input tag.
$thattr	string	A string of additional attributes to be used in the `<th>` element of the row.
$tdattr	string	A string of additional attributes to be used in the `<td>` element of the row.

displayFile

Displays a file-upload input type.

```
void displayFile(string $name [, integer $maxsize = HTML_FORM_MAX_FILE_SIZE]
                    [, integer $size = HTML_FORM_TEXT_SIZE]
                    [, string $accept = ''] [, string $attr = ''])
```

Parameter	Type	Description
$name	string	The name to give the file upload element.
$maxsize	integer	An integer that limits the maximum size that the file upload can be (in bytes).
$size	integer	An integer to use in the form element size attribute.
$accept	string	A string that specifies which MIME types are allowed to be uploaded.
$attr	string	A string of any additional attributes to use in the form element tag.

displayFileRow

Displays a file-upload input type in a table row.

```
void displayFileRow(string $name, string $title
                        [, integer $maxsize = HTML_FORM_MAX_FILE_SIZE]
                        [, integer $size = HTML_FORM_TEXT_SIZE]
                        [, string $accept = ''] [, string $attr = '']
                        [, string $thattr = HTML_FORM_TH_ATTR]
                        [, string $tdattr = HTML_FORM_TD_ATTR])
```

Parameter	Type	Description
$name	string	The name to give the file upload element.
$title	string	The title to give the table row added.
$maxsize	integer	An integer that limits the maximum size that the file upload can be (in bytes).
$size	integer	An integer to use in the form element size attribute.
$accept	string	A string that specifies which MIME types are allowed to be uploaded.
$attr	string	A string of any additional attributes to use in the form element tag.
$thattr	string	A string of additional attributes to be used in the <th> element of the row.
$tdattr	string	A string of additional attributes to be used in the <td> element of the row.

displayHidden

Outputs a hidden form-input element.

```
void displayHidden(string $name, string $value[, string $attr = ''])
```

Parameter	Type	Description
$name	string	The name to give the hidden form element.
$value	string	The value to give the hidden form element.
$attr	string	A string of any additional attributes to include in the form input tag.

displayImage

Prints out an image input element.

```
void displayImage(string $name, string $src [, string $attr = ''])
```

Parameter	Type	Description
$name	string	The name to give the image input element.
$src	string	A string specifying the path to the image to use in the input element.
$attr	string	A string of any additional attributes to be included in the form input element.

displayImageRow

Outputs an image input element in a table row.

```
void displayImage(string $name, string $title, string $src [, string $attr = '']
                  [, string $thattr = HTML_FORM_TH_ATTR]
                  [, string $tdattr = HTML_FORM_TD_ATTR])
```

Parameter	Type	Description
$name	string	The name to give the image input element.
$title	string	A string to use as the label for the table row.
$src	string	A string specifying the path to the image to use in the input element.
$attr	string	A string of any additional attributes to be included in the form input element.
$thattr	string	A string of additional attributes to be used in the \<th> element of the row.
$tdattr	string	A string of additional attributes to be used in the \<td> element of the row.

displayPassword

Prints out a password input element.

```
void displayPassword(string $name [, mixed $default = null]
                            [, integer $size = HTML_FORM_PASSWD_SIZE]
                            [, integer $maxlength = 0] [ string $attr = ''])
```

Parameter	Type	Description
$name	string	The name to give the password input element.
$default	mixed	The default value for the password element.
$size	integer	The value for the size attribute of the password input.
$maxlength	integer	The maximum length that the password can be.
$attr	string	A string of any additional attributes to be used in the input tag.

displayPasswordRow

Displays a password input element and password confirmation in a table row.

```
void displayPasswordRow(string $name, string $title [, mixed $default = null]
                               [, integer $size = HTML_FORM_PASSWD_SIZE]
                               [, integer $maxlength = 0]
                               [ string $attr = '']
                               [, string $thattr = HTML_FORM_TH_ATTR]
                               [, string $tdattr = HTML_FORM_TD_ATTR])
```

Parameter	Type	Description
$name	string	The name to give the password input element.
$title	string	The label to give the table row.
$default	mixed	The default value for the password element.
$size	integer	The value for the size attribute of the password input.
$maxlength	integer	The maximum length that the password can be.
$attr	string	A string of any additional attributes to be used in the input tag.
$thattr	string	A string of additional attributes to be used in the <th> element of the row.
$tdattr	string	A string of additional attributes to be used in the <td> element of the row.

displayPasswordOneRow

Displays a password input in a table row.

```
void displayPasswordOneRow(string $name, string $title [, mixed $default = null]
                                        [, integer $size = HTML_FORM_PASSWD_SIZE]
                                        [, integer $maxlength = 0]
                                        [ string $attr = '']
                                        [, string $thattr = HTML_FORM_TH_ATTR]
                                        [, string $tdattr = HTML_FORM_TD_ATTR])
```

Parameter	Type	Description
$name	string	The name to give the password input element.
$title	string	The label to give the table row.
$default	mixed	The default value for the password element.
$size	integer	The value for the size attribute of the password input.
$maxsize	integer	The maximum length that the password can be.
$attr	string	A string of any additional attributes to be used in the input tag.
$thattr	string	A string of additional attributes to be used in the <th> element of the row.
$tdattr	string	A string of additional attributes to be used in the <td> element of the row.

displayPlaintext

Prints out the text provided.

```
void displayPlaintext([string $text = ' '])
```

Parameter	Type	Description
$text	string	The text string to display.

displayPlaintextRow

Prints out the text provided in a table row.

```
void displayPlaintextRow(string $title [, string $text = ' ']
                    [, string $thattr ='align=''right'' valign=''top''']
                    [, string $tdattr = HTML_FORM_TD_ATTR])
```

Parameter	Type	Description
$title	string	The label to give the table row.
$text	string	The text string to display.
$thattr	string	A string of additional attributes to be used in the <th> element of the row.
$tdattr	string	A string of additional attributes to be used in the <td> element of the row.

displayRadio

Displays a radio button input type.

```
void displayRadio(string $name, string $value [, boolean $default = false]
                    [, string $attr = ''])
```

Parameter	Type	Description
$name	string	The name to give the radio button.
$value	string	The value to give the radio button.
$default	boolean	If this is set to true, then the radio button will be selected when displayed.
$attr	string	A string of any additional attributes to be included in the input tag.

displayRadioRow

Displays a radio button in a table row.

```
void displayRadioRow(string $name, string $title, string $value
                            [, boolean $default = false]
                            [, string $attr = '']
                            [, string $thattr = HTML_FORM_TH_ATTR]
                            [, string $tdattr = HTML_FORM_TD_ATTR])
```

Parameter	Type	Description
$name	string	The name to give the radio button.
$title	string	The label to give the table row.
$value	string	The value to give the radio button.
$default	boolean	If this is set to `true`, then the radio button will be selected when displayed.
$attr	string	A string of any additional attributes to be included in the input tag.
$thattr	string	A string of additional attributes to be used in the `<th>` element of the row.
$tdattr	string	A string of additional attributes to be used in the `<td>` element of the row.

displayReset

Displays a reset input button.

```
void displayReset([string $title = 'Clear contents'] [, string $attr = ''])
```

Parameter	Type	Description
$title	string	The caption to display on the reset button.
$attr	string	A string of any additional attributes to include with the input tag.

displayResetRow

Displays a reset input button in a table row.

```
void displayResetRow([string $title = 'Clear contents'] [, string $attr = '']
                     [, string $thattr = HTML_FORM_TH_ATTR]
                     [, string $tdattr = HTML_FORM_TD_ATTR])
```

Parameter	Type	Description
$title	string	The caption to display on the reset button.
$attr	string	A string of any additional attributes to include with the input tag.
$thattr	string	A string of additional attributes to be used in the `<th>` element of the row.
$tdattr	string	A string of additional attributes to be used in the `<td>` element of the row.

displaySelect

Displays a select input type, either as a drop-down menu or as a list of selectable options.

```
void displaySelect(string $name, array $entries [, mixed $default = null]
                   [, integer $size = 1] [, string $blank = '']
                   [, boolean $multiple = false] [, string $attr = ''])
```

Parameter	Type	Description
$name	string	The name of the form field.
$entries	array	An associative array of the entries, where the key is used as the option value, and the value of the array is used as the displayed text.
$default	mixed	A default value for the element.
$size	integer	The number of rows in the select element to display. A value of 1 shows a drop-down list; any other value shows that many rows of data.
$blank	string	If this is set to anything, it will be used as the text of the first option, and will have a blank value.
$multiple	boolean	If this is set to true, then multiple options can be selected simultaneously.
$attr	string	A string of any additional attributes to be included in the select tag.

displaySelectRow

Displays a select input type in a table row.

```
void displaySelectRow(string $name, string $title,
                      array $entries[, mixed $default = null]
                      [, integer $size = 1] [, string $blank ='']
                      [, boolean $multiple = false] [, string $attr = '']
                      [, string $thattr = HTML_FORM_TH_ATTR]
                      [, string $tdattr = HTML_FORM_TD_ATTR])
```

Parameter	Type	Description
$name	string	The name of the form field.
$title	string	The label to give the form field.
$entries	array	An associative array of the entries, where the key is used as the option value, and the value of the array is used as the displayed text.
$default	mixed	A default value for the element.
$size	integer	The number of rows in the select element to display. A value of 1 shows a drop-down list; any other value shows that many rows of data.

Parameter	Type	Description
$blank	string	If this is set to anything, it will be used as the text of the first option, and will have a blank value.
$multiple	boolean	If this is set to true, then multiple options can be selected simultaneously.
$attr	string	A string of any additional attributes to be included in the select tag.
$thattr	string	A string of additional attributes to be included in the <th> element.
$tdattr	string	A string of additional attributes to be included in the <td> element.

displaySubmit

Prints out a submit button.

```
void displaySubmit([string $title = ''Submit Changes] [, string $name = 'submit']
                [, string $attr = ''])
```

Parameter	Type	Description
$title	string	The caption to include on the submit button.
$name	string	The name to give the submit button.
$attr	string	A string of any additional attributes for the element.

displaySubmitRow

Prints out a submit button within a table row.

```
void displaySubmitRow([string $name = 'submit'] [, string $title = 'Submit Changes']
                    [, string $attr = '']
                    [, string $thattr = HTML_FORM_TH_ATTR]
                    [, string $tdattr = HTML_FORM_TD_ATTR])
```

Parameter	Type	Description
$name	string	The name to give the submit button.
$title	string	The caption to include on the submit button.
$attr	string	A string of any additional attributes for the element.
$thattr	string	A string of additional attributes to be included in the <th> element.
$tdattr	string	A string of additional attributes to be included in the <td> element.

displayText

Prints out a text input element.

```
void displayText (string $name, [, mixed $default = null]
                            [, integer $size = HTML_FORM_TEXT_SIZE]
                            [, integer $maxlength = 0] [, string $attr = ''])
```

Parameter	Type	Description
$name	string	The name of the form field.
$default	mixed	A default value to use for the text field.
$size	integer	A value to use in the field's size attribute.
$maxlength	integer	The maximum number of characters that the field can contain.
$attr	string	A string of any additional attributes to be included in the text input tag.

displayTextarea

Displays a textarea input type.

```
void displayTextarea(string $name, [, mixed $default = null']
                             [, integer $width = 40] [, integer $height = 5]
                             [, integer $maxlength = ''] [, string $attr = ''])
```

Parameter	Type	Description
$name	string	The name of the form field.
$default	mixed	A default value to use for the textarea field.
$width	integer	A value to specify how many characters wide the textarea should be.
$height	integer	A value to specify how many rows high the textarea should be.
$maxlength	integer	The maximum number of characters that the field can contain.
$attr	string	A string of any additional attributes to be included in the textarea tag.

displayTextareaRow

Displays a textarea input type within a table row.

```
void displayTextareaRow(string $name, string $title [, mixed $default = null]
                        [, integer $width = 40] [, integer $height = 5]
                        [, integer $maxlength = 0]
                        [, string $attr = '']
                        [, string $thattr = HTML_FORM_TH_ATTR]
                        [, string $tdattr = HTML_FORM_TD_ATTR])
```

Parameter	Type	Description
$name	string	The name of the form field.
$title	string	The label to give the form field.
$default	mixed	A default value to use for the textarea field.
$width	integer	A value to specify how many characters wide the textarea should be.
$height	integer	A value to specify how many rows high the textarea should be.
$maxlength	integer	The maximum number of characters that the field can contain.
$attr	string	A string of any additional attributes to be included in the textarea tag.
$thattr	string	A string of additional attributes to be included in the <th> element.
$tdattr	string	A string of additional attributes to be included in the <td> element.

displayTextRow

Prints out a text input element within a table row.

```
void displayTextRow(string $name, string $title [, mixed $default = null]
                    [, integer $size = HTML_FORM_TEXT_SIZE]
                    [, integer $maxlength = 0] [, string $attr = '']
                    [, string $thattr = HTML_FORM_TH_ATTR]
                    [, string $tdattr = HTML_FORM_TD_ATTR])
```

Parameter	Type	Description
$name	string	The name of the form field.
$title	string	The label to give to the form field.
$default	mixed	A default value to use for the text field.
$size	integer	A value to use in the field's size attribute.
$maxlength	integer	The maximum number of characters that the field can contain.
$attr	string	A string of any additional attributes to be included in the text input tag.
$thattr	string	A string of additional attributes to be included in the <th> element.
$tdattr	string	A string of additional attributes to be included in the <td> element.

end

Prints out the ending tags for both the table that's laying out the form structure, and for the form itself.

```
void end()
```

returnBlank

Returns a string containing an   character.

```
string returnBlank()
```

returnBlankRow

Returns a string containing a blank table row.

```
string returnBlankRow(integer $i [, string $title = '']
                                 [, string $thattr = HTML_FORM_TH_ATTR]
                                 [, string $tdattr = HTML_FORM_TD_ATTR])
```

Parameter	Type	Description
$i	integer	The number of blank rows to return. If $caption is set, then this will be ignored, and only one row will be displayed.
$title	string	A string to be used as the label for the table row.
$thattr	string	A string of additional attributes to be used in the <th> element of the row.
$tdattr	string	A string of additional attributes to be used in the <td> element of the row.

returnCheckbox

Returns a string containing a checkbox input.

```
string returnCheckbox(string $name [, boolean $default = false]
                                   [, string $attr = ''])
```

Parameter	Type	Description
$name	string	The name to give the checkbox.
$default	boolean	If this is set to true, then the checkbox will be checked when displayed.
$attr	string	A string of any additional attributes to be included in the input tag.

returnCheckboxRow

Returns a string containing a checkbox form element in a table row.

```
string returnCheckboxRow(string $name, string $title [, boolean $default = false]
                                     [, string $attr = '']
                                     [, string $thattr = HTML_FORM_TH_ATTR]
                                     [, string $tdattr = HTML_FORM_TD_ATTR])
```

Parameter	Type	Description
$name	string	The name to give the checkbox.
$title	string	A string to be used as the label for the table row.
$default	boolean	If this is set to true, then the checkbox will be checked when displayed.
$attr	string	A string of any additional attributes to be included in the input tag.
$thattr	string	A string of additional attributes to be used in the <th> element of the row.
$tdattr	string	A string of additional attributes to be used in the <td> element of the row.

returnEnd

Returns a string containing closing tags for the form and table.

```
string returnEnd()
```

returnFile

The returnFile method returns a string containing a file-upload input type.

```
string returnFile([string $name = 'userfile']
                  [, integer $maxsize = HTML_FORM_MAX_FILE_SIZE]
                  [, integer $size = HTML_FORM_TEXT_SIZE]
                  [, string $accept = '']
                  [, string $attr = ''])
```

Parameter	Type	Description
$name	string	The name to give the file upload element.
$maxsize	integer	An integer that limits the maximum size that the file upload can be (in bytes).
$size	integer	An integer to use in the form element size attribute.
$accept	string	A string that specifies which MIME types are allowed to be uploaded.
$attr	string	A string of any additional attributes to use in the form element tag.

returnFileRow

Returns a string containing a file-upload input type in a table row.

```
string returnFileRow(string $name, string $title
                     [, integer $maxsize = HTML_FORM_MAX_FILE_SIZE]
                     [, integer $size = HTML_FORM_TEXT_SIZE]
                     [, string $accept = ''] [, string $attr = '']
                     [, string $thattr = HTML_FORM_TH_ATTR]
                     [, string $tdattr = HTML_FORM_TD_ATTR])
```

Parameter	Type	Description
$name	string	The name to give the file upload element.
$title	string	The title to give to the table row added.
$maxsize	integer	An integer that limits the maximum size that the file upload can be (in bytes).
$size	integer	An integer to use in the form element size attribute.
$accept	string	A string that specifies which MIME types are allowed to be uploaded.
$attr	string	A string of any additional attributes to use in the form element tag.
$thattr	string	A string of additional attributes to be used in the <th> element of the row.
$tdattr	string	A string of additional attributes to be used in the <td> element of the row.

returnHidden

Returns a string containing a hidden form input element.

```
string returnHidden(string $name, string $value [, string $attr = ''])
```

Parameter	Type	Description
$name	string	The name to give the hidden form element.
$value	string	The value to give the hidden form element.
$attr	string	A string of any additional attributes to include in the form input tag.

returnImage

Returns a string containing an image input element.

```
string returnImage(string $name, string $src [, string $attr = ''])
```

Parameter	Type	Description
$name	string	The name to give the image input element.
$src	string	A string specifying the path to the image to use in the input element.
$attr	string	A string of any additional attributes to be included in the form input element.

returnImageRow

Returns a string containing an image input element in a table row.

```
string returnImageRow(string $name, string $title, string $src [, string $attr = '']
                      [, string $thattr = HTML_FORM_TH_ATTR]
                      [, string $tdattr = HTML_FORM_TD_ATTR])
```

Parameter	Type	Description
$name	string	The name to give the image input element.
$title	string	A string to use as the label for the table row.
$src	string	A string specifying the path to the image to use in the input element.
$attr	string	A string of any additional attributes to be included in the form input element.
$thattr	string	A string of additional attributes to be used in the <th> element of the row.
$tdattr	string	A string of additional attributes to be used in the <td> element of the row.

returnMultipleFiles

Returns a string containing multiple file upload elements.

```
string returnMultipleFiles([string $name = 'userfile']
                           [, integer $maxsize = HTML_FORM_MAX_FILE_SIZE]
                           [, integer $files = 3]
                           [, integer $size = HTML_FORM_TEXT_SIZE]
                           [, string $accept = ''] [, string $attr = ''])
```

Parameter	Type	Description
$name	string	The name to give the file upload element.
$maxsize	integer	An integer that limits the maximum size that the file upload can be (in bytes).
$files	integer	Specifies how many file input form elements to display.
$size	integer	An integer to use in the form element size attribute.
$accept	string	A string that specifies which MIME types are allowed to be uploaded.
$attr	string	A string of any additional attributes to use in the form element tag.

returnPassword

Returns a string containing a password input element.

```
string returnPassword(string $name [, mixed $default = null]
                      [, integer $size = HTML_FORM_PASSWD_SIZE]
                      [, integer $maxlength = 0] [ string $attr = ''])
```

Parameter	Type	Description
$name	string	The name to give the password input element.
$default	mixed	The default value for the password element.
$size	integer	The value for the size attribute of the password input.
$maxlength	integer	The maximum length that the password can be.
$attr	string	A string of any additional attributes to be used in the input tag.

returnPasswordOneRow

Returns a string containing a password input in a table row.

```
string returnPasswordOneRow(string $name, string $title [, mixed $default = null]
                            [, integer $size = HTML_FORM_PASSWD_SIZE]
                            [, integer $maxlength = 0] [ string $attr = '']
                            [, string $thattr = HTML_FORM_TH_ATTR]
                            [, string $tdattr = HTML_FORM_TD_ATTR])
```

Parameter	Type	Description
$name	string	The name to give the password input element.
$title	string	The label to give the table row.
$default	mixed	The default value for the password element.
$size	integer	The value for the size attribute of the password input.
$maxlength	integer	The maximum length that the password can be.
$attr	string	A string of any additional attributes to be used in the input tag.
$thattr	string	A string of additional attributes to be used in the <th> element of the row.
$tdattr	string	A string of additional attributes to be used in the <td> element of the row.

returnPasswordRow

Returns a string containing a password input element and password confirmation in a table row.

```
string returnPasswordRow(string $name, string $title [, mixed $default = null]
                         [, integer $size = HTML_FORM_PASSWD_SIZE]
                         [, integer $maxlength = 0] [ string $attr = '']
                         [, string $thattr = HTML_FORM_TH_ATTR]
                         [, string $tdattr = HTML_FORM_TD_ATTR])
```

Parameter	Type	Description
$name	string	The name to give the password input element.
$title	string	The label to give the table row.
$default	mixed	The default value for the password element.
$size	integer	The value for the size attribute of the password input.
$maxlength	integer	The maximum length that the password can be.
$attr	string	A string of any additional attributes to be used in the input tag.
$thattr	string	A string of additional attributes to be used in the <th> element of the row.
$tdattr	string	A string of additional attributes to be used in the <td> element of the row.

returnPlaintext

Returns a string containing the text provided.

```
string returnPlaintext([string $text = ' '])
```

Parameter	Type	Description
$text	string	The text string to display.

returnPlaintextRow

Returns a string containing the text provided in a table row.

```
string returnPlaintextRow(string $title [, string $text = ' ']
                          [, string $thattr =HTML_FORM_TH_ATTR]
                          [, string $tdattr = HTML_FORM_TD_ATTR])
```

Parameter	Type	Description
$title	string	The label to give the table row.
$text	string	The text string to display.
$thattr	string	A string of additional attributes to be used in the <th> element of the row.
$tdattr	string	A string of additional attributes to be used in the <td> element of the row.

returnRadio

Returns a string containing a radio button input type.

```
string returnRadio(string $name, string $value [, boolean $default = false]
                   [, string $attr = ''])
```

Parameter	Type	Description
$name	string	The name to give the radio button.
$value	string	The value to give the radio button.
$default	boolean	If this is set to true, then the radio button will be selected when displayed.
$attr	string	A string of any additional attributes to be included in the input tag.

returnRadioRow

Returns a string containing a radio button in a table row.

```
string returnRadioRow(string $name, string $title, string $value
                      [, boolean $default = false] [, string $attr = '']
                      [, string $thattr = HTML_FORM_TH_ATTR]
                      [, string $tdattr = HTML_FORM_TD_ATTR])
```

Parameter	Type	Description
$name	string	The name to give the radio button.
$title	string	The label to give the table row.
$value	string	The value to give the radio button.
$default	boolean	If this is set to true, then the radio button will be selected when displayed.
$attr	string	A string of any additional attributes to be included in the input tag.
$thattr	string	A string of additional attributes to be used in the <th> element of the row.
$tdattr	string	A string of additional attributes to be used in the <td> element of the row.

returnReset

Returns a string containing a reset input button.

```
string returnReset([string $title = 'Clear contents'] [, string $attr = ''])
```

Parameter	Type	Description
$title	string	The caption to display on the reset button.
$attr	string	A string of any additional attributes to include with the input tag.

returnResetRow

Returns a string containing a reset input button in a table row.

```
string returnResetRow([string $title = 'Clear contents'] [, string $attr = '']
                      [, string $thattr = HTML_FORM_TH_ATTR]
                      [, string $tdattr = HTML_FORM_TD_ATTR])
```

Parameter	Type	Description
$title	string	The caption to display on the reset button.
$attr	string	A string of any additional attributes to include with the input tag.
$thattr	string	A string of additional attributes to be used in the <th> element of the row.
$tdattr	string	A string of additional attributes to be used in the <td> element of the row.

returnSelect

Returns a string containing a select input type, either as a drop-down menu or as a list of selectable options.

```
string returnSelect(string $name, array $entries [, mixed $default = null]
                               [, integer $size = 1] [, string $blank = '']
                               [, boolean $multiple = false] [, string $attr = ''])
```

Parameter	Type	Description
$name	string	The name of the form field.
$entries	array	An associative array of the entries, where the key is used as the option value, and the value of the array is used as the displayed text.
$default	mixed	A default value for the element.
$size	integer	The number of rows in the select element to display. A value of 1 shows a drop-down list; any other value shows that many rows of data.
$blank	string	If this is set to anything, it will be used as the text of the first option, and will have a blank value.
$multiple	boolean	If this is set to true, then multiple options can be selected simultaneously.
$attr	string	A string of any additional attributes to be included in the select tag.

returnSelectRow

Returns a string containing a select input type in a table row.

```
string returnSelectRow(string $name, string $title,
                           array $entries[, mixed $default = null] [, integer $size = 1]
                           [, string $blank =''] [, boolean $multiple = false]
                           [, string $attr = ''] [, string $thattr = HTML_FORM_TH_ATTR]
                           [, string $tdattr = HTML_FORM_TD_ATTR])
```

Parameter	Type	Description
$name	string	The name of the form field.
$title	string	The label to give the form field.
$entries	array	An associative array of the entries, where the key is used as the option value and the value of the array is used as the displayed text.
$default	mixed	A default value for the element.
$size	integer	The number of rows in the select element to display. A value of 1 shows a drop-down list; any other value shows that many rows of data.
$blank	string	If this is set to anything, it will be used as the text of the first option, and will have a blank value.
$multiple	boolean	If this is set to true, then multiple options can be selected simultaneously.
$attr	string	A string of any additional attributes to be included in the select tag.
$thattr	string	A string of additional attributes to be included in the <th> element.
$tdattr	string	A string of additional attributes to be included in the <td> element.

returnStart

Returns a string containing the opening tags for the form and table.

```
string returnStart([boolean $multipart = false])
```

Parameter	Type	Description
$multipart	boolean	If this is set to true, then the form will be submitted using multi-part format.

returnSubmit

Returns a string containing a submit button.

```
string returnSubmit([string $title = ''Submit Changes] [, string $name = 'submit']
                    [, string $attr = ''])
```

Parameter	Type	Description
$title	string	The caption to include on the submit button.
$name	string	The name to give the submit button.
$attr	string	A string of any additional attributes for the element.

returnSubmitRow

Returns a string containing a submit button within a table row.

```
string returnSubmitRow([string $name = 'submit']
                       [, string $title = ''Submit Changes]
                       [, string $attr = '']
                       [, string $thattr = HTML_FORM_TH_ATTR]
                       [, string $tdattr = HTML_FORM_TD_ATTR])
```

Parameter	Type	Description
$name	string	The name to give the submit button.
$title	string	The caption to include on the submit button.
$attr	string	A string of any additional attributes for the element.
$thattr	string	A string of additional attributes to be included in the <th> element.
$tdattr	string	A string of additional attributes to be included in the <td> element.

returnText

Returns a string containing a text input element.

```
string returnText (string $name, [, mixed $default = null]
                       [, integer $size = HTML_FORM_TEXT_SIZE]
                       [, integer $maxlength = 0] [, string $attr = ''])
```

Parameter	Type	Description
$name	string	The name of the form field.
$default	mixed	A default value to use for the text field.
$size	integer	A value to use in the field's size attribute.
$maxlength	integer	The maximum number of characters that the field can contain.
$attr	string	A string of any additional attributes to be included in the text input tag.

returnTextarea

Returns a string containing a textarea input type.

```
string returnTextarea(string $name, [, mixed $default = null]
                       [, integer $width = 40] [, integer $height = 5]
                       [, integer $maxlength = 0] [, string $attr = ''])
```

Parameter	Type	Description
$name	string	The name of the form field.
$default	mixed	A default value to use for the textarea field.
$width	integer	A value to specify how wide the textarea should be.
$height	integer	A value to specify how many rows high the textarea should be.
$maxlength	integer	The maximum number of characters that the field can contain.
$attr	string	A string of any additional attributes to be included in the textarea tag.

returnTextareaRow

Returns a string containing a textarea input type within a table row.

```
string returnTextareaRow(string $name, string $title [, mixed $default = null]
                         [, integer $width = 40] [, integer $height = 5]
                         [, integer $maxlength = 0] [, string $attr = '']
                         [, string $thattr = HTML_FORM_TH_ATTR]
                         [, string $tdattr = HTML_FORM_TD_ATTR])
```

Parameter	Type	Description
$name	string	The name of the form field.
$title	string	The label to give the form field.
$default	mixed	A default value to use for the textarea field.
$width	integer	A value to specify how wide the textarea should be.
$height	integer	A value to specify how many rows high the textarea should be.
$maxlength	integer	The maximum number of characters that the field can contain.
$attr	string	A string of any additional attributes to be included in the textarea tag.
$thattr	string	A string of additional attributes to be included in the <th> element.
$tdattr	string	A string of additional attributes to be included in the <td> element.

returnTextRow

Returns a string containing a text input element within a table row.

```
string returnTextRow(string $name, string $title [, mixed $default = null]
                     [, integer $size = HTML_FORM_TEXT_SIZE]
                     [, integer $maxlength = 0] [, string $attr = '']
                     [, string $thattr = HTML_FORM_TH_ATTR]
                     [, string $tdattr = HTML_FORM_TD_ATTR])
```

Parameter	Type	Description
$name	string	The name of the form field.
$title	string	The label to give the form field.
$default	mixed	A default value to use for the text field.
$size	integer	A value to use in the field's size attribute.
$maxlength	integer	The maximum number of characters that the field can contain.
$attr	string	A string of any additional attributes to be included in the text input tag.
$thattr	string	A string of additional attributes to be included in the `<th>` element.
$tdattr	string	A string of additional attributes to be included in the `<td>` element.

setDefaultFromInput

Enables or disables any data already submitted by the user from showing up as the values for the form fields.

```
void setDefaultFromInput(boolean $bool)
```

Parameter	Type	Description
$bool	boolean	If set to TRUE, then data in the $_GET and/or $_POST variables will be used to set the value of corresponding form fields. FALSE sets them to an empty string.

setEscapeDefaultFromInput

Enables or disables the escaping of data from the $_GET and/or $_POST variables.

```
void setEscapeDefaultFromInput(boolean $bool)
```

Parameter	Type	Description
$bool	boolean	If set to TRUE, then data will be escaped using the PHP htmlspecialcharacters() function.

start

Prints the opening tags for the form and table in which the form will be displayed.

```
void start([boolean $multipart = FALSE])
```

Parameter	Type	Description
$multipart	boolean	If this is set to TRUE, then the form will be submitted using multi-part format.

Examples

Building a Simple Form

The HTML_Form package provides a quick interface for building simple forms quickly. Take a look at this script:

```php
<?php
require_once "HTML/Form.php";

$form = new HTML_Form('05_formhandler.php');

$form->addText('name', 'Name:');
$form->addText('email', 'Email:');
$form->addSelect('industry', 'Industry:', array('adv' => 'Advertising',➡
 'it' => 'Information Technology', 'web' => 'Web Development'), '', 1, ➡
'Please Select');
$form->addCheckbox('subscribe', 'Subscribe:', true);
$form->addSubmit("submit", "Submit");

$form->display();
?>
```

The constructor function for the HTML_Form object takes the form that will be handling the form as an argument, and then it's a simple matter of adding the form elements to the form in the order in which you want them to be displayed.

The HTML code that's generated is a standard HTML table containing the form elements:

```html
<form action="05_formhandler.php" method="get" >
<table >
 <tr>
  <th align="right" valign="top">Name:</th>
  <td >
   <input type="text" name="name" size="20" value="" />
  </td>
 </tr>
 <tr>
  <th align="right" valign="top">Email:</th>
  <td >
   <input type="text" name="email" size="20" value="" />
  </td>
 </tr>
```

```
<tr>
 <th align="right" valign="top">Industry:</th>
 <td >
  <select name="industry" size="1" >
   <option value="">Please Select</option>
   <option value="adv">Advertising</option>
   <option value="it">Information Technology</option>
   <option value="web">Web Development</option>
  </select>
 </td>
</tr>
<tr>
 <th align="right" valign="top">Subscribe:</th>
 <td >
  <input type="checkbox" name="subscribe" checked="checked" />
 </td>
</tr>
<tr>
 <th align="right" valign="top"> </th>
 <td >
  <input type="submit" name="submit" value="Submit" />
 </td>
</tr>
</table>
<input type="hidden" name="_fields" value="name:email:industry:subscribe:submit" />
</form>
```

Styling a Simple Form

The standard display method for HTML_Form outputs the form as a table, but there are methods for returning the code for individual form elements if you want to style the form yourself, perhaps by using CSS. Let's take a look at the same example, this time using methods to return the individual form elements so that you can lay them out using CSS.

```
<!DOCTYPE HTML PUBLIC "-//W3C//DTD HTML 4.01 Transitional//EN">
<html>
<head>
        <title>CSS Styled Form</title>
        <style>
        dl{}
        dt{
                font-family:    Tahoma,Verdana;
                font-size:      13px;
        }
```

```
        dd{
                margin-top:      -15px;
                margin-left:     200px;
        }
        dd input{
                width:           200px;
                border:          1px solid #dddddd;
        }
        </style>
</head>

<body>
<?php
require_once "HTML/Form.php";
$form = new HTML_Form('05_formhandler.php');
$form->start();
?>
<dl>
        <dt>Name:</dt>
        <dd><?php $form->displayText('name'); ?></dd>
        <dt>Email:</dt>
        <dd><?php $form->displayText('email'); ?></dd>
        <dt>Industry:</dt>
        <dd><?php $form->displaySelect('industry', ➥
        array('adv' => 'Advertising', 'it' => 'Information Technology',➥
        'web' => 'Web Development'), '', 1, 'Please Select'); ?></dd>
        <dt>Subscribe:</dt>
        <dd><?php $form->displayCheckbox('subscribe', true); ?></dd>
        <dt> </dt>
        <dd><?php $form->displaySubmit('submit', 'Submit'); ?></dd></dl>
<?php
$form->end();
?>
</body>
</html>
```

As you can see, in this version of the form you aren't using the display shortcut method for displaying the form, but rather displaying the HTML code for each of the individual form elements as you need them in the form.

HTML_JavaScript

The HTML_JavaScript package facilitates the generation of client-side JavaScript code that can perform basic actions.

Common Uses

The HTML_JavaScript package has the following common uses:

- Displaying JavaScript notification messages
- Displaying JavaScript prompts
- Popping up new browser windows

Related Packages

None

Dependencies

HTML_JavaScript has the following dependencies.

Required Packages

None

Optional Packages

None

API

alert

Outputs the JavaScript to display an alert dialog box. If the script hasn't been started, it will return a PEAR_Error; otherwise the JavaScript script string will be returned.

```
mixed alert(string $message [, boolean $var = false])
```

Parameter	Type	Description
$message	string	The string that appears as the message.
$var	boolean	This is set to true if $message is a variable name and not an actual string.

confirm

Returns the script string to display a JavaScript confirmation box with Yes and No buttons.

```
string confirm(string $message, string $assign [, boolean $var = false])
```

Parameter	Type	Description
$message	string	The message to display in the confirmation box.
$assign	string	The JavaScript variable to which the result (the button pushed) is assigned.
$var	boolean	Set this to true if $message is a variable and not an actual string.

endScript

Ends the JavaScript script block. If this wasn't first started with startScript, a PEAR_Error is returned.

```
mixed endScript()
```

getOutputMode

Returns the output mode for the script. The output mode is set with the setOutputMode method, and can be set either to return the script as a string, echo it directly to the browser, or write it to a file. On failure, a PEAR_Error is returned.

```
getOutputMode()
```

popup

Helps easily generate the JavaScript to display popup windows.

```
mixed popup(string $assign, string $file, string $title, integer $width,
            integer $height, mixed $attr [, integer $top = 300]
            [, integer $left = 300])
```

Parameter	Type	Description
$assign	string	The JavaScript variable to assign the window to.
$file	string	The filename of the file that appears in the window.
$title	string	The title of the new window.
$width	integer	The width of the new window in pixels.
$height	integer	The height of the new window in pixels.
$attr	mixed	An array containing the attributes for the new window, using either 1/0 or yes/no to turn attributes on or off. The attributes appear in order as resizable, scrollbars, menubar, toolbar, status, and location. If $attr is set to a boolean, then all attributes will be set to the value of $attr.
$top	integer	The distance from the top of the screen in pixels.
$left	integer	The distance from the left of the screen in pixels.

popupWrite

Opens a new popup window, the contents of which are the string provided.

```
mixed popupWrite(string $assign, string $file, string $title, integer $width,
                 integer $height, mixed $attr [, integer $top = 300]
                 [, integer $left = 300])
```

Parameter	Type	Description
$assign	string	The JavaScript variable to assign the window to.
$file	string	The string to display in the browser (typically an HTML message).
$title	string	The title of the new window.
$width	integer	The width of the new window in pixels.
$height	integer	The height of the new window in pixels.
$attr	mixed	An array containing the attributes for the new window, using either 1/0 or yes/no to turn attributes on or off. The attributes appear in order as resizable, scrollbars, menubar, toolbar, status, and location. If $attr is set to a boolean, then all attributes will be set to the value of $attr.
$top	integer	The distance from the top of the screen in pixels.
$left	integer	The distance from the left of the screen in pixels.

prompt

Returns the JavaScript for displaying a prompt dialog box into which the user can enter some information. Returns a PEAR_Error on failure.

```
mixed prompt(string $message, string $assign [, string $default = '']
                    [, boolean $var = false])
```

Parameter	Type	Description
$message	string	The message to display in the prompt dialog box.
$assign	string	The name of the JavaScript variable into which the entered value is assigned.
$default	string	The default value prefilled in the text box of the prompt dialog.
$var	boolean	If this is set to true, then $message will be a variable name and not a string.

setOutputMode

Sets the output mode for the script. Valid modes can be to return the script as a string (HTML_JAVASCRIPT_OUTPUT_RETURN), write to the browser (HTML_JAVASCRIPT_OUTPUT_ECHO), or write to a file (HTML_JAVASCRIPT_OUTPUT_FILE).

```
mixed setOutputMode([integer $mode = HTML_JAVASCRIPT_OUTPUT_RETURN]
                    [, string $file = null])
```

Parameter	Type	Description
$mode	integer	The output mode to set.
$file	string	If $mode is set to HTML_JAVASCRIPT_OUTPUT_FILE, then this will contain the name of the file to output the script to.

startScript

Returns or outputs the opening script code. If the script has already been started, a PEAR_Error will be returned.

```
mixed startScript([boolean $defer = true])
```

Parameter	Type	Description
$defer	boolean	If this is set to true, then the script will only execute after the page has finished loading.

write

The write method is a simple wrapper around the JavaScript document.writeln function. If the script hasn't previously been started with startScript, a PEAR_Error will be returned.

```
mixed write(string $str [, boolean $var = false])
```

Parameter	Type	Description
$str	string	The string to write out.
$var	boolean	If this is set to true, then $str will be a variable name and not a string.

writeLine

The writeLine method is a wrapper around the JavaScript document.writeln function, but it includes an additional <br /> tag. If the script hasn't previously been started with startScript, a PEAR_Error will be returned.

```
mixed writeLine(string $str [, boolean $var = false])
```

Parameter	Type	Description
$str	string	The string to write out.
$var	boolean	If this is set to true, then $str will be a variable name and not a string.

Examples

Personalizing a Page

When you're outputting JavaScript into the page and using the write methods, the contents that you write to the page will replace any existing content that you already have in the page. As you can see in the following example, the content of the page is also built using the write methods, so it isn't overwritten by the JavaScript write methods:

```php
<?php
require_once 'HTML/Javascript.php';
$javascript = new HTML_Javascript();
$javascript->setOutputMode(HTML_JAVASCRIPT_OUTPUT_RETURN);
$js = $javascript->startScript();
$js .= $javascript->write('<html><body>Welcome ');
$js .= $javascript->alert('Please tell us who you are...');
$js .= $javascript->prompt('What is your name?','clientname');
$js .= $javascript->write('clientname',true);
$js .= $javascript->write('</body></html>');
$js .= $javascript->endScript();
echo $js;
?>
```

Once you've created the new JavaScript object, set the output mode to return the script contents rather than output it directly to the browser. Then, write out the opening HTML tags and pop up a message. The prompt that you display returns the values entered into a JavaScript variable called clientname. In the next write method, pass the string clientname and the boolean true, meaning that clientname is the name of a JavaScript variable and not a literal string. You then close off the HTML tags and end the script.

Because it was all returned into the $js variable, you simply echo that to the browser.

HTML_Menu

You use the HTML_Menu package to build and maintain navigation structures for your website by taking a multidimensional hash of the structure and outputting it in different navigation formats.

Common Uses

The HTML_Menu package has the following common uses:

- Building breadcrumb navigation for your website
- Building a site map of your website

Related Packages

None

Dependencies

HTML_Menu has the following dependencies.

Required Packages

None

Optional Packages

None

API

HTML_Menu

The HTML_Menu constructor initializes the menu object and sets the menu type, the structure, and the variable that are used to determine the current page. All the arguments are optional and can be set later with setter methods.

```
void HTML_Menu([array $menu = null] [, string $type = 'tree']
                        [, string $urlEnvVar = 'PHP_SELF'])
```

Parameter	Type	Description
$menu	array	The menu structure with which to initialize the menu.
$type	string	The type of menu structure to create.
$urlEnvVar	string	The PHP variable to use to determine what the current page is.

forceCurrentIndex

Forces the menu item with the provided index to the current URL rather than one extracted from the script name or server variable.

```
void forceCurrentIndex(mixed $index)
```

Parameter	Type	Description
$index	mixed	The index of the menu item to be made current.

forceCurrentUrl

Forces the provided URL to the current URL, rather than one extracted from the script name or server variable.

```
void forceCurrentUrl(string $url)
```

Parameter	Type	Description
$url	string	The URL to be made current.

get

Returns the HTML menu in the format specified. The get method uses the default templates for building the output. If you want to customize the output, you'll need to build the menu with the render method instead.

```
string get([string $menuType = ''])
```

Parameter	Type	Description
$menuType	string	The type of menu to return. Valid types are tree, urhere, rows, prevnext, and sitemap.

getCurrentURL

Returns the URL of the currently selected page.

```
string getCurrentURL()
```

getPath

Returns the path of the currently selected page within the menu structure. The path is returned as an array, the elements of which are the steps within the path to reach the current page.

```
array getPath()
```

render

Renders the menu using the renderer specified. By using this method and not `get`, you can use a different rendering engine to the default provided. For example, if you were using the Sigma templating system on your site, you could specify the `render` method using the `HTML_Menu_SigmaRenderer` so that it fits easily into your site. This method returns a `PEAR_Error` on failure.

```
mixed render(HTML_Menu_Renderer &$renderer [, string $type = ''])
```

Parameter	Type	Description
$renderer	HTML_Menu_Renderer	The renderer to use.
$type	string	The type of menu to build.

setMenu

Sets the array for the menu structure to be built from. If you didn't provide the structure to the constructor function, you could set it with this method. The array is a multidimensional hash where submenus are array elements themselves. The array structure is explained in the example later in this section.

```
void setMenu(array $menu)
```

Parameter	Type	Description
$menu	array	The array to use for the menu.

setMenuType

Sets the type of the menu that should be built. Valid types are tree, rows, urhere (breadcrumb style), prevnext, and sitemap.

void setMenuType(string $type)

Parameter	Type	Description
$type	string	The type of menu to set.

setURLEnvVar

Sets the PHP variable that should be used to determine what the current URL is.

void setURLEnvVar(string $urlVar)

Parameter	Type	Description
$urlVar	string	The PHP variable to use.

setUrlPrefix

Allows you to use relative URLs in the menu structure array. Then, by specifying a URL prefix, the prefix is appended to all URLs in the structure when comparing to the current URL.

void setURLPrefix(string $prefix)

Parameter	Type	Description
$prefix	string	The prefix to add before URLs in the menu.

show

Prints out the HTML menu. This works in the same way as get, except the HTML is sent directly to the browser and not returned into a variable. The renderer that the show method uses is HTML_Menu_DirectRenderer, so if you want to use a different rendering engine, you'll need to use the render method and output the result to the browser manually.

void show([string $type = ''])

Parameter	Type	Description
$type	string	The type of menu to output.

Examples

Navigating a Site Map

When building a multilevel site map, a nice navigation to use is previous/next–type navigation. This kind of navigation is often seen on websites that contain online documentation. The previous and next navigation items allow you to move from one section to the next, and there's also an option to move up a level. In the following example, we've used a basic menu structure that's common across a number of applications.

```php
<?php
$structure = array(
        1       =>      array(
                'title' =>      'File',
                'url'   =>      '05_menu.php?nav=file',
                'sub'   =>      array(
                        11      =>      array(
                                'title' =>      'Open',
                                'url'   =>      '05_menu.php?nav=fileopen'
                        ),
                        12      =>      array(
                                'title' =>      'Save',
                                'url'   =>      '05_menu.php?nav=filesave'
                        ),
                        13      =>      array(
                                'title' =>      'Print',
                                'url'   =>      '05_menu.php?nav=fileprint'
                        )
                )
        ),
        2       =>      array(
                'title' =>      'Edit',
                'url'   =>      '05_menu.php?nav=edit',
                'sub'   =>      array(
                        21      =>      array(
                                'title' =>      'Cut',
                                'url'   =>      '05_menu.php?nav=editcut'
                        ),
                        22      =>      array(
                                'title' =>      'Copy',
                                'url'   =>      '05_menu.php?nav=editcopy'
                        ),
```

```
                    23      =>      array(
                            'title' =>      'Paste',
                            'url'   =>      '05_menu.php?nav=editpaste'
                    )
            )
    ),
    3       =>      array(
            'title' =>      'Help',
            'url'   =>      '05_menu.php?nav=help'
    )
);

require_once('HTML/Menu.php');

$menu =& new HTML_Menu($structure, 'prevnext');
$menu->setUrlPrefix('/Apress/');
$menu->forceCurrentUrl('/Apress/05_menu.php?nav='.$_GET['nav']);

$menu->show();
?>
```

The preceding array creates a File, Edit, and Help menu structure. The File menu has sub-items for Open, Save, and Print, while the Edit menu has sub-items for Cut, Copy, and Paste. Because the script lives in an Apress folder on our server, we had to specify that the URL prefix of /Apress/ be included. Also, to keep the navigation within a single script, all the navigation items point to the same script, just with different query strings. Because the current URL is determined by the URL excluding the query string, we had to specify the current URL manually by including the query string onto the end.

HTML_Progress2_Lite

The HTML_Progress2_Lite package implements an HTML loading bar using PHP and JavaScript. The target browser needs to support DHTML , and the loading bar is implemented only as either a horizontal or vertical bar. For more complex loading animations, HTML_Progress2 is also available.

Common Uses

The HTML_Progress2_Lite package has the following common use:

Including a loading bar in your page

Related Packages

HTML_Progress2

Dependencies

HTML_Progress2_Lite has the following dependencies.

Required Packages

None

Optional Packages

None

API

HTML_Progress2_Lite

The `HTML_Progress2_Lite` constructor function create a new progress bar object. At this point, you can provide the parameters for the progress bar, or you can set them later with setter functions.

```
HTML_Progress2_Lite HTML_Progress2_Lite([array $options = array()]
                                   [, string $id = null])
```

Parameter	Type	Description
$options	array	An array of style parameters to be applied to the progress bar.
$id	string	A unique identifier string for the progress bar.

addButton

Adds a new button to the progress bar.

```
void addButton(string $name, string $value, string $action
                       [, string $target = 'self'])
```

Parameter	Type	Description
$name	string	The name to give the button.
$value	string	The label that will appear on the button.
$action	string	The action that the button will perform.
$target	string	The target frame for the button action.

addLabel

Adds a new label to the progress bar.

```
void addLabel(string $type, string $name [, string $value = ' '])
```

Parameter	Type	Description
$type	string	The type of label to add. Valid options are text, button, step, percent, and crossbar.
$name	string	The name to give the label.
$value	string	The default label value.

display

Shows and renders the progress bar.

```
void display()
```

hide

Hides the progress bar.

```
void hide()
```

moveMin

Changes the value of the progress bar to the minimum step set.

```
void moveMin()
```

moveNext

Changes the value of the progress bar to the next step in the series.

```
void moveNext()
```

moveStep

Changes the value of the progress bar to the step value provided.

```
void moveStep(integer $step)
```

Parameter	Type	Description
$step	integer	The new step value to move the progress bar to.

removeButton

Removes a previously added button from the progress bar.

```
void removeButton(string $name)
```

Parameter	Type	Description
$name	string	The name given to the button when it was added initially.

removeLabel

Removes a previously added label from the progress bar.

```
void removeLabel(string $name)
```

Parameter	Type	Description
$name	string	The name given to the label when it was added initially.

setBarAttributes

Allows you to define the main style of the progress bar. If you didn't set this up when initializing the progress bar, you can use this method to set the style later.

```
void setBarAttributes([array $attributes = array()])
```

Parameter	Type	Description
$attributes	array	An indexed array of style attributes to apply to the progress bar.

setDirection

Sets the direction in which the progress bar fills up.

```
void setDirection(string $direction)
```

Parameter	Type	Description
$direction	string	The direction to fill the bar up. Valid options are left, right, up, or down.

setFrameAttributes

Sets the style attributes of the frame around the progress bar.

```
void setFrameAttributes([array $attributes = array()])
```

Parameter	Type	Description
$attributes	array	An indexed array of style attributes to apply to the progress bar frame.

setLabelAttributes

Sets the style attributes of a label on the progress bar.

```
void setLabelAttributes(string $name [, array $attributes = array()])
```

Parameter	Type	Description
$name	string	The name of the label to which you want to apply these styles.
$attributes	array	An indexed array of style attributes to apply to the progress bar label.

show

Shows the progress bar after it has previously been hidden.

```
void show()
```

toHtml

Renders the entire progress bar and returns it as HTML.

```
string toHtml()
```

Examples

Showing a Loading Bar

With the prevalence of social networking sites that allow you to upload images and video, we more often encounter forms that take some time to process the files that are submitted by users. If we had a form that allowed the user to upload ten files, and then created thumbnail versions of each of those images, the script might sit for some time while the files were converted. Using the HTML_Progress2_Lite package, we can show a progress indicator so that users know how far along in the process they are.

This is your hypothetical function that converts the images. You simply put a sleep function in it to cause the script to wait for a second before continuing:

```
<html>
<body>
<?php
require_once 'HTML/Progress2_Lite.php';

function imageConvert()
{
        sleep(1);
}
```

The options array specifies the size and position of the progress bar, as well as the minimum and maximum values of the bar. Here it is set to 10, but this would need to correspond to the number of iterations that you'll be performing:

```
$options = array(
        'position'      =>      'absolute',
        'left'  =>      100,
        'top'   =>      50,
        'width' =>      300,
        'height'        =>      30,
        'padding'       =>      5,
        'min'   =>      0,
        'max'   =>      10
);
```

The percent label shows a percentage complete, in addition to the visual indicator of the progress bar:

```
$progress = new HTML_Progress2_Lite($options);
$progress->addLabel('text', 'text1', 'Converting images...');
$progress->addLabel('percent','step1');
```

The direction that the bar fills up can be up, down, left, or right:

```
$progress->setDirection('right');
```

To style the bar itself, simply pass it an associative array of style elements:

```
$progress->setBarAttributes(array('background-color' => '#ff0000', 'color' => ➥
'#00ff00'));
```

Finally, the progress bar is displayed:

```
$progress->display();
```

Once the bar has been displayed, you then loop through your iterations, calling moveStep each time to update the progress bar. The imageConvert function is the time-consuming function you need to call each time:

```
for($i=1; $i<=10; $i++) {
    $progress->moveStep($i);
    imageConvert();
}
```

Once the process is complete, you can simply hide the progress bar:

```
$progress->hide();
?>
</body>
</html>
```

HTML_QuickForm

The HTML_QuickForm package provides another way of building HTML forms. The added advantage of the HTML_QuickForm package is that it also builds the JavaScript or server-side code to validate the form.

Common Uses

The HTML_QuickForm package has the following common uses:

- Building HTML forms
- Validating HTML forms

Related Packages

HTML_Form

Dependencies

HTML_QuickForm has the following dependencies.

Required Packages

HTML_Common

Optional Packages

None

API

HTML_QuickForm

The HTML_QuickForm constructor function creates the QuickForm object and sets up the HTML form tags for the form.

```
HTML_QuickForm HTML_QuickForm([string $formName = ''] [, string $method = 'post']
                             [, string $action = ''] [, string $target = '']
                             [, mixed $attributes = null]
                             [, boolean $trackSubmit = false])
```

Parameter	Type	Description
$formName	string	The name to give the form.
$method	string	Either get or post—the method to use when submitting the form.
$action	string	The action attribute of the form—the script that's called when the form is submitted.
$target	string	The target frame for the submitted action.
$attributes	mixed	Any additional attributes to set for the form tag.
$trackSubmit	boolean	If this is set to true, then a special hidden field will be set in the form to track whether the form has been submitted or not.

accept

Tells the HTML_QuickForm to render using a specific HTML_QuickForm_Renderer object. Eight different renderers are available, including renderers for outputting arrays, Smarty code, and Sigma templates.

```
void accept(HTML_QuickForm_Renderer &$renderer)
```

Parameter	Type	Description
$renderer	HTML_QuickForm_Renderer	The renderer object to use to render the form.

addElement

Adds an element to the form.

```
object &addElement(mixed $element)
```

Parameter	Type	Description
$element	mixed	Either an element object or a string specifying the type of element. If a string, then you can include additional parameters that vary depending on the type of element to add, and that are used to create the element.

addFormRule

Adds a global validation rule to the form. A global rule is used if you want to define your own custom JavaScript validation function to use, rather than the HTML_QuickForm validation methods. The JavaScript function that you build should return true if validation was successful. On error, the function should return an associative array of problematic form elements, where the key is the element name and the value is the error message for that form element.

```
void addFormRule(mixed $rule)
```

Parameter	Type	Description
$rule	mixed	The validation function to call, either a function name or an array containing the callback object.

addGroup

Adds an element group to the form. A reference to the new group object created is returned.

```
object &addGroup(array $elements [, string $name = null] [, string $groupLabel = '']

                               [, string $separator = null]
                               [, string $appendName = true])
```

Parameter	Type	Description
$elements	array	An array of the elements composing the group. This array is made up of the object references returned by the addElement method.
$name	string	The name to give the group.
$groupLabel	string	A label for the group.
$separator	string	A string that's used to separate the elements within the group.
$appendName	string	If this is set to true, then the group name will be used in the form element name in the form groupName[elementName].

addGroupRule

Adds a validation rule that's applied to all the elements within a group. The group needs to have been assigned a name for this to work.

```
void addGroupRule(string $group, mixed $arg1 [, string $type = '']
                         [, string $format = null] [, integer $howmany = 0]
                         [, string $validation = 'server']
                         [, boolean $reset = false])
```

Parameter	Type	Description
$group	string	The name of the group to which this rule is being added.
$arg1	mixed	An error message string for a single element or an array of error message strings for multiple elements.
$type	string	The type of rule to use. The getRegisteredRules method returns the types.
$format	string	Required for extra rule data.
$howmany	integer	How many valid elements should be in the group.
$validation	string	Whether to perform client-side or server-side validation. Valid values are client or server.
$reset	boolean	If client-side validation is used, this will be used to set the form values back to default if validation fails.

addRule

Adds a validation rule for a specific form element. If the element name provided is a group, then the group will be considered as a whole and the validation applied.

```
void addRule(string $name, string $message, string $type [, string $format = null]
             [, string $validation = 'server'] [, boolean $reset = false]
             [, boolean $force = false])
```

Parameter	Type	Description
$name	string	The name of the element to which this rule is being added.
$message	string	An error message string for the element when validation fails.
$type	string	The type of rule to add. The getRegisteredRules method returns the types.
$format	string	Required for extra rule data.
$validation	string	Whether to perform client-side or server-side validation. Valid values are client or server.
$reset	boolean	If client-side validation is used, this will be used to set the form values back to default if validation fails.
$force	boolean	If this is set to true, then this will force the rule to be applied, even if the form element doesn't exist.

apiVersion

Returns the current API version of the HTML_QuickForm object.

```
float apiVersion()
```

applyFilter

Applies a data filter to the elements specified.

```
void applyFilter(mixed $element, mixed $filter)
```

Parameter	Type	Description
$element	mixed	The form element or array of form elements to apply the filter to.
$filter	mixed	Either callback function to use: a function name or an array containing an object and the method name to use within the object.

arrayMerge

Merges two arrays in the same way as the PHP array_merge function does, except it does so recursively.

```
array arrayMerge(array $a, array $b)
```

Parameter	Type	Description
$a	array	The original array.
$b	array	The array that will be merged into the $a array.

createElement

Creates a new form element of the given type. Just like addElement, this method can take a variable number of parameters, depending on the type of element you're creating.

```
object &createElement(mixed $element)
```

Parameter	Type	Description
$element	mixed	Either an element object or a string specifying the type of element. If a string, then additional parameters can be included that vary depending on the type of element to add and that are used to create the element.

defaultRenderer

Returns a reference to the default renderer object for the current form object.

```
object &defaultRenderer()
```

elementExists

Returns true or false depending on whether the named element already exists in the form or not.

```
boolean elementExists([string $element = null])
```

Parameter	Type	Description
$element	string	The name to check for.

errorMessage

Returns a text error message for an HTML_QuickForm error code.

```
string errorMessage(integer $code)
```

Parameter	Type	Description
$code	integer	The error code to return the message for.

exportValue

Returns a safe value for the form element named, first by looking for a cleaned-up value submitted through the form, and then by checking if one was set using setValue, setDefaults, or setConstants.

```
mixed exportValue(string $element)
```

Parameter	Type	Description
$element	string	The name of the element for which to return the value.

exportValues

Returns safe values for the elements named. The result is searched for in the same way as for exportValue. If no elements are named, then the values for all the form elements will be returned.

```
array exportValues([mixed $elementList = null])
```

Parameter	Type	Description
$elementList	mixed	Either an array or string of the element names for which you want to return the values.

freeze

Causes the elements named to be displayed as text only, and not editable in the form element type as they were originally added.

```
void freeze([mixed $elementList = null])
```

Parameter	Type	Description
$elementList	mixed	Either an array or string of the element names that you want to make read-only.

getElement

Returns a reference to the form element named.

```
object &getElement(string $name)
```

Parameter	Type	Description
$name	string	The name of the element for which you want to return the object reference.

getElementError

Returns the error for the named element. Errors are set for each of the elements when they fail validation.

```
string getElementError(string $element)
```

Parameter	Type	Description
$element	string	The name of the form element to check for the error on.

getElementType

Returns the element type of the named element.

```
string getElementType(string $element)
```

Parameter	Type	Description
$element	string	The name of the form element to return the type of.

getElementValue

Returns the raw value for the form field, as submitted, before it has been filtered.

```
mixed &getElementValue(string $element)
```

Parameter	Type	Description
$element	string	The name of the form element to return the raw value of.

getMaxFileSize

Returns the value of the MAX_FILE_SIZE hidden form element. The maximum file size is returned in bytes.

```
integer getMaxFileSize()
```

getRegisteredRules

Returns an array of all the registered validation rules for the form.

```
array getRegisteredRules()
```

getRegisteredTypes

Returns an array of all the registered element types for the form.

```
array getRegisteredTypes()
```

getRequiredNote

Returns the required note that's displayed with the form when the form contains required fields.

```
string getRequiredNote()
```

getSubmitValue

Returns the value for a specific element after the form has been submitted and the value passed through the filter for that element.

```
mixed getSubmitValue(string $element)
```

Parameter	Type	Description
$element	string	The name of the form element to return the value of.

getSubmitValues

Returns an array of all the values submitted in the form.

```
array getSubmitValues([boolean $mergeFiles = false])
```

Parameter	Type	Description
$mergeFiles	boolean	If this is set to true, then uploaded files will also be returned.

getValidationScript

Returns the JavaScript that will do the client-side validation of the form.

```
string getValidationScript()
```

insertElementBefore

Allows you to add an element to the form and place it before an already existing element.

```
object &insertElementBefore(HTML_QuickForm_element &$element, string $before)
```

Parameter	Type	Description
$element	HTML_QuickForm_element	The form element to insert into the form.
$before	string	The name of the element before which to add this element.

isElementFrozen

Returns whether or not the element named has been frozen in the form.

```
boolean isElementFrozen(string $element)
```

Parameter	Type	Description
$element	string	The name of the form element for which you want to check whether it's frozen or not.

isElementRequired

Checks to see whether the element named is a required form element or not.

```
boolean isElementRequired(string $element)
```

Parameter	Type	Description
$element	string	The name of the form element for which you want to check whether it's required or not.

isError

Returns whether the result returned from one of the QuickForm methods is an error or not.

```
boolean isError(mixed $result)
```

Parameter	Type	Description
$result	mixed	The result from an HTML_QuickForm method.

isFrozen

Returns whether the entire form has been frozen or not.

```
boolean isFrozen()
```

isRuleRegistered

Tells whether a given rule has been registered or not.

```
boolean isRuleRegistered(string $name [, boolean $autoRegister = false])
```

Parameter	Type	Description
$name	string	The name of the validation rule you're checking for.
$autoRegister	boolean	If this is set to true, then the named rule will automatically be registered if it doesn't already exist.

isSubmitted

Returns whether the form has already been submitted or not. This is useful to know, because the filters applied to elements might result in no usable results being set after a form has been submitted.

```
boolean isSubmitted()
```

isTypeRegistered

Tells whether an element type has been registered or not.

```
boolean isTypeRegistered(string $type)
```

Parameter	Type	Description
$type	string	The form element type.

process

Performs the form data processing. The callback processing function is called, and all the form values are submitted to it.

```
void process(mixed $callback [, boolean $mergeFiles])
```

Parameter	Type	Description
$callback	mixed	The callback function to call to process the form. This parameter is either a function name or an array containing the callback object and the name of the method within the object to use.
$mergeFiles	boolean	If this is set to true, then uploaded files will also be processed.

registerElementType

Registers a new element type to use in the form. If you need a custom form element that hasn't already been catered for with createElement, you can define it here, and once defined, create new elements of this type with createElement.

```
void registerElementType(string $name, string $include, string $className)
```

Parameter	Type	Description
$name	string	The name of the new element type.
$include	string	The path to the include file that defines this element type.
$className	string	The class name of the new element.

registerRule

You use the `registerRule` method to add a new validation rule to the form.

```
void registerRule(string $ruleName, string $type, string $data1 [, string $data2])
```

Parameter	Type	Description
$ruleName	string	The name to give this validation rule.
$type	string	The type of rule to add. Can be regex, function, or rule.
$data1	string	The name of the function, regular expression, or HTML_QuickForm_Rule to apply.
$data2	string	The object parent of the rule in $data1 if it's a function or HTML_QuickForm_Rule.

removeElement

Removes a form's elements. If there's more than one element in the form with the same name, then the first one will be removed.

```
void &removeElement(string $elementName [, boolean $removeRules - true])
```

Parameter	Type	Description
$elementName	string	The name of the element to remove.
$removeRules	boolean	If this is set to true, then any rules associated with the element will be removed as well.

setConstants

Initializes constant form values that cannot be overridden by $_GET and $_POST variables.

```
void setConstants([array $constantValues = null] [, mixed $filter = null])
```

Parameter	Type	Description
$constantValues	array	An associative array of constant values that cannot be changed. The key of the array is the element name; the value is the value to apply to that element.
$filter	mixed	Filters to apply to all the constant values.

setDatasource

Sets a data source object for this form. If the data source object implements the `defaultValues()` and `constantValues()` methods, then these will be used to set these values on the QuickForm.

```
void setDatasource(object &$datasource [, mixed $defaultsFilter = null]
                              [, mixed $constantsFilter = null])
```

Parameter	Type	Description
$datasource	object	A data source object.
$defaultsFilter	mixed	A string or array of filters to apply to the default values returned from the data source.
$constantsFilter	mixed	A string or array of filters to apply to the constant values returned from the data source.

setDefaults

Initializes the form with default form values.

```
void setDefaults([array $defaultValues = null] [, mixed $filter = null])
```

Parameter	Type	Description
$defaultValues	array	An indexed array where the key is the form element name and the value is the default value for that element.
$filter	mixed	A filter or set of filters to apply to all the default values. A filter is simply a PHP function that you have written, and the value is passed to this function before being used in the form.

setElementError

Sets up the error message for a specific form element.

```
void setElementError(string $element, string $message)
```

Parameter	Type	Description
$element	string	The name of the element for which you want to set the error message.
$message	string	The error message to display.

setJsWarnings

Sets up strings that can be included before and after generated JavaScript warning messages.

```
void setJsWarnings(string $pre, string $post)
```

Parameter	Type	Description
$pre	string	A string to prefix onto any JavaScript warning.
$post	string	A string to append to any JavaScript warning.

setMaxFileSize

Creates and sets the value of the MAX_FILE_S17F hidden form element that's used when uploading files with a file form element.

```
void setMaxFileSize([integer $bytes = 0]
```

Parameter	Type	Description
$bytes	integer	The maximum size in bytes that a file can be to upload.

setRequiredNote

Sets a message that's displayed to indicate when form elements are required.

```
void setRequiredNote(string $note)
```

Parameter	Type	Description
$note	string	The required field message.

toArray

Returns the form as a multidimensional array.

```
array toArray([boolean $collectHidden = false])
```

Parameter	Type	Description
$collectHidden	boolean	If this is set to true, then hidden form elements will be included in the array.

toHtml

Returns the HTML code for showing the form in the browser.

```
string toHtml([string $extraData = null])
```

Parameter	Type	Description
$extraData	string	Any extra data that you want to insert into the page before the form is rendered and displayed.

updateElementAttr

Updates the HTML attributes of a number of elements in the form.

```
void updateElementAttr(mixed $elements, mixed $attributes)
```

Parameter	Type	Description
$elements	mixed	Either the name of an element to update or an array of element names when updating multiple elements at the same time.
$attributes	mixed	Either an array or a string of HTML attributes to update.

validate

Performs the server-side validation of the form.

```
booolean validate()
```

Examples

Validating a Form on the Client

In this example, you'll re-create the example form that you created for the HTML_Form package, but this time using HTML_QuickForm. This will enable you to look at the differences between the two, and also include client-side validation of the form.

```php
<?php
require_once 'HTML/QuickForm.php';
$form = new HTML_QuickForm('subscribeform');
```

The first difference is that you can test to see if the form has been submitted, or if the user got to this page in error. In this case, this is important because you're using the same script to display both the form and the results of the form submission. You can also test whether the form validated or not, but this isn't strictly necessary in this example, because you're validating on the client.

```
if ($form->isSubmitted()) {
        if ($form->validate()) {
                echo '<pre>';
```

If the form has been submitted, you simply display the results from the form:

```
                print_r($form->getSubmitValues());
                echo '</pre>';
        }
} else {
```

The form hasn't been submitted, so let's build the form. In the HTML_Form package, we had methods for adding each of the form elements, but in HTML_QuickForm, a standard addElement method is used, passing the type of element to add as an argument to the method:

```
                $form->addElement('text', 'name', 'Name:');
                $form->addElement('text', 'email', 'Email:');
```

Because the addElement method is used for a number of different input types, it cannot have input-type–specific parameters. With the select, you cannot set up the blank element, so you need to add it to the options array:

```
                $form->addElement('select', 'industry', 'Industry', ➥
                array('' => 'Please select', ➥
                'adv' => 'Advertising', 'it' => 'Information Technology', 'web' => ➥
                'Web Development'));
```

The same goes for the checkbox—to make sure it's checked you need to include the HTML attributes for displaying it with a check mark:

```
                $form->addElement('checkbox', 'subscribe', 'Subscribe:', null, ➥
                array('checked' => 'checked'));
                $form->addElement('submit', null, 'Submit');
```

You can then apply some filters to the name and e-mail so that extraneous white space is removed:

```
                $form->applyFilter('name', 'trim');
                $form->applyFilter('email', 'trim');
```

You can also include validation. First you make sure that both the name and e-mail fields are filled in. You're adding two validation rules to the e-mail field, the first to make it a required field, the second to make sure that users have entered a valid e-mail address. If they've filled nothing in the e-mail field, the first validation message will be displayed, but if they enter rubbish in the mail field, the second validation message will be displayed:

```
$form->addRule ➥
('name', 'Please enter your name', 'required', null, 'client');
$form->addRule ➥
('email', 'Please enter your email address', 'required', null,➥
'client');
$form->addRule ➥
('email', 'Please enter a valid email address', 'email', null,➥
'client');
$form->addRule ➥
('industry', 'Please select the industry in which you work', ➥
'required', null, 'client');
$form->display();
}
?>
```

HTML_Safe

The HTML_Safe package parses a text string and removes any potentially dangerous HTML tags and other script elements. It searches for things such as unclosed `<li>` tags, object or applet tags, and `javascript` or `vbscript` elements.

Common Uses

Following are the common uses of the HTML_Safe package:

- Making sure that HTML is XHTML-compliant before outputting it to a browser
- Stripping potentially troublesome HTML code from user-submitted input

Related Packages

HTML_Tidy

Dependencies

HTML_Safe has the following dependencies.

Required Packages

XML_HtmlSax3

Optional Packages

None

API

HTML_Safe

The HTML_Safe constructor function simply returns a new HTML_Safe parser object.

```
HTML_Safe HTML_Safe()
```

clear

Clears the HTML_Safe object of any current document data.

```
boolean clear()
```

getXHTML

Returns the parsed content as an XHTML-compliant string with all potentially problematic tokens removed.

```
string getXHTML()
```

parse

Takes an HTML string and parses it for potentially problematic tokens, returning the parsed XHTML string.

```
string parse(string $html)
```

Parameter	Type	Description
$html	string	The HTML string to parse.

HTML_Table

The HTML_Table package provides a spreadsheet-like interface for creating HTML tables. When building a table in HTML, you have to work from top to bottom, left to right, but with HTML_Table you can address and populate any table cells wherever you want.

Common Uses

The HTML_Table package has the following common use:

Dynamically building an HTML table

Related Packages

None

Dependencies

HTML_Table has the following dependencies.

Required Packages

HTML_Common

Optional Packages

None

API

HTML_Table

The HTML_Table constructor builds a new HMTL_Table object.

```
HTML_Table HTML_Table([array $attributes = null] [, integer $tabOffset = 0]
                [, boolean $useTGroups = false])
```

Parameter	Type	Description
$attributes	array	An associative array of table tag attributes to use in the table tag.
$tabOffset	integer	The tab offset (indent) of the table.
$useTGroups	boolean	If this is set to true, then the parts of the table will be grouped in thead, tbody, and tfoot tags.

addCol

Adds a column to the table and returns the identifier of the new column.

```
integer addCol([array $contents = null] [, mixed $attributes = null]
            [, string $type = 'td'])
```

Parameter	Type	Description
$contents	array	An indexed array of cell contents to include in the column.
$attributes	mixed	An associative array or a string of the table row attributes.
$type	string	The cell type to use—either th or td.

addRow

Adds a row to the table and returns the identifier of the new row.

```
integer addCol([array $contents = null] [, mixed $attributes = null]
            [, string $type = 'td'] [, boolean $inTR = false])
```

Parameter	Type	Description
$contents	array	An indexed array of cell contents to include in the column.
$attributes	mixed	An associative array or a string of the table row attributes.
$type	string	The cell type to use—either th or td.
$inTR	boolean	If this is set to true, then the attributes will be applied to the tr tag; otherwise, the attributes will be applied to the td tags.

altRowAttributes

Allows you to specify a different set of attributes that are then applied to alternate rows in the table. Using this method, you could set the table up so that alternating rows have different background colors.

```
void altRowAttributes(integer $start, mixed $attributes1, mixed $attributes2
                    [, boolean $inTR = false])
```

Parameter	Type	Description
$start	integer	The row index at which the alternating of attributes should begin.
$attributes1	mixed	An associative array or a string of the table row attributes.
$attributes2	mixed	An associative array or a string of the alternate table row attributes.
$inTR	boolean	If this is set to true, then the attributes will be applied to the tr tag; otherwise the attributes will be applied to the td tags.

apiVersion

Returns the API version of HTML_Table.

```
double apiVersion()
```

getAutoFill

Returns the value that's used to autofill table cells that haven't had specific content defined.

```
mixed getAutoFill()
```

getAutoGrow

Returns the value of the autoGrow flag. When autoGrow is set to true, new rows and columns will be automatically added when a nonexisting cell is referenced.

```
boolean getAutoGrow()
```

getBody

Returns the tbody section of the table as an HTML_Table_Storage object, which can then be independently manipulated and output.

```
HTML_Table_Storage &getBody()
```

getCellAttributes

Returns the attributes for a specific cell as an array.

```
array getCellAttributes(integer $row, integer $column)
```

Parameter	Type	Description
$row	integer	The row index for the cell.
$column	integer	The column index for the cell.

getCellContents

Returns the contents for a specific table cell.

```
mixed getCellContents(integer $row, integer $column)
```

Parameter	Type	Description
$row	integer	The row index for the cell.
$column	integer	The column index for the cell.

getColCount

Returns the number of columns in the table. If you specify a specific row, then the getColCount method won't take into account cells that are spanning multiple columns.

```
integer getColCount([integer $row = null])
```

Parameter	Type	Description
$row	Integer	The row index in which to count the columns.

getFooter

Returns the footer of the table as an HTML_Table_Storage object.

```
HTML_Table_Storage &getFooter()
```

getHeader

Returns the header of the table as an HTML_Table_Storage object.

```
HTML_Table_Storage &getHeader()
```

getRowAttributes

Returns the attributes for a specific row as contained in the tr tag. The attributes are returned as an array.

```
array getRowAttributes(integer $row)
```

Parameter	Type	Description
$row	integer	The index of the row for which you want to return the attributes.

getRowCount

Returns the number of rows in the table.

```
integer getRowCount()
```

setAllAttributes

Sets the attributes globally for all cells in the table.

```
void setAllAttributes([mixed $attributes = null])
```

Parameter	Type	Description
$attributes	mixed	Either an associative array or a string of attributes to apply to all table cells.

setAutoFill

Sets the autofill value to be used in cells that haven't had values explicitly set.

```
void setAutoFill(mixed $fill)
```

Parameter	Type	Description
$fill	mixed	The value with which to fill cells.

setAutoGrow

Sets the autoGrow flag for the table. If this is set to true, then additional rows and columns will be added when nonexisting cells are referenced.

```
void setAutoGrow(boolean $grow)
```

Parameter	Type	Description
$grow	boolean	Whether to grow the table automatically to accommodate additional cells or not.

setCaption

Sets the caption for the table.

```
void setCaption(string $caption [, mixed $attributes = null])
```

Parameter	Type	Description
$caption	string	The caption to set for the table.
$attributes	mixed	An associative array or a string of attributes to include with the table caption tag.

setCellAttributes

Sets the attributes for a specific cell in the table.

```
void setCellAttributes(integer $row, integer $column, mixed $attributes)
```

Parameter	Type	Description
$row	integer	The row in which the cell you want to set the attributes for is found.
$column	integer	The column in which the cell you want to set the attributes for is found.
$attributes	mixed	Either an associative array or a string of attributes to use for the table cell.

setCellContents

Sets the contents for a cell. Setting the contents of a cell that doesn't exist returns an error, unless the autoGrow flag is set to true.

```
mixed setCellContents(integer $row, integer $column, mixed $contents
                                  [, string $type = 'td'])
```

Parameter	Type	Description
$row	integer	The row in which the cell you want to set the attributes for is found.
$column	integer	The column in which the cell you want to set the attributes for is found.
$contents	mixed	HTML or any object that has a toHTML method. Can also be an array, in which case $column is used as an offset and the cell contents are filled from that point down.
$type	string	The cell type, either a th or td.

setColAttributes

Sets the attributes for an existing column in the table.

```
void setColAttributes(integer $column [, mixed $attributes = null])
```

Parameter	Type	Description
$column	integer	The index of the column for which you want to set the attributes.
$attributes	mixed	Either an associative array or a string of attributes to use for the column.

setColCount

Sets the number of columns in the table.

```
void setColCount(integer $columns)
```

Parameter	Type	Description
$columns	integer	The number of columns to create in the table.

setColType

Sets the specified column to be either td- or th-type cells.

```
void setColType(integer $column, string $type)
```

Parameter	Type	Description
$column	integer	The index of the column that you want to set.
$type	string	Either td or th, depending on what you want to set the column to.

setHeaderContents

Allows you to set the contents of the header cell. This sets the contents of the specified cell and sets it as a th type at the same time.

```
void setHeaderContents(integer $row, integer $column, mixed $contents
                                [, mixed $attributes = null])
```

Parameter	Type	Description
$row	integer	The row in which the cell you want to set the attributes for is found.
$column	integer	The column in which the cell you want to set the attributes for is found.
$contents	mixed	HTML or any object that has a toHTML method. Can also be an array, in which case $column is used as an offset and the header contents are filled from that point down.
$attributes	mixed	Either an associative array or a string of attributes to use for the header cell.

setRowAttributes

Sets the attributes for an existing row in the table.

```
void setRowAttributes(integer $row , mixed $attributes [, boolean $inTR = false])
```

Parameter	Type	Description
$row	integer	The index of the column for which you want to set the attributes.
$attributes	mixed	Either an associative array or a string of attributes to use for the column.
$inTR	boolean	If this is set to true, then the attributes will be applied to the tr tag; otherwise they will be applied in the td tags.

setRowCount

Sets the number of rows in the table. If the autoGrow flag is set to false, then this will be the maximum number of rows that will appear in the table.

```
void setRowCount(integer $rows)
```

Parameter	Type	Description
$rows	integer	The number of rows to set the table to.

setRowType

Sets the row type to be either td or th.

```
void setRowType(integer $row, string $type)
```

Parameter	Type	Description
$row	integer	The row index of the row for which you wish to set the type.
$type	string	The type of cells that you want the row to have, either td or th.

toHtml

Returns the table structure as HTML.

```
string toHtml()
```

updateAllAttributes

Updates the attributes of all the cells in the table.

```
void updateAllAttributes([mixed $attributes = null])
```

Parameter	Type	Description
$attributes	mixed	Either an associative array or a string of attributes to apply to all table cells.

updateCellAttributes

Updates the attributes for a specific cell in the table.

```
void updateCellAttributes(integer $row, integer $column, mixed $attributes)
```

Parameter	Type	Description
$row	integer	The row in which the cell you want to update the attributes for is found.
$column	integer	The column in which the cell you want to update the attributes for is found.
$attributes	mixed	Either an associative array or a string of attributes to use for the table cell.

updateColAttributes

Updates the attributes for an existing column in the table.

```
void setColAttributes(integer $column [, mixed $attributes = null])
```

Parameter	Type	Description
$column	integer	The index of the column for which you want to update the attributes.
$attributes	mixed	Either an associative array or a string of attributes to use for the column.

updateRowAttributes

Updates the attributes for an existing row in the table.

```
void updateRowAttributes(integer $row , mixed $attributes [, boolean $inTR = false])
```

Parameter	Type	Description
$row	integer	The index of the column for which you want to update the attributes.
$attributes	mixed	Either an associative array or a string of attributes to use for the column.
$inTR	boolean	If this is set to true, then the attributes will be applied to the tr tag; otherwise they will be applied in the td tags.

Examples

Building a Monthly Calendar

Following is an interesting table to build that shows off a number of the features of the HTML_Table package. What you'll do is build a calendar of the current month.

```php
<?php
require_once "HTML/Table.php";
$weekDays = array('Sunday', 'Monday', 'Tuesday', 'Wednesday', 'Thursday', ➡
'Friday', 'Saturday');
```

You'll use this array of the days of the week to build the headings for the columns. You then need to get some information about the current month:

```php
$data = array();
$data['numDays'] = date('t');
$data['curDay'] = date('j');
$data['curMonth'] = date('F');
$data['firstDay'] = date('w', strtotime('1 ' . $data['curMonth']));
```

You need to know how many days are in the current month, as well as the current day, because you'll want to style it differently. You'll use the month name that you store in the curMonth array element as the caption for the table. You also need to know what day of the week the first day of the month fell on, because that's where you'll start displaying your dates from.

You don't want a border between your cells, so you put that into an array of options:

```
$tAttributes = array(
            'border'=>'0',
);
```

You then create a new HTML_Table object using the options array you just set up:

```
$dateTable = new HTML_Table($tAttributes);
```

The autoGrow feature of the table is great for this because now you don't need to work out how many weeks the month falls over, and therefore how many rows:

```
$dateTable->setAutoGrow(true);
$dateTable->setAutoFill('');
```

You can then go ahead and put the weekday headings in the table:

```
for($i=0; $i < count($weekDays); $i++) {
            $dateTable->setHeaderContents(0, $i, $weekDays[$i]);
}
```

The first row (row 0) contains the headers, so your actual dates begin at row 1. The column that you begin in relates to the day of the week on which the first of the month fell:

```
$row = 1;
$col = $data['firstDay'];
```

You can then loop through the number of days in the month, adding a cell to the table for each of the days:

```
for ($i=1; $i<=$data['numDays']; $i++) {
            $dateTable->setCellContents($row, $col, $i);
```

When you reach today, you want to style that cell differently, so create an array of the options for that cell (make the background red) and use the setCellAttributes method to set them:

```
            if ($i == $data['curDay']) {
$todayAttrs = array(
                              'bgcolor' => '#ff0000'
);
$dateTable->setCellAttributes($tRow, $tCol, $todayAttrs);
            }
```

After each cell has been added, you increment the column to which you're writing the cell information. If you move past 6 (Saturday, the last column in the table), increment the row number and reset the column count to 0. If you were relying on HTML to output this information, at this point you'd need to end the table row with a `<tr>` tag and start the next row. Also, once you reached the end of the month, you'd need to add empty cells to complete the current row. The `autoGrow` feature eliminates this problem.

```
        $col++;
        if ($col>6) {
                $row++;
                $col = 0;
        }
}
```

You'd also like to style the weekend differently—columns 0 and 6:

```
$weekendAttrs = array(
            'bgcolor' => '#cccccc'
);
$dateTable->setColAttributes(0, $weekendAttrs);
$dateTable->setColAttributes(6, $weekendAttrs);
```

You can then set the caption for the table and output the result:

```
$dateTable->setCaption($data['curMonth']);
echo $dateTable->toHTML();
?>
```

Images and Text

The packages in this section provide ways of working with both images and text. Although you can access all these packages directly, many of them are there to be used as assistance in other packages. We'll look at these packages:

- The Image_Color package provides a set of methods for working with color.

- The Image_Text package lets you manipulate text for inclusion and display in images.

- The Text_CAPTCHA package implements the CAPTCHA functionality. CAPTCHA are Completely Automated Public Turing tests to tell Computers and Humans Apart.

- The Text_Password package provides a way to generate different kinds of passwords.

- The Text_Wiki package lets you convert wiki-style markup into structured plain text.

Image_Color

The Image_Color package provides a quick and easy way to work with color in your application. The methods provided allow you to convert color representations from one type to another, as well as mix colors together to get a single resultant color.

Note The Image_Color package requires the GD extension to function. For more information about the GD extension, see http://www.php.net/gd.

Common Uses

The Image_Color package has the following common uses:

- Mixing colors together

- Retrieving a web-safe version of your color

- Converting color from one type to another (for example, RGB to hex)

Related Packages

- None

Dependencies

Image_Color has the following dependencies.

Required Packages

- None

Optional Packages

- None

API

allocateColor()

Allocates a color in the given image. Essentially, this method is a wrapper to the PHP `imagecolorallocate()` function, which expects the color to be provided as RGB values. With this method, you provide the colors as either a named color, an RGB array, or a hex value.

```
im allocateColor(im $image, mixed $color)
```

Parameter	Type	Description
$image	im	The image resource that you want the color to be allocated in.
$color	mixed	Either an RGB array or a string containing a hex value or color name to allocate to the image.

changeLightness()

The `changeLightness()` method simply changes the lightness of the class's two colors.

```
void changeLightness([integer $degree = 10])
```

Parameter	Type	Description
$degree	integer	The amount to change the lightness by. Positive values will lighten the two colors contained in the class, while negative values will darken them.

color2RGB()

Converts a named color or a hex string to an RGB array.

```
array color2RGB(string $color)
```

Parameter	Type	Description
$color	string	Either a hex color value or a named color. Values starting with the # character are treated as hex values; all other values are treated as named colors. Named colors not known are returned as black.

getRange()

Returns an array of hex strings that provide a series of steps between the two colors set in the `Image_Color` class.

```
array getRange([integer $degrees = 2])
```

Parameter	Type	Description
$degrees	integer	The number of steps to take between the two colors.

getTextColor()

You use the getTextColor() method to determine whether a light or dark text color would be more readable if the provided color were used as a background. By default, the light and dark colors are white and black, but you can provide alternate light and dark colors if you wish.

```
string getTextColor(string $color [, string $light = '#FFFFFF']
                                   [, string $dark = '#000000'])
```

Parameter	Type	Description
$color	string	The hex value of the color that you want to use as a background color.
$light	string	The hex value of the color that you want to test as the light color.
$dark	string	The hex value of the color that you want to test as the dark color.

hex2rgb()

Converts a hex color string to an RGB array. The returned array has four elements, the fourth element being the original hex string that was converted.

```
array hex2rgb(string $hex)
```

Parameter	Type	Description
$hex	string	The hex color value that you want to convert.

hsv2hex()

Converts an HSV color (Hue, Saturation, Value) to hex.

```
string hsv2hex(integer $h, integer $s, integer $v)
```

Parameter	Type	Description
$h	integer	The hue value of the color.
$s	integer	The saturation value of the color.
$v	integer	The brightness value of the color.

hsv2rgb()

Converts an HSV color to an RGB color array.

```
array hsv2hex(integer $h, integer $s, integer $v)
```

Parameter	Type	Description
$h	integer	The hue value of the color.
$s	integer	The saturation value of the color.
$v	integer	The brightness value of the color.

mixColors()

Mixes two colors together by simply working out their average. If the colors to mix together aren't provided, the class's colors will be used instead.

```
string mixColors([string $color1 = false] [,string $color2 = false])
```

Parameter	Type	Description
$color1	string	The first color to mix, as a hex string.
$color2	string	The second color to mix, as a hex string.

namedColor2RGB()

Converts a named color to an RGB color array. If a named color is not known, black is returned.

```
array namedColor2RGB(string $color)
```

Parameter	Type	Description
$color	string	Either a hex value beginning with //, or a named color. The value is not case sensitive.

percentageColor2RGB()

Converts an RGB percentage string into an RGB array. An RGB percentage string is a comma-separated list of percentages that correspond to RGB values.

```
array percentageColor2RGB(string $color)
```

Parameter	Type	Description
$color	string	An RGB percentage string—"20%,60%,15%".

rgb2hex()

Converts an RGB color array to a hex string.

```
string rgb2hex(array $color)
```

Parameter	Type	Description
$color	array	A three-element array that contains the RGB color values to convert.

setColors()

Takes two colors in hex format and sets them as the colors that the Image_Color class should use when mixing colors together. By setting the colors for the class with this method, you don't have to provide the mixColors() method with the colors to mix.

```
void setColors(string $color1, string $color2)
```

Parameter	Type	Description
$color1	string	The first color to use.
$color2	string	The second color to use.

setWebSafe()

Determines whether a color that is returned will be as is, or rounded to the nearest web-safe color.

```
void setWebSafe([boolean $bool = true])
```

Parameter	Type	Description
$bool	boolean	If true, the color returned should be limited to the web-safe palette.

Examples

Building Color Ranges

In this example, you'll use a simple form to let the user build a range of stepped colors. The form will provide a list of named colors to select the start and end colors, and also the number of color steps to build between the two. You'll look at the functions to convert named colors to RGB and to convert RGB arrays to hexadecimal color string. You'll learn how to build a stepped array of colors between two points, and also how to return web-safe colors.

```
<!DOCTYPE html PUBLIC "-//W3C//DTD XHTML 1.0 Strict//EN"➥
"http://www.w3.org/TR/xhtml1/DTD/xhtml1-strict.dtd">
<html xmlns="http://www.w3.org/1999/xhtml">
<head>
<title>Color Example</title>
</head>
<body>
<?php
$colorList = array('aliceblue', 'antiquewhite', 'aqua', 'aquamarine', 'azure',
                   'beige', 'bisque', 'black', 'blanchedalmond', 'blue',
                   'blueviolet', 'brown', 'burlywood', 'cadetblue', 'chartreuse',
                   'chocolate', 'coral', 'cornflowerblue', 'cornsilk', 'crimson',
                   'cyan', 'darkblue', 'darkcyan', 'darkgoldenrod', 'darkgray',
                   'darkgreen', 'darkkhaki', 'darkmagenta', 'darkolivegreen',
                   'darkorange', 'darkorchid', 'darkred', 'darksalmon',
                   'darkseagreen', 'darkslateblue', 'darkslategray',
                   'darkturquoise', 'darkviolet', 'deeppink', 'deepskyblue',
                   'dimgray', 'dodgerblue', 'firebrick', 'floralwhite',
                   'forestgreen', 'fuchsia', 'gainsboro', 'ghostwhite', 'gold',
                   'goldenrod', 'gray', 'green', 'greenyellow', 'honeydew',
                   'hotpink', 'indianred', 'indigo', 'ivory', 'khaki', 'lavender',
                   'lavenderblush', 'lawngreen', 'lemonchiffon', 'lightblue',
                   'lightcoral', 'lightcyan', 'lightgoldenrodyellow', 'lightgreen',
                   'lightgrey', 'lightpink', 'lightsalmon', 'lightseagreen',
                   'lightskyblue', 'lightslategray', 'lightsteelblue', 'lightyellow',
                   'lime', 'limegreen', 'linen', 'magenta', 'maroon',
                   'mediumaquamarine', 'mediumblue', 'mediumorchid', 'mediumpurple',
                   'mediumseagreen', 'mediumslateblue', 'mediumspringgreen',
                   'mediumturquoise', 'mediumvioletred', 'midnightblue', 'mintcream',
                   'mistyrose', 'moccasin', 'navajowhite', 'navy', 'oldlace',
                   'olive', 'olivedrab', 'orange', 'orangered', 'orchid',
                   'palegoldenrod', 'palegreen', 'paleturquoise', 'palevioletred',
                   'papayawhip', 'peachpuff', 'peru', 'pink', 'plum', 'powderblue',
                   'purple', 'red', 'rosybrown', 'royalblue', 'saddlebrown',
                   'salmon', 'sandybrown', 'seagreen', 'seashell',
                   'sienna', 'silver', 'skyblue', 'slateblue', 'slategray', 'snow',
                   'springgreen', 'steelblue', 'tan', 'teal', 'thistle', 'tomato',
                   'turquoise', 'violet', 'wheat', 'white', 'whitesmoke', 'yellow',
                   'yellowgreen');

$cString = '';

foreach ($colorList as $color) {
    $cString .= "<option value='$color'>$color</option>\n";
}
?>
```

```php
<form action="<?php echo $_SERVER['PHP_SELF']; ?>" method="POST">
<p>Color start: <select name="cStart"><?php echo $cString; ?></select></p>
<p>Color end: <select name="cEnd"><?php echo $cString; ?></select></p>
<p>Steps: <select name="cSteps">
<?php
for ($i = 1; $i <= 10; $i++) {
    echo "<option value='$i'>$i</option>\n";
}
?>
</select></p>
<p><input type="submit" name="submit" value="Build Steps"></p>
</form>
<?php
if (isset($_POST['submit'])) {
    require_once("Image/Color.php");
    $c = new Image_Color;
    $hexStart = $c->rgb2hex($c->namedColor2RGB($_POST['cStart']));
    $hexEnd = $c->rgb2hex($c->namedColor2RGB($_POST['cEnd']));
    $c->setColors($hexStart, $hexEnd);

    $nRange = $c->getRange($_POST['cSteps']);

    $c->setWebSafe(true);

    $wRange = $c->getRange($_POST['cSteps']);
?>
<table border="0">
<tr>
    <th></th>
    <th>Standard</th>
    <th>Websafe</th>
</tr>
<tr>
    <td>Start Color</td>
    <td bgcolor="#<?php echo $hexStart; ?>">#<?php echo $hexStart; ?></td>
    <td bgcolor="#<?php echo $hexStart; ?>">#<?php echo $hexStart; ?></td>
</tr>
<?php
for ($i = 0; $i < count($nRange); $i++) {
?>
```

```
<tr>
    <td></td>
    <td bgcolor="#<?php echo $nRange[$i]; ?>">#<?php echo $nRange[$i]; ?></td>
    <td bgcolor="#<?php echo $wRange[$i]; ?>">#<?php echo $wRange[$i]; ?></td>
</tr>
<?php
}
?>
<tr>
    <td>End Color</td>
    <td bgcolor="#<?php echo $hexEnd; ?>">#<?php echo $hexEnd; ?></td>
    <td bgcolor="#<?php echo $hexEnd; ?>">#<?php echo $hexEnd; ?></td>
</tr>
</table>
<?php
}
?>
</body>
</html>
```

Displaying the RGB Value of a Color

In this example, a simple web form is used to display the RGB value of a color from its name. The names for the colors appear in a select box, and when the form is submitted, the color2RGB() method will be used to return an array of the RGB values. The values from this array are printed along with a table with the background color, so you can view the color as well.

```
<!DOCTYPE html PUBLIC "-//W3C//DTD XHTML 1.0 Strict//EN"➥
"http://www.w3.org/TR/xhtml1/DTD/xhtml1-strict.dtd">
<html xmlns="http://www.w3.org/1999/xhtml">
<head>
<title>Displaying the RGB value of a color</title>
<style type="text/css">
table.swatch {width:200px;border-style:solid;border-width:1px}
</style>
</head>
<body>
<?php
```

```
$colorList = array('aliceblue', 'antiquewhite', 'aqua', 'aquamarine', 'azure',
                   'beige', 'bisque', 'black', 'blanchedalmond', 'blue',
                   'blueviolet', 'brown', 'burlywood', 'cadetblue', 'chartreuse',
                   'chocolate', 'coral', 'cornflowerblue', 'cornsilk', 'crimson',
                   'cyan', 'darkblue', 'darkcyan', 'darkgoldenrod', 'darkgray',
                   'darkgreen', 'darkkhaki', 'darkmagenta', 'darkolivegreen',
                   'darkorange', 'darkorchid', 'darkred', 'darksalmon',
                   'darkseagreen', 'darkslateblue', 'darkslategray',
                   'darkturquoise', 'darkviolet', 'deeppink', 'deepskyblue',
                   'dimgray', 'dodgerblue', 'firebrick', 'floralwhite',
                   'forestgreen', 'fuchsia', 'gainsboro', 'ghostwhite', 'gold',
                   'goldenrod', 'gray', 'green', 'greenyellow', 'honeydew',
                   'hotpink', 'indianred', 'indigo', 'ivory', 'khaki', 'lavender',
                   'lavenderblush', 'lawngreen', 'lemonchiffon', 'lightblue',
                   'lightcoral', 'lightcyan', 'lightgoldenrodyellow', 'lightgreen',
                   'lightgrey', 'lightpink', 'lightsalmon', 'lightseagreen',
                   'lightskyblue', 'lightslategray', 'lightsteelblue', 'lightyellow',
                   'lime', 'limegreen', 'linen', 'magenta', 'maroon',
                   'mediumaquamarine', 'mediumblue', 'mediumorchid', 'mediumpurple',
                   'mediumseagreen', 'mediumslateblue', 'mediumspringgreen',
                   'mediumturquoise', 'mediumvioletred', 'midnightblue', 'mintcream',
                   'mistyrose', 'moccasin', 'navajowhite', 'navy', 'oldlace',
                   'olive', 'olivedrab', 'orange', 'orangered', 'orchid',
                   'palegoldenrod', 'palegreen', 'paleturquoise', 'palevioletred',
                   'papayawhip', 'peachpuff', 'peru', 'pink', 'plum', 'powderblue',
                   'purple', 'red', 'rosybrown', 'royalblue', 'saddlebrown',
                   'salmon', 'sandybrown', 'seagreen', 'seashell', 'sienna',
                   'silver', 'skyblue', 'slateblue', 'slategray', 'snow',
                   'springgreen', 'steelblue', 'tan', 'teal', 'thistle', 'tomato',
                   'turquoise', 'violet', 'wheat', 'white', 'whitesmoke', 'yellow',
                   'yellowgreen');
```

```php
$cString = '';

foreach ($colorList as $color) {
    if ((isset($_POST['submit'])) &&
        (isset($_POST['color1'])) &&
        ($_POST['color1'] == $color)) {
        $cString .= "<option value='$color' selected>$color</option>\n";
    } else {
        $cString .= "<option value='$color'>$color</option>\n";
    }
}
?>
<form action="<?php echo $_SERVER['PHP_SELF']; ?>" method="POST">
<p>Select a color:  <select name="color1"><?php echo $cString; ?></select></p>
<p><input type="submit" name="submit" value="Show RGB values"></p>
</form>
<?php
if (isset($_POST['submit'])) {
    require once("Image/Color.php");
    $c = new Image_Color;
    $rgbArray = $c->color2RGB($_POST['color1']);

    print sprintf("<p><b>Color is:  </b> rgb(%s, %s, %s)</p>",
        $rgbArray[0],
        $rgbArray[1],
        $rgbArray[2]);
    print sprintf
    ("<table class=\"swatch\"><tr><td style=\"background-color:rgb(%s,%s,%s)\">",
        $rgbArray[0],
        $rgbArray[1],
        $rgbArray[2]);
    print " </td></tr></table>";

}
?>
</body>
</html>
```

Image_Text

The Image_Text package provides advanced text manipulation methods for use when writing text to PHP GD image resources. With this package you can rotate, align, and wrap text within the constraints of your image size.

Common Uses

The Image_Text package has the following common uses:

- Displaying rotated text in an image
- Wrapping long lines of text within an image
- Fitting text within a specific area of an image

Related Packages

- None

Dependencies

Image_Text has the following dependencies.

Required Packages

- PHP GD extension

Optional Packages

- None

API

autoMeasurize()

Tries to determine the best font size to fit the text provided within the area box that you've set. Be careful when using this method, as it can overload your web server by testing out all the different font sizes. If no possible font size is found, the method will return PEAR_Error.

```
integer autoMeasurize([integer $start = false] [, integer $end = false])
```

Parameter	Type	Description
$start	integer	A font size to start testing with.
$end	integer	A font size to stop testing at. By using the $start and $end parameters, you can limit the range of font sizes the method tests, thereby limiting the usage and impact on your web server.

construct()

Constructs and initializes the Image_Text object. It calls init(), so if you set an option using set() after you've called construct(), you'll need to call init() manually again.

```
Image_Text &construct(string $text, array $options)
```

Parameter	Type	Description
$text	string	The text to render in the image.
$options	array	An array of options that specify how the text is to be rendered within the image.

The following table shows the possible options that you can set to control how the text is rendered.

Text Rendering Options

Option	Description
angle	The angle at which the text is to be printed.
antialias	Defaults to true. Set to false to turn antialiasing off for the text rendering.
canvas	The canvas to use, either a GD image resource or an array with width and height values.
color	This is an array of color values that are rotated through depending on the color_mode setting.
color_mode	Set this to rotate through colors for each rendered line or paragraph. Set to line for lines and paragraphs for paragraphs.
cx	The center *x* position of the text box.
cy	The center *y* position of the text box.
dest_file	The destination filename to save the image to.
font_file	The font file to use for printing the text.
font_path	The location of the font to use. The path only gives the directory path (ending with a /).

Text Rendering Options (Continued)

Option	Description
font_size	The font size to use when rendering the text. If autoMeasurize is used, this setting is overwritten.
halign	The horizontal alignment of the text within your box.
height	The height of the text box.
image_type	The type of image to build.
line_spacing	The line spacing to use.
max_font_size	The maximum font size to use with autoMeasurize.
min_font_size	The minimum font size to use with autoMeasurize.
valign	The vertical alignment of the text within your box.
width	The width of the text box.
x	The position of the left side of your text box.
y	The top position of your text box.

display()

Outputs the current image to the browser, optionally saving it to disk at the same time. It will return true if it's successful or a PEAR_Error if it fails.

```
boolean display([boolean $save = false] [, boolean $free = false])
```

Parameter	Type	Description
$save	boolean	If set to true and you have specified a destination filename in the options, the image will be saved to disk.
$free	boolean	If this is set to true, the image resource will be freed.

getImg()

Returns the current image as a GD image resource. Use this method if you want to perform your own additional manipulations on the image before saving or outputting it.

```
image &getImg()
```

init()

Initializes the Image_Text object and needs to be called after you've set the options for your Image_Text object.

```
boolean init()
```

measurize()

Takes the text and font size provided and measures it all up to fit within the area you defined. The array returned contains the measured lines.

```
array measurize([boolean $force = false])
```

Parameter	Type	Description
$force	boolean	Determines whether to force the measuring within the area defined.

render()

Renders the text onto the canvas using the options provided through the init or set methods.

```
boolean render([boolean $force = false])
```

Parameter	Type	Description
$force	boolean	Determines whether to turn on measuring problems or not. If you set this to true, you might cause text to be rendered outside the available or given area.

save()

Saves the current image canvas to a file on disk.

```
boolean save([string $destination = false])
```

Parameter	Type	Description
$destination	string	The name of the file to save the image to. You can leave this parameter out if you have previously set the destination filename option.

set()

Lets you set or reset single or multiple options for the Image_Text object. The options that you can set are the same options that are passed through with the construct() method. You must call init() again after setting options.

```
boolean set(mixed $option [, mixed $value = null])
```

Parameter	Type	Description
$option	mixed	A single option name or an array of options to set.
$value	mixed	The value for the option name provided if $option is a string.

setColor()

Sets a color for a specific ID in the Image_Text object color array. The color formats understood by the method are HTML-style hex values, with or without the leading # character. An eight-character hex value is also understood, the fourth part being the alpha channel for the color. You can also pass an indexed array with 'r', 'g', 'b', and optionally 'a' keys.

```
boolean setColor(mixed $color [, mixed $id = 0])
```

Parameter	Type	Description
$color	mixed	The color value to set. Examples are ff0000, 08ffff00, or array('r'=>200, 'g'=>200, 'b'=>255).
$id	mixed	The ID in the color array to set the color of.

setColors()

Sets up the colors to be used in the Image_Text object.

```
boolean setColors(mixed $colors)
```

Parameter	Type	Description
$colors	mixed	A single color value or an array of colors to set.

Examples

Saving an Image with Text to Disk

This example takes a small amount of text, writes it to an image, and saves it to disk.

```php
<?php
require_once 'Image/Text.php';

$options = array (
    'cx' => 200,
    'cy' => 100,
    'canvas' => array (
        'width' => 400,
        'height' => 200
    ),
    'width' => 200,
    'height' => 100,
    'color' => '#ffffff0',
    'line_spacing' => 1,
    'max_lines' => 100,
    'antialias' => true,
    'font_file' => './Chalkboard.ttf',
    'font_size' => 12,
    'halign' => 'center',
    'valign' => 'center'
);

$text = "That's no moon.  That's a space station!";

$itext = new Image_Text($text, $options);
$itext->init();
$itext->render();
$itext->save('/tmp/file.png');
?>
```

Filling an Image with Text

This example takes a paragraph of text and fills the available space of the image with it. To do this, you use the autoMeasurize() method to determine the correct font size.

The $options array determines the settings that are used. As you can see, we've used a width and height that are slightly smaller than the canvas width and height so that there's some padding between the area of the text and the sides of the images. By specifying the minimum and maximum font size, you restrict the Image_Text object within a font size range to save on processor usage. The font file specified must exist.

```php
<?php
require_once 'Image/Text.php';

$options = array(
            'cx'            => 200,
            'cy'            => 100,
            'canvas'        => array('width'=> 400,'height'=> 200),
            'width'         => 380,
            'height'        => 180,
            'color'          => '#fce88b',
            'line_spacing'  => 1,
            'min_font_size' => 5,
            'max_font_size' => 20,
            'max_lines'      => 100,
            'antialias'     => true,
            'font_file'     => 'arial.ttf'
        );

$text = "PHP succeeds an older product, named PHP/FI. PHP/FI was created by
Rasmus Lerdorf in 1995, initially as a simple set of Perl scripts for tracking
accesses to his online resume. He named this set of scripts 'Personal Home Page
Tools.' As more functionality was required, Rasmus wrote a much larger C
implementation, which was able to communicate with databases, and enabled users
to develop simple dynamic Web applications.";

$itext = new Image_Text($text, $options);
$itext->init();
$itext->autoMeasurize();
$itext->render();
$itext->display();
?>
```

Text_CAPTCHA

The Text_CAPTCHA package is a great package to install and use if you want to secure your web forms against automated form submission bots. The package builds a small graphic image, into which is embedded a text string. The user of the form is then prompted to provide the string or phrase that he or she can read in the image; by testing whether this phrase has been entered correctly, you can ascertain whether this form has been submitted by a real live person or a computer program running somewhere on the Internet.

Common Uses

The Text_CAPTCHA package has the following common use:

- Securing your web forms against automated submissions

Related Packages

- None

Dependencies

Because the Text_CAPTCHA package is building an image, you also need to have the PHP GD extension along with these packages.

Required Packages

- Text_Password
- Image_Text

Optional Packages

- None

API

factory()

Creates a new Text_CAPTCHA object. Once the object has been initialized, you can then apply the options that you want it to have and build the physical image. The method returns either a Text_CAPTCHA object if it was initialized correctly, or a PEAR_Error object if there was a problem.

```
mixed &factory(string $driver)
```

Parameter	Type	Description
$driver	string	The driver name of the class to initialize. Currently this is only 'Image'.

getCAPTCHA()

Returns the raw GD image resource that was created. Use this method if you want to manipulate the CAPTCHA further before outputting it to the browser.

```
im getCAPTCHA()
```

getCAPTCHAAsJPEG()

Returns the CAPTCHA object as JPEG data. A physical file isn't created on the disk; you'll have to handle that yourself. If an error occurs, the method will return a PEAR_Error.

```
string getCAPTCHAAsJPEG()
```

getCAPTCHAAsPNG()

Returns the CAPTCHA object as PNG data. If an error occurs, the method will return PEAR_Error.

```
string getCAPTCHAAsPNG()
```

getPhrase()

Returns the random phrase that the Text_CAPTCHA object generated to use in the CAPTCHA image. You need to retrieve this and store it in a session variable so that you can test against it in the target script.

```
string getPhrase()
```

init()

Once the Text_CAPTCHA object has been initialized with the driver you specified, the init()
method initializes the Text_CAPTCHA_Driver_Image object, generates the random phrase if
necessary, and creates the physical GD image. The init method will either return true if it was
created successfully, or a PEAR_Error if there was a problem.

```
mixed init([integer $width = 200] [, integer $height = 80] [, string $phrase = null]
        [, array $options = null])
```

Parameter	Type	Description
$width	integer	The width of the image to create.
$height	integer	The height of the image to create.
$phrase	string	The secret phrase to be used in the CAPTCHA image. If this isn't specified, then the Text_CAPTCHA object will generate one for you.
$options	array	Any further options that you want to pass to the Image_Text object.

Examples

Validating That the CAPTCHA is Readable

This simple example displays an Image_CAPTCHA–generated JPEG with a text input for the
user to supply the phrase that he or she can read in the image. When the form is submitted, the
entered phrase will be tested against the phrase stored in the session variable.

```php
<?php
    session_start();
?>
<!DOCTYPE html PUBLIC "-//W3C//DTD XHTML 1.0 Strict//EN"➥
"http://www.w3.org/TR/xhtml1/DTD/xhtml1-strict.dtd">
<html xmlns="http://www.w3.org/1999/xhtml">
<head>
<title>CAPTCHA Example</title>
</head>
<body>
<?php
if (!isset($_POST['captcha'])) {
    // Form has not been submitted, display the form
    require_once 'Text/CAPTCHA.php';
    // These are the options for the CAPTCHA object.  The physical font file
    // must exist
```

```php
    $options = array(
        'font_size' => 32,
        'font_path' => './',
        'font_file' => 'arial.ttf'
    );
    $formCAPTCHA = Text_CAPTCHA::factory('Image');
    $result = $formCAPTCHA->init(300, 120, null, $options);
    if (PEAR::isError($result)) {
        echo 'Sorry, there was a problem generating the CAPTCHA Object';
        exit;
    }
    // Store the generated phrase in a session
    // variable so that we can get to it later
    $_SESSION['secretCAPTCHA'] = $formCAPTCHA->getPhrase();

    $imageCAPTCHA = $formCAPTCHA->getCAPTCHAAsJPEG();
    if (PEAR::isError($imageCAPTCHA)) {
        echo 'Sorry, there was a problem generating the CAPTCHA Image';
        exit;
    }
    // We use an MD5 of the generated phrase as a unique filename
    file_put_contents(md5($formCAPTCHA->getPhrase()) . '.jpg', $imageCAPTCHA);
?>
<p>
Enter the phrase in the box below:
<form action="<?php echo $_SERVER['PHP_SELF']; ?>" method="POST">
<img src="<?php echo md5($formCAPTCHA->getPhrase()); ?>.jpg" width="300"
    height="120" /><br />
<input type="text" name="captcha" /><br />
<input type="submit" value="Validate" />
</form>
</p>
<?php
```

```
    } else {
        // Form has been submitted with a CAPTCHA value
        if (isset($_POST['captcha']) && isset($_SESSION['secretCAPTCHA']) &&
                strlen($_POST['captcha']) > 0 && strlen($_SESSION['secretCAPTCHA']) > 0
                && $_POST['captcha'] == $_SESSION['secretCAPTCHA']) {
            echo "Congratulations!";
            unlink(md5($_SESSION['secretCAPTCHA']) . '.jpg');
        } else {
            echo "Sorry, that is not correct.";
        }
    }
}
?>
</body>
</html>
```

Note You'll notice that the image is being stored using a filename that is an MD5 of the generated phrase. This is then unlinked when the form is submitted. If the user continuously refreshes the page, visits the page and does not submit the phrase, or simply provides an incorrect phrase, the generated images won't be removed and will begin to build up. To get around this, you can write your own simple session-handling functions and use those to clean up any files related to that session when the session expires.

Text_Password

In any web application that requires people to log in and authenticate, you need to be able to generate passwords for them. The Text_Password package enables you to generate passwords in any one of three possible ways: producing a pronounceable password, an unpronounceable password, or one that's based on an existing string.

Common Uses

The Text_Password class has the following common use:

- Creating passwords for your application

Related Packages

- None

Dependencies

Text_Password requires the following other PEAR packages.

Required Packages

- None

Optional Packages

- None

API

create()

Creates a single password.

```
string create([integer $length = 10] [, string $type = 'pronounceable']
              [, string $chars = ''])
```

Parameter	Type	Description
$length	integer	Length of the password to generate.
$type	string	Type of password to generate (pronounceable or unpronounceable).
$chars	string	Characters which may be used in generating the unpronounceable password.

createMultiple()

Creates a number of unique passwords in an array.

```
array createMultiple(integer $number [, integer $length = 10]
                               [, string $type = 'pronounceable']
                               [, string $chars = ''])
```

Parameter	Type	Description
$number	integer	Sets the number of passwords to return.
$length	integer	Length of the passwords that are generated.
$type	string	Type of password to generate.
$chars	string	Characters which may be used in generating the unpronounceable password.

createFromLogin()

Returns a password that's based on an existing username or login. You can specify how the function must use the login name to build the password; this can be anything from simply reversing the username to performing a rotx on the text. The password is returned as a string.

```
string createFromLogin(string $login, string $type[, integer $key = 0])
```

Parameter	Type	Description
$login	string	The login name that the password is based on.
$type	string	Specifies how to convert the username into a password. Valid types are reverse, shuffle, xor, rot13, rotx, rotx++, rotx--, ascii_rotx, ascii_rotx++, and ascii_rotx--. The reverse type simply reverses the login; shuffle mixes the characters up. The xor and rot13 types perform xor and rot13 on the logins, respectively. The remaining types apply the optional key that you provide to the rot encoding in different ways to provide differing results.
$key	integer	A value that's applied in the encoding to provide less predictable results.

createMultipleFromLogin()

The createMultipleFromLogin() method works in the same way as the createFromLogin method, except it returns an array of multiple passwords instead of just the single one.

```
array createMultipleFromLogin(array $login, string $type [, integer $key = 0])
```

Parameter	Type	Description
$login	array	An array of logins for which passwords must be generated.
$type	string	The type of encoding to use for generating the passwords.
$key	integer	A value applied to the encoding to provide different results.

Examples

Creating a Random Password

This example shows you how to return passwords that are entirely random. For this example, you'll look first at how to create a simple pronounceable password, and then look at returning a number of unpronounceable passwords.

Listing 1. *The code for this example is all contained in a single PHP script.*

```
<!DOCTYPE html PUBLIC "-//W3C//DTD XHTML 1.0 Strict//EN"➥
"http://www.w3.org/TR/xhtml1/DTD/xhtml1-strict.dtd">
<html xmlns="http://www.w3.org/1999/xhtml">
<head>
<title>Password Example</title>
```

```
<style>
    li {
        font-style: italic;
    }
</style>
</head>
<body>
<?php
// require the Text_Password package to be included in the page
require_once "Text/Password.php";
?>
<p>
<strong>Here is a pronounceable password, defaulting to 10 characters:</strong>
<br />
<em><?php echo Text_Password::create(); ?></em>
</p>
<p>
<strong>Here are 5 unpronounceable passwords, with a
  length of 15 characters each:</strong>
<br />
<ul>
<?php
    $passwords = Text_Password::createMultiple(5, 15, 'unpronounceable');
    foreach ($passwords as $password) {
    ?>
    <li><?php echo $password; ?></li>
    <?php
    }
?>
</ul>
</p>
</body>
</html>
```

Creating Passwords Based on Existing Usernames

This next example takes an existing list of usernames and applies three types of encoding to them to generate passwords. If you refresh the script, you'll see that only the Shuffle column changes—the other types of encoding are predictable in the results they return.

```
<!DOCTYPE html PUBLIC "-//W3C//DTD XHTML 1.0 Strict//EN"➥
"http://www.w3.org/TR/xhtml1/DTD/xhtml1-strict.dtd">
<html xmlns="http://www.w3.org/1999/xhtml">
<head>
<title>Password Example</title>
</head>
<body>
<?php
```

```php
// require the Text_Password package to be included in the page
require_once "Text/Password.php";
// Create an array of usernames
$usernames = array("allan", "nathan", "wendy");
?>
<p>
<strong>Here are our usernames and their corresponding passwords:</strong>
<br />
<table>
<tr><th>Username</th><th>Reversed</th><th>ROT13</th><th>Shuffled</th></tr>
<?php
    // Return three arrays of the usernames encoded in different ways
    $passwordsRev = Text_Password::createMultipleFromLogin($usernames, 'reverse');
    $passwordsROT13 = Text_Password::createMultipleFromLogin($usernames, 'rot13');
    $passwordsShuffle =
    Text_Password::createMultipleFromLogin($usernames, 'shuffle');
    for ($i = 0; $i < count($usernames); $i++) {
    ?>
    <tr>
        <td><?php echo $usernames[$i]; ?></td>
        <td><?php echo $passwordsRev[$i]; ?></td>
        <td><?php echo $passwordsROT13[$i]; ?></td>
        <td><?php echo $passwordsShuffle[$i]; ?></td>
    </tr>
    <?php
    }
?>
</table>
</p>

</body>
</html>
```

Text_Wiki

The Text_Wiki package takes text that has been marked up using the tags used in a Wiki and transforms it into another marked-up format. If you've ever used a Wiki, you'll know that there are a set of standard characters that you can use to do fairly complex markup—headings, text styles, and even tables. By using the Text_Wiki package, you'll be able to provide users of your application with an easy method of marking up text that leverages an existing user base that might already be familiar with these standards.

You can extend the Text_Wiki package to parse other common markup languages such as BBCode, as popularized by the phpBB bulletin board.

Common Uses

The Text_Wiki package has the following common uses:

- Converting existing wiki-style text to another usable format

- Giving users of your web application an easy way of formatting text

Related Packages

- None

Dependencies

Text_Wiki has the following dependencies.

Required Packages

- None

Optional Packages

- None

API

addPath()

Adds a path to an array of paths stored inside the Text_Wiki object. This array of paths is used when searching for a file to load.

`void addPath(string $type, string $dir)`

Parameter	Type	Description
$type	string	The path type to add—either a parse or render type.
$dir	string	The directory to add to the path.

addToken()

An array of tokens is created when the Text_Wiki object parses your source—each of the objects or renderings that it understands is stored as a new token. The addToken() method adds a token to this array of tokens.

`string|integer addToken(string $rule [, array $options] [,boolean $id_only])`

Parameter	Type	Description
$rule	string	The rule to add as a token.
$options	array	An array of options to use for the new token element.
$id_only	boolean	If true, then only the new token number will be returned. If false, the newly created token element will be returned as a string.

changeRule()

Within the Text_Wiki object is an array of rules that are applied in order and are used to parse the source that was provided. The changeRule() method changes an existing rule to a new one.

`void changeRule(string $old, string $new)`

Parameter	Type	Description
$old	string	The name of the rule you're changing from.
$new	string	The name of the rule it's changing to.

deleteRule()

With this method, you can delete an existing rule from the parser.

```
void deleteRule(string $name)
```

Parameter	Type	Description
$name	string	The name of the rule you want to remove.

disableRule()

There's an array of rules that shouldn't be applied when parsing the source. The `disableRule()` method adds a rule to this list of rules.

```
void disableRule(string $name)
```

Parameter	Type	Description
$name	string	The name of the rule you want to disable.

enableRule()

There's an array of rules that shouldn't be applied when parsing the source. The `enableRule()` method removes a rule from this list of rules, effectively enabling it.

```
void enableRule(string $name)
```

Parameter	Type	Description
$name	string	The name of the rule you want to enable.

error

This method simply raises an error.

```
PEAR_Error &error(string $message)
```

Parameter	Type	Description
$message	string	The error message to use.

factory()

Returns a copy of the Text_Wiki object.

```
Text_Wiki &factory([string $parser = 'Default'] [, array $rules = null])
```

Parameter	Type	Description
$parser	string	The name of the parser to use. The Default parser is the only one included in the package.
$rules	array	The rules to use when instantiating the object.

findFile()

Searches through the internal array of paths for the file specified. If the file isn't found, the method will return false. The method returns the full path to the file if it finds the file.

```
string|boolean findFile(string $type, string $file)
```

Parameter	Type	Description
$type	string	The type of path to search.
$file	string	The name of the file you're searching for.

getFormatConf()

Although the Text_Wiki object can render the tokens, some output formats might need specific configuration. The getFormatConf() method returns the configuration for a specific format and key.

```
mixed getFormatConf(string $format [, string $key = null])
```

Parameter	Type	Description
$format	string	The format to retrieve the config for.
$key	string	The key to return the config for. If no key is provided, then the entire configuration array will be returned.

getParseConf()

Returns the configuration for a specific rule and key for the parser.

```
mixed getParseConf(string $rule [, string $key = null])
```

Parameter	Type	Description
$rule	string	The parser rule to return the config for.
$key	string	The key to return the config for. If no key is provided, then the entire configuration array will be returned.

getPath()

Returns the array of current paths stored in the internal array of paths.

```
array getPath([string $type = null])
```

Parameter	Type	Description
$type	string	The path type to return. If not provided or null, all paths will be returned.

getRenderConf()

Just as you can have special configurations for specific parsers, so you can have configurations for specific renderers. The getRenderConf() method returns the configuration for a renderer, rule, and key.

```
mixed getRenderConf(string $format, string $rule [, string $key = null])
```

Parameter	Type	Description
$format	string	The render format to retrieve the config for.
$rule	string	The render format rule to retrieve the config for.
$key	string	The key to return the config for. If the key isn't supplied, then the entire configuration array will be returned.

getSource()

Returns the source text that was parsed to build the array of tokens.

```
string getSource()
```

getTokens()

Returns an array of the tokens that were parsed out of the source text.

```
array getTokens([array $rules = null])
```

Parameter	Type	Description
$rules	array	An optional array of rule names. If an array is supplied, the method will return the tokens matching the rule names. If null is supplied, all tokens will be returned.

insertRule()

Inserts a rule into the current rule set.

```
void insertRule(string $name [, string $tgt = null])
```

Parameter	Type	Description
$name	string	A unique name for the rule to add.
$tgt	string	If $tgt is provided, the rule specified by $name will be inserted after $tgt. If $tgt isn't provided or is null, the $name will be added at the end of the rule set.

isError()

Checks if an error has been generated.

```
boolean isError(mixed $obj)
```

Parameter	Type	Description
$obj	mixed	The object to test if it is a PEAR_Object or not. Will return true if it is, otherwise false.

loadFormatObj()

The format rules can be stored in an external file. The `loadFormatObj()` method loads the format rules from the file specified.

```
boolean loadFormatObj(string $rule)
```

Parameter	Type	Description
$rule	string	The format rule class name to load.

loadParseObj()

Loads a set of parser rules from the file specified.

```
boolean loadParseObj(string $rule)
```

Parameter	Type	Description
$rule	string	The parser rule class name to load.

loadRenderObj()

Loads a set of renderer rules from the file specified.

```
boolean loadRenderObj(string $rule)
```

Parameter	Type	Description
$rule	string	The render rule class name to load.

parse()

Parses the source text into an array of tokens using either the default set of rules, or the rules that you specify.

```
void parse(string $text)
```

Parameter	Type	Description
$text	string	The source text containing wiki markup that you wish to parse.

render()

Renders the array of tokens into the target format you specified.

```
string render([string $format = 'Xhtml'])
```

Parameter	Type	Description
$format	string	The target output format.

setFormatConf()

Sets the format configuration for a specific rule and key.

```
void setFormatConf(string $format, string $key [, string $val = null])
```

Parameter	Type	Description
$format	string	The format you're setting the config for.
$key	string	The config key you're setting.
$val	string	The config value for the key.

setParseConf()

Sets the parser configuration for a specific rule and key.

```
void setParseConf(string $rule, array|string $arg1 [, string $arg2 = null])
```

Parameter	Type	Description
$rule	string	The parse rule you want to set the config for.
$arg1	array|string	Either an array to use for the parse rule config, or a config key.
$arg2	string	The config value for the key passed as $arg1.

setRenderConf()

Sets the renderer configuration for a specific rule and key.

```
void setRenderConf(string $format, string $rule, array|string $arg1
                   [, string $arg2 = null])
```

Parameter	Type	Description
$format	string	The render format you're setting the config for.
$rule	string	The render rule you're setting the config for.
$arg1	array|string	Either an array to use for the render config, or a config key.
$arg2	string	The config value for the key passed as $arg1.

setToken()

Lets you set or reset a token within the tokens array. By using this method, you can add or alter a token with different rules to those that were used when initially parsing the source.

```
void setToken(integer $id, string $rule [, array $options])
```

Parameter	Type	Description
$id	integer	The token number you want to reset.
$rule	string	The rule name.
$options	array	An array of options to use for this token element.

singleton()

Returns the instance of the Text_Wiki object. If there is no instance already created, the method will create a new instance. A singleton means that only one instance of the class is created.

```
Text_Wiki &singleton([string $parser - 'Default'] [,array $rules - null])
```

Parameter	Type	Description
$parser	string	The parser to be used.
$rules	array	The set of rules to use when instantiating the object.

transform()

Does both a parse and a render in the same step. Use this method if you simply want to transform your source text into the output format without manipulating any of the tokens that are parsed.

```
string transform(string $text [, string $format = 'Xhtml'])
```

Parameter	Type	Description
$text	string	Your source text containing wiki markup.
$format	string	The target output format.

Examples

Converting Standard Wiki Text to XHTML

This example is a single XHTML and PHP page that contains a textarea form input. When the form is submitted, you simply assume that the text contains wiki-style markup and convert it to XHTML.

```
<!DOCTYPE html PUBLIC "-//W3C//DTD XHTML 1.0 Strict//EN"➥
"http://www.w3.org/TR/xhtml1/DTD/xhtml1-strict.dtd">
<html xmlns="http://www.w3.org/1999/xhtml">
<head>
<title>Wiki to XHTML Example</title>
</head>
<body>
<p>
<form action="<?php echo $_SERVER['PHP_SELF']; ?>" method="POST">
<textarea name="source" rows="10" cols="40">
<?php
if (isset($_POST['source'])) {
    echo $_POST['source'];
} else {
?>
**This text is bold**
||Table Cell 1||Table Cell 2||
<?php
}
?>
</textarea>
<br />
<input type="submit" value="Transform!">
</form>
</p>
<?php
if (isset($_POST['source']) && strlen($_POST['source']) > 0) {
?>
<hr />
<strong>Here are the XHTML results of your Wiki code:</strong>
<p>
<?php
    // The base Pear class is needed for error reporting
    require_once 'PEAR.php';
    // Require the Text_Wiki package to do the actual transforming
    require_once 'Text/Wiki.php';
    $wiki = & Text_Wiki::factory();
```

```php
    $result = $wiki->transform($_POST['source']);

// display the transformed text

    if (PEAR::isError($result)) {
?>
<em>Sorry, there was a problem converting the text:</em>
<pre>
<?php var_dump($result); ?>
</pre>
<?php
    } else {
        echo '<pre>' . htmlentities($result) . '</pre>';
    }
?>
</p>
<?php
}
?>
</body>
</html>
```

Transforming with a Subset of Parsing Rules

In this next example, you'll use the exact same code as in the previous example, but here you provide parameters when calling the factory method. By doing this, you can provide the Text_Wiki object with a custom set of parsing rules to apply to the text. This is useful if you're building a way for users of your application to apply markup, but you want to limit the kinds of markup that they can use.

In the previous example, you built the Text_Wiki object with the following line:

```php
$wiki = & Text_Wiki::factory();
```

In this example, you provide the two parameters, the first being the parser to use, and the second an array of valid parsing rules:

```php
$wiki = & Text_Wiki::
factory('Default',array('Strong','Bold','Emphasis','Italic','Underline'));
```

As you can see in this instance, you only want to allow the user to apply bold, italic, and underline formatting to the text. In the earlier example, you took the following wiki text:

```
**This text is bold**
||Table Cell 1||Table Cell 2||
```

You got the following XHTML result:

```
<p><strong>This text is bold</strong><br />

<table>
    <tr>
        <td>Table Cell 1</td>
        <td>Table Cell 2</td>
    </tr>
</table>

</p>
```

In this second example, the same source text now provides the following XHTML:

```
<strong>This text is bold</strong>
||Table Cell 1||Table Cell 2||
```

Database

The packages in this section help you to connect and interact with databases. The most common function that they provide is database abstraction—a common way of working with different types of databases. We'll discuss the following packages in this section:

- The DB package provides a database abstraction layer.

- The DB_DataObject package contains tools to build SQL statements, and also acts as a data store for your table rows.

- The DB_Pager package lets you easily create paginated displays of your query results.

- The DB_Table package provides a way of automating data capture.

DB

The PEAR DB package provides a database abstraction layer for your PHP application. As you might know from working with databases in PHP, PHP can connect to and interact with a number of different types of databases, and each of these databases has a different set of functions and methods. A database abstraction layer provides a common technique for connecting to and working with a variety of different databases. The DB package is made up of the main DB class, which contains some basic functionality; the DB_common class, which contains the standard functions and methods for working with databases; and then a driver file specific to the database you're working with. This driver file contains the database-specific code to implement the standard interfaces set out in the DB_common class.

Common Uses

The DB package has the following common use:

- Connecting to and interacting with online databases

Related Packages

The following package is related to the DB package:

- MDB2

Dependencies

DB has the following dependencies.

Required Packages

- None

Optional Packages

- None

API

affectedRows()

Determines how many rows are affected by a query. If an error occurs, the method will return PEAR_Error.

```
integer affectedRows()
```

apiVersion()

Returns the current API version of the DB package.

```
string apiVersion()
```

autoCommit()

Turns automatic commit on or off. If the driver doesn't support autocommitting transactions, the method will return a PEAR_Error object. If successful, it will return DB_OK.

```
integer autoCommit([boolean $onoff = false])
```

Parameter	Type	Description
$onoff	boolean	If true, automatic commit will be turned on; if false, automatic commit will be turned off.

autoExecute()

Generates a query and calls prepare() and query(). If the query is a SELECT query, the method returns a DB_Result object containing the results of the query. DB_OK is returned if the query is an UPDATE, DELETE, or INSERT query. If an error occurs, the method will return a PEAR_Error.

```
mixed autoExecute(string $table, array $fields_values
                  [, integer $mode = DB_AUTOQUERY_INSERT]
                  [, string $where = false])
```

Parameter	Type	Description
$table	string	The table name.
$fields_values	array	An associative array where the key is the field name and the value is the value for that database field, escaped and quoted automatically in the method.
$mode	integer	The type of query to make, either DB_AUTOQUERY_INSERT or DB_AUTOQUERY_UPDATE.
$where	string	For use in UPDATE queries; this is the WHERE clause to use in the query. It is not escaped.

■Caution The data sent into the $where parameter is not escaped—it's sent to the database as is. Make sure to escape it first before sending it to autoExecute()!

---

autoPrepare()

Generates either an insert or an update query and passes it on to the prepare() method. It will return a PEAR_Error if an error occurs.

```
resource autoPrepare(string $table, array $table_fields
                               [, integer $mode = DB_AUTOQUERY_INSERT]
                               [, string $where = false])
```

Parameter	Type	Description
$table	string	The table name.
$table_fields	array	An associative array where $key is the field name and $value is the value for that database field.
$mode	integer	The type of query to make, either DB_AUTOQUERY_INSERT or DB_AUTOQUERY_UPDATE.
$where	string	For use in UPDATE queries; this is the WHERE clause to use in the query.

commit()

Commits the current database transaction. The method returns either DB_OK if it was successful or PEAR_Error if an error occurred.

```
integer commit()
```

connect()

Creates a new DB object and connects to the database specified. If an error occurs while attempting to connect to the database, a PEAR_Error will be returned.

```
DB connect(mixed $dsn [, array $options = array()])
```

Parameter	Type	Description
$dsn	mixed	Either a string containing the DSN or an array that has been returned by the parseDSN() method.
$options	array	An associative array of option names and their respective values.

Data Source Names (DSNs)

The format of a DSN in PHP is shown here. The DSN is a specially formatted URI that tells the DB package everything it needs to connect to the database, including user account information and additional options.

```
phptype(dbsyntax)://username:password@protocol+hostspec/database?option=value
```

The valid values for phptype are listed here for different database vendors. This type, along with an optional dbsyntax type, is different for each database vendor.

Available phptypes for Connecting to Databases

PhpType Value	Database
dbase	dBASE.
fbsql	FrontBase (functional since DB 1.7.0).
ibase	InterBase (functional since DB 1.7.0).
ifx	Informix.
msql	Mini SQL (functional since DB 1.7.0).
mssql	Microsoft SQL Server. (*Not* for Sybase. Compile PHP --with-mssql.)
mysql	MySQL (for MySQL <= 4.0).
mysqli	MySQL (for MySQL >= 4.1). Requires PHP 5 since DB 1.6.3.
oci8	Oracle 7/8/9
odbc	ODBC (Open Database Connectivity).
pgsql	PostgreSQL.
sqlite	SQLite.
sybase	Sybase.

For example, mysql://myuser:password1@db.example.com/mydb is an example of connecting to a MySQL database called mydb on the host db.example.com with username myuser and password password1. More examples are available in the "Introduction—DSN" section of the DB package documentation online at http://pear.php.net.

createSequence()

Generates a new sequence. A sequence is an incrementing ID that can be used with a row of data so that you have a unique identifier for that specific row of data. It's similar to an AUTO_INCREMENT column in MySQL or an IDENTITY column in Microsoft SQL Server.

```
integer createSequence(string $sequence_name)
```

Parameter	Type	Description
$sequence_name	string	The name for the sequence. The name for the sequence should start with a letter and only contain letters, numbers, and an underscore.

disconnect()

Disconnects from the database. It returns true if it disconnected from the database successfully, false if an error occurred.

```
boolean disconnect()
```

dropSequence()

Deletes a sequence.

```
integer dropSequence(string $sequence_name)
```

Parameter	Type	Description
$sequence_name	string	The sequence name to drop.

errorMessage()

Returns a human-readable error message string for the error code provided.

```
string errorMessage(integer $value)
```

Parameter	Type	Description
$value	integer	The DB error code.

errorNative()

Returns the error code produced by your last query directly from the database system you're using. This bypasses the error codes that might be returned through the PEAR_Error object.

```
mixed errorNative()
```

escapeSimple()

Escapes and returns a string according the standards of the database system you're using.

```
string escapeSimple(string $str)
```

Parameter	Type	Description
$str	string	The string to be escaped.

execute()

Executes a database statement that has been prepared with the prepare() method. If the number of data elements specified in the $data_array doesn't match the number of placeholders (the ? character) in the statement, the method will return a PEAR_Error. It will return a DB_result if successful in running a SELECT statement; DB_OK if successful in running a DELETE, UPDATE, or INSERT statement; or a PEAR_Error if an error occurs during execution.

```
mixed execute(resource $statement[, mixed $data_array = array()])
```

Parameter	Type	Description
$statement	resource	The database statement as returned by the prepare() method.
$data_array	mixed	The data to be used in the execution of the statement.

executeMultiple()

Calls execute() a number of times with the same statement resource, once for each element of the supplied array. The method returns DB_OK on success and PEAR_Error if an error occurred.

```
integer executeMultiple(resource $statement, array $data)
```

Parameter	Type	Description
$statement	resource	The query resource returned by the prepare() method.
$data	array	A multidimensional array containing the data to insert into the query.

fetchInto()

Returns a row of data from a result set into a variable you provide, either as an array or as an object. Once the row of data has been returned, the result pointer is moved to the next row.

```
boolean fetchInto(mixed $arr [, integer $fetchmode = DB_FETCHMODE_DEFAULT]
                             [, integer $rownum = null])
```

Parameter	Type	Description
$arr	mixed	The variable into which to return the data.
$fetchmode	integer	The fetch mode to use when returning the data. Valid fetch modes are DB_FETCHMODE_DEFAULT, DB_FETCHMODE_ORDERED, DB_FETCHMODE_ASSOC, DB_FETCHMODE_OBJECT, and DB_FETCHMODE_FLIPPED.
$rownum	integer	The row number to fetch.

fetchRow()

Returns a row of data from a result set and advances to the next row.

```
mixed fetchRow([ integer $fetchmode = DB_FETCHMODE_DEFAULT]
              [, integer $rownum = null])
```

Parameter	Type	Description
$fetchmode	integer	The fetch mode to use when returning the data.
$rownum	integer	The row number to fetch.

Modes for Fetching Data

Mode	Description
DB_FETCHMODE_ASSOC	Returns data in an array of rows, containing nested arrays with the column names as the index.
DB_FETCHMODE_DEFAULT	Specifies that the current fetch mode should be used.
DB_FETCHMODE_FLIPPED	Returns data with the column names as the index of the outer array and the row number of the key of the nested array.
DB_FETCHMODE_OBJECT	Returns column data as object properties.
DB_FETCHMODE_ORDERED	Returns data in columns indexed by their position (zero-based) instead of column name.

* Use these modes in methods that expect $fetchmode as a parameter.

free()

Frees up the result set and any resources associated with it.

```
boolean free()
```

freePrepared()

Frees up any internal resources that are associated with a prepared query, but leaves any DB_result returned by the query alone. The method returns true if successful and false if the result is invalid.

```
boolean freePrepared(resource $statement[, boolean $free_resource = true])
```

Parameter	Type	Description
$statement	resource	The resource identifier returned by the prepare() method.
$free_resource	boolean	Whether the PHP resource should be freed as well. Set to false if you'll need to retrieve data from it at a later stage.

getAll()

Returns all the rows from a query result as an array. It frees any resources used inside the method. If an error occurs, getAll() will return a PEAR_Error.

```
array getAll(string $query[, mixed $params = array()]
                  [, integer $fetchmode = DB_FETCHMODE_DEFAULT])
```

Parameter	Type	Description
$query	string	The SQL query.
$params	mixed	An array of the data to be used in the execution of the statement.
$fetchmode	integer	The fetch mode to be used, which determines what kind of array to return. Valid values are DB_FETCHMODE_ORDERED, DB_FETCHMODE_ASSOC, and DB_FETCHMODE_FLIPPED.

getAssoc()

Fetches an entire query result set as an associative array using the column as the key. It frees any resources used inside the method. If an error occurs, getAssoc() will return a PEAR_Error.

```
array getAssoc(string $query[, boolean $force_array = false]
                      [, mixed $params = array()]
                      [, integer $fetchmode = DB_FETCHMODE_DEFAULT]
                      [, boolean $group = false])
```

Parameter	Type	Description
$query	string	The SQL query to use.
$force_array	boolean	If the query returns only two columns and $force_array is set to true, the values will be returned as one-element arrays and not scalars.
$params	mixed	Data to be used in the execution of the statement. The data can be in the form of an array of values, a string, or numeric data.
$fetchmode	integer	The fetch mode to use.
$group	boolean	If set to true, then the values returned will be wrapped in another array that groups repeated keys.

getCol()

Returns a single column from a query result as an indexed array. It frees any resources used inside the method. If an error occurs, getCol() will return a PEAR_Error.

```
array getCol(string $query[, mixed $column = 0] [, mixed $params = array()])
```

Parameter	Type	Description
$query	string	The SQL query to use.
$column	mixed	The column to return, either as column number or column name.
$params	mixed	An array of data to be used in the query.

getListOf()

Returns internal database information.

```
array getListOf(string $type)
```

Parameter	Type	Description
$type	string	The type of information you want to return: tables, databases, users, views, or functions. The types of data that can be returned are database dependent.

getOne()

Returns the first column of the first row of a query result set. This method does the query and frees up the results.

```
mixed getOne(string $query[, mixed $params = array()])
```

Parameter	Type	Description
$query	string	The SQL query.
$params	mixed	Data to be used in the query. The data can be in the form of an array, a string, or numeric data.

getOption()

Returns the value of an option for the PEAR DB runtime configuration.

```
mixed getOption(string $option)
```

Parameter	Type	Description
$option	string	The name of the option that you want the value of.

Configuration Options

Option	Description
Autofree	If true, results will be freed automatically if there are no more rows in the result.
debug	Integer value that specifies the level of debugging.
persistent	If true, the connection to the database will be persistent.
portability	A portability constant that sets the portability mode.
seqname_format	A string format (such as %s_seq, which is the default value) for the sequence names used in createSequence(), nextID(), and dropSequence().
ssl	If true, Secure Sockets Layer (SSL) will be used to connect to the database.

* *For more information about the portability constants, see the DB package documentation's "Introduction—Portability" section found in the online documentation at* http://pear.php.net.

getRow()

Returns the first row of data from a query result set as an array, freeing the results when complete. The method will return PEAR_Error if an error occurs.

```
array getRow(string $query[, mixed $params = array()]
                        [, integer $fetchmode = DB_FETCHMODE_DEFAULT])
```

Parameter	Type	Description
$query	string	The SQL query to use.
$params	mixed	Data to be used in the execution of the query. The data can be in the form of an array, string, or number.
$fetchmode	integer	The fetch mode to use when returning the data.

isConnection()

The isConnection() method can determine whether a given value is a DB connection object or not.

```
boolean isConnection(mixed $value)
```

Parameter	Type	Description
$value	mixed	The possible connection value to test.

isError()

Tests whether a given value is a DB error object or not.

```
boolean isError(mixed $value)
```

Parameter	Type	Description
$value	mixed	The possible error value to test.

isManip()

The isManip() method can determine the type of query provided, returning true if the query will manipulate data in your database. Manipulation queries are INSERT, UPDATE, and DELETE queries.

```
boolean isManip(string $query)
```

Parameter	Type	Description
$query	string	The query string to test.

limitQuery()

Generates and executes a query on your database and returns, at most, the number of rows specified by $count. The behavior is similar to using LIMIT in MySQL or TOP in Microsoft SQL Server.

```
mixed limitQuery(string $query, integer $from, integer $count
               [, mixed $params = array()])
```

Parameter	Type	Description
$query	string	The SQL query.
$from	integer	The zero-based index of the first row that will be included in the result.
$count	integer	The number of rows to fetch.
$params	mixed	An array of data to be used in the execution of the statement.

nextId()

Returns the next free ID in a sequence.

```
integer nextId(string $sequence_name[, boolean $ondemand = true])
```

Parameter	Type	Description
$sequence_name	string	The name of the sequence. The sequence name should begin with a letter and thereafter contain only letters, numbers, or underscores.
$ondemand	boolean	If set to true, the named sequence will be created if it doesn't already exist.

nextResult()

For database systems that support executing more than one query at the same time, the nextResult() method lets you move on to the next result set returned by your query.

```
Boolean nextResult()
```

numCols()

Returns the number of columns in a result set.

```
integer numCols()
```

numRows()

Returns the number of rows in a result set.

```
integer numRows()
```

parseDSN()

Parses a DSN and returns an associative array that can be used in the connect method.

```
array parseDSN(string $dsn)
```

Parameter	Type	Description
$dsn	string	The DSN to be parsed. For more information about DSNs, see "Data Source Names" earlier in this chapter.

prepare()

Prepares a query for execution with the execute() method and returns a DB statement resource.

```
mixed prepare(string $query)
```

Parameter	Type	Description
$query	string	The SQL query string to be prepared.

provides()

You use the provides() method to determine whether the database driver you're using supports a particular feature.

```
boolean provides(string $feature)
```

Parameter	Type	Description
$feature	string	The feature you'd like to check for. Possible features to test for are prepare, pconnect, transaction, and limit.

query()

Sends a SQL query to the database. The query() method will return DB_OK if a manipulation query is successful, a DB_result if a SELECT query is successful, or PEAR_Error if an error occurs. It calls prepare() and execute(), then frees resources after calling execute().

```
DB_result query(string $query[, mixed $params = array()])
```

Parameter	Type	Description
$query	string	The SQL query.
$params	mixed	An array of data to use in the execution of the statement.

quoteIdentifier()

Takes a string and returns it quoted so that it can be used safely as a column or table name in your current database.

```
string quoteIdentifier(string $str)
```

Parameter	Type	Description
$str	string	The string to be quoted.

quoteSmart()

Quotes user-provided input so that it can be used safely within your database.

```
mixed quoteSmart(mixed $input)
```

Parameter	Type	Description
$input	mixed	The data to be quoted.

rollback()

Reverts the current database transaction.

```
integer rollback()
```

setFetchMode()

Sets the fetch mode to be used as the default fetch mode with query results.

```
void setFetchMode(integer $fetchmode[, string $object_class = 'stdClass'])
```

Parameter	Type	Description
$fetchmode	integer	The fetch mode to use: DB_FETCHMODE_ORDERED, DB_FETCHMODE_ASSOC, or DB_FETCHMODE_OBJECT.
$object_class	string	If the fetch mode is set to DB_FETCHMODE_OBJECT, then this will be the class name to use.

setOption()

Sets a runtime configuration option for the PEAR DB. Valid options are autofree, debug, persistent, portability, seqname_format, and ssl.

```
integer setOption(string $option, mixed $value)
```

Parameter	Type	Description
$option	string	The option name to set.
$value	mixed	The value to set the option to.

tableInfo()

Returns information about a table.

```
array tableInfo(mixed $result[, integer $mode = null])
```

Parameter	Type	Description
$result	mixed	The DB_result object or a table name.
$mode	integer	The mode to use when returning the table info. Can be null, DB_TABLEINFO_ORDERTABLE, DB_TABLEINFO_ORDER, or DB_TABLEINFO_FULL.

Examples

Connecting to and Querying a Database

For this first example, you'll create a simple database table in both MySQL and in SQLite (available at http://www.sqlite.org). You'll then write some code to connect to each of the databases, run a query to return some data, and then display the data on the screen. You'll see that migrating the code from the MySQL database to the SQLite database involves changing the connection string to the database, and that's it.

The first thing you'll need to do is create the database in MySQL. We're assuming that you're familiar with creating databases and tables in MySQL, so here's the SQL script for creating the table:

```
create table mustsee (
  ms_id integer auto_increment primary key,
  ms_rank integer,
  ms_name varchar(100),
  ms_year year
);
```

```
insert into mustsee values (1, 1, "The Godfather", "1972");
insert into mustsee values (2, 2, "The Shawshank Redemption", "1994");
insert into mustsee values (3, 3, "The Godfather: Part II", "1974");
insert into mustsee values (4, 4, "The Lord of the Rings: The Return of the King",
                                   "2003");
insert into mustsee values (5, 5, "Casablanca", "1942");
insert into mustsee values (6, 6, "Schindler's List", "1993");
insert into mustsee values (7, 7, "Shichinin no samurai", "1954");
insert into mustsee values (8, 8, "Star Wars: Episode V - The Empire Strikes Back",
                                   "1980");
insert into mustsee values (9, 9, "Buono, il brutto, il cattivo, Il", "1966");
insert into mustsee values (10, 10, "Pulp Fiction", "1994");
```

To build the SQLite database, you use a similar script:

```
create table mustsee (
  ms_id integer primary key,
  ms_rank integer,
  ms_name varchar(100),
  ms_year year
);

insert into mustsee values (1, 1, "The Godfather", "1972");
insert into mustsee values (2, 2, "The Shawshank Redemption", "1994");
insert into mustsee values (3, 3, "The Godfather: Part II", "1974");
insert into mustsee values (4, 4, "The Lord of the Rings: The Return of the King",
                                   "2003");
insert into mustsee values (5, 5, "Casablanca", "1942");
insert into mustsee values (6, 6, "Schindler's List", "1993"),
insert into mustsee values (7, 7, "Shichinin no samurai", "1954");
insert into mustsee values (8, 8, "Star Wars: Episode V - The Empire Strikes Back",
                                   "1980");
insert into mustsee values (9, 9, "Buono, il brutto, il cattivo, Il", "1966");
insert into mustsee values (10, 10, "Pulp Fiction", "1994");
```

As you can see, the only difference is that the column you're using for the primary key doesn't include the auto_increment directive, because SQLite automatically increments a column in the database that's an integer flagged as a primary key. You've retained the same field types that you used in MySQL, because SQLite is typeless. The types you assign in the database schema are simply for documentation purposes.

The list data that we've used are the top ten entries from the http://www.imdb.com top 250 movies. The full list is viewable at http://www.imdb.com/chart/top, but for the sake of saving a few trees, only the top ten are presented here.

The following code connects to the MySQL database, returns the records, and displays them simply in the page:

```php
<?php
require_once 'DB.php';

$dataSource = array(
    'phptype'  => 'mysql',
    'username' => 'apress',
    'password' => 'apress',
    'hostspec' => 'localhost',
    'database' => 'apress'
);

$dataOptions = array(
);

$database =& DB::connect($dataSource, $dataOptions);
if (PEAR::isError($database)) {
    die($database->getMessage());
}

$dataResult = &$database->query('SELECT * FROM mustsee ORDER BY ms_rank');

while ($dataRow = &$dataResult->fetchRow()) {
    echo $dataRow[2] . "<br>\n";
}

$database->disconnect();
?>
```

The first line includes the DB class into your current script. Then you build an array that contains all the information that the DB class needs to connect to the database. You then proceed to connect to the database and execute a query on the database with query(). This returns a result set to you, which you can then work your way through using the fetchRow() method. Because you aren't passing any parameters to fetchRow(), it simply returns an indexed array of the columns. You could have asked for an associative array where the keys were the column names and the values the row values for each column. You simply display the information and disconnect.

That simple example could have just as easily been created using the native PHP MySQL functions, but what would have happened then if you decided that you needed to run your database off SQLite, or any other database for that matter? You would have had to go through all your code where you were using MySQL-specific calls and replace them with the SQLite-specific functions, possibly changing the arguments and parameters as you went along. With PEAR DB this becomes easy. Here's the same script, this time using a SQLite database:

```php
<?php
require_once 'DB.php';

$dataSource = array(
    'phptype'  => 'sqlite',
    'database' => 'apress.db',
    'mode'     => '0666'
);

$dataOptions = array(
);

$database =&DB::connect($dataSource, $dataOptions);
if (PEAR::isError($database)) {
    die($database->getMessage());
}

$dataResult = &$database->query('SELECT * FROM mustsee ORDER BY ms_rank');

while ($dataRow = &$dataResult->fetchRow()) {
    echo $dataRow[2] . "<br>\n";
}
$database->disconnect();
?>
```

As you can see, the only part of the script that has changed is the $dataSource array. Here you just include SQLite-specific database connection options, and the DB class takes care of the rest of it for you.

DB_DataObject

The DB_DataObject package works as both a SQL builder and a data modeling layer. Besides providing an API to access and work with data, the package lets you build and execute SQL statements based on the variables within the object.

Common Uses

The DB_DataObject package has the following common uses:

- Accessing and manipulating data in your database tables
- Building complex queries to join multiple tables
- Providing basic data validation of your database data

Related Packages

- None

Dependencies

DB_DataObject has the following dependencies.

Required Packages

- None

Optional Packages

- None

API

count()

Returns the number of results generated by a SQL query. The method will return `PEAR_Error` if an error occurs.

```
integer count([boolean $countWhat = false] [, boolean $whereAddOnly = false])
```

Parameter	Type	Description
$countWhat	boolean	If set, will do a DISTINCT count on the table's key column.
$whereAddOnly	boolean	If set to DB_DATAOBJECT_WHEREADD_ONLY, then the condition of the query will be built using the properties of the whereAdds only.

database()

The database() method either returns or sets the name of the current database. If no parameter is supplied, the name will be returned; otherwise the name will be set to the value provided.

```
string database([string $database =''])
```

Parameter	Type	Description
$database	string	The name to set for the current database.

databaseStructure()

Loads the table definitions according to an INI file or an array of the table structure.

```
boolean databaseStructure([string $dbName = ''] [, array $dbStruc = array()]
                                               [, array $tblLinks = array()]))
```

Parameter	Type	Description
$dbName	string	Name of the database to assign.
$dbStruc	array	The structure of the database.
$tblLinks	array	Any table links (foreign keys).

debug()

Allows you to debug your DataObject classes by providing a way of outputting debug information.

```
void debug(string $message [, string $logtype = 0] [, string $level =1])
```

Parameter	Type	Description
$message	string	The debug message to output.
$logtype	string	The format to use when outputting the message (defaults to bold).
$level	string	The output level of the debug message.

debugLevel()

The debugLevel() method either sets or returns the current debug level, depending on whether a parameter is passed to the method or not.

```
void debugLevel([integer $dLevel = null])
```

Parameter	Type	Description
$dLevel	integer	The level at which to set the debug level.

delete()

Removes entries from the table according to matches with current object variables, or with conditions set up using the whereAdd() method.

```
mixed delete([boolean $useWhere = false])
```

Parameter	Type	Description
$useWhere	boolean	If set to true, then the delete() method will limit the rows affected using the conditions added with the whereAdd() method.

escape()

The escape() method simply acts as a wrapper to the DB package's escapeSimple() method. It escapes a string to be used in a database query.

```
string escape(string $string)
```

Parameter	Type	Description
$string	string	The string value that you want to escape.

fetch()

Fetches the next row into the object as variables.

```
boolean fetch()
```

fetchRow()

The fetchRow() method also returns a row into the object as variables, but allows you to specify which row to return. It's better to use fetch() in a loop to move through your results than to try and target specific rows.

```
boolean fetchRow([integer $row = null])
```

Parameter	Type	Description
$row	integer	The index of the row to return.

find()

Finds results in your database for you, either from a single table or across multiple tables. It builds the current query and executes it, returning the number of rows found.

```
mixed find([boolean $n = false])
```

Parameter	Type	Description
$n	boolean	If this is set to true, then the find() method will execute a fetch() to return the first row of the result set automatically.

free()

Frees up the resources allocated for storing the result sets generated by the DataObject. This frees up all resources, irrespective of whether you're using them or not.

```
void free()
```

get()

Returns (usually one) row, based on a specific key value.

```
integer get([string $key = null] [, string $value = null])
```

Parameter	Type	Description
$key	string	The name of the key to use in the lookup.
$value	string	The value to match for the key. If no value for $value is provided, $key is assumed to be the value and the lookup will do the lookup with the first key in the DataObject's keys() array.

getDatabaseConnection()

Gets the database connection information related to the object. You can then use this to do specific database tasks.

```
DB getDatabaseConnection()
```

getDatabaseResult()

Returns the current DB result object so that you can use standard DB methods with it.

```
DB_Result getDatabaseResult()
```

getLink()

Loads a related object, as set up by the objects' relationship in the links.ini file.

```
mixed getLink(string $column [, string $table = null] [, string $link = false])
```

Parameter	Type	Description
$column	string	Name of the column.
$table	string	Name of the table within which to look up the value.
$link	string	Name of the column in the related table.

getLinks()

Loads all the related database objects into the main object using relationships set up in the links.ini file.

```
boolean getLinks([string $format = '_%s'])
```

Parameter	Type	Description
$format	string	The formatting to apply to variable names imported into the object. The default is to prepend an underscore character to their row names.

groupBy()

Adds a GROUP BY condition to your query. It adds to any previous grouping, so to reset the group, just call the method without a parameter.

```
void groupBy([string $group = false])
```

Parameter	Type	Description
$group	string	The grouping to add. Passing no parameter resets the groupings for your query.

having()

Adds a HAVING clause to your query. It adds to any previous values already in the HAVING clause. To reset the HAVING clause, just call the method without specifying any parameters.

```
void having([string $having = false])
```

Parameter	Type	Description
$having	string	The HAVING clause to add. Passing no parameter resets the HAVING clauses in your query.

insert()

Inserts the current object variables into the database. If your database table uses primary keys, the ID of the newly inserted record will be returned. Basic type checking is done and values are quoted correctly.

```
mixed insert()
```

joinAdd()

Adds another DataObject to the current one, to build a joined query.

```
void joinAdd([DB_DataObject $object = false] [, string $joinType = 'INNER']
            [, string $joinAs = false] [, string $joinCol = false])
```

Parameter	Type	Description
$object	DB_DataObject	The data object to join with the current one.
$joinType	string	The type of join to use. Possible values are 'LEFT', 'INNER', or 'RIGHT'.
$joinAs	string	The name to join the joining table as.
$joinCol	string	The column on this object's table to match.

limit()

Sets the limit for this query on databases that support the LIMIT clause.

```
void limit([string $start = null] [, string $limit = null])
```

Parameter	Type	Description
$start	string	The number to start the limit at.
$limit	string	The number of records to include in the limit. Passing no parameters resets the LIMIT clause on the query.

orderBy()

Adds an ORDER BY condition to your query. Passing no parameters resets any ORDER BY clauses within your query.

```
void orderBy([string $order = false])
```

Parameter	Type	Description
$order	string	The ORDER BY condition to add to any previous condition.

query()

Sends a raw SQL query to the database.

```
void query(string $query)
```

Parameter	Type	Description
$query	string	The raw SQL to send to the database.

selectAdd()

Adds columns to return from your query. By default all columns in the table are returned, so to return only specific columns, you first need to call selectAdd() with no parameters to reset the column list, and then add the columns you want returned using selectAdd(). You can also pass a comma-separated list of column names into the method.

```
void selectAdd([string $column = null])
```

Parameter	Type	Description
$column	string	The column to add to your SELECT statement.

setFrom()

Copies items from another array or object into the current object. If you named form fields correctly, you'd be able to copy them from a form's POST object into your current object to insert or update the table. Be careful when using raw user input, because you could potentially be making your application vulnerable to SQL injection attacks.

```
boolean setFrom(mixed $from [, string $format = '%s']
                             [, boolean $skipEmpty = false])
```

Parameter	Type	Description
$from	mixed	Array or object from which to copy values.
$format	string	Naming convention to use when copying object variables across. Defaults to use the existing name.
$skipEmpty	boolean	If set to true, then empty column values will be ignored and not copied across.

table()

The table() method either returns the current table schema, or sets it according to the array passed to it.

```
array table([array $tableData = null])
```

Parameter	Type	Description
$tableData	array	An associative array of the table columns to set.

tableName()

The tableName() method either returns or sets the current table name. Passing no parameter returns the table name.

```
string tableName([string $tableName = null])
```

Parameter	Type	Description
$tableName	string	The table name to set.

toArray()

Returns an associative array of the current result set. This can then be passed to other PEAR packages that require data as arrays.

```
array toArray([string $format = '%s'] [, boolean $hideEmpty = false])
```

Parameter	Type	Description
$format	string	Format string to use when building the array.
$hideEmpty	boolean	If set to true, then only elements that have a value assigned to them will be returned.

update()

Updates the database with the values in the current object's variables. If you provide a DB_DataObject as a parameter, the update will only update the differences between the two.

```
integer update([object $dataObject = false])
```

Parameter	Type	Description
$dataObject	object	The DB_DataObject to compare with for determining what to update.

validate()

Validates the values of the object's variables according to simple rules. Returns an array of validation results.

```
array validate()
```

whereAdd()

Adds a WHERE condition to your SQL query. Passing no parameters resets the current whereAdd() entries.

```
string whereAdd([string $condition = false] [, string $logic = 'AND'])
```

Parameter	Type	Description
$condition	string	The condition to add.
$logic	string	How the condition should be added into the query—AND or OR.

Examples

Setting up and Using DB_DataObject

In this example, you'll step your way through setting up and using the DataObject, as it involves a few extra steps and isn't as straightforward as using other PEAR classes.

Because the DataObject needs to have an understanding of the database structure that it's working with, the first step in using it is to build a series of files that it will use when working with your database. The DataObject comes with a PHP script createTables.php that can be used to set everything up. The createTables script takes an INI file as input and generates the INI and class files necessary for interacting with your database.

Before you can run the script, you need to build the INI file that it will use. Our files are stored in the C:\xampp\htdocs\Apress directory on our machine, so we created the C:\xampp\htdocs\Apress\apress.ini file as follows:

```
[DB_DataObject]

database       = mysql://apress:apress@localhost/apress
schema_location = c:/xampp/htdocs/Apress/DataObjects
class_location  = c:/xampp/htdocs/Apress/DataObjects
require_prefix  = DataObjects/
class_prefix    = DataObjects_
```

The first line sets up the database connection using the DSN format:

```
phptype://username:password@hostname/databasename
```

You then set up some directories in which to store the schema and class files that the script will create. In this case, we're using a DataObject directory within our Apress website directory. These directories don't need to exist; the script creates them for you.

The last two lines just set up the prefixes that will be used for the classes.

You then run the createTables script using the shell or command line PHP:

```
C:\xampp\php\pear\DB\DataObject>c:\xampp\php\php.exe ➥
createTables.php c:\xampp\htdocs\Apress\apress.ini
```

This script then creates an INI and a class file for your tables (see Listing 1).

Listing 1. *The generated apress.ini file*

```
[mustsee]
ms_id = 129
ms_rank = 1
ms_name = 2
ms_year = 1

[mustsee__keys]
ms_id = N
```

The numbers following each of the column names are binary values indicating the column type and any additional column properties.

A class file is then generated for each of the tables in your database:

```php
<?php
/**
 * Table Definition for mustsee
 */
require_once 'DB/DataObject.php';

class DataObjects_Mustsee extends DB_DataObject
{
    ###START_AUTOCODE
    /* the code below is auto generated - do not remove the above tag */

    public $__table = 'mustsee';            // table name
    public $ms_id;                  // integer(11)  not_null primary_key auto_increment
    public $ms_rank;                // integer(11)
    public $ms_name;                // string(100)
    public $ms_year;                // year(4)   unsigned zerofill

    /* Static get */
    function staticGet($k,$v=NULL) { return
DB_DataObject::staticGet('DataObjects_Mustsee',➥
$k,$v); }

    /* the code above is auto generated - do not remove the tag below */
    ###END_AUTOCODE
}
```

Now that that's all done, you can create the script that uses these files to connect to the database:

```php
<?php
include_once('DB/DataObject.php' );

$options = &PEAR::getStaticProperty('DB_DataObject','options');

$options = array(
        'database' => 'mysql://apress:apress@localhost/apress',
        'schema_location' => 'C:/xampp/htdocs/Apress/DataObjects/',
        'class_location' => 'C:/xampp/htdocs/Apress/DataObjects/',
        'require_prefix' => 'DataObjects/',
        'class_prefix' => 'DataObjects_',
);
```

```
$movies = DB_DataObject::factory('MustSee');

$movies->selectAdd();
$movies->selectAdd('ms_rank');
$movies->selectAdd('ms_name');
$movies->whereAdd("ms_name LIKE 'S%'");
$movies->orderBy('ms_rank');
$movies->find();

while($movies->fetch())
{
    echo $movies->ms_rank . ' - ' . $movies->ms_name . '<br>';
}
?>
```

Because the INI file and the class file that createTables.php created for us doesn't include any connection information, you still need to include that in any scripts that connect to the database. Build the static properties with getStaticProperty() and then assign the values to them. You could either create an INI file, read it using the PHP parse_ini_file() function, and then assign the individual values that way, or simply pass through an array as you have in this example. You then build the DB_DataObject object using the MustSee class file that was generated earlier. The MustSee.php file contains all the details of the structure of the database tables.

By default, any select query will contain all the columns from the tables selected, so you first clear all the columns from the select by calling selectAdd() with no parameters. You can then add only the columns you want selected, in this case the ms_rank and ms_name columns. To filter out only specific records, in this case those that start with "S," you can use whereAdd() to add the criteria to the query. Adding the orderBy() makes sure that the records that are returned are ordered by rank. Calling find() fires off the select query, and you can then move through the records by calling fetch(). Notice how values of the columns are propagated into the object as properties of the object, making it easy to work with and display them. This is what's output from the script:

```
6 - Schindler's List
7 - Shichinin no samurai
8 - Star Wars: Episode V - The Empire Strikes Back
```

Inserting Data into the Database

Inserting data into your tables is just as simple as selecting it. The difficult part of using the DB_DataObject is getting it set up initially—once you've overcome that hurdle, it all falls into place. Take a look at this example that adds a new record to your mustsee table:

```php
<?php
include_once('DB/DataObject.php' );

$options = &PEAR::getStaticProperty('DB_DataObject','options');

$options = array(
        'database' => 'mysql://apress:apress@localhost/apress',
        'schema_location' => 'C:/xampp/htdocs/Apress/DataObjects/',
        'class_location' => 'C:/xampp/htdocs/Apress/DataObjects/',
        'require_prefix' => 'DataObjects/',
        'class_prefix' => 'DataObjects_',
);

$movies = DB_DataObject::factory('MustSee');

$movies->ms_rank = 11;
$movies->ms_name = "Star Wars";
$movies->ms_year = 1977;

$movies->insert();
?>
```

The first half of the script is just as you have seen in the previous example—you set up the options and create the DB_DataObject object. All that you need to do then is set the object's properties that correspond to the column names in your table and call the insert() method.

If you then run the previous example again, you'll get a different set of results:

```
6 - Schindler's List
7 - Shichinin no samurai
8 - Star Wars: Episode V - The Empire Strikes Back
11 - Star Wars
```

The new Star Wars entry that you just added is now included in the query result set.

DB_Pager

The DB_Pager package is a way of displaying paginated results from your queries. All the data needed to build pages like the Google search results page are included within the DB_Pager package.

Common Uses

The DB_Pager package has the following common uses:

- Limiting your search results
- Displaying search results in a manageable fashion

Related Packages

The following package is related:

- Pager

Dependencies

DB_Pager has the following dependencies.

Required Packages

- DB

Optional Packages

- None

API

build()

Calculates all the data that's needed for the pager to work. The method returns an associative array with all the data. If an error occurs in the method, PEAR_Error will be returned.

```
mixed build()
```

getData()

Returns an associative array filled with all the data you need to paginate results. PEAR_Error will be returned if an error occurs in the method.

```
array getData(integer $from, integer $limit, integer $numrows
          [, integer $maxpages = false])
```

Parameter	Type	Description
$from	integer	The row to start fetching the data from.
$limit	integer	The number of results to return per page.
$numrows	integer	The DB_Pager will automatically find the value for this if you don't supply it.
$maxpages	integer	The maximum number of pages to show in the navigation.

Contents of Array Returned by getData()

Array key	Description
current	The current page you're in.
numrows	The total number of results.
next	The row number where the next page starts.
prev	The row number where the previous page starts.
remain	The number of results remaining in the next page.
numpages	The total number of pages.
from	The row to start fetching from.
to	The row to stop fetching at.
limit	The number of results per page.
maxpages	The number of pages to show.
firstpage	The row number of the first page.
lastpage	The row number where the last page starts.
pages	An associative array where each element has the row number as a key and the row number where that page starts as the value.

Examples

Paginating Through Results

The DB_Pager package has a simple API, and it's just as easy to use.

```
<html>
<head>
<title>DB_Pager example</title>
</head>
<body>
<?php
require 'DB/Pager.php';

$dataSource = 'mysql://apress:apress@localhost/apress';
if (DB::isError($connection = DB::connect($dataSource))){
    die (DB::errorMessage($connection));
}

$sql = "select * from mustsee";
if (DB::isError($result = $connection->query($sql))){
    die (DB::errorMessage($result));
}
```

At this point, you've set up and connected to the MySQL database and you've returned a result set of all the records in your table. You'll now be able to use this to break the results out into pages and return only the rows you need for each page.

The first thing to do then is set up the limit—how many records are displayed per page. In this example you're displaying 3 records per page, as your example database currently only has 11 records in it. You also need to know where you're starting the rows from, and this is coming in via the from parameter on the query string. You grab the value and put it into the $from variable:

```
$limit = 3;
if (isset($_GET['from'])) {
        $from = intval($_GET['from']);
} else {
        $from = 0;
}
```

Now that you have all the information you need, you can go ahead and create the new DB_Pager object:

```
$pager = new DB_Pager($result, $from, $limit);
```

Once the pager has been created, you return the data into the $pagerData array:

```
$pagerData = $pager->build();
if (DB::isError($pagerData)){
    die (DB::errorMessage($pagerData));
}
?>
```

You can then go ahead and display the data that has been returned. All the information that you need should be included in the $pagerData array:

```
<p><strong>Found <?php echo $pagerData['numrows']; ?> results</strong></p>
<p><em>Displaying page <?php echo $pagerData['current']; ?> of
<?php echo $pagerData['numpages']; ?> pages</em></p>
<table border="0">
 <tr>
  <td><strong>Rank</strong></td>
  <td><strong>Name</strong></td>
  <td><strong>Year</strong></td>
 </tr>
<?php
while ($dataRow = $pager->fetchRow(DB_FETCHMODE_ASSOC)){
?>
 <tr>
  <td><?php echo $dataRow['ms_rank']; ?></td>
  <td><?php echo $dataRow['ms_name']; ?></td>
  <td><?php echo $dataRow['ms_year']; ?></td>
 </tr>
<?php
}
?>
 <tr>
  <td colspan="3" align="center">
```

The pages element in the array contains an entry for each of the pages to which you can navigate. The number of pages is determined by the number of results and the results per page. You simply loop through each of the elements, displaying a link to that specific page, including the from parameter in the query string:

```
<?php
foreach ($pagerData['pages'] as $pageNumber => $startRow) {
?>
[ <a href="<?php echo $_SERVER['PHP_SELF']; ?>?from=<?php echo $startRow; ?>">
<?php echo $pageNumber; ?></a> ]
<?php
}
?>
  </td>
 </tr>
</table>
</body>
```

DB_Table

The DB_Table package provides an object-oriented interface into your database tables. With this package, you'll be able to build SQL functionality for CREATE, INSERT, UPDATE, DELETE, and SELECT SQL methods, and well as use the HTML_QuickForm package to build input forms dynamically for your data.

Common Uses

The DB_Table package has the following common uses:

- Creating a database table automatically based on a described column schema

- Working easily with abstracted date and time formats

- Building forms to input and manage data in your database tables

Related Packages

The following package is related:

- MDB2

Dependencies

DB_Table has the following dependencies.

Required Packages

- Date

Optional Packages

- HTML_QuickForm

API

DB_Table Constructor

Returns a new instance of a DB_Table object.

```
DB_Table DB_Table(DB $db, string $table [, mixed $flag])
```

Parameter	Type	Description
$db	DB	The PEAR DB object to connect with.
$table	string	The table name to connect to in the database.
$flag	mixed	A flag that defines how to go about creating the table. A boolean false causes table creation to abort, or you can specify any one of the options specified in the following "DB_Table Constructor Flags" table.

You can pass the following values into the $flag parameter in the DB_Table constructor.

DB_Table Constructor Flags

Flag	Description
safe	Creates the table only if it doesn't already exist.
drop	Drops the table if it already exists, and re-creates it.
verify	Checks to make sure the table already exists, along with the columns and the column types, and indexes and index types.
alter	Checks to see if the table and columns exist. Creates a new table only if one doesn't already exist. Makes any necessary changes to the table.

addFormElements()

The addFormElements() method works with an existing HTML_QuickForm object and adds elements and rules to it based on the database columns you provide.

```
void addFormElements(HTML_QuickForm $form [, array $columns = null]
                                         [, string $array_name = null]
                                         [, s $clientValidate = null])
```

Parameter	Type	Description
$form	HTML_QuickForm	The existing HTML_QuickForm object.
$columns	array	An array of column names to use in the form. If this is null, then all columns will be used.
$array_name	string	By default, the HTML_QuickForm class uses the column names as form element names. If this parameter is passed, the column names will be included as keys in an array named with this parameter.
$clientValidate	string	Whether the form must validate these fields or not.

autoRecast()

Turns on or off the automatic recasting of insert and update data.

```
void autoRecast([boolean $flag = true])
```

Parameter	Type	Description
$flag	boolean	Set to true to recast data automatically.

autoValidInsert()

Turns on or off the automatic validation of inserted data.

```
void autoValidInsert([boolean $flag = true])
```

Parameter	Type	Description
$flag	boolean	If set to true, then automatic validation of inserted data will be turned on.

autoValidUpdate

Turns on or off the automatic validation of updated data.

```
void autoValidUpdate([boolean $flag = true])
```

Parameter	Type	Description
$flag	boolean	If set to true, then automatic validation of updated data will be turned on.

buildSQL

Builds a SQL command based on an internal SQL element. The method will return a PEAR_Error if an error occurs.

```
mixed buildSQL(string $sqlkey [, string $filter = null] [, string $order = null]
                              [, integer $start = null] [, integer $count = null])
```

Parameter	Type	Description
$sqlkey	string	The internal SQL key to use as the basis of the SQL query string.
$filter	string	A filter to add to the WHERE clause of the query.
$order	string	An ORDER clause to override any predefined order in the internal SQL object.
$start	integer	The row number to start returning result rows from.
$count	integer	The number of rows to return in the result set.

create

Creates a table based on the internal column and index objects. If an error occurs, the method will return PEAR_Error.

```
mixed create(mixed $flag)
```

Parameter	Type	Description
$flag	mixed	A flag that defines how to go about creating the table. A boolean false causes table creation to abort. You can specify other flags— see the "DB_Table Constructor Flags" table previously in this section.

delete

Deletes rows based on the WHERE clause provided. If an error occurs, the method will return a PEAR_Error.

```
mixed delete(string $where)
```

Parameter	Type	Description
$where	string	The WHERE clause for the delete command.

getBlankRow()

Returns a blank row array based on the column map provided. The array keys are the column names, and the values are all set to `null`.

```
array getBlankRow()
```

getColumns()

Returns all or part of the object's `$col` array.

```
mixed getColumns([mixed $col = null])
```

Parameter	Type	Description
$col	mixed	If set to `null`, the entire array will be returned. If set to a string, `getColumns()` will return a column with a matching name from the `$col` array. If the parameter is an array, then the columns that have names matching the entries in the array will be returned.

getForm()

Creates and returns an `HTML_QuickForm` object based on the table columns provided.

```
HTML_QuickForm getForm([array $columns = null] [, string $array_name = null]
                                                [, array $args = array()]
                                                [, string $clientValidate = null]
                                                [, array $formFilters = null])
```

Parameter	Type	Description
$columns	array	An array of column names to use in the form. If this is `null`, then all columns will be used.
$array_name	string	By default, the HTML_QuickForm uses the column names as form element names. If this parameter is passed, then the column names will be included as keys in an array named with this parameter.
$args	array	An associative array of optional arguments to pass to the HTML_QuickForm object.
$clientValidate	string	Whether to provide client validation or not.
$formFilters	array	An array of filter method names and callbacks that will be applied to all form elements.

getFormElement()

Returns a single HTML_QuickForm element based on a DB_Table.

HTML_QuickForm getFormElement(string $column, string $elementname)

Parameter	Type	Description
$column	string	The column name to be used from the DB_Table.
$elementname	string	The name to be used for the generated HTML_QuickForm element.

getFormElements()

Creates and returns an array of HTML_QuickForm elements based on a DB_Table.

HTML_QuickForm getFormElements(array $cols [, string $array_name = null])

Parameter	Type	Description
$cols	array	An array of DB_Table column names to use.
$array_name	string	The name to be used for the generated HTML_QuickForm elements.

getFormGroup()

Creates and returns an array of HTML_QuickForm elements in a group, based on an array of DB_Table column names.

array getFormGroup([array $columns = null] [, string $array_name = null])

Parameter	Type	Description
$columns	array	An array of column names to use to create the form.
$array_name	string	By default, the HTML_QuickForm uses the column names as form element names. If this parameter is passed, the column names will be included as keys in an array named with this parameter.

getIndexes()

Returns the internal index's property array.

array getIndexes([string $index = null])

Parameter	Type	Description
$index	string	If specified, returns only this index key from the array.

insert()

Inserts a single table row into the database table after validating it with the `validInsert()` method. Returns a `PEAR_Error` if an error occurred during the insert.

```
mixed insert(array $data)
```

Parameter	Type	Description
$data	array	An associative array of key–value pairs, where the key is the column name and the value is the data to use for that column.

isRequired()

Checks to see whether a specified column is required or can be set to null.

```
boolean isRequired(string $column)
```

Parameter	Type	Description
$column	string	The column name to check.

isValid()

The `isValid()` method only tests to see if a value's variable type works with the data type for the given column. It will throw a `PEAR_Error` if an error occurs during validation.

```
boolean isValid(mixed $val, string $col)
```

Parameter	Type	Description
$val	mixed	A value to check against the DB Table's column type.
$col	string	The column name to test against.

nextID()

Generates a sequence value with the sequence name based on the table name. The method will throw a `PEAR_Error` if the name of the sequence is greater than 26 characters.

```
integer nextID([string $seq_name = null])
```

Parameter	Type	Description
$seq_name	string	The sequence name to use. If not set, will default to the table name.

quote()

Escapes and quotes a value for use in a SQL query.

```
string quote(string $val)
```

Parameter	Type	Description
$val	string	The string value to escape.

recast()

Forces array elements to the proper data types for their columns.

```
void recast(array $data)
```

Parameter	Type	Description
$data	array	The array of data to recast.

select()

Selects rows of data from the table. If an error occurs, the method will return a PEAR_Error.

```
mixed select(string $sqlkey [, string $filter = null] [, string $order = null]
                           [, integer $start = null] [, integer $count = null]
                           [, array $params = array()])
```

Parameter	Type	Description
$sqlkey	string	The internal SQL key to use as the basis of the SQL query string.
$filter	string	A filter to add to the WHERE clause of the query.
$order	string	An ORDER clause to override any predefined order in the internal SQL object.
$start	integer	The row number to start returning result rows from.
$count	integer	The number of rows to return in the result set.
$params	array	Any parameters to use in placeholder substitutions.

selectCount()

Returns the number of rows that would be returned by a select query. If an error occurs, PEAR_Error will be returned.

```
integer selectCount(string $sqlkey [, string $filter = null]
                                   [, string $order = null]
                                   [, integer $start = null]
                                   [, integer $count = null]
                                   [, array $params = array())
```

Parameter	Type	Description
$sqlkey	string	The internal SQL key to use as the basis of the SQL query string.
$filter	string	A filter to add to the WHERE clause of the query.
$order	string	An ORDER clause to override any predefined order in the internal SQL object.
$start	integer	The row number to start returning result rows from.
$count	integer	The number of rows to return in the result set.
$params	array	Any parameters to use in placeholder substitutions.

selectResult()

Selects rows of data from the table and returns them as a DB_result or MDB2_Result_* object if successful. If an error occurs, the method will return PEAR_Error.

```
mixed selectResult(string $sqlkey [, string $filter = null] [, string $order = null]
                                  [, integer $start = null] [, integer $count = null]
                                  [, array $params = array())
```

Parameter	Type	Description
$sqlkey	string	The internal SQL key to use as the basis of the SQL query string.
$filter	string	A filter to add to the WHERE clause of the query.
$order	string	An ORDER clause to override any predefined order in the internal SQL object.
$start	integer	The row number to start returning result rows from.
$count	integer	The number of rows to return in the result set.
$params	array	Any parameters to use in placeholder substitutions.

supported()

Checks to see if a particular database system is supported.

```
boolean supported(string $phptype [, string $dbsyntax = ''])
```

Parameter	Type	Description
$phptype	string	The database system to check.
$dbsyntax	string	The chosen database syntax.

throwError()

Throws an error with a DB_Table error message.

```
PEAR_Error throwError(string $code [, string $extra = null])
```

Parameter	Type	Description
$code	string	A DB_Table error code constant.
$extra	string	Any extra text for the error that you want to provide.

update()

Updates table rows matching a custom WHERE clause. It first checks the data with validUpdate().

```
void update(array $data, string $where)
```

Parameter	Type	Description
$data	array	An associative array of key–value pairs, where the key is the column name and the value is the data to be used in the column.
$where	string	A SQL WHERE clause to limit which records are updated.

validInsert()

Validates an array of data for insertion into a table.

```
boolean validInsert(array $data)
```

Parameter	Type	Description
$data	array	An associative array of key–value pairs, where the key is the column name and the value is the data to be used in the column. Data is checked against the column type for validity.

validUpdate()

Validates an array of data for updating a table.

```
boolean validUpdate(array $data)
```

Parameter	Type	Description
$data	array	An associative array of key–value pairs, where the key is the column name and the value is the data to be used in the column. Data is checked against the column type for validity.

Examples

Creating a New Table and Inserting Some Data

The DB_Table package makes creating new tables in your database straightforward to manage. You cannot use the DB_Table package directly; you need to extend it and build your own class that describes your database table.

You want to create a new table in the database to store actor information. At this stage, you'll keep it simple and only include an actor name and a unique ID for each record. The file actors.php contains the extended class information.

```php
<?php
class actors extends DB_Table {
    var $col = array(
        'act_id' => array(
            'type'    => 'integer',
            'require' => true
        ),
            'act_name' => array(
            'type'    => 'varchar',
            'size'    => 100
        )
    );
    var $idx = array(
            'act_id' => array(
            'type' => 'unique',
            'cols' => 'act_id'
        )
    );
}
?>
```

The class contains two arrays initially—$col describes the columns in the table and $idx describes any indexes that you need for the table.

The script to create the table is as follows:

```php
<?php
require_once 'DB.php';
require_once 'DB/Table.php';
require_once 'actors.php';

$dataSource = "mysql://apress:apress@localhost/apress";
if (DB::isError($connection = DB::connect($dataSource))){
    die (DB::errorMessage($connection));
}
$actor = &new actors($connection, 'actors', 'safe');

$rowID = $actor->nextID();
$insertData = array(
        'act_id'        => $rowID,
        'act_name'      => 'Uma Thurman'
);
$insertResult = $actor->insert($insertData);

$rowID = $actor->nextID();
$insertData = array(
        'act_id'        => $rowID,
        'act_name'      => 'Morgan Freeman'
);
$insertResult = $actor->insert($insertData);
?>
```

You've included the DB, DB_Table, and your new actors class files. You then connect to the database and create a new instance of your actors class. The parameters passed to the constructor method are the connection that you've created, the name of the table, and the mode to use when creating the table. The options for that are safe or drop. The safe mode won't try to create the table if it already exists, while drop drops an existing table before re-creating it. It's best to use safe unless you want to lose any data you've stored in the new table. Use drop when testing your script initially.

After creating the new actors object, the table will have been created.

The MySQL database supports an AUTO_INCREMENT field, but because not all databases do, the PEAR DB package manages and uses sequences for using as indexes on the tables. To insert data into the table, call nextID() to return a unique ID for your new record, and build an associative array that has keys for the column names and the values you want as the associated values in the array. You then pass that info to the insert() method to insert the data.

After running this script, you have the following tables in MySQL:

```
mysql> show tables;
```

```
+------------------+
| Tables_in_apress |
+------------------+
| actors           |
| actors_seq       |
| mustsee          |
+------------------+
```

The actors_seq table has the following structure:

```
mysql> describe actors_seq;
```

```
+-------+---------------------+------+-----+---------+----------------+
| Field | Type                | Null | Key | Default | Extra          |
+-------+---------------------+------+-----+---------+----------------+
| id    | integer(10) unsigned | NO  | PRI | NULL    | auto_increment |
+-------+---------------------+------+-----+---------+----------------+
```

The DB package uses this table to maintain an internal unique ID for the actors table. The actors table has been created as per your definition in the actors class file:

```
mysql> describe actors;
```

```
+----------+--------------+------+-----+---------+-------+
| Field    | Type         | Null | Key | Default | Extra |
+----------+--------------+------+-----+---------+-------+
| act_id   | integer(11)  | NO   | PRT | NULL    |       |
| act_name | varchar(100) | YES  |     | NULL    |       |
+----------+--------------+------+-----+---------+-------+
```

If you take a look at the contents of the actors table, the information that you wanted to insert is all there:

```
mysql> select * from actors;
```

```
+--------+----------------+
| act_id | act_name       |
+--------+----------------+
|      1 | Uma Thurman    |
|      2 | Morgan Freeman |
+--------+----------------+
```

Building a Form Based on the Table Structure and Inserting Data

The DB_Table package can build HTML_QuickForm objects for you based on your table structure. For this to work, you need to add QuickForm-specific elements into the table definition array in your class file. For this example, you'll build a form for the mustsee table that you used earlier in the chapter. This is the full mustsee.php class file:

```php
<?php
class mustsee extends DB_Table {
    var $col = array(
            'ms_id' => array(
            'type'     => 'integer'
        ),
            'ms_rank' => array(
            'type'     => 'integer',
            'size'     => 3,
            'qf_label' => 'Movie Ranking',
            'qf_type'  => 'text',
            'qf_rules' => array(
                'required' => 'Please enter a movie ranking',
                'numeric'    => 'Please enter a numeric value'
            )
        ),
            'ms_name'     => array(
            'type'        => 'varchar',
            'size'        => 100,
            'qf_label'    => 'Movie name',
            'qf_type'     => 'text',
            'qf_rules'    => array(
                'required'    => 'Please enter a movie name'
            )
        ),
            'ms_year'     => array(
            'type'        => 'year',
            'size'        => 4,
            'qf_label'    => 'Movie Year',
            'qf_type'     => 'text',
            'qf_rules'    => array(
                'required'    => 'Please enter the movie year',
                'numeric' => 'Please enter a numeric value',
                'minlength' => array(
                    'Please enter a 4 digit year',
                    4
                ),
```

```
            'maxlength' => array(
                'Please enter a 4 digit year',
                4
            )
        )
    )

    );
}
?>
```

You've added array elements prepended with qf_; these are the QuickForm-specific elements.

QuickForm-Specific Elements

Element	Description
qf_label	The label to use with the form element.
qf_type	The type of input element to output for this column.
qf_rules	Validation rules that are applied to the input element.

The rules that you add include both the type of validation that must be applied, as well as an error message to display when the input element doesn't validate.

The code to display the form from this is fairly straightforward (see Listing 2).

Listing 2. *Form input example*

```
f
<head>
<title>DB_Table - form input example</title>
</head>
<body>
<?php
require_once 'DB.php';
require_once 'DB/Table.php';
require_once 'mustsee.php';

$dataSource = "mysql://apress:apress@localhost/apress";
if (DB::isError($connection = DB::connect($dataSource))){
    die (DB::errorMessage($connection));
}

$mustsee = &new mustsee($connection, 'mustsee', 'safe');
```

```
$columns = array('ms_rank','ms_name','ms_year');
$form = &$mustsee->getForm($columns,null,null,true);

$form->addElement('submit', 'submit', 'Add');

$form->display();
?>
</body>
</html>
```

After creating the mustsee object, you then create an array of the column names that you want included in the form. These are passed to getForm(), along with two null parameters (for the array name to give to the form elements and any additional arguments to pass to QuickForm—these are both null, as you don't need either of these), and then true to specify that you want client-side validation for your form. This causes it to write out JavaScript validation for your form based on the rules you applied.

Because getForm() only returns form elements for the columns you specified, you need to add a submit button with addElement() and then simply display the form.

Files and Formats

At some point in building dynamic web content, web services, and other applications, you'll run into situations where dealing with files is necessary. You can use the packages in this section to deal with files in all kinds of different formats. Many of the packages in this section have extensive classes and methods available, but most of them allow you to do the majority of the work from one or two central classes.

- You use two packages to write and read files in the vCard format: Contact_Vcard_Build and Contact_Vcard_Parse, respectively.

- The Archive_Tar and Archive_Zip packages are similar, except that they allow you to work with different file formats: `.tar` and `.zip`.

- The File package provides convenient methods for reading and writing to files.

- File_Bittorrent includes classes that allow you to work with files in the `.torrent` format. The File_Find package provides powerful functions that allow you to find files and directories on the file system.

- File_HtAccess allows you to work with `.htaccess` files.

- File_SearchReplace provides the ability to perform a variety of different search and replace functions in files and directories.

Contact_Vcard_Build

The vCard format is used to store personal information, sometimes in the form of electronic business cards. RFC 2426 describes the vCard format in detail. The Contact_Vcard_Build package allows you to build valid vCards by setting values and then saving the information to a file.

The keys for pieces of information about a contact in a vCard are called *identifiers*. You won't have to worry about the identifiers in a vCard file, but you will set the values that are labeled by the identifiers. An example is setting the name of the contact with the setName() method, which automatically files the information you give it under the FN identifier in the vCard.

To learn more about the various components and their identifiers in a vCard file, see the RFC at http://www.faqs.org/rfcs/rfc2426.html.

Common Uses

The classes in this package have the following common use:

- Dynamically building electronic business cards

Related Packages

- Contact_Vcard_Parse

Dependencies

Contact_Vcard_Build has the following dependencies.

Required Packages

- None

Optional Packages

- None

API

> **Note** Many of the parameters in the methods here are mixed, which in most cases can be either a single string or an array of strings. If a single string is supplied, a single value is added. Multiple values can be specified in arrays. Although the vCard format supports multiple values for a single component, you might have trouble with the vCard importing cleanly into different programs. Unless you're very familiar with the vCard specification, we recommend you stick to using single values.

Contact_Vcard_Build()

The constructor for creating a new instance of Contact_Vcard_Build. The constructor will throw an error if the version isn't supported.

```
void Contact_Vcard_Build([string $version = '3.0'])
```

Parameters	Type	Description
$version	string	The version of the vCard format supported by the object. Valid values are 3.0 and 2.1 only.

addAddress()

Adds the specified address to the Contact_Vcard_Build instance. Each parameter may be either a single string or an array of strings.

```
void addAddress(mixed $pob, mixed $extend, mixed $street, mixed $locality,
                mixed $region, mixed $postcode, mixed $country)
```

Parameters	Type	Description
$pob	mixed	The value of the post office box for the contact's address.
$extend	mixed	Any extended information contained in the contact's address.
$street	mixed	The street name of the contact's address.
$locality	mixed	The locality of the contact's address. For many addresses, this is the city.
$region	mixed	The region of the contact's address. For many addresses, this is the state or province.
$postcode	mixed	The postal code of the contact's address.
$country	mixed	The country part of the contact's address.

addCategories()

Adds the specified category. The $text parameter may be a string or an array of strings.

```
void addCategories(mixed $text [, $append = true])
```

Parameters	Type	Description
$text	mixed	The name of the category to be added.
$append	boolean	If true, the category or categories are appended to what is already there.

addEmail()

Adds an e-mail address to the Contact_Vcard_Build object.

```
void addEmail(string $text)
```

Parameters	Type	Description
$text	string	The e-mail address.

addLabel()

Adds the specified label to the Contact_Vcard_Build object.

```
void addLabel(string $text)
```

Parameters	Type	Description
$text	string	The label.

addNickname()

Adds a nickname to the contact stored in the Contact_Vcard_Build object. You can specify multiple values by passing an array of strings instead of a single string value.

```
void addNickname(mixed $text)
```

Parameters	Type	Description
$text	mixed	A nickname for the contact.

addOrganization()

Adds an organization to the `Contact_Vcard_Build` object. You can specify multiple values by passing an array of strings instead of a single string value.

```
void addOrganization(mixed $text)
```

Parameters	Type	Description
$text	mixed	An organization to which the contact belongs.

addParam()

Adds the specified parameter to the `Contact_Vcard_Build` object.

```
mixed addParam(string $param_name, string $param_value [, string $comp = null]
               [, mixed $iter = null])
```

Parameters	Type	Description
$param_name	string	The name of the parameter to add.
$param_value	string	The value of the parameter.
$comp	string	The component of the contact to which the parameter will be added. If the value is null, the component last modified will be used.
$iter	mixed	A key for the *iteration* of the component. Some components, such as the address component, allow more than one iteration. It's zero-based, so a value of 0 refers to the first address.

addTelephone()

Adds a telephone number to the `Contact_Vcard_Build` object.

```
void addTelephone(string $text)
```

Parameters	Type	Description
$text	string	The contact's telephone number.

addValue()

Adds the given value to the `Contact_Vcard_Build` object.

```
void addValue(string $comp, integer $iter, integer $part, mixed $text)
```

Parameters	Type	Description
$comp	string	The identifier for the component to which this value will be added.
$iter	integer	The iteration, if the component allows more than one iteration. The address is an example of a component that can occur more than once.
$part	integer	The number of the part to set the value.
$text	mixed	The value that will be assigned to the part. You can pass in multiple values by using an array of strings; otherwise use a single string.

escape()

Escapes the text.

```
string escape(string $text)
```

Parameters	Type	Description
$text	string	The text that will be escaped, so any characters that mean something to the vCard format will be escaped.

getAddress()

Returns the address of the contact in the Contact_Vcard_Build object.

```
mixed getAddress(integer $iter)
```

Parameters	Type	Description
$iter	integer	The iteration of the address to be returned.

getEmail()

Returns the e-mail address in the Contact_Vcard_Build object.

```
mixed getEmail(integer $iter)
```

Parameters	Type	Description
$iter	integer	The iteration of the e-mail address to be returned.

getLabel()

Returns the label.

```
mixed getLabel(integer $iter)
```

Parameters	Type	Description
$iter	integer	The iteration of the label to be returned.

getMeta()

Returns metadata for the Contact_Vcard_Build object.

```
string getMeta(string $comp [, integer $iter = 0])
```

Parameters	Type	Description
$comp	string	The identifier of the component.
$iter	integer	The iteration of the component, because some components allow more than one iteration.

getParam()

Returns the parameter for a given iteration of a given component.

```
string getParam(string $comp [, integer $iter = 0])
```

Parameters	Type	Description
$comp	string	The name of the component.
$iter	integer	The iteration of the component.

getTelephone()

Returns the telephone number for the Contact_Vcard_Build object.

```
mixed getTelephone(integer $iter)
```

Parameters	Type	Description
$iter	integer	The iteration of the telephone number to get.

getValue()

Returns the value.

```
string getValue(string $comp [, integer $iter = 0] [, integer $part = 0]
                              [, mixed $rept = null])
```

Parameters	Type	Description
$comp	string	The component for which to get the value.
$iter	integer	The iteration of the component.
$part	integer	The number of the part of the component.
$rept	mixed	The repetition number inside the part to return.

reset()

Resets the Contact_Vcard_Build object by setting all the values blank.

```
void reset([string $version = null])
```

Parameters	Type	Description
$version	string	The version of the vCard format to support. Can be either one of 2.1 or 3.0.

send()

Persists the Contact_Vcard_Build object to a file.

```
void send(string $filename [, string $disposition = 'attachment']
                           [, string $charset = 'us-ascii'])
```

Parameters	Type	Description
$filename	string	The filename of the vCard file.
$disposition	string	Determines if the file is sent inline or as an attachment.
$charset	string	The character set to support.

setAgent()

Sets the agent (AGENT) for the Contact_Vcard_Build object.

```
void setAgent(string $text)
```

Parameters	Type	Description
$text	string	The value of the agent.

setBirthday()

Sets the birthday (BDAY) of the Contact_Vcard_Build object.

```
void setBirthday(string $text)
```

Parameters	Type	Description
$text	string	The contact's birthday.

setClass()

Sets the class (CLASS) of the Contact_Vcard_Build object.

```
void setClass(string $text)
```

Parameters	Type	Description
$text	string	This can be used for security to specify access classification. Examples are PUBLIC, PRIVATE, and CONFIDENTIAL.

setFormattedName()

Sets the formatted name (FN) of the Contact_Vcard_Build object.

```
mixed setFormattedName([string $text = null])
```

Parameters	Type	Description
$text	string	The name of the contact; for example, Joe Q. User.

setFromArray()

Sets the values of the Contact_Vcard_Build object by using an array such as the one returned in the Contact_Vcard_Parse object. Be careful only to send in a single parsed object.

```
void setFromArray(array $src)
```

Parameters	Type	Description
$src	array	The array containing contact information.

setGeo()

Sets the geography (GEO) of the Contact_Vcard_Build object, allowing you to define the global positioning of the contact.

void setGeo(string $lat, string $lon)

Parameters	Type	Description
$lat	string	The latitude.
$lon	string	The longitude.

setKey()

Sets the public key (KEY) or authentication certificate of the Contact_Vcard_Build object.

void setKey(string $text)

Parameters	Type	Description
$text	string	String value of the public key or authentication certificate.

setLogo()

Sets the logo (LOGO) of the Contact_Vcard_Build object.

void setLogo(string $text)

Parameters	Type	Description
$text	string	Binary encoded image data.

setMailer()

Sets the mailer (MAILER) of the Contact_Vcard_Build object.

void setMailer(string $text)

Parameters	Type	Description
$text	string	The name of the mailer program associated with the contact.

setName()

Sets the name (N) of the `Contact_Vcard_Build` object.

`void setName(mixed $family, mixed $given, mixed $addl, mixed $prefix, mixed $suffix)`

Parameters	Type	Description
$family	mixed	The family name (last name) of the contact.
$given	mixed	The given name (first name) of the contact.
$addl	mixed	Additional names, separated by commas, such as the contact's middle name.
$prefix	mixed	A prefix, such as Dr.
$suffix	mixed	A suffix, such as Sr. or III.

setNote()

Sets the note (NOTE) of the `Contact_Vcard_Build` object.

`void setNote(string $text)`

Parameters	Type	Description
$text	string	The value assigned to the note.

setPhoto()

Sets the photo (PHOTO) of the `Contact_Vcard_Build` object.

`void setPhoto(string $text)`

Parameters	Type	Description
$text	string	Binary data encoded as a string.

setProductID()

Sets the product ID (PRODID) of the `Contact_Vcard_Build` object.

`void setProductID(string $text)`

Parameters	Type	Description
$text	string	An identifier for the application that was used to generate the vCard.

setRevision()

Sets the revision (REV) of the Contact_Vcard_Build object.

void setRevision(string $text)

Parameters	Type	Description
$text	string	A string that's used to identify the revision of the information for this contact. For example, it could be a timestamp when the card was created.

setRole()

Sets the role (ROLE) of the Contact_Vcard_Build object.

void setRole(string $text)

Parameters	Type	Description
$text	string	A string describing the contact's role within the organization.

setSortString()

Sets the sort string (SORT-STRING) of the Contact_Vcard_Build object.

void setSortString(string $text)

Parameters	Type	Description
$text	string	A value that can be used to sort the vCard.

setSound()

Sets the sound (SOUND) of the Contact_Vcard_Build object.

void setSound(string $text)

Parameters	Type	Description
$text	string	Any sound that can be associated with the contact. The RFC suggests recording the correct pronunciation of the contact's name.

setSource()

Sets the data source (SOURCE) of the Contact_Vcard_Build object.

void setSource(string $text)

Parameters	Type	Description
$text	string	The name of the data source for the vCard.

setSourceName()

Sets the display name of the data source for the Contact_Vcard_Build object. If it cannot set a source name because no name is specified and no source is set, the method will throw a PEAR_Error.

mixed setSourceName([string $text = null])

Parameters	Type	Description
$text	string	The name of the data source for the vCard. If the value is null, the value from SOURCE will be used; see setSource().

setTitle()

Sets the title (TITLE) of the Contact_Vcard_Build object.

void setTitle(string $text)

Parameters	Type	Description
$text	string	The contact's job title.

setTZ()

Sets the time zone (TZ) of the Contact_Vcard_Build object.

void setTZ(string $text)

Parameters	Type	Description
$text	string	The time zone where the contact lives.

setUniqueID()

Sets the unique identifier (UID) of the `Contact_Vcard_Build` object.

`void setUniqueID(string $text)`

Parameters	Type	Description
$text	string	A unique identifier for the contact, such as a globally unique identifier (GUID) or a universally unique identifier (UUID).

setURL()

Sets the Uniform Resource Locator (URL) of the `Contact_Vcard_Build` object.

`void setURL(string $text)`

Parameters	Type	Description
$text	string	A URL associated with the vCard.

setValue()

Provides a generic method of storing any value for any component of the `Contact_Vcard_Build` object. Any prior values will be overridden.

`void setValue(string $comp, integer $iter, integer $part, mixed $text)`

Parameters	Type	Description
$comp	string	The identifier for the component (FN, N, ADDR).
$iter	integer	The iteration of the component, for those that can appear more than once in a vCard, such as ADDR and TEL.
$part	integer	The index of the part. For FN, a value of 0 would specify the family (last) name, because that is the first part in the value.
$text	mixed	The value to set for the specified part.

setVersion()

Sets the version of the `Contact_Vcard_Build` object.

```
mixed setVersion([string $text = '3.0'])
```

Parameters	Type	Description
$text	string	The version of the vCard that's supported by this `Contact_Vcard_Build` object. Can be one of 2.1 or 3.0.

validateParam()

Validates the parameter names and values of the `Contact_Vcard_Build`'s vCard version, which is either 2.1 or 3.0. The method will return `true` if the parameter name is valid; otherwise it will return a `PEAR_Error`.

```
mixed validateParam(string $name, string $text [, string $comp = null]
              [, string $iter = null])
```

Parameters	Type	Description
$name	string	The name of the parameter to validate.
$text	string	The text value of the parameter.
$comp	string	The name of the component, or vCard part, that's being validated.
$iter	string	The iteration of the component.

Examples

Building a Simple vCard

This example shows you how to build a simple vCard for a contact. The `Contact_Vcard_Build` object is created, then the properties are set on the object to fill out the information that will be in the card. A few components in the card allow more than one iteration, such as the e-mail address. That means that after a function such as `addEmail()` is called, you should follow it up with a call to `addParam()` to tell the object what type of e-mail address was added. The same goes for the address in this example.

```php
<?php
/* Building a simple vCard */

require_once 'Contact_Vcard_Build.php';

/* Note:  The RFC for the vCard format can be located at:
 * http://www.ietf.org/rfc/rfc2426.txt
 */

$card = new Contact_Vcard_Build();

$card->setFormattedName('Joe User');
$card->setName('User', 'Joe', 'Q.', 'Mr.', '');
$card->addEmail('juser@example.com');
$card->addParam('TYPE', 'WORK');

$card->addAddress('P.O. Box 111', '', '', 'Anytown', 'NE', '55555', 'US');
$card->addParam('TYPE', 'WORK');

$text = $card->fetch();

/* Right now we will just print it out to the console */
printf("%s\n", $text);

?>
```

When the text is printed out, it looks like this:

```
BEGIN:VCARD
VERSION:3.0
FN:Joe User
N:User;Joe;Q.;Mr.;
PROFILE:VCARD
ADR;TYPE=WORK:P.O. Box 111;;;Anytown;NE;55555;US
EMAIL;TYPE=WORK:juser@example.com
END:VCARD
```

Saving a New vCard to a File

This similar example shows you how to save the output to a file. In this example, the fopen()
function is used to open a file, and fwrite() is used to write to the file. Later in this section,
you'll see that in the File chapter the same functionality can be done with fewer lines of code.

```php
<?php
/* Building a vcard and saving it to a file. */

require_once 'Contact_Vcard_Build.php';

$card = new Contact_Vcard_Build();
$card->setFormattedName('John Q. User');
$card->setName('User', 'John', 'Q.', 'Mr.', 'Jr.');
$card->addEmail('john.user@example.com');
$card->addParam('TYPE', 'WORK');

$card->addAddress('P.O. Box 111', '', '', 'Anytown', 'NE', '55555', 'US');
$card->addParam('TYPE', 'WORK');

/* Now save the text that we've just created to a
 * file
 */
$file = 'JohnQUser.vcf';

if ($cardFile = fopen($file, 'w')) {
    fwrite($cardFile, $card->fetch());
    fclose($cardFile);
}

?>
```

Contact_Vcard_Parse

The Contact_Vcard_Parse package provides the ability to parse vCard files into arrays.

Common Uses

Common uses for the classes in this package are as follows:

- Writing applications that allow end users to upload vCard files to be parsed and used
- Writing applications that allow end users to import vCard files into an existing data structure

Related Packages

- Contact_Vcard_Build

Dependencies

Contact_Vcard_Parse has the following dependencies.

Required Packages

- None

Optional Packages

- None

API

convertLineEndings()

Converts the line endings in the specified text to Unix line endings.

```
void convertLineEndings(&$text)
```

Parameters	Type	Description
&$text	string	The text with line endings to convert.

fileGetContents()

Reads in the contents of a file.

```
string fileGetContents(string $filename)
```

Parameters	Type	Description
$filename	string	The name of the file.

fromFile()

Parses the vCard information from a given file.

```
array fromFile(string $filename [, $decode_qp = true])
```

Parameters	Type	Description
$filename	string	The name of the file to parse.
$decode_qp	boolean	true if the vCard contains values that are encoded QUOTED-PRINTABLE.

fromText()

Parses the vCard information from the given text.

```
array fromText(array $text [, boolean $decode_qp = true])
```

Parameters	Type	Description
$text	array	The text to parse.
$decode_qp	boolean	true if the vCard contains values that are encoded QUOTED-PRINTABLE.

splitByComma()

Splits a string separated by commas into an array.

```
mixed splitByComma(string $text [, boolean $convertSingle = false])
```

Parameters	Type	Description
$text	string	The string that will be split into an array.
$convertSingle	boolean	If true and there is only one element in the array, the element will be returned as a single string instead of an array with only one element.

splitBySemi()

Splits a string separated by semicolons into an array.

```
mixed splitBySemi(string $text [, boolean $convertSingle = false])
```

Parameters	Type	Description
$text	string	The string that will be split into an array.
$convertSingle	boolean	If true and there is only one element in the array, the element will be returned as a single string instead of an array with only one element.

unescape()

Removes escape characters from the given text.

```
void unescape(string &$text)
```

Parameters	Type	Description
&$text	string	Text from which to remove escape characters.

Examples

Parsing the Contents of a vCard File

This example demonstrates how to parse the file created in the `Contact_Vcard_Build` examples and print the output to the console.

```php
<?php
/* Parsing a vCard file */

require_once 'Contact_Vcard_Parse.php';

$file = 'JohnQUser.vcf';
$card = new Contact_Vcard_Parse();
```

```
if (file_exists($file)) {

    $content = $card->fromFile($file);

    print_r($content);

    /* By examining the printed content, you will see that you
     * can get to the first name by typing:
     */

    $firstName = $content[0]["FN"][0]["value"][0][0];

    printf("First name is:  \"%s\"\n", $firstName);
}

?>
```

The result of this script looks like this:

```
Array
(
    [0] => Array
        (
            [VERSION] => Array
                (
                    [0] => Array
                        (
                            [param] => Array
                                (
                                )

                            [value] => Array
                                (
                                    [0] => Array
                                        (
                                            [0] => 3.0
                                        )

                                )

                        )

                )

            [FN] => Array
                (
                    [0] => Array
```

```
                    (
                        [param] => Array
                            (
                            )

                        [value] => Array
                            (
                                [0] => Array
                                    (
                                        [0] => John Q. User
                                    )

                            )

                    )

            )

    [N] => Array
        (
            [0] => Array
                (
                    [param] => Array
                        (
                        )

                    [value] => Array
                        (
                            [0] => Array
                                (
                                    [0] => User
                                )

                            [1] => Array
                                (
                                    [0] => John
                                )

                            [2] => Array
                                (
                                    [0] => Q.
                                )

                            [3] => Array
                                (
                                    [0] => Mr.
                                )
```

```
                              [4] => Array
                                  (
                                      [0] => Jr.
                                  )


                      )


              )


      )

  [PROFILE] => Array
      (
          [0] => Array
              (
                  [param] => Array
                      (
                      )

                  [value] => Array
                      (
                          [0] => Array
                              (
                                  [0] => VCARD
                              )


                      )


              )


      )

  [ADR] => Array
      (
          [0] => Array
              (
                  [param] => Array
                      (
                          [TYPE] => Array
                              (
                                  [0] => WORK
                              )


                      )
```

```
[value] => Array
    (
        [0] => Array
            (
                [0] => P.O. Box 111
            )

        [1] => Array
            (
                [0] =>
            )

        [2] => Array
            (
                [0] =>
            )

        [3] => Array
            (
                [0] => Anytown
            )

        [4] => Array
            (
                [0] => NE
            )

        [5] => Array
            (
                [0] => 55555
            )

        [6] => Array
            (
                [0] => US
            )

    )

)

)
```

```
[EMAIL] => Array
    (
        [0] => Array
            (
                [param] => Array
                    (
                        [TYPE] => Array
                            (
                                [0] => WORK
                            )

                    )

                [value] => Array
                    (
                        [0] => Array
                            (
                                [0] => john.user@example.com
                            )

                    )

            )

    )

)
First name is:  "John Q. User"
```

Archive_Tar

You use the Archive_Tar package to work with .tar files, including creating, extracting, and listing the file contents.

Common Uses

The classes in this package have the following common uses:

- Providing functionality to an application to extract files from .tar archives
- Creating dynamic .tar archives

Related Packages

- Archive_Zip
- File_Archive

Dependencies

Archive_Tar has the following dependencies.

Required Packages

- None

Optional Packages

- None

API

Note If an error occurs that causes the methods of Archive_Tar to return false, you can find more information about the error by examining the PEAR_Error that is raised.

Archive_Tar()

Creates a new instance of the Archive_Tar class.

```
Archive_Tar Archive_Tar(string $p_tarname [, string $p_compress = null])
```

Parameters	Type	Description
$p_tarname	string	The name of the .tar archive file.
$p_compress	string	The compression type of the file, if any. It's either gz or bz2.

add()

Adds the files specified by the filenames included in the file list and returns true if the operation was successful.

```
boolean add(array $p_filelist)
```

Parameters	Type	Description
$p_filelist	array	An array of filenames.

addModify()

Adds the specified files or directories indicated in the file list to the end of the archive, returning true if the operation was successful.

```
boolean addModify(array $p_filelist, string $p_add_dir
                [, string $p_remove_dir = ''])
```

Parameters	Type	Description
$p_filelist	array	A list of file or directory names as an array of strings.
$p_add_dir	string	The directory name that will be added in front of the files in the archive.
$p_remove_dir	string	The name of the directory to remove from the files that are archived.

addString()

Adds the provided string in a file to the archive, returning true if the operation was successful. The archive is created if it doesn't already exist.

```
boolean addString(string $p_filename, string $p_string)
```

Parameters	Type	Description
$p_filename	string	The name of the file that will contain the string.
$p_string	string	The string to put inside the file.

create()

Creates a new archive file with the files or directories included in the list.

```
boolean create(array $p_filelist)
```

Parameters	Type	Description
$p_filelist	array	An array of file or directory names expressed as strings.

createModify()

Creates a new archive file with the specified files or directories, and at the same time modifies the names of the files.

```
boolean createModify(array $p_filelist, string $p_add_dir
                [, string $p_remove_dir = ''])
```

Parameters	Type	Description
$p_filelist	array	An array of file or directory names expressed as strings.
$p_add_dir	string	A directory name to be added to the files inside the archive.
$p_remove_dir	string	A directory name to be removed from the files inside the archive.

extract()

Extracts the archive to the given path.

```
void extract([string $p_path = ''])
```

Parameters	Type	Description
$p_path	string	The path where the files will be extracted.

extractInString()

Extracts the given file and returns the contents of the file as a string. The method returns null if an error occurs.

```
string extractInString(string $p_filename)
```

Parameters	Type	Description
$p_filename	string	The name of the file to extract.

extractList()

Extracts the specified files and returns true if it was successful.

```
boolean extractList(array $p_filelist [, string $p_path = '']
                  [, string $p_remove_path = ''])
```

Parameters	Type	Description
$p_filelist	array	A list of files to extract as an array of strings.
$p_path	string	The path to extract the files.
$p_remove_path	string	The path to remove from the files as they are extracted.

extractModify()

Extracts the files in the archive, and at the same time modifies the files' original paths. It returns true if the operation was successful. If the extraction is aborted, the result might be a partial extraction that might need to be cleaned up manually. An extraction can be aborted under the following conditions:

- If a file being extracted already exists but is write protected.

- If a directory being extracted already exists.

- If a file being extracted has the same name as a directory that already exists, or vice versa.

- If a file is being extracted into a directory that already exists but is write protected.

- If a file doesn't have the correct size after extraction.

  The PEAR_Error text is set if the method is aborted.

```
boolean extractModify(string $p_path, string $p_remove_path)
```

Parameters	Type	Description
$p_path	string	The path to extract the files.
$p_remove_path	string	The path that will be removed from the names of the files, if it's present.

listContent()

Lists the files and directories contained in the archive file.

```
void listContent()
```

setAttribute()

Sets attributes of the .tar file.

```
true setAttribute(mixed $argv)
```

Parameters	Type	Description
$argv	mixed	A list of attribute values.

Examples

Creating a .tar File

This example demonstrates how to create a simple .tar file containing three files. The names of the files are specified in an array called $files (a lot of time was spent coming up with the variable names in this book) and passed to the addModify() function.

```php
<?php
/*  Creating a .tar file */

require_once 'Archive/Tar.php';

$archive = new Archive_Tar('/tmp/my_archive.tar');

/* If these files don't exist, either change the names
 * to files that do exist or create the files.  If the
 * files don't exist, you'll get an empty archive.
 */
$files = array('/tmp/file1.txt', '/tmp/file2.txt', '/tmp/file3.txt');

$archive->addModify($files, '', '');

?>
```

The output of tar -tvf /tmp/my_archive.tar looks like this:

```
-rw-r--r-- 100/101         627 2006-05-21 17:35:03 /tmp/file1.txt
-rw-r--r-- 100/101         627 2006-05-21 17:35:13 /tmp/file2.txt
-rw-r--r-- 100/101         627 2006-05-21 17:35:18 /tmp/file3.txt
```

Printing the Contents of a .tar File

This example demonstrates how to get and display information about the contents of an archive.

```php
<?php
/* Printing the contents of a .tar file */

require_once 'Archive/Tar.php';

$archive = new Archive_Tar('/tmp/my_archive.tar');

$content = $archive->listContent();

foreach($content as $entry) {
    printf("Found file: \"%s\" of size %d\n", $entry["filename"], $entry["size"]);
}

?>
```

The output of the script looks like this:

```
Found file: "/tmp/file1.txt" of size 627
Found file: "/tmp/file2.txt" of size 627
Found file: "/tmp/file3.txt" of size 627
```

Extracting a .tar File

This example demonstrates how to extract the files inside an archive into a directory.

```php
<?php

/* Extracting a .tar file */

require_once 'Archive/Tar.php';

$archive = new Archive_Tar('/tmp/my_archive.tar');

$archive->extract('/tmp/files');

?>
```

The output of `ls -l /tmp/files/tmp` looks like this:

```
-rw-r--r--  1 user1  group1  627 May 02 17:35 file1.txt
-rw-r--r--  1 user1  group1  627 May 02 17:35 file2.txt
-rw-r--r--  1 user1  group1  627 May 02 17:35 file3.txt
```

Archive_Zip

The Archive_Zip package provides methods for working with ZIP files, including methods for reading, writing, and getting the contents of ZIP archives.

Common Uses

The classes in this package have the following common uses:

- Building applications that dynamically build ZIP files
- Building applications that allow end users to upload ZIP files and dynamically unpack them in a home directory on a server

Related Packages

- Archive_Tar
- File_Archive

Dependencies

Archive_Zip has the following dependencies.

Required Packages

- None

Optional Packages

- None

API

Archive_Zip()

Creates a new instance of the Archive_Zip class.

```
Archive_Zip Archive_Zip(string $p_zipname)
```

Parameters	Type	Description
$p_zipname	string	The name of the ZIP file.

add()

Adds the files specified in the list to the ZIP archive.

```
mixed add(mixed $p_filelist [, mixed $p_params = 0])
```

Parameters	Type	Description
$p_filelist	mixed	The names of the files or directories, expressed either as an array of strings or as a comma-delimited string.
$p_params	mixed	Parameters to use for adding the files.

Parameters for add()

Parameter	Description
add_path	Adds the specified path to the names of the archived files.
remove_path	Removes the specified root path from the names of the archived files.
remove_all_path	Removes the entire path from the names of the archived files.
no_compression	Doesn't compress the archived files.
callback_pre_add	Specifies a callback function to be called before adding each file to the archive.
callback_post_add	Specifies a callback function to be called after adding each file to the archive.

create()

Creates a new ZIP archive with the specified files or directories.

```
mixed create(mixed $p_filelist [, mixed $p_params = 0])
```

Parameters	Type	Description
$p_filelist	mixed	The names of the files or directories expressed either as an array of strings or as a comma-delimited string.
$p_params	mixed	Parameters to use for adding the files.

Parameters for create()

Parameter Name	Description
add_path	Adds the specified path to the names of the archived files.
remove_path	Removes the specified root path from the names of the archived files.
remove_all_path	Removes the entire path from the names of the archived files.
no_compression	Doesn't compress the archived files.

delete()

Deletes files from the ZIP archive.

```
mixed delete(mixed $p_params)
```

Parameters	Type	Description
$p_filelist	mixed	An array of parameters and their values.

Parameters for delete()

Parameter Name	Description
by_name	Specifies the name of the file or directories. Multiple names can be separated by a comma or by sending in an array.
by_index	Specifies the indexes of the file or directories. Ranges such as 1-4 may be used.
by_ereg	Specifies a POSIX regular expression to use for identifying the file.
by_preg	Specifies a Perl-compatible regular expression (PCRE) to use for identifying files.

duplicate()

Copies the contents of the current Archive_Zip instance into the one specified.

```
integer duplicate(mixed $p_archive)
```

Parameters	Type	Description
$p_archive	mixed	The archive to copy files into.

errorCode()

Returns the last error code.

```
integer errorCode()
```

errorInfo()

Returns the information about the last error.

```
string errorInfo([boolean $p_full = false])
```

Parameters	Type	Description
$p_full	boolean	If true, the information will include the error name along with the code and description. If false, the information won't include the error name.

errorName()

The name of the latest error.

```
string errorName([boolean $p_with_code = false])
```

Parameters	Type	Description
$p_with_code	boolean	If true, the method will also provide the error code.

extract()

Extracts the files and directories from the ZIP archive.

```
mixed extract([mixed $p_params = 0])
```

Parameters	Type	Description
$p_params	mixed	An array of parameters and their values.

Parameters for extract()

Parameter Name	Description
add_path	Adds the specified path to the names of the archived files.
remove_path	Removes the specified root path from the names of the archived files.
remove_all_path	Removes the entire path from the names of the archived files.
extract_as_string	Extracts the contents of the archive as a string.

Parameters for extract() (Continued)

Parameter Name	Description
set_chmod	Specifies the mode of the file (executable, writeable, readable) after extraction.
by_name	Specifies the name of the file or directories. Multiple names can be separated by a comma or by sending in an array.
by_index	Specifies the indexes of the file or directories. Ranges such as 1-4 may be used.
by_ereg	Specifies a POSIX regular expression to use for identifying the file.
by_preg	Specifies a PCRE to use for identifying files.

listContent()

Returns the content of the ZIP archive.

```
mixed listContent()
```

merge()

Merges two ZIP archives together by combining the archive provided as a parameter with the current Archive_Zip instance. If the archive $this doesn't exist, the merge becomes a duplicate of the archive supplied as a parameter.

```
integer merge(mixed $p_archive_to_add)
```

Parameters	Type	Description
$p_archive_to_add	mixed	An archive to merge.

properties()

Returns the properties of the ZIP archive.

```
mixed properties(mixed $p_params)
```

Parameters	Type	Description
$p_params	mixed	An array of parameters and their values.

Examples

Creating a New ZIP File

Using the Archive_Zip class, this example shows how to add files to an archive. The filenames are specified in an array and passed into the add() method.

```php
<?php
/* Creating a new ZIP file. */

require_once 'Archive/Zip.php';

$zipfile = new Archive_Zip('/tmp/my_archive.zip');

$files = array('/tmp/file1.txt', '/tmp/file2.txt', '/tmp/file3.txt');

$zipfile->add($files);

?>
```

Listing the Contents of a ZIP File

This is an example of listing the contents of a ZIP file. The example uses the ZIP file created in the first example, containing three files named file1.txt, file2.txt, and file3.txt.

```php
<?php
/* Listing the contents of a zip file */
require_once 'Archive/Zip.php';

$zipfile = new Archive_Zip('/tmp/my_archive.zip');

$fileInfo = $zipfile->listContent();

foreach ($fileInfo as $file)
{
    printf("Found file:  '%s'.\n", $file['filename']);
}

?>
```

The output of the example looks like this:

```
Found file:   '/tmp/file1.txt'.
Found file:   '/tmp/file2.txt'.
Found file:   '/tmp/file3.txt'.
```

Extracting Files from a ZIP file

This example shows how to extract files from a ZIP file into a directory, /tmp/zipfiles. It removes the path that is remembered for the files and adds /tmp/zipfiles. The options are built into an array and then passed to the extract() method.

```php
<?php
/* Extracting files from a ZIP file */

require_once 'Archive/Zip.php';

$zipfile = new Archive_Zip('/tmp/my_archive.zip');

$options = array (
    'remove_all_path' => 'true',
    'add_path' => '/tmp/zipfiles/'
);

$zipfile->extract($options);

?>
```

The output of ls /tmp/zipfiles looks like this:

```
file1.txt        file2.txt        file3.txt
```

File

The File package provides the ability to read and write from files easily, without having to know anything about what PHP functions are being called under the hood. The File class in this package includes numerous methods for reading and writing files in different ways, from byte-sized chunks to gobbling in the entire file at once.

Common Uses

The classes in this package have the following common uses:

- Writing files
- Reading files

Related Packages

- File_SearchReplace
- File_Find

Dependencies

File has the following dependencies.

Required Packages

- None

Optional Packages

- None

API

■**Note** The online documentation for the `File` class shows many other methods, but they are marked DEPRECATED. We've left them off here because we don't want to encourage getting in the habit of using deprecated functions.

---

close()

Closes the open file pointer or returns `PEAR_Error` if an error occurs.

```
mixed close(string $filename, string $mode)
```

Parameters	Type	Description
$filename	string	The name of the file.
$mode	string	The mode used to open the file.

closeAll()

Closes all open file pointers.

```
void closeAll()
```

read()

Returns a specific number of bytes from a file or returns `PEAR_Error` if an error occurs.

```
mixed read(string $filename [, integer $size = FILE_DEFAULT_READSIZE]
                            [, mixed $lock = false])
```

Parameters	Type	Description
$filename	string	The name of the file.
$size	integer	The number of bytes to return.
$lock	mixed	The type of file lock to use.

readAll()

Reads the entire contents of a file or returns `PEAR_Error` if an error occurs.

```
mixed readAll(string $filename [, mixed $lock = false])
```

Parameters	Type	Description
$filename	string	The name of a file.
$lock	mixed	The type of file lock to use when reading the file.

readChar()

Reads a single character from a file or returns PEAR_Error if an error occurs.

```
mixed readChar(string $filename [, mixed $lock = false])
```

Parameters	Type	Description
$filename	string	The name of the file.
$lock	mixed	The file lock to use when reading the file.

readLine()

Reads a single line from a file or returns PEAR_Error if an error occurs. The trailing Carriage Return, Line Feed (CRLF) characters aren't included in the line.

```
mixed readLine(string $filename [, boolean $lock = false])
```

Parameters	Type	Description
$filename	string	The name of the file.
$lock	boolean	The file lock to use when reading the file.

rewind()

Rewinds the open file pointer to the start of the file or returns PEAR_Error if an error occurs.

```
mixed rewind(string $filename, string $mode)
```

Parameters	Type	Description
$filename	string	The name of the file.
$mode	string	The mode used when the file was opened.

unlock()

Unlocks a locked file or returns PEAR_Error if an error occurs.

```
mixed unlock(string $filename, string $mode)
```

Parameters	Type	Description
$filename	string	The name of the file.
$mode	string	The mode used when the file was opened.

write()

Writes the given data to the file or returns PEAR_Error if an error occurs.

```
mixed write(string $filename, string $data [, string $mode = FILE_MODE_APPEND]
            [, mixed $lock = false])
```

Parameters	Type	Description
$filename	string	The name of the file.
$data	string	The data to write to the file.
$mode	string	The mode to use when writing to the file.
$lock	mixed	The type of lock to use when writing to the file.

writeChar()

Writes the character to the file or returns PEAR_Error if an error occurs.

```
mixed writeChar(string $filename, string $char [, string $mode = FILE_MODE_APPEND]
                [, mixed $lock = false])
```

Parameters	Type	Description
$filename	string	The name of the file.
$char	string	The character to write to the file.
$mode	string	The mode to use when writing to the file.
$lock	mixed	The type of lock to use when writing to the file.

writeLine()

Writes the given line to the file, along with a line feed, or returns PEAR_Error if an error occurs.

```
mixed writeLine(string $filename, string $line [, string $mode = FILE_MODE_APPEND]
                [, string $crlf = "\n"] [, mixed $lock = false])
```

Parameters	Type	Description
$filename	string	The name of the file.
$line	string	The line of text to write to the file.
$mode	string	The mode to use when writing to the file.
$crlf	string	The CRLF your system is using. Unix uses \n, Windows uses \r\n, and Mac uses \r.
$lock	mixed	The type of lock to use when writing to the file.

Examples

Reading Lines in a File

You can use the File::readLine() function to read a single line from a file. A pointer inside the File object keeps track of the last position, so it's safe to call it over and over in a while loop, as is the case here. You can use the rewind() method (not shown in this example) to reset the pointer back to the beginning of the file.

```php
<?php

/* Reading the lines in a file. */

require_once 'File.php';

$file = "/tmp/myfile.txt";

while($line = File::readLine($file)) {
    print $line . "\n";
}

?>
```

The script's output looks like this (assuming, of course, that this is the content of /tmp/myfile.txt):

```
Hello
world
```

Writing to a File

This example demonstrates how to write lines to a file. It uses the `File::writeLine()` method to append to the file, which is specified with the `$file` variable.

```php
<?php
/* Writing to a file */

require_once 'File.php';

$file = '/tmp/mynewfile.txt';

for ($i = 0; $i < 5; $i++) {
    File::writeLine($file, sprintf("%s", $i), FILE_MODE_APPEND);
}

?>
```

The contents of the file that was created by this example look like this:

```
0
1
2
3
4
```

Note Simple text editors, such as Notepad, might not display this file correctly. The file displays fine in WordPad, or other text editors such as TextPad or Vim.

Reading an Entire File at Once

Reading a file all in one shot is probably the simplest method, but it can present major problems if the files are large. If the file is small, though, reading the file with the readAll function can be a quick approach to loading up file contents into a variable. Here that variable is called $contents.

```php
<?php
/* Reading an entire file at once. */

require_once 'File.php';

$file = "/tmp/myfile.txt";

$contents = File::readAll($file);

echo $contents;

?>
```

When the preceding script executes, it prints the results shown here:

```
Hello
world
```

File_Archive

The File_Archive package includes a large number of classes that are used to read and write file archives in a wide variety of sources and output formats. The package is well designed from an object-oriented approach, so that just by changing the `File_Archive_Writer` object type, the archive is written to a different output. These writers include ones that allow you to send output to the file system, memory, `STDOUT`, and as e-mail attachments.

Common Uses

The classes in this package have the following common uses:

- Dynamically creating archive files for download
- Creating archive files in a large number of supported formats
- Extracting archive files to a variety of different output devices, including e-mail

Related Packages

- Archive_Tar
- Archive_Zip

Dependencies

File_Archive has the following dependencies.

Required Packages

- MIME_Type

Optional Packages

- Mail_MIME
- Mail
- Cache_Lite

API

appender()

Returns a writer that appends the output to an existing archive.

```
File_Archive_Writer appender(string $URL [, $unique = null] [, $type = null]
            [, $stat = array()], File_Archive_Reader $source)
```

Parameters	Type	Description
$URL	string	The URL of the archive file to be written.
$unique	boolean	true if duplicates aren't allowed, false if duplicates are to be appended. If the value is null, false will be used.
$type	string	The type of archive, which is usually the extension of the archive file. Possible values are tar, tbz, tgz, gz, gzip, zip, bz2, bzip2, deb, and ar.
$stat	array	If provided, the array will be populated with statistics about the archive.

appenderFromSource()

Returns an appender using the provided &$toConvert parameter as a reader for reading the archive.

```
File_Archive_Writer appenderFromSource(File_Archive_Reader &$toConvert
            [, string $URL = null] [, boolean $unique = null]
            [, string $type = null]
            [, array $stat = array()], File_Archive_Reader $source)
```

Parameters	Type	Description
&$toConvert	File_Archive_Reader	The object used as a source of the files that will be written to the archive by the writer.
$URL	string	The URL of the archive file to be written.
$unique	boolean	true if duplicates aren't allowed, false if duplicates are to be appended. If the value is null, false will be used.
$type	string	The type of archive, which is usually the extension of the archive file. Possible values are tar, tbz, tgz, gz, gzip, zip, bz2, bzip2, deb, and ar.
$stat	array	If provided, the array is populated with statistics about the archive.

cache()

Caches the contents of the writer specified by &$toConvert to a local file, and reads the local file on subsequent reads.

```
void cache(File_Archive_Reader &$toConvert)
```

Parameters	Type	Description
&$toConvert	File_Archive_Reader	The reader that contains the contents to be cached.

extract()

Extracts files using the supplied reader into the supplied writer. The name of this method can be a little confusing, because you can use it to create an archive by extracting the files from a file reader and writing them using an archive writer.

```
null extract(&$sourceToConvert,  &$destToConvert [, boolean $autoClose = true]
             [, integer $bufferSize = 0])
```

Parameters	Type	Description
&$sourceToConvert	File_Archive_Reader	The reader to use for the source of the files.
&$destToConvert	File_Archive_Writer	The writer to use to create or append the archive.
$autoClose	boolean	true if the writer should be closed when the call is complete.
$bufferSize	integer	The size of the buffer to use when transferring data. Under most circumstances, you can leave this one 0, as the block size will be used.

filter()

Uses the supplied filter predicate to remove files from the archive.

```
void filter(File_Archive_Predicate $predicate, File_Archive_Reader &$toConvert)
```

Parameters	Type	Description
$predicate	File_Archive_Predicate	A predicate object that's used to filter the reader.
&$toConvert	File_Archive_Reader	The reader that will be filtered by the supplied File_Archive_Predicate object.

getOption()

Returns the value of the specified option.

```
void getOption(string $name)
```

Parameters	Type	Description
$name	string	The name of the option. Available options are zipCompressionLevel, gzCompressionLevel, tmpDirectory, cache, appendRemoveDuplicates, blockSize, and cacheCondition.

isKnownExtension()

Returns true if the extension is one that the File_Archive package knows how to handle. Available extensions are ar, bz2, bzip2, deb, gz, tar, tbz, tgz, and zip. The method is case sensitive.

```
boolean isKnownExtension(string $extension)
```

Parameters	Type	Description
$extension	string	A file extension to verify.

predAnd()

Builds an array of File_Archive_Predicate_And objects given the list of arguments.

```
void predAnd(array args)
```

Parameters	Type	Description
args	array	A list of one or more File_Archive_Predicate_And objects.

predCustom()

Returns a File_Archive_Predicate_Custom object that uses the given expression as a predicate.

```
void predCustom(string $expression)
```

Parameters	Type	Description
$expression	string	A string that contains an expression that can be evaluated to a boolean value. You can use $name to specify the name of the current filename, such as predCustom("strlen($name)<100;");.

predEreg()

Returns a `File_Archive_Predicate_Ereg` object that uses the given regular expression to filter filenames.

`void predEreg(string $ereg)`

Parameters	Type	Description
$ereg	string	A regular expression that's used to evaluate the filename being filtered by the predicate.

predEregi()

Returns a case-insensitive version of the `File_Archive_Predicate_Ereg` object.

`void predEregi(string $ereg)`

Parameters	Type	Description
$ereg	string	A regular expression that's used to evaluate the filename being filtered by the predicate, ignoring case.

predExtension()

Returns a `File_Archive_Predicate_Extension` object that uses the supplied list of file extensions.

`void predExtension(mixed $list)`

Parameters	Type	Description
$list	mixed	A list of file extensions to use when applying this predicate in a filter.

predFalse()

Returns a `File_Archive_Predicate_False` object, which always evaluates to false.

`void predFalse()`

predIndex()

Returns a `File_Archive_Predicate_Index` object using the given indexes.

`void predIndex(array $indexes)`

Parameters	Type	Description
$indexes	array	An array of integers that's used to filter files by the position that they are located in the list of files.

predMaxDepth()

Returns a `File_Archive_Predicate_MaxDepth` object that can be used to filter files by how many directories are in their full path names.

`void predMaxDepth(integer $depth)`

Parameters	Type	Description
$depth	integer	The number of directories to allow in the full path name of the file.

predMIME()

Returns a `File_Archive_Predicate_MIME` object that's used to filter files by MIME type.

`void predMIME(array $list)`

Parameters	Type	Description
$list	array	An array of MIME types expressed as strings.

predMinSize()

Returns a `File_Archive_Predicate_MinSize` object that's used to filter files by size.

`void predMinSize(integer $size)`

Parameters	Type	Description
$size	integer	The minimum file size for files that will be included after `File_Archive_Predicate_MinSize` is finished evaluating the files.

predMinTime()

Returns a File_Archive_Predicate_MinTime object that's used to filter files by their modification time.

```
void predMinTime(integer $time)
```

Parameters	Type	Description
$time	integer	The minimum (earliest) modification time, in Unix timestamp format, allowed for files included in the archive.

predNot()

Returns a File_Archive_Predicate_Not object, which is used to negate a given predicate.

```
void predNot(File_Archive_Predicate $pred)
```

Parameters	Type	Description
$pred	File_Archive_Predicate	The predicate that will be negated. Any value that would normally evaluate to false by the given predicate will now return true.

predOr()

Returns a File_Archive_Predicate_Or predicate that uses the supplied list of predicates in its evaluation.

```
void predOr(list args)
```

Parameters	Type	Description
args	list	A list of predicates that will be added to an OR condition.

predTrue()

Returns a File_Archive_Predicate_True object, which is a predicate that always evaluates to true.

```
void predTrue()
```

read()

Returns a File_Archive_Reader object using the given information to specify the source of the reader.

```
File_Archive_Reader read(string $URL [string, $symbolic = null]
                    [, $uncompression = 0] [, $directoryDepth = -1])
```

Parameters	Type	Description
$URL	string	The location from which to read files.
$symbolic	string	A symbolic name to use when reading the files.
$uncompression	integer	The level of compression to use when uncompressing the files.
$directoryDepth	integer	The number of directories to allow in the full path name of the file.

readArchive()

Returns a File_Archive_Reader that reads the specified archive.

```
File_Archive_Reader readArchive(string $extension, File_Archive_Reader &$toConvert
                    [, boolean $sourceOpened = false], File_Archive_Reader $source)
```

Parameters	Type	Description
$extension	string	The extension of the archive file, which also determines what type of archive it is.
&$toConvert	File_Archive_Reader	The reader to use when reading the archive.
$sourceOpened	boolean	true if the specified archive is already opened.

readConcat()

Returns a File_Archive_Reader object that reads the content of all of its files as if it were one large file.

```
File_Archive_Reader readConcat(File_Archive_Reader &$toConvert, string $filename
                    [, array $stat - array()] [, string $mime = null])
```

Parameters	Type	Description
&$toConvert	File_Archive_Reader	The reader to use for the source of the files.
$filename	string	The name of the single file that contains the contents of concatenating all the files in the File_Archive_Reader specified by &$toConvert.
$stat	array	If it's not null, then this array will be populated with statistics about the archive.
$mime	string	The MIME type to use for the file in the returned reader.

readMemory()

Returns a File_Archive_Reader that contains a single file residing in memory.

```
File_Archive_Reader readMemory(string $memory, string $filename
                [, array $stat = array()] [, string $mime = null])
```

Parameters	Type	Description
$memory	string	The contents of the file in memory.
$filename	string	Because the content is treated as if it were in a file on the file system, it requires a name that's the "public name" of the file.
$stat	array	If supplied, this array will be populated with statistics about the file.

readMulti()

Returns a File_Archive_Reader object that contains other readers. This allows you to read from more than one source at the same time, but treat the contents of all the readers as if they were being read from one source.

```
File_Archive_Reader readMulti([array $sources = array()])
```

Parameters	Type	Description
$sources	array	An array of File_Archive_Reader objects that will be read.

readSource()

Returns a File_Archive_Reader that reads from a specific reader and not the file system.

```
File_Archive_Reader readSource(File_Archive_Reader &$source, string $URL
                [, string $symbolic = null] [, integer $uncompression = 0]
                [, integer $directoryDepth = -1])
```

Parameters	Type	Description
&$source	File_Archive_Reader	The reader to use.
$URL	string	The URL to use for the source of the reader, expressed as a string.
$symbolic	string	A symbolic name for the files read by the reader, which will override the real names of the files. You can use this if you want to hide the real filenames.

Parameters	Type	Description
$uncompression	integer	The level of compression to use when uncompressing the files.
$directoryDepth	integer	The maximum number of directories to allow in the full path name of the files read by the reader.

readUploadedFile()

Returns a `File_Archive_Reader` object that reads temporary files.

```
File_Archive_Reader readUploadedFile(string $name)
```

Parameters	Type	Description
$name	string	The name of the file's key in the $_FILES array.

remove()

Uses the provided `File_Archive_Predicate` to remove files from the source specified by the $URL parameter.

```
void remove(File_Archive_Predicate $pred,  $URL)
```

Parameters	Type	Description
$pred	File_Archive_Predicate	The object to use as a filter to remove files.
$URL	string	The location of the source.

removeDuplicates()

Removes duplicate file entries from the specified source URL.

```
void removeDuplicates(string $URL)
```

Parameters	Type	Description
$URL	string	The location, as a URL, of the source.

removeDuplicatesFromSource()

Removes duplicates from the provided File_Archive_Reader.

```
void removeDuplicatesFromSource(File_Archive_Reader &$toConvert
            [, string $URL = null])
```

Parameters	Type	Description
&$toConvert	File_Archive_Reader	The reader from which to remove duplicates.
$URL	string	An optional URL location to use as a source.

removeFromSource()

Removes files from the provided File_Archive_Reader using the given File_Archive_Predicate to filter the files.

```
void removeFromSource(File_Archive_Predicate &$pred, File_Archive_Reader &$toConvert
            [, string $URL = null])
```

Parameters	Type	Description
&$pred	File_Archive_Predicate	The object to use as a filter when removing files.
&$toConvert	File_Archive_Reader	The reader to use for reading the source.
$URL	string	The location, as a URL, of the source for the reader.

setOption()

Sets the specified option to a given value.

```
void setOption(string $name, mixed $value)
```

Parameters	Type	Description
$name	string	The name of the option to set.
$value	mixed	The value of the option.

Supported Options

Option	Description	Default
cache	An instance of `Cache_Lite` used to cache compressed data.	`null`
zipCompressionLevel	Value, between 0 as the lowest and 9 as the highest, used by ZIP writers.	9
gzCompressionLevel	Value, between 0 as the lowest and 9 as the highest, used by GZ writers.	9
tmpDirectory	Directory where temporary files are created.	current directory
appendRemoveDuplicates	If set to `true`, any file that already exists in the archive will be replaced by the new file if the names are the same.	`false`
blockSize	Specifies the size of the chunks read from the source and written to the archive.	64K
cacheCondition	Allows a cache to be used when reading compressed files or download files. Can be either `false`, which means the cache won't be used, or a regular expression that specifies the cache will be used if the URL matches the regular expression.	`false`

toArchive()

Returns the appropriate `File_Archive_Writer`, given the extension of the file or the specified type.

```
File_Archive_Writer toArchive(string $filename, File_Archive_Writer &$toConvert
                [, string $type = null] [, array $stat = array()]
                [, boolean $autoClose = true])
```

Parameters	Type	Description
$filename	string	The name of the archive file.
&$toConvert	File_Archive_Writer	The writer to use when writing the archive.
$type	string	The type of archive to write, if the file extension is not to be used to set the type automatically.
$stat	array	If supplied, statistics about the archive will be populated into this array.
$autoClose	boolean	If `true`, the archive will be closed when this method completes.

toFiles()

Returns a `File_Archive_Writer` that writes the files to the specified location.

```
File_Archive_Writer_Files toFiles([string $baseDir = ""])
```

Parameters	Type	Description
$baseDir	string	The base directory into which the files will be written.

toMail()

Returns a `File_Archive_Writer_Mail` object that's used to write the files to an e-mail message.

```
File_Archive_Writer_Mail toMail(string $to, array $headers, string $message
                [, Mail $mail = null])
```

Parameters	Type	Description
$to	string	The e-mail address of the recipient of the message.
$headers	array	An array of header information that will be used with MIME type e-mail attachments.
$message	string	The message to include in the e-mail.
$mail	Mail	The `Mail` object to use for mailing the message.

toMemory()

Returns a `File_Archive_Writer_Memory` object that's used to write the contents to memory.

```
File_Archive_Writer_Memory toMemory(out $data)
```

Parameters	Type	Description
$data	out	The data to write to memory.

toMulti()

Returns a `File_Archive_Writer_Multi` object, which can contain one or more writers and is used to write the contents of the source to more than one writer at the same time.

```
File_Archive_Writer_Multi toMulti(File_Archive_Writer &$aC,
                File_Archive_Writer &$bC)
```

Parameters	Type	Description
&$aC	File_Archive_Writer	A File_Archive_Writer to use.
&$bC	File_Archive_Writer	Another File_Archive_Writer to use.

toOutput()

Returns a File_Archive_Writer_Output object, which is used to write the contents to standard output (STDOUT).

```
File_Archive_Writer_Output toOutput([boolean $sendHeaders = true])
```

Parameters	Type	Description
$sendHeaders	boolean	If true, the header information about the archive will be printed to STDOUT.

toVariable()

Similar to the toMemory() method, this method writes the contents to the provided variable.

```
File_Archive_Writer_Memory toVariable(mixed &$v)
```

Parameters	Type	Description
&$v	mixed	The variable that holds the contents of the writer.

Examples

Creating a .tgz File

This example demonstrates how to create a .tgz file using the File_Archive class. The extract() function is being used here to extract the files from the File_Archive_Reader, which is created with the File_Archive::read() function using the file URL /tmp/sampledir. The archive is written using the File_Archive_Writer object that's returned by the File_Archive::toArchive() function, using the extension of the filename as the archive type. The File_Archive::toFiles() function specifies the type of writer that's used to write the archive.

■Note You might get an error that says the following:

```
Notice: Use of undefined constant filename - assumed 'filename' in ➥
C:\php\PEAR\File\Archive\Writer\Files.php on line 201.
```

If you get that error, change line 201 to `$this->filename = $filename;` and re-run the example.

```php
<?php

/* Creating a .tgz file. */

require_once 'File/Archive.php';

/* The method name, extract, is a little confusing here.
 * But think of it as the File_Archive class is extracting
 * the files from the directory named here and placing them
 * into the archive writer.
 */

File_Archive::extract(
    File_Archive::read('/tmp/sampledir'),
    File_Archive::toArchive(
        '/tmp/archive.tgz',
        File_Archive::toFiles())
);

?>
```

Downloading a Dynamically Created ZIP File

This example is nearly identical to the previous example, but the purpose is to demonstrate the difference made by just changing the archive writer to the File_Archive_Writer_Output object that's returned by the File_Archive::toOutput() function. Instead of the archive file being persisted to the file system, the output is sent to STDOUT. If this file is called in a web browser, the archive is dynamically created and sent out to the browser. This is a wonderful capability if you're building a website where archive files might be dynamically built and downloaded by users.

```php
<?php

/* Downloading a dynamically created zip file.  */

require_once 'File/Archive.php';

/* The contents of the archive are printed to STDOUT.
 */

File_Archive::extract(
    File_Archive::read('/tmp/sampledir'),
    File_Archive::toArchive(
        'archive.zip',
        File_Archive::toOutput(true))
);

?>
```

File_Bittorrent

The File_Bittorrent package contains three classes that help you to build your own .torrent files, encode .torrent files, and decode existing .torrent files. BitTorrent files are used for peer-to-peer sharing of files.

You can learn more about BitTorrent at http://www.bittorrent.com.

Common Uses

The classes in this package have the following common use:

- Dynamically creating .torrent files

Related Packages

- NameFile

Dependencies

File_Bittorent has the following dependencies.

Required Packages

- NameNone

Optional Packages

- NameNone

API

File_Bittorrent_MakeTorrent()

Constructor for the File_Bittorrent_MakeTorrent object.

File_Bittorrent_MakeTorrent File_Bittorrent_MakeTorrent(mixed $path)

Parameters	Type	Description
$path	mixed	The path of the .torrent file to create from.

buildTorrent()

Builds the .torrent file for the file specified in the constructor.

```
mixed buildTorrent()
```

setAnnounce()

Sets the announce location, as a URL, of the .torrent file and returns true if the operation was successful.

```
boolean setAnnounce(string $announce)
```

Parameters	Type	Description
$announce	string	The URL of the .torrent file.

setAnnounceList()

Sets the announce location to more than one URL at the same time, and returns true if the operation was successful.

```
boolean setAnnounceList(array $announce_list)
```

Parameters	Type	Description
$announce_list	array	An array of string URLs that specify the locations to announce the .torrent file.

setComment()

Sets the comment on the .torrent file and returns true if the operation was successful.

```
boolean setComment(string $comment)
```

Parameters	Type	Description
$comment	string	The comment.

setPath()

Sets the path of the file for the .torrent.

```
boolean setPath(string $path)
```

Parameters	Type	Description
$path	string	The file and directory names of the file for the .torrent.

setPieceLength()

Sets the piece length, in kilobytes (KBs) for the .torrent file.

```
boolean setPieceLength(mixed $piece_length)
```

Parameters	Type	Description
$piece_length	mixed	The length of the file piece, in kilobytes.

Examples

Building a .torrent File

Using the File_Bittorrent_Maketorrent class, you can create your own .torrent file. In this example, the data is held in a variable called $meta and printed to a file using the File::write() method.

■**Note** You might get an error running this script on a computer with Microsoft Windows installed until you change the path to look like a conventional Windows path instead of a Unix-style path. For instance, for this script, change the path passed to the constructor to C:\\tmp\\myfile.iso instead of /tmp/myfile.iso.

```php
<?php
/* Make a BitTorrent file. */

require_once 'File/Bittorrent/Maketorrent.php';
require_once 'File.php';

PEAR::setErrorHandling(PEAR_ERROR_PRINT);

$torrent = new File_Bittorrent_Maketorrent('/tmp/myfile.iso');
$torrent->setAnnounce('http://localhost/~user1/torrents');
$torrent->setComment('This is my test!');
$torrent->setPieceLength(256);
$meta = $torrent->buildTorrent();

File::write('test.torrent', $meta, FILE_MODE_WRITE);

?>
```

Decoding a .torrent File

This example demonstrates how to decode a .torrent file using the File_Bittorrent_Decode class. It loads the contents of the .torrent file into an array, called $fileInfo here. The contents of $fileInfo are printed out using the print_r() function.

```php
<?php
/* Decoding a torrent file */

require_once 'File/Bittorrent/Decode.php';

$decode = new File_Bittorrent_Decode();

$fileInfo = $decode->decodeFile('/home/user1/test.torrent');

print_r($fileInfo);

?>
```

The output of the script looks like this:

```
Array
(
    [name] => my.iso
    [filename] => test.torrent
    [comment] => This is my test!
    [date] => 1129175581
    [created_by] =>
    [files] => Array
        (
            [0] => Array
                (
                    [filename] => myiso.iso
                    [size] => 675827712
                )

        )

    [size] => 675827712
    [announce] => http://localhost/~user1/torrents
    [announce_list] => Array
        (
        )

)
```

File_Find

The File_Find package provides a class that allows you to perform advanced searches for files and directories. Also, you can use convenient mapping functions such as `maptree()` to get a list of all the subdirectories and files found in a directory for easy display on an interface.

Common Uses

The classes in this package have the following common uses:

- Searching for files in directories
- Applying regular expression searches for files
- Mapping directories and files under a base directory

Related Packages

- File
- File_SearchReplace

Dependencies

File_Find has the following dependencies.

Required Packages

- None

Optional Packages

- None

API

glob()

Searches the given directory and returns an array of files that match the pattern.

```
array &glob(string $pattern, string $dirpath [, string $pattern_type = 'php'])
```

Parameters	Type	Description
$pattern	string	A pattern to use when matching file and directory names.
$dirpath	string	The directory path to search.
$pattern_type	string	The type of pattern to use in the search. Valid values are shell, perl, and php.

mapTreeMultiple()

Returns an array with the matching files mapped as elements of the array. Subdirectories are added as arrays, with their files included as elements inside them.

```
array &mapTreeMultiple(string $directory [, integer $maxrecursion = 0]
              [, integer $count = 0])
```

Parameters	Type	Description
$directory	string	The directory to search.
$maxrecursion	integer	The number of directories to recurse into.
$count	integer	The current directory level, used to evaluate against the max recursion.

search()

Returns an array of files that match the specified pattern.

```
array &search(string $pattern, string $directory [, string $type = 'php']
              [, boolean $fullpath = true] [, string $match = 'files'])
```

Parameters	Type	Description
$pattern	string	The pattern to use when finding files.
$directory	string	The directory to search.
$type	string	The type of expression to use. Can be one of shell, perl, and php.
$fullpath	boolean	true if the expression should be matched against the full path of the filename.
$match	string	Specifies the type of results to return. Valid values are directories, files, or both.

isError()

Returns true if the specified object is a PEAR_Error.

```
boolean isError(object &$var)
```

Parameters	Type	Description
&$var	object	The object to check.

maptree()

Creates a map, in the form of an array containing filenames and directory names, of the directory specified by $directory.

```
array maptree(string $directory)
```

Parameters	Type	Description
$directory	string	The directory to map.

Examples

Searching for a File

This example uses the perl method of matching filenames to take advantage of a regular expression search, which can be a little more powerful than a simple shell search. The files that are being searched for will match the expression file[0-2]\.txt, which means that any file with the name file0.txt, file1.txt, or file2.txt will match.

```php
<?php
/* Searching for a file */

require_once 'File/Find.php';

/* The 'perl' option will use PCREs to find the
 * files.  This is very powerful, because it offers the ability
 * to use regular expressions as criteria instead of the more
 * simple shell wildcard characters.
 */
$results = File_Find::glob('/file[0-2]\.txt/', '/tmp', 'perl');

foreach($results as $result) {
    printf("Found file: '%s'\n", $result);
}

?>
```

The results look like this:

```
Found file: 'file1.txt'
Found file: 'file2.txt'
```

Displaying the Entire Contents of a Directory

The example shown here demonstrates how to display the entire contents of a directory by using the maptree() function to populate two arrays. One array, $directories, contains a list of directory names, while the $files array contains a list of files found in the directory that is being mapped. Two loops at the end of the example iterate through the two arrays and print their contents.

```php
<?php
/* Displaying the entire contents of a directory */

require_once 'File/Find.php';

/* This example will recursively search through an entire
 * directory and find all of the files/directories contained
 * in the directory.
 */

list($directories, $files) = File_Find::maptree('/tmp');

foreach ($directories as $directory) {
    printf("Found directory:  '%s'\n", $directory);
}
```

```php
foreach ($files as $file) {
    printf("Found file:  '%s'\n", $file);
}

?>
```

Because the script prints out the contents of the /tmp directory, your results will vary, but they'll look something like this:

```
Found directory:  '/tmp'
Found directory:  '/tmp/pear'
Found directory:  '/tmp/pear/cache'
Found directory:  '/tmp/hsperfdata_Nathan'
Found directory:  '/tmp/503'
Found file:  '/tmp/cs_cache_lock_92'
Found file:  '/tmp/cups_noproof_log'
Found file:  '/tmp/objc_sharing_ppc_26'
Found file:  '/tmp/objc_sharing_ppc_4294967294'
Found file:  '/tmp/objc_sharing_ppc_502'
Found file:  '/tmp/objc_sharing_ppc_503'
Found file:  '/tmp/objc_sharing_ppc_92'
```

Searching for a Directory

This example shows how to search for a directory using wild cards. It will find any directory named mydir, and will start in the /tmp directory, looking in subdirectories as it performs the search.

```php
<?php
/* Searching for a directory */

require_once 'File/Find.php';

$results = File_Find::search('*/mydir', '/tmp', 'shell', 'false', 'directories');

foreach ($results as $result) {
    printf("Found directory:  '%s'\n", $result);
}

?>
```

The results look like this:

```
Found directory:  '/tmp/mydir'
```

File_HtAccess

The File_HtAccess package includes a single class, File_HtAccess, that you can use for reading and writing .htaccess files. The .htaccess files are special files used by the Apache web server to add authentication to directories. An example .htaccess file looks like this:

```
AuthType Basic*
AuthName "Password Required"*
AuthUserFile /www/passwords/password.file*
AuthGroupFile /www/passwords/group.file*
Require Group siteadmins
```

For more information about .htaccess files, see the tutorial on the Apache website at http://httpd.apache.org/docs/2.0/howto/htaccess.html.

Common Uses

The classes in this package have the following common uses:

- Reading .htaccess files to display group access

- Writing .htaccess files to allow more easily administered permissions on websites

Related Packages

- None

Dependencies

File_HtAccess has the following dependencies.

Required Packages

- None

Optional Packages

- None

API

addAdditional()

Adds a value for the Additional property of the .htaccess file.

void addAdditional([string $additional = ''])

Parameters	Type	Description
$additional	string	The value to set.

addRequire()

Adds a value for the Require property of the .htaccess file.

void addRequire(string $require)

Parameters	Type	Description
$require	string	The value to set.

delRequire()

Deletes the value from the Require property of the .htaccess file.

void delRequire(string $require)

Parameters	Type	Description
$require	string	The value to delete.

getAdditional()

Returns the value of the Additional property of the .htaccess file.

mixed getAdditional([string $type = ''])

Parameters	Type	Description
$type	string	Whether to return an array or a string. Specify string to return the property value as a string.

getAuthDigestFile()

Gets the value for the `AuthDigestFile` directive from the `.htaccess` file.

```
string getAuthDigestFile()
```

getAuthDigestGroupFile()

Gets the value for the `AuthDigestGroupFile` directive from the `.htaccess` file.

```
string getAuthDigestGroupFile()
```

getAuthGroupFile()

Gets the value for the `AuthGroupFile` directive from the `.htaccess` file.

```
string getAuthGroupFile()
```

getAuthName()

Gets the value for the `AuthName` directive from the `.htaccess` file.

```
string getAuthName()
```

getAuthType()

Gets the value for the `AuthType` directive from the `.htaccess` file.

```
string getAuthType()
```

getAuthUserFile()

Gets the value for the `AuthUserFile` directive from the `.htaccess` file.

```
string getAuthUserFile()
```

getFile()

Gets the name of the `.htaccess` file.

```
string getFile()
```

getRequire()

Gets the value for the `Require` directive from the `.htaccess` file.

```
mixed getRequire([string $type = ''])
```

Parameters	Type	Description
$type	string	Whether to return an array or a string. Specify `string` to return the property value as a string.

load()

Loads the .htaccess file by reading the file and setting the values in the file to the object properties.

```
mixed load()
```

save()

Saves the object to an .htaccess file.

```
mixed save()
```

setAdditional()

Sets additional information in the .htaccess file.

```
void setAdditional([array $additional = ''])
```

Parameters	Type	Description
$additional	array	The additional values.

setAuthDigestFile()

Sets the AuthDigestFile directive in the .htaccess file.

```
void setAuthDigestFile([string $file = ''])
```

Parameters	Type	Description
$file	string	The new value of the AuthDigestFile directive.

setAuthDigestGroupFile()

Sets the AuthDigestGroupFile directive in the .htaccess file.

```
void setAuthDigestGroupFile([string $file = ''])
```

Parameters	Type	Description
$file	string	The new value of the AuthDigestGroupFile directive.

setAuthGroupFile()

Sets the `AuthGroupFile` directive in the `.htaccess` file.

```
void setAuthGroupFile([string $file = ''])
```

Parameters	Type	Description
$file	string	The new value of the `AuthGroupFile` directive.

setAuthName()

Sets the `AuthName` directive in the `.htaccess` file.

```
void setAuthName([string $name = 'Restricted'])
```

Parameters	Type	Description
$name	string	The new value of the `AuthName` directive.

setAuthType()

Sets the `AuthType` directive in the `.htaccess` file.

```
void setAuthType([string $type = 'Basic'])
```

Parameters	Type	Description
$type	string	The new value of the `AuthType` directive.

setAuthUserFile()

Sets the `AuthUserFile` directive in the `.htaccess` file.

```
void setAuthUserFile([string $file = ''])
```

Parameters	Type	Description
$file	string	The new value of the `AuthUserFile` directive.

setFile()

Sets the name of the .htaccess file.

```
void setFile(string $file)
```

Parameters	Type	Description
$file	string	The new value of the filename.

setProperties()

Sets many properties at one time, using an array. The keys are the names of the directives in the .htaccess file.

```
void setProperties(array $params)
```

Parameters	Type	Description
$params	array	An array containing one or more properties and their values.

setRequire()

Sets the Require directive in the .htaccess file.

```
void setRequire([mixed $require = ''])
```

Parameters	Type	Description
$require	mixed	The new value of the Require directive.

Examples

Writing an .htaccess File

This example demonstrates writing an .htaccess file using the File_HtAccess class. Here, all the major options are specified ahead of time in the $options array and passed to the class's constructor. However, you can also set each of these options using the appropriate accessor functions. For example, you can use the setAuthType() function to set the AuthType directive (the option authtype in the $options array).

```php
<?php
/* Writing an .htaccess file */

require_once('File/HtAccess.php');

/* create a new .htaccess file with given parameters */

$options = array(
    'authname' => 'Private',
    'authtype' => 'Basic',
    'authuserfile' => '/tmp/.htpasswd',
    'authgroupfile' => '/tmp/.htgroup',
    'require' => array ('group', 'users')
);

$htaccess = new File_HtAccess('.htaccess', $options);
$result = $htaccess->save();

if (PEAR::isError($result)) {
    echo "An error occurred while trying to save the file\n";
} else {
    // continue processing
}

?>
```

The contents of the new file look like this:

```
AuthName Private
AuthType Basic
AuthUserFile /tmp/.htpasswd
AuthGroupFile /tmp/.htgroup
Require group users
```

Reading an .htaccess File

This is an example of reading the .htaccess file using the File_HtAccess class. The value is printed to the console using the printf() function.

```php
<?php
/* Reading the entries in an .htaccess file */

require_once 'File/Htaccess.php';

$htaccess = new File_HtAccess('.htaccess');
$result = $htaccess->load();
```

```php
if (PEAR::isError($result)) {
    echo "An error occurred while trying to load the file\n";
} else {
    /* No error while loading the file, so it is okay
     * to get properties from the file.
     */
    printf("The AuthType is: '%s'\n", $htaccess->getAuthType());
}

?>
```

The script will display the output shown here:

```
The AuthType is: 'Basic'
```

Changing the Properties of an .htaccess File

This example shows you how to load an existing .htaccess file, change a property, and save the file. The property that's being modified is the value of the AuthName directive.

```php
<?php
/* Changing the properties on an .htaccess file */

/* First, load the file up. */
require_once 'File/Htaccess.php';

$htaccess = new File_HtAccess('.htaccess');
$result = $htaccess->load();

if (PEAR::isError($result)) {
    echo "An error occurred while trying to load the file\n";
} else {
    /* Now set some properties */
    $htaccess->setAuthName('My Secret Zone');
}

/* Then save the file.  */
$result = $htaccess->save();

if (PEAR::isError($result)) {
    echo "An error occurred while trying to save the file\n";
} else {
    // continue processing
}

?>
```

The contents of the changed file look like this:

```
AuthName My Secret Zone
AuthType Basic
AuthUserFile /tmp/.htpasswd
AuthGroupFile /tmp/.htgroup
Require group users
```

File_SearchReplace

The File_SearchReplace package performs search and replace routines on lists of files and also in files found in lists of directories. You can tailor the search and replace function to be one of normal, quick, preg, or ereg. Each function provides its own advantages. The normal, or default search allows you to specify lines to ignore. The quick search does a straight search and replace and is the fastest method to use. The preg search uses preg_replace(), so you can use Perl-compatible regular expressions. Lastly, the ereg search uses ereg_replace(), which is PHP's POSIX regular-expression replace function.

Common Uses

The classes in this package have the following common uses:

- Searching through files for text
- Replacing text in files

Related Packages

- File

Dependencies

File_SearchReplace has the following dependencies.

Required Packages

- None

Optional Packages

- None

API

File_SearchReplace()

This constructor allows you to create a new instance of a File_SearchReplace object.

```
File_SearchReplace File_SearchReplace(string $find, string $replace,
            array $files [, array $directories = '']
            [, boolean $include_subdir = TRUE]
            [, array $ignore_lines = array()])
```

Parameters	Type	Description
$find	string	The string or regex to find.
$replace	string	The string or regex to use as a replacement.
$files	array	The files in which to perform the search and replace action.
$directories	array	The directory to search.
$include_subdir	boolean	true if the function should recurse into subdirectories.
$ignore_lines	array	Specifies lines to ignore, which only works for a search that doesn't use regexes or isn't a quick search.

doReplace()

Performs the replacement.

```
void doReplace()
```

doSearch()

Performs the search.

```
void doSearch()
```

getLastError()

Returns the last error that occurred.

```
string getLastError()
```

getNumOccurences()

Returns the number of times the replacement was made.

```
integer getNumOccurences()
```

setDirectories()

Sets the directories that will be searched.

```
void setDirectories(array $directories)
```

Parameters	Type	Description
$directories	array	An array of string directory names.

setFiles()

Sets the files that will be searched.

```
void setFiles(array $files)
```

Parameters	Type	Description
$files	array	An array of string filenames.

setFind()

Sets the string to find.

```
void setFind(string $find)
```

Parameters	Type	Description
$find	string	The string or regex to find in the search.

setIgnoreLines()

Sets an array of lines to ignore in the search.

```
void setIgnoreLines(array $ignore_lines)
```

Parameters	Type	Description
$ignore_lines	array	An array of lines.

setIncludeSubdir()

Sets the on/off switch for recursing into subdirectories.

void setIncludeSubdir(boolean $include_subdir)

Parameters	Type	Description
$include_subdir	boolean	true if subdirectories will be searched.

setReplace()

Sets the replacement string.

void setReplace(string $replace)

Parameters	Type	Description
$replace	string	The string or regex to use as a replacement.

setSearchFunction()

Sets the type of function that's used for the search and replace. Valid values are normal, quick, preg, or ereg.

void setSearchFunction(mixed $search_function)

Parameters	Type	Description
$search_function	mixed	The search function that will be used to perform the search.

Examples

Making Replacements in a List of Files

This example demonstrates how to do a search and replace through a list of files. You specify the list of files by the $files array, and you use the full path names to the files. In this example, the files are in INI file format, and the string [servername] is replaced with example.com.

```php
<?php

/* Making replacements in a list of files. */

include 'File/SearchReplace.php';

$files = array (
    "/tmp/config.ini",
    "/tmp/config2.ini",
    "/tmp/config3.ini"
);

$search = new File_SearchReplace( "[servername]", "example.com", $files);
$search->doSearch();

?>
```

Before this script is executed, one of the files looks like this:

```
[MyConfiguration]
dbserver = [servername]
dbname = mydb
dbuser = user1
dbpass = secret
```

After the script is executed, the same file has the new values:

```
[MyConfiguration]
dbserver = example.com
dbname = mydb
dbuser = user1
dbpass = secret
```

Making Replacements in Directories

This example performs the same search and replace that's found in the previous example, except this search iterates through every single file in the provided directories.

```php
<?php

/* Making replacements in a list of directories. */

include 'File/SearchReplace.php';

$files = array ();

$directories = array (
    "/tmp/mydir1/",
    "/tmp/mydir2/"
);

$search = new File_SearchReplace( "[servername]", "example.com", $files,
    $directories, true);
$search->doSearch();

?>
```

HTTP

The PEAR packages in this section present ways in which you can use the web (HTTP) protocol to connect to and transfer information with Internet web servers.

- The HTTP package contains miscellaneous HTTP utilities.

- The HTTP_Client package provides a simple client class that can perform as a normal web client application.

- The HTTP_Download package allows you to control when and how downloads are sent to the client browsers.

- The HTTP_Header package lets you interrogate, manipulate, and send HTTP headers.

- The HTTP_Request package contains methods to generate HTTP requests, and has the added advantage of being able to work through proxy servers.

- The HTTP_Upload package provides interfaces into managing files uploaded via web forms.

HTTP

The HTTP package contains a number of miscellaneous utility methods for doing tasks such as redirecting the client, selecting an appropriate language, and formatting date headers.

Common Uses

The HTTP package has the following common uses:

- Redirecting the client
- Retrieving the HTTP headers for a server or page
- Selecting a language appropriate to the client

Related Packages

- None

Dependencies

HTTP has the following dependencies.

Required Packages

- None

Optional Packages

- None

API

absoluteURI()

Takes a partial URL and returns the absolute URI. When returning the absolute URI, you can choose a new protocol to return and redirect the user at the same time.

```
string absoluteURI([string $url = null] [, string $protocol = null]
                   [, integer $port = null])
```

Parameter	Type	Description
$url	string	The URI that you want to go to.
$protocol	string	The protocol that the new URI should use.
$port	integer	The port that the new URI should use.

Date()

Converts a Unix timestamp into an RFC-compliant GMT date HTTP header line. The y2k_compliance directive in the php.ini file is honored when determining how to format the returned date.

```
mixed Date([mixed $time = null])
```

Parameter	Type	Description
$time	mixed	Either a Unix timestamp or date. Defaults to the current time.

head()

Sends an HTTP HEAD command to the web server and returns the headers as an associative array. If an error occurs, the method will return PEAR_Error.

```
array head(string $url [, integer $timeout = 10])
```

Parameter	Type	Description
$url	string	A valid URL from which to fetch the headers.
$timeout	integer	Timeout in seconds; defaults to 10.

negotiateLanguage()

Uses the Accept-Language HTTP header as well as the user's host address to determine which language to use. Language codes take the form of a two-character code for the language, followed by an optional two-character code for the country the language is spoken in. This is to differentiate between, for example, English spoken in the UK and English spoken in the US. When the country portion is present, the two parts are joined with a dash.

```
string negotiateLanguage(array $supported [, string $default = 'en-US'])
```

Parameter	Type	Description
$supported	array	An associative array of the supported languages. Each of the supported languages in the array should have its value set to true.
$default	string	The default language to use if no match is found.

redirect()

Redirects the client browser by sending a Location header.

```
mixed redirect(string $url [, boolean $exit = true] [, boolean $rfc2616 = false])
```

Parameter	Type	Description
$url	string	The URL that the redirect should go to.
$exit	boolean	If this is set to true, then the script will exit immediately after the redirect.
$rfc2616	boolean	If set to true, then a redirect message will be printed before redirecting.

Examples

Viewing the Headers

In this first example, you'll simply return the headers for a top-level domain and display them.

```php
<?php
require_once "PEAR.php";
require_once "HTTP.php";

$headers = HTTP::head("http://localhost/");

if (PEAR::isError($headers)) {
    echo "Error: " . $headers->getMessage();
} else {
    echo "<pre>";
    print_r($headers);
    echo "</pre>";
}
?>
```

As you can see, you're also including PEAR.php, as you'll need it for the error checking. You then statically call the head() method and return its output into the $headers variable. You can then check if it has generated a PEAR_Error and display any error it might have had. Otherwise, you can simply output the array that was returned. Running this on our machine, we get the following output:

```
Array
(
    [response_code] => 200
    [response] => HTTP/1.1 200 OK
    [Date] => Sun, 02 Jul 2006 08:23:29 GMT
    [Server] => Apache/2.2.2 (Win32) DAV/2 mod_ssl/2.2.2 OpenSSL/0.9.8b➡
    mod_autoindex_color PHP/5.1.4
    [X-Powered-By] => PHP/5.1.4
    [Connection] => close
    [Content-Type] => text/html
)
```

The headers include all sorts of interesting information about the server, including the version of PHP that you're running. If you set the expose_php directive in the php.ini to Off and run the same script again, you'll get the same results, but this time without any PHP information in it:

```
Array
(
    [response_code] => 200
    [response] => HTTP/1.1 200 OK
    [Date] => Sun, 02 Jul 2006 08:24:54 GMT
    [Server] => Apache/2.2.2 (Win32) DAV/2 mod_ssl/2.2.2 OpenSSL/0.9.8b➡
    mod_autoindex_color
    [Connection] => close
    [Content-Type] => text/html
)
```

If you choose to return the headers for a specific page, you'll get some additional information. Change the line that's returning the $headers array to point to a file on your server:

```
$headers = HTTP::head("http://localhost/Apress/test.txt");
```

You get back the following result:

```
Array
(
    [response_code] => 200
    [response] => HTTP/1.1 200 OK
    [Date] => Sun, 02 Jul 2006 08:27:42 GMT
    [Server] => Apache/2.2.2 (Win32) DAV/2 mod_ssl/2.2.2 OpenSSL/0.9.8b➥
    mod_autoindex_color
    [Last-Modified] => Sun, 02 Jul 2006 08:20:15 GMT
    [ETag] => "1c1de-13-f391ca32"
    [Accept-Ranges] => bytes
    [Content-Length] => 19
    [Connection] => close
    [Content-Type] => text/plain
)
```

HTTP_Client

The HTTP_Client package acts as a wrapper for the HTTP_Request package, allowing you to perform multiple HTTP requests.

Common Uses

The HTTP package has the following common uses:

- Managing cookies
- Redirecting the client

Related Packages

- HTTP
- HTTP Request

Dependencies

HTTP has the following dependencies.

Required Packages

- HTTP_Request

Optional Packages

- None

API

HTTP_Client Constructor

Sets up and returns an HTTP_Client object.

```
HTTP_Client HTTP_Client([array $defaultRequestParams = null]
                        [, array $defaultHeaders = null]
                        [, object $cookieManager = null])
```

Parameter	Type	Description
$defaultRequestParams	array	The parameters to pass to the HTTP_Request constructor.
$defaultHeaders	array	An array of default headers to send with every request.
$cookieManager	object	The object to use for managing cookies.

attach()

Adds a listener to the listeners that are notified of the object's events. The listeners are notified of the events in the following table.

Events for Notification

Event	Description
request	Event is sent before an HTTP request that isn't a result of a previous redirect.
httpSuccess	Sent when a successful 200-range response code is returned.
httpRedirect	Sent when a 300-range response is received, before the redirect is followed.
httpError	Sent when a 400- or 500-range response is received.

```
boolean attach(HTTP_Request_Listener &&$listener[, boolean $propagate = false])
```

Parameter	Type	Description
$listener	HTTP_Request_Listener	The listener object to attach to.
$propagate	boolean	Whether the listener should be attached to the created HTTP_Request objects.

currentResponse()

Returns the most recent HTTP response as an array. The array has the keys code, headers, and body.

```
array currentResponse()
```

detach()

Removes a listener that was previously attach()ed.

```
boolean detach(HTTP_Request_Listener $listener)
```

Parameter	Type	Description
$listener	HTTP_Request_Listener	The HTTP_Request_Listener object that was previously attached to.

enableHistory()

Sets whether the object should retain all the responses it has received, or only the most recent one.

```
void enableHistory(boolean $enable)
```

Parameter	Type	Description
$enable	boolean	Set to true to enable a full history of the responses received.

get()

Sends a GET HTTP request. The HTTP response code is returned.

```
integer get(string $url[, mixed $data = null] [, boolean $encoded = false]
                [, $headers = array()])
```

Parameter	Type	Description
$url	string	The URL to GET.
$data	mixed	Any additional data that you want to send with the GET.
$encoded	boolean	Whether the data has been URL encoded or not.
$headers	array	Additional data to send with the header.

getCookieManager()

Returns the HTTP_Client_CookieManager object, which manages cookies.

getCookieManager()

head()

Sends a HEAD HTTP request. The HTTP response code is returned.

integer head(string $url [, $headers = array()])

Parameter	Type	Description
$url	string	The URL to send the HEAD response to.
$headers	array	Additional information to send with the header.

post()

Sends an HTTP POST request. The HTTP response code is returned.

integer post(string $url, mixed $data [, boolean $encoded = false]
              [, array $files = array()] [, $headers = array()])

Parameter	Type	Description
$url	string	The URL to post the data to.
$data	mixed	The data to send with the POST.
$encoded	boolean	Specifies whether the data has already been URL encoded or not.
$files	array	An array of files to upload. The array elements should have the form array(name, filename()[, content-type()]). This is the same format as passed to the HTTP_Request::addFile() method.
$headers	array	Additional information to send with the header.

reset()

The reset() method clears the HTTP_Client object's internal properties.

void reset()

setDefaultHeader()

Sets the default headers for HTTP requests.

```
void setDefaultHeader(mixed $name[, string $value = null])
```

Parameter	Type	Description
$name	mixed	Either a string of the header name to set, or an array of header=>value pairs to set.
$value	string	The value to set the header named in the first parameter, or null if an array was passed for the name.

setMaxRedirects()

Sets the maximum number of redirects that the object will follow when performing one of the requests. The method will raise an error if the number of redirects is greater than the number passed into this method.

```
void setMaxRedirects(integer $redirects)
```

Parameter	Type	Description
$redirects	integer	The maximum number of redirects to follow. Setting this to 0 will disable redirect processing.

setRequestParameter()

Sets the parameters for HTTP requests.

```
void setRequestParameter(mixed $name[, string $value = null])
```

Parameter	Type	Description
$name	mixed	Either a string of the parameter name to set, or an array of parameter=>value pairs to set.
$value	string	The value to set the parameter named, or null if an array was passed for the name.

Examples

Sending Data Using the POST Method

In this example, you'll take a look at how you can send data to a URL using the POST method. This is especially useful if you want to submit details programmatically to a script that only accepts details that have been submitted from a form using the POST method. As long as you know what the script expects to receive, you can send those details from your script:

```php
<?php
require_once 'HTTP/Client.php';
$client = new HTTP_Client();
$data = array();
$data['name'] = 'allan';
$data['email'] = 'allan@mediafrenzy.co.za';

$response_code = $client->post('http://localhost/apress/postdata.php', $data);

echo $response_code;

?>
```

The methods in the HTTP_Client package cannot be called statically, so you have to instantiate an HTTP_Client object first before calling any of its methods. After creating the object, create an associative array of the data that you want to send through to the script. You then call the POST method, passing the URL of the script and the data variable as parameters.

All you need to do now is create the postdata.php script; otherwise your response code will be a 404.

For the sake of brevity, here's a simple postdata.php script. In a real-world situation you'd want to write this information to a database and implement error checking on the data that you're being sent.

```php
<?php
$data = serialize($_POST);
$fp = fopen('postdata.log','a');
fwrite($fp, $data);
fclose($fp);
?>
```

After running the first script, you're presented with a 200 response code—the file was found OK.

The contents of postdata.log look like the following:

```
a:2:{s:4:"name";s:5:"allan";s:5:"email";s:23:"allan@mediafrenzy.co.za";}
```

Running a simple unserialize and var_dump on it gives you the following result:

```
array(2) {
  ["name"]=>
  string(5) "allan"
  ["email"]=>
  string(23) "allan@mediafrenzy.co.za"
}
```

This is what you sent through initially.

HTTP_Download

The HTTP_Download package provides an easy-to-use interface for sending data to clients. Data can come from anywhere—files, streams, or variables—and can be sent using compression, using caching, or in chunks. HTTP_Download also supports resuming of downloads.

Common Uses

The HTTP_Download package has the following common uses:

- Sending downloads to the client
- Caching download data
- Compressing download data
- Sending partial downloads and resuming

Related Packages

- None

Dependencies

HTTP_Download has the following dependencies.

Required Packages

- PEAR Installer
- HTTP_Header
- pcre PHP extension

Optional Packages

- Archive_Tar
- Archive_Zip
- MIME_Type

- `mime_magic` PHP extension

- `pgsql` PHP extension

API

guessContentType()

Attempts to guess the content type of the file. It uses the PEAR_Mime package if installed, otherwise the `mime_magic` PHP extension. Either returns `true` if the content type was found or `PEAR_Error` if it couldn't work it out for some reason.

`mixed guessContentType()`

HTTP_Download

The `HTTP_Download()` constructor method builds a new `HTTP_Download` object and returns it. The parameters array that is passed to the constructor must contain any one of the first three parameters that follow, and can optionally contain any of those that follow.

Parameter	Description
file	Path to the file for the download.
data	Raw data for the download
resource	The resource handle for the download.
cache	Whether to allow caching or not.
gzip	Whether to use gzip compression on the download.
lastmodified	Unix timestamp of when the file was last modified.
contenttype	The content type of the download.
contentdisposition	The content disposition of the download.
buffersize	The number of bytes to buffer.
throttledelay	The number of seconds to sleep when throttling the download.
cachecontrol	Cache privacy and validity.

`HTTP_Download HTTP_Download([array $params = array()])`

Parameter	Type	Description
$params	array	An array of parameters to use when building the object.

send()

Sends the download to the client. Returns `true` on success or a `PEAR_Error` on failure.

```
mixed send([boolean $setContentDisposition = true])
```

Parameter	Type	Description
$setContentDisposition	boolean	This determines whether to set the Content-Disposition header if it isn't already set.

sendArchive()

Sends a number of files as a single archive file. The `sendArchive` method is deprecated in favor of using `send()`.

send()

The `send` method is a static method of the `HTTP_Download_Archive` class. This replaces the `sendArchive()` method. This method is called statically.

```
mixed send(string $name, mixed $files [, string $type = HTTP_DOWNLOAD_TGZ]
           [, string $add_path = ''] [, string $strip_path = ''])
```

Parameter	Type	Description
$name	string	The name that the archive file should have.
$files	mixed	The files or directories that should make up the archive to send.
$type	string	The type of archive to send. Valid types are TAR, TGZ, BZIP2, or ZIP.
$add_path	string	A path that should be prepended onto the files.
$strip_path	string	A path that should be stripped from the files.

setBufferSize()

Sets the maximum amount of data that can be read at once from your file or resource. This is set in bytes. If the file size is zero length, the method will return a `PEAR_Error`.

```
mixed setBufferSize([integer $bytes = 2097152])
```

Parameter	Type	Description
$bytes	integer	The maximum size of the buffer. Defaults to 2MB.

setCache()

Specifies whether to allow caching or not. If caching is enabled, then common cache headers will be sent first. If set to `false`, then the download will be sent to the client irrespective of whether the client might have cached it or not.

```
void setCache([boolean $cache = true])
```

Parameter	Type	Description
$cache	boolean	Whether to use the client's cached copy or not.

setCacheControl()

Determines whether proxies are allowed to cache this data or not.

```
boolean setCacheControl([string $cache = 'public'] [, integer $maxage = 0])
```

Parameter	Type	Description
$cache	string	If this is set to `private`, then proxy servers should not cache this response. Setting it to `public` allows proxies to cache the data.
$maxage	integer	The maximum age of the client cache entry.

setContentDisposition()

The `setContentDisposition()` method describes the content of the download. The Content-Disposition header isn't HTTP compliant, but most browsers will acknowledge and use its contents.

```
void setContentDisposition([string $disposition = HTTP_DOWNLOAD ATTACHMENT]
                            [, $filename = null])
```

Parameter	Type	Description
$disposition	string	Whether to send the download as an attachment or inline to the page. Valid values are `HTTP_DOWNLOAD_ATTACHMENT` or `HTTP_DOWNLOAD_INLINE`.
$filename	string	The filename that's displayed in the client download dialog.

setContentType()

Sets the content type of the download. By default this is `application/x-octetstream`. The method will return `PEAR_Error` if an error occurs.

```
mixed setContentType([string $content_type = 'application/x-octetstream'])
```

Parameter	Type	Description
$content_type	string	The content type to set the download to.

setData()

Sets the data for the download. This is for sending raw data as the content for the download. Set this to null if you want to remove the data from the download.

```
void setData([mixed $data = null])
```

Parameter	Type	Description
$data	mixed	The raw data to send as the download.

setETag()

Sets a user-defined entity tag for use in cache validation. This is usually generated by HTTP_Download as part of its data, but you can use this method to set it manually.

```
void setETag([string $etag = null])
```

Parameter	Type	Description
$etag	string	The entity tag to use for the cache validation.

setFile()

Sets the physical file that will be sent as the download.

```
mixed setFile(string $file [, boolean $send404 = true])
```

Parameter	Type	Description
$file	string	The path to the file to use as the download.
$send404	boolean	If this is set to true and the path set in the $file parameter isn't found, then a 404 error will be sent to the browser.

setGzip()

Specifies whether to use gzip compression on the download file or not. If gzip compression isn't available, the method will return PEAR_Error.

```
mixed setGzip([boolean $gzip = false])
```

Parameter	Type	Description
$gzip	boolean	If this is set to true, then the file will be compressed with gzip before being sent to the client.

setLastModified()

Sets the Last-Modified header for the file that is being sent to the client. Usually the PHP filemtime() method is used to determine this from the actual file, but if you're sending raw data as the download, you'll have to set this yourself.

```
void setLastModified(integer $last_modified)
```

Parameter	Type	Description
$last_modified	integer	The Unix timestamp to use as the last modification date of the download file.

setParams()

Sets the parameters for the download. This array is the same as the parameters array passed in the HTTP_Download constructor.

```
mixed setParams(array $params)
```

Parameter	Type	Description
$params	array	An array of parameters to set for the download.

setResource()

Sets a PHP resource handle as the source for the download. Once the download has been sent, the handle to the resource will be closed. If $handle doesn't refer to a valid resource, which is determined by the PHP method is_resource(), the method will return PEAR_Error.

```
mixed setResource([integer $resource = null])
```

Parameter	Type	Description
$resource	integer	The resource handle to the data to send as the download. Set this to null to clear the resource from the download.

setThrottleDelay()

Sets a delay in seconds after each chunk of data has been sent. By adjusting the buffer size and the throttle delay, you can control the rate that data is downloaded from your server.

```
void setThrottleDelay([float $delay = 0])
```

Parameter	Type	Description
$delay	float	The number of seconds to wait before sending the next chunk of data.

staticSend()

Provides a method of sending a download that can be called statically without creating an HTTP_Download object. The method will return PEAR_Error if an error occurs.

```
mixed staticSend(array $params [, boolean $guess = false])
```

Parameter	Type	Description
$params	array	An array of parameters that set up the send. This is the same array as used in the HTTP_Download constructor.
$guess	boolean	If this is set to true, then the guessContentType method will be called.

Examples

Sending a File, Throttled to Save Bandwidth

In this first example, you'll send a single file to the client, but by setting up the HTTP_Download object correctly first, you'll be able to control the speed at which the client receives the download. You could do this either because you need to conserve the bandwidth usage on your site, or if you wanted visitors to your site to have full access but have to subscribe for unthrottled downloads. With this, guests can have the content delivered via a controlled mechanism and members can be unrestricted.

```php
<?php
require_once('HTTP/Download.php');
$download = new HTTP_Download();
$download->setFile('datafile.dat');
$download->setCache(false);
$download->setBufferSize(10000);
$download->setThrottleDelay(1);
$download->send();
?>
```

Rather than pass all the parameters for the download through to the constructor, we've used the individual setter methods for the different options. After creating the new HTTP_Download object, you set the file to send to a large file that you created to test with. Caching is set to false so that you can test multiple times and not get a cached version of the file. You then set the buffer size to 10,000 bytes of 10K. Only 10K of the file will be read at a time. The throttle delay is then set to 1 second so that each 10K chunk is only sent after a second has passed. This should limit your download speed to roughly 10K per second. You can then fire off the send() method to send the actual file.

Sending an Archive Download

In this example, you'll send a whole bunch of files as a single download for the user, saving users from having to download each file individually.

```php
<?php
require_once('HTTP/Download/Archive.php');
HTTP_Download_Archive::send(
    'apress.zip',
    array('c:/work/Apress/7397/PHP-PEAR_outline.doc',
            'c:/work/Apress/7397/Author_information.doc'),
    HTTP_DOWNLOAD_ZIP,
    '',
    'c:/work/Apress/'
);
?>
```

When sending an archive, unlike for the HTTP_Download, the send method of HTTP_Download_Archive is called statically. This means you don't have to set anything up initially; you just have to call the method and pass the correct parameters through.

For the multiple files you pass through an array, each element is a separate file that needs to be included in the archive. As you can see, the files are coming from the C:\work\Apress directory. You don't want to include this directory path within the archive, so the last parameter strips C:\work\Apress from the path included in the archive.

HTTP_Header

The HTTP_Header package allows you to set and alter HTTP headers. It provides HTTP caching and also a way of looking up status types.

Common Uses

The HTTP package has the following common uses:

- Managing cookies
- Redirecting the client

Related Packages

- None

Dependencies

HTTP_Header has the following dependencies.

Required Packages

- PEAR Installer
- HTTP

Optional Packages

- None

API

dateToTimestamp()

Converts formatted date strings into a Unix timestamp. Either returns the Unix timestamp as an integer, or `false` if the date could not be parsed.

For later versions of PHP, you can use the `strtotime()` method to perform the same method.

```
mixed dateToTimestamp(string $date)
```

Parameter	Type	Description
$date	string	The date string to convert.

getHeader()

Returns a specific HTTP header string. If you don't pass any parameters to the method, then an array of all the headers will be returned.

```
mixed getHeader([string $key = null])
```

Parameter	Type	Description
$key	string	The name of the header to fetch.

getHttpVersion()

Returns the current HTTP version.

```
string getHttpVersion()
```

getStatusText()

Returns the message for a particular status code.

```
string getStatusText(integer $status_code)
```

Parameter	Type	Description
$status_code	integer	The status code that you want to return the message for.

getStatusType()

Returns the type of the provided status code. Valid types are
HTTP_HEADER_STATUS_INFORMATIONAL, HTTP_HEADER_STATUS_SUCCESSFUL,
HTTP_HEADER_STATUS_REDIRECT, HTTP_HEADER_STATUS_CLIENT_ERROR, and
HTTP_HEADER_STATUS_SERVER_ERROR.

```
integer getStatusType(integer $status_code)
```

Parameter	Type	Description
$status_code	integer	The status code that you want to return the type of.

isClientError()

Checks if the status code is in the 400 range, and therefore a client error (HTTP_HEADER_STATUS_CLIENT_ERROR).

boolean isClientError(integer $status_code)

Parameter	Type	Description
$status_code	integer	The status code that you want to check.

isError()

Checks if the status code is in either the 400 or the 500 range, and therefore a client error (HTTP_HEADER_STATUS_CLIENT_ERROR) or a server error (HTTP_HEADER_STATUS_SERVER_ERROR).

boolean isError(integer $status_code)

Parameter	Type	Description
$status_code	integer	The status code that you want to check.

isInformational()

Checks if the status code is in the 100 range, and therefore an informational message (HTTP_HEADER_STATUS_INFORMATIONAL).

boolean isInformational(integer $status_code)

Parameter	Type	Description
$status_code	integer	The status code that you want to check.

isRedirect()

Checks if the status code is in the 300 range, and therefore a client redirect (HTTP_HEADER_STATUS_REDIRECT).

boolean isRedirect(integer $status_code)

Parameter	Type	Description
$status_code	integer	The status code that you want to check.

isServerError()

Checks if the status code is in the 500 range, and therefore a server error (HTTP_HEADER_
STATUS_SERVER_ERROR).

```
boolean isServerError(integer $status_code)
```

Parameter	Type	Description
$status_code	integer	The status code that you want to check.

isSuccessful()

Checks if the status code is in the 200 range, and therefore successful (HTTP_HEADER_
STATUS_SUCCESSFUL).

```
boolean isSuccessful(integer $status_code)
```

Parameter	Type	Description
$status_code	integer	The status code that you want to check.

redirect()

Redirects the client using a Location header and exiting. Use this method if you want to add
parameters to the URL you're redirecting to; otherwise use HTTP:redirect.

```
void redirect([string $url = null] [, array $param = array()]
            [, boolean $session = false])
```

Parameter	Type	Description
$url	string	The URL to redirect to. If this is not set, the redirect will point to the current page.
$param	array	An associative array of key=>value pairs that form the parameters to add.
$session	boolean	If set to true, then the session name and ID will be added.

sendHeaders()

Sends all the headers that have been set using the setHeader() method.

```
boolean sendHeader([array $keys = array()] [, boolean $include = true])
```

Parameter	Type	Description
$keys	array	An array of headers to test against when sending the set headers.
$include	boolean	If this is set to true, then only the headers that match those in $keys will be sent. If set to false, then only the headers not matching those in $keys will be sent.

sendStatusCode()

Sends the given HTTP status code to the client. Returns true on success or false if other headers have already been sent.

```
boolean sendStatusCode(integer $status_code)
```

Parameter	Type	Description
$status_code	integer	The status code to send.

setHcader()

Sets a header value. Once you've set a number of these, you can send them all to the browser with the sendHeaders() method.

```
boolean setHeader(string $key [, string $value = null])
```

Parameter	Type	Description
$key	string	The name of the header to set.
$value	string	The value to set the header to. Setting this to null unsets the header named in $key, unless the key is the Last-Modified key. If the key is the Last-Modified key, then the value will get set to the current date and time.

setHttpVersion()

Sets the HTTP version. Returns true if successful or false if the version provided doesn't match 1.0 or 1.1.

```
boolean setHttpVersion(mixed $version)
```

Parameter	Type	Description
$version	mixed	Either 1.0 or 1.1.

Examples

Checking the Validity of a URL

Using the HTTP_Header class, you can interrogate the headers returned from a specific URL and determine whether the page existed or not, had been redirected to a new location, or caused the server to have an error. Your script also makes use of the HTTP_Client class to get a URL and return the status code of that URL:

```php
<?php
require_once('HTTP/Client.php');
require_once('HTTP/Header.php');
$client = new HTTP_Client();
$response_code = $client->get('http://localhost/apress/test.php');
$status = HTTP_Header::getStatusType($response_code);
switch ($status) {
    case HTTP_HEADER_STATUS_INFORMATIONAL:
        echo "The page that you requested contains informational data";
        break;
    case HTTP_HEADER_STATUS_REDIRECT:
        echo "The page that you requested redirected to another location";
        break;
    case HTTP_HEADER_STATUS_CLIENT_ERROR:
        echo "There was an error requesting that page";
        break;
    case HTTP_HEADER_STATUS_SERVER_ERROR:
        echo "There was an error on the server requesting the page";
        break;
    case HTTP_HEADER_STATUS_SUCCESSFUL:
    default:
        echo "The page was returned successfully";
}
?>
```

The getStatusType() method returns the type of the status code, so you don't have to try and cover each of the specific status codes. Depending on the type returned, you can display a different message. Without first creating the test.php script, this code returns the following string:

```
There was an error requesting that page
```

If you then create an empty test.php, the following message will be returned:

```
The page was returned successfully
```

You can test.php again, this time to use the HTTP_Header class to send a specific header, in this case a 500 server error:

```php
<?php
require_once('HTTP/Header.php');
$header = new HTTP_Header();
$header->sendStatusCode(500);
?>
```

You can test that your earlier script displays the correct message:

```
There was an error on the server requesting the page
```

HTTP_Request

The HTTP_Request package lets you easily perform GET, POST, HEAD, TRACE, PUT, and DELETE HTTP requests. It supports proxy authentication and can handle file uploads. Most of the tasks that a normal web browser can perform are duplicated in the HTTP_Request package.

Common Uses

The HTTP_Request package has the following common uses:

- Checking the validity of links
- Grabbing remote pages and parsing the contents

Related Packages

- HTTP
- HTTP_Client

Dependencies

HTTP_Request has the following dependencies.

Required Packages

- None

Optional Packages

- None

API

HTTP_Request Constructor

Sets up the HTTP_Request object. The constructor will return an HTTP_Request object. You can set the object up initially by passing an associative array of parameters to the constructor.

```
HTTP_Request HTTP_Request([string $url =''] [, array $params = array()])
```

Parameter	Type	Description
$url	string	The URL to fetch, access, or post information to.
$params	array	An associative array of the parameters for the object.

The parameters that can be passed into the constructor in an associative array are listed in the table "Constructor Parameters."

Constructor Parameters

Array Key	Purpose
method	The method to use when accessing the URL. Examples are GET, POST, and PUT.
http	The HTTP version to use—1.0 or 1.1.
user	The username to use in basic authentication.
pass	The password to use for basic authentication.
proxy_host	The proxy server to use.
proxy_port	The port for the proxy server.
proxy_user	The username to authenticate with to the proxy server.
proxy_pass	The password for authenticating to the proxy server.
timeout	The connection timeout in seconds.
allowRedirects	Set to true to allow the HTTP_Request object to follow redirects on the server.
maxRedirects	The maximum number of redirects to follow.
useBrackets	Set to true to append [ ] to array variable names.
saveBody	Set to true to save the response body in the response body object property.
readTimeout	Timeout for reading and writing data over the socket. Pass this through as an array (seconds, microseconds).
socketOptions	Any options that you want to pass to the Net_Socket object, as an array.

addCookie()

Adds a cookie to the Cookie header.

```
void addCookie(string $name, string $value)
```

Parameter	Type	Description
$name	string	The cookie name to add.
$value	string	The value to give the cookie.

addFile()

Adds a file to upload and changes the content-type to multipart/form-data at the same time. If an error occurs, the method will return PEAR_Error.

```
boolean addFile(string $inputName, mixed $fileName
                        [, mixed $contentType = 'application/octet-stream'])
```

Parameter	Type	Description
$inputName	string	The name of the file upload field.
$fileName	mixed	The name or names in an array of the files to upload.
$contentType	mixed	The content-type or content-types in an array of the files to upload.

addHeader()

Adds a header.

```
void addHeader(string $name, string $value)
```

Parameter	Type	Description
$name	string	The name of the header to add.
$value	string	The value to set the header to.

addPostData()

Adds items to include in the POST data array.

```
void addPostData(string $name, string $value[, boolean $encoded = false])
```

Parameter	Type	Description
$name	string	The name of the POST data items to add.
$value	string	The value to set $name to.
$encoded	boolean	If set to true, then the data has already been URL encoded. Default is that it hasn't yet been URL encoded.

addQueryString()

Adds a query string parameter.

```
void addQueryString(string $name, string $value[, boolean $encoded = false])
```

Parameter	Type	Description
$name	string	The query string parameter name.
$value	string	The value to set $name to.
$encoded	boolean	If set to true, then the data has already been URL encoded. Default is that it hasn't yet been URL encoded.

addRawQueryString()

Sets the query string to the exact string that you provide.

```
void addRawQueryString(string $query[, boolean $encoded = false])
```

Parameter	Type	Description
$query	string	The query string data. You have to make sure that it's in the correct format.
$encoded	boolean	If set to true, then the data has already been URL encoded. Default is that it has been URL encoded.

attach()

Adds a listener to the listeners that are notified of the object's events.

```
void attach(HTTP_Request_Listener $listener)
```

Parameter	Type	Description
$listener	HTTP_Request_Listener	The listener object you're attaching to.

detach()

Removes a listener from the listeners notified of the object's events.

```
void detach(HTTP_Request_Listener $listener)
```

Parameter	Type	Description
$listener	HTTP_Request_Listener	The listener object you're detaching from.

getResponseBody()

Returns the body of the response after the sendRequest method has been called. If the body isn't set, the method will return false.

```
mixed getResponseBody()
```

getResponseCode()

Returns the status code of the response. If it hasn't been set by the response, then false will be returned.

```
mixed getResponseCode()
```

getResponseCookies()

Returns an array of the cookies that have been set in the response. If none have been set, then false will be returned.

```
mixed getResponseCookie()
```

getResponseHeader()

Either returns the value of the named header, or an array of all the headers if no header name is given.

```
mixed getResponseHeader([string $headername = null])
```

Parameter	Type	Description
$headername	string	The header to return.

removeHeader()

Removes a request header.

```
void removeHeader(string $name)
```

Parameter	Type	Description
$name	string	The name of the response header to remove.

sendRequest()

Sends the request, using the parameters that have either been set up when initializing the object, or through the various set methods. Returns `true` on success or a `PEAR_Error` if there was a problem.

```
mixed sendRequest([boolean $saveBody = true])
```

Parameter	Type	Description
$saveBody	boolean	Determines whether to save the response body in the response object's property or not. You'd set this to `false` if you were downloading a large file and using a listener.

setBasicAuth()

Sets up the username and password required for basic authentication.

```
void setBasicAuth(string $user, string $pass)
```

Parameter	Type	Description
$user	string	The username to use when authenticating.
$pass	string	The password to use when authenticating.

setBody()

Sets the body for the request.

```
void setBody(string $body)
```

Parameter	Type	Description
$body	string	The data to set the request body to.

setHttpVer()

Sets the HTTP version to either 1.0 or 1.1.

```
void setHttpVer(string $version)
```

Parameter	Type	Description
$version	string	The version to set the request to.

setMethod()

Sets the method to use when sending the request—GET, POST, and so on.

```
void setMethod(string $method)
```

Parameter	Type	Description
$method	string	The method to set the request to.

setProxy()

Sets up the HTTP_Request object to use a proxy server.

```
void setProxy(string $host [, integer $port = 8080] [, string $username = null]
                      [, string $password = null])
```

Parameter	Type	Description
$host	string	The proxy server to use.
$port	integer	The port to use when connecting to the proxy server.
$username	string	The username to use when authenticating to the proxy server.
$password	string	The password to use when authenticating to the proxy server.

setURL()

Sets the URL to be accessed.

```
void setURL(string $url)
```

Parameter	Type	Description
$url	string	The URL you want the HTTP_Request object to connect to.

Examples

Connecting Through a Proxy Server

In one of the first examples in this chapter, you used the HTTP class to return the headers of a page. The example connected to a page on the localhost machine, but in many instances you might be sitting behind a proxy server, and in these situations the HTTP or HTTP_Client packages won't suffice. In this instance you'd need to use the HTTP_Request package, which lets you set up and connect through a proxy server. The original script you used was the following:

```php
<?php
require_once "PEAR.php";
require_once "HTTP.php";
$headers = HTTP::head("http://localhost/");
if (PEAR::isError($headers)) {
    echo "Error: " . $headers->getMessage();
} else {
    echo "<pre>";
    print_r($headers);
    echo "</pre>";
}
?>
```

Let's change that to connect to a site on the Internet through a proxy server:

```php
<?php
require_once "PEAR.php";
require_once "HTTP/Request.php";
$request =& new HTTP_Request('http://www.google.com/');
/* Make sure to change the proxy IP address to one in your network.  */
$request->setProxy('172.16.24.253',8080);
$request->sendRequest(false);
$headers = $request->getResponseHeader();
 if (PEAR::isError($headers)) {
    echo "Error: " . $headers->getMessage();
 } else {
    echo "<pre>";
    print_r($headers);
    echo "</pre>";
}
?>
```

Here you create a new HTTP_Request object, and then use the setProxy() method to tell the HTTP_Request object which proxy server to use. sendRequest() sends the request, and the false parameter tells it not to bother keeping the body of the page (because you're just interested in the headers).

You then retrieve the headers with the getResponseHeader() method and display them:

```
Array
(
    [location] => http://www.google.co.za/
    [cache-control] => private
    [content-type] => text/html
    [server] => GWS/2.1
    [content-length] => 221
    [date] => Wed, 05 Jul 2006 15:58:27 GMT
    [x-cache] => MISS from cproxy.saatchi.co.za
    [x-cache-lookup] => MISS from cproxy.saatchi.co.za:8080
    [proxy-connection] => close
)
```

HTTP_Upload

The HTTP_Upload package provides an easy and secure environment to manage uploading files from web forms.

Common Uses

The HTTP_Upload package has the following common uses:

- Handling multiple simultaneous uploads
- Safe handling of uploaded files
- Returning information about the uploaded file

Related Packages

- None

Dependencies

HTTP_Upload has the following dependencies.

Required Packages

- HTTP_Request

Optional Packages

- None

API

HTTP_Upload Constructor

The HTTP_Upload constructor returns a new HTTP_Upload object.

```
HTTP_Upload HTTP_Upload([string $language = null])
```

Parameter	Type	Description
$language	string	The language to use for error reporting. Uses the two-character country code.

getFiles()

Gets the files uploaded via the web form. It will return either an HTTP_Upload_File object, or an array of HTTP_Upload_File objects, or PEAR_Error if an error occurs in the method.

```
mixed getFiles([mixed $file = null])
```

Parameter	Type	Description
$file	mixed	If $file is left as null, an array of HTTP_Upload_File objects will be returned, one for each file upload form element. If $file is set to a string, only a single object will be returned that corresponds to the form upload element of that name. Setting $file to an integer will return the object in the array of objects that has $file as an index.

isMissing()

Checks to see if the user submitted a file or not. Returns false if there are files, or a PEAR_Error when files are missing.

```
mixed isMissing()
```

setChmod()

Sets the file access mask (chmod) to be used for uploaded files.

```
void setChmod(integer $mode)
```

Parameter	Type	Description
$mode	integer	The mode to set the files to.

The following API methods are all part of the HTTP_Upload_File class. You'll remember the name of this as the object that the previous methods returned as an object of the HTTP_Upload_File class. You use these methods on the uploaded file objects to get information about them, move them into place, and name them correctly.

getMessage()

Returns the error message for the error that occurred. Check if an error has occurred with the isError() method.

```
string getMessage()
```

getProp()

Returns the properties of the uploaded file.

```
mixed getProp([string $name = null])
```

Parameter	Type	Description
$name	string	If set to null, then an associative array of all the properties of the file will be returned; otherwise the value of the named property will be returned.

isError()

Tests to see if an error occurred during the upload. Returns true if there were errors. You can then display the exact error message by returning it with getMessage().

```
boolean isError()
```

isMissing()

Returns true if the user didn't submit a file in the form.

```
boolean isMissing()
```

isValid()

Tests to see if the file was submitted correctly.

```
boolean isValid()
```

moveTo()

Moves the uploaded file from the temporary directory that PHP uploaded it to, to the destination directory you specify. If an error occurs, the method will return PEAR_Error.

```
mixed moveTo(string $destination [, boolean $overwrite = true])
```

Parameter	Type	Description
$destination	string	The directory to move the file to.
$overwrite	boolean	If this is set to true, then existing files will be overwritten by like-named new uploads.

nameToSafe()

Changes an uploaded filename so it's safe to be written as that name to the file system. Extended characters (such as those with accent characters) are replaced with similar nonaccented characters. This method is normally called by the setName method.

```
string nameToSafe(string $name [, integer $maxlen = 250])
```

Parameter	Type	Description
$name	string	The filename to make safe.
$maxlen	integer	The maximum permitted name length.

nameToUniq()

Returns a unique filename for your uploaded file. This method is normally called by the setName method.

```
string nameToUniq()
```

setName()

Sets the destination name of your uploaded file. The new name is returned as a string.

```
string setName(string $mode [, $prepend = null] [, $append = null])
```

Parameter	Type	Description
$mode	string	The mode to use when naming the file. uniq creates a new unique name for the file, safe removes extended characters from the filename, and real keeps the existing filename.
$prepend	string	A string to prepend to the new filename.
$append	string	A string to append to the filename.

setValidExtensions()

Restricts the extensions of files that people can upload.

```
void setValidExtensions(array $extensions [, string $mode = 'deny'])
```

Parameter	Type	Description
$extensions	array	An array of file extensions to validate.
$mode	string	If set to deny, then the array will be treated as a blacklist of file extensions; if set to accept, then the array will be treated as a whitelist of file extensions.

Examples

Uploading a File

The HTTP_Upload package makes the PHP code for handling a file upload more accessible by wrapping the required code into the HTTP_Upload class and providing meaningful error checking and helper methods for it. Let's take a look at how an upload will work using HTTP_Upload:

```
<html>
<body>
<form enctype="multipart/form-data" action="<?php echo $_SERVER['PHP_SELF']; ?>"
method="POST">
    <input type="hidden" name="MAX_FILE_SIZE" value="20000" />
    File to upload: <input name="myFile" type="file" />
    <input type="submit" name="submit" value="Upload" />
</form>
```

The form is your standard form with a file upload element. The important bit to remember for the following code is that you've named the upload element myFile.

First you create a new HTTP_Upload object. The parameter you pass it is the language code for the language that you want any error messages to be displayed in. You can use this in conjunction with an HTTP::negotiateLanguage call to display the error messages automatically in the correct language.

```
<?php
require_once('HTTP/Upload.php');
if (isset($_POST['submit']) && $_POST['submit'] == 'Upload') {
            $upload = new HTTP_Upload('en');
```

The getFiles() method returns the information about the file uploaded through a specific upload form element—in this case myFile:

```
            $file = $upload->getFiles('myFile');
```

The error checking you do uses the getMessage() method to return and display the appropriate error message:

```
            if (PEAR::isError($file)) {
                        die ($file->getMessage());
            }
            if ($file->isValid()) {
                $upload_directory = 'c:/xampp/htdocs/Apress/uploads/';
```

The setName method creates a new filename for the uploaded file. In this case, you simply want to remove unwanted characters from the existing filename:

```
$file->setName('safe');
```

The moveTo() method moves the file from the temporary upload directory (as defined by your php.ini file) to the directory of your choice, renaming it to the name determined by setName at the same time:

```
$upload_name = $file->moveTo($upload_directory);
if (PEAR::isError($upload_name)) {
                die ($upload_name->getMessage());
}
```

You can then use the getProp() method to return any details about the file you just handled, and display a message to the user:

```
echo 'The file <strong>' . $file->getProp('real')
. '</strong> has been uploaded to the <em>'
. $upload_directory . '</em> directory and renamed to <strong>'
. $upload_name . '</strong>.';
        }
}
?>
</body>
</html>
```

XML

Extensible Markup Language (XML) is a file format that's gaining more and more acceptance as a file format to transfer data. You can use the classes in this section to work with XML files and strings.

You can use the XML_Beautifier package to format XML files and strings.

You can use the SOAP and Services_WebService packages to build clients and servers that transport XML messages back and forth, in the form of Simple Object Access Protocol (SOAP).

XML_Beautifier

The XML_Beautifier package contains classes that you can use to format XML files and XML strings into output that's easier to read by a human. Because space outside of elements isn't important in XML, it's common for XML to have no spacing or indenting between the elements to save space. However, this makes it difficult to read the XML if something is wrong or if the data inside the file needs to be viewed by a human.

XML_Beautifier has several options that allow you to adjust exactly how the XML is formatted, including how it's indented, the maximum line length in comments, and whether or not an XML element should be printed across more than one line.

Common Uses

The classes in this package have the following common use:

- Printing XML in a more easily read format.

Related Packages

- None

Dependencies

XML_Beautifier has the following dependencies.

Required Packages

- XML_Parser
- XML_Util

Optional Packages

- None

API

XML_Beautifier()

The constructor for the XML_Beautifier class creates a new instance of the class and can initialize it to options, if they're provided.

```
XML_Beautifier XML_Beautifier([array $options = array()])
```

Parameters	Type	Description
$options	array	An array containing options to set for the new object.

formatFile()

This method allows you to format a file.

```
mixed formatFile(string $file [, mixed $newFile = null]
                              [, string $renderer = "Plain"])
```

Parameters	Type	Description
$file	string	The name of the file to format.
$newFile	mixed	The name of the new file to write, unless you want to over-write the original file. If you want to write over the original file, use the XML_BEAUTIFIER_OVERWRITE constant. If nothing is provided here, the formatted XML will be returned as a string
$renderer	string	Specifies the renderer to use, which by default is the XML renderer.

formatString()

This method allows you to format a string.

```
string formatString(string $string [, string $renderer = "Plain"])
```

Parameters	Type	Description
$string	string	The string to format.
$renderer	string	Specifies the renderer to use, which by default is the XML renderer.

resetOptions()

Resets all the options back to the default options.

```
void resetOptions()
```

setOption()

Sets the given option to the given value.

```
void setOption(string $name,  string $value)
```

Parameters	Type	Description
$name	string	The name of the option to set.
$value	string	The value of the option to set.

setOptions()

Allows you to set more than one option at a time by allowing you to send the options and their values in as an array.

```
void setOptions(array $options)
```

Parameters	Type	Description
$options	array	An array containing option name and value pairs.

Several options are available that allow you to tailor the way that XML_Beautifier formats the XML. You can set these options individually using setOption(), or in an array using setOptions() or the constructor.

Options

Option Name	Description	Default Value
removeLineBreaks	If true, line breaks will be removed.	true
indent	Specifies the string to use for indenting.	" " (four spaces)
linebreak	Specifies the character used for the line break.	\n
caseFolding	Changes the case of the tags.	false
caseFoldingTo	Specifies the case to use for the tags.	uppercase
normalizeComments	Removes extra white space in comments and combines lines if possible.	false

Options

Option Name	Description	Default Value
maxCommentLine	Specifies the maximum length of a comment line. A value of -1 means that the comment line has no maximum length.	-1
multilineTags	If true, tags are allowed to span across multiple lines.	false

Examples

Formatting XML in a File

This example demonstrates how to format an XML file.

```php
<?php
/* Formatting an XML document */

require_once 'XML/Beautifier.php';

$beautifier = new XML_Beautifier();

$result = $beautifier->formatFile('samples/ugly.xml', 'samples/pretty.xml');

if (PEAR::isError($result)) {
    printf("An error has occured:  \"%s\"\n", $result->getMessage());
    exit(1);
}

print "All done!\n";

?>
```

The XML that is found in the ugly.xml file is shown in Listing 1 in all its glory, with multiple elements on one line, no indenting, and hideously formatted comments.

Listing 1. *ugly.xml*

```xml
<?xml version="1.0"?>
<!--
    This
    is a      comment
    that spans quite a few lines and has a lot of white space that
    could be condensed and made smaller.
    Because it's not very readable spanning this many lines and having a lot of ➡
    characters in one line.
```

```
-->
<xml>    <element1><childElement/>
</element1>
</xml>
```

The "prettied" version of the XML in Listing 2 now has elements nested and indented properly, and is much easier to read. However, the comments are still formatted poorly. That's because the normalizeComments option defaults to false. See the last example in this chapter to see how to specify different options that allow you to customize how the XML is formatted.

Listing 2. *pretty.xml*

```
<!--
    This
    is a      comment
    that spans quite a few lines and has a lot of white space that
    could be condensed and made smaller.
    Because it's not very readable spanning this many lines and having a lot ➡
    of characters in one line.
-->
<xml>
    <element1>
        <childElement />
    </element1>
</xml>
```

Formatting XML in a String

This example demonstrates how to format a string of XML. This can be handy if you're formatting input for a text area on a web page, where a user can cut and paste XML into a form and it isn't put into a file. Another use for this is storing XML in a compact, nonindented format and displaying it in a format that's easier to read.

```php
<?php
/* Formatting an XML string */

require_once 'XML/Beautifier.php';

$xml = "<root><elements><element1/></elements></root>";

$beautifier = new XML_Beautifier();

$result = $beautifier->formatString($xml);

print($result);

?>
```

The output of the script looks like this:

```
<root>
    <elements>
        <element1 />
    </elements>
</root>
```

Formatting XML with Different Options

This example demonstrates how to set options to tailor how the XML is formatted. Other than the options being specified, it's identical to the first example.

```php
<?php
/* Formatting XML with options */

require_once 'XML/Beautifier.php';

$options = array (
    'indent' => '  ' , /* Only indent each element 2 spaces */
    'normalizeComments' => 'true' , /* Combine comments into one line */
    'maxCommentLine' => 50 , /* Maximum length of a comment line */
    'multiLineTags' => false , /* Tags are not multiline */
    );

$beautifier = new XML_Beautifier($options);

$result = $beautifier->formatFile('samples/ugly.xml', 'samples/pretty.xml');

if (PEAR::isError($result)) {
    printf("An error has occured:  \"%s\"\n", $result->getMessage());
    exit(1);
}

print "All done!\n";

?>
```

With the `normalizeComments` option set to `true`, the lines will be combined if possible. The maximum length of each comment line is set to 50 characters (see Listing 3).

Listing 3. *ugly.xml*

```
<?xml version="1.0"?>
<!--
    This
    is a      comment
    that spans quite a few lines and has a lot of white space that
    could be condensed and made smaller.
    Because it's not very readable spanning this many lines and having a lot of ➡
    characters in one line.
-->
<xml>    <element1><childElement/>
</element1>
</xml>
```

After the XML is formatted, the elements once again are neatly indented and the comments are easier to read than they were before (see Listing 4).

Listing 4. *pretty.xml*

```
<!--
  This is a comment that spans quite a few lines and
  has a lot of white space that could be condensed
  and made smaller. Because it's not very readable
  spanning this many lines and having a lot of
  characters in one line.
-->
<xml>
  <element1>
    <childElement />
  </element1>
</xml>
```

SOAP

The SOAP package contains classes that allow you to create clients and servers for SOAP requests. SOAP is one of the most common methods for transporting messages back and forth between web services and their clients.

The classes in this package, namely SOAP_Server and SOAP_Client, allow you to create servers and clients without having to deal with the details of putting the SOAP requests and responses together. The classes hide the implementation details to the point where the examples of using the clients appear as though you're calling methods on a local object instead of a web service located out on the Net.

Common Uses

The classes in this package have the following common uses:

- Creating SOAP servers on systems that don't have PHP SOAP extensions enabled
- Creating SOAP clients on systems that don't have PHP SOAP extensions enabled

Related Packages

- Services_WebService

Dependencies

SOAP has the following dependencies.

Required Packages

- Net_Socket-1.0.6
- Net_URL-1.0.14
- HTTP_Request-1.3.0

Optional Packages

- None

SOAP_Server API

SOAP_Server()

This constructor creates a new instance of the SOAP_Server class.

```
SOAP_Server SOAP_Server([array $options = null])
```

Parameters	Type	Description
$options	array	An optional array of options to use when creating a new instance.

addObjectMap()

Adds an object map, which allows SOAP_Server to generate WSDLs automatically from the object and properties.

```
void addObjectMap(object &$obj [, string $namespace = null]
                               [, string $service_name = 'Default']
                               [, string  $service_desc - ''])
```

Parameters	Type	Description
&$obj	object	The object to use when creating the map.
$namespace	string	The namespace to use for the web service.
$service_name	string	The name of the service.
$service_desc	string	A description for the service, which will be used in the documentation that's generated for the service.

addToMap()

Adds the given method to the map of methods that the SOAP server supports.

```
void addToMap(string $methodname, array $in, array $out [, string $namespace = null]
                                                         [, string $alias = null])
```

Parameters	Type	Description
$methodname	string	The name of the method.
$in	array	An array that describes the input parameters for the method.
$out	array	An array that describes the output of the method.
$namespace	string	An optional namespace for the method.
$alias	string	An optional alias for the method.

bindWSDL()

Allows the server to use a WSDL to define the methods that are supported by the server instead of using an object via the addObjectMap() method.

```
void bindWSDL(string $wsdl_url)
```

Parameters	Type	Description
$wsdl_url	string	The URL of the WSDL.

service()

Executes the service, calling whatever method is specified by the SOAP message being posted by the client.

```
void service(mixed $data [, string $endpoint = ''] [, boolean $test = false])
```

Parameters	Type	Description
$data	mixed	The data that's posted by the client; for example, $HTTP_RAW_POST_DATA.
$endpoint	string	The name of the web service endpoint, which is optional.
$test	boolean	If true, the service is being called in test mode and the actual code won't be called.

setCallHandler()

Sets the call handler for the SOAP server.

```
void setCallHandler(string $callHandler [, boolean $validation = true])
```

Parameters	Type	Description
$callHandler	string	The method that will be called when the web service is called.
$validation	boolean	If true, the callHandler will be validated to see if the method name is a real method name.

SOAP_Client API

SOAP_Client()

This is the constructor for the SOAP_Client class, which exposes methods for making SOAP requests.

```
SOAP_Client SOAP_Client(string $endpoint [, boolean $wsdl = false]
                                          [, string $portName = false]
                                          [, array $proxy_params = array()])
```

Parameters	Type	Description
$endpoint	string	A URL.
$wsdl	boolean	If true, the resource located at the provided URL is a WSDL file.
$portName	string	The name of the port to use for the call.
$proxy_params	array	Parameters that can be passed to the HTTP_Request class.

addHeader()

Adds the provided header to the request that will be sent in the SOAP request.

```
void addHeader(SOAP_Header $soap_value)
```

Parameters	Type	Description
$soap_value	mixed	A SOAP_Header object or an array of values that can be sent in the header.

&call()

Makes the actual call to the SOAP method.

```
mixed &call(string $method,  &$params [, mixed $namespace = false]
                                      [, $soapAction = false])
```

Parameters	Type	Description
$method	string	The name of the method to call.
$params	array	An array of parameters to pass to the method.
$namespace	mixed	The namespace of the web service, or an array of options. The options are documented in the table "Options for call() Method." If an array is passed into $namespace, the SOAP action must be supplied as an option in the array and not in the $soapAction parameter. If an array is passed to $namespace, $soapAction will be ignored.
$soapAction	string	The type of SOAP action to use when making the SOAP request.

Options for call() method

Option	Description
namespace	The namespace for the SOAP request.
soapAction	The type of SOAP action.
timeout	The time the HTTP socket will stay open before timing out.
transfer-encoding	The value used for the SMTP Content-Transfer-Encoding header.
from	The value used for the SMTP From header.
subject	The value used for the SMTP Subject header.
headers	Additional SMTP headers.

* *These options may be passed into the $namespace parameter as an array.*

setEncoding()

Sets the type of encoding to use when making the SOAP requests. The setEncoding() method returns a SOAP_Fault if the encoding is invalid. Valid encoding types are UTF-8, US_ASCII, and ISO-8859-1.

mixed setEncoding(string $encoding)

Parameters	Type	Description
$encoding	string	The name of the encoding to use.

setOpt()

Sets options for use with the client. These options can be used by the transport classes, such as SOAP_Transport_HTTP, SOAP_Transport_SMTP, and SOAP_Transport_TCP.

void setOpt(string $category, string $option [, string $value = null])

Parameters	Type	Description
$category	string	The category of the option or the name of the option.
$option	string	The name of the option.
$value	string	The option's value.

Examples

Calling a Simple SOAP Method

This example demonstrates how to call a SOAP web service using an automatically generated proxy. The ease of use for the client rivals that of the SoapClient class, but unlike the SoapClient class, using the PEAR::SOAP package classes doesn't require SOAP extensions to be enabled in PHP.

```php
<?php

/* Calling a SOAP method.*/

require_once 'SOAP/Client.php';

/* Calling this URL will get an automatically generated WSDL file
 * from the "Exposing a Simple Web Service" example in the
 * Services_WebService package section . . .
 */
$wsdl = new SOAP_WSDL('http://localhost/~user1/pear_ch10/➡
services_webservice_cx01.php?wsdl');

$proxy = $wsdl->getProxy();

print ($proxy->getTime());
?>
```

Implementing a SOAP Server

This example demonstrates how to implement a SOAP server.

At first glance, using the SOAP_Server class found in the PEAR::SOAP package might seem like it's more difficult to use than the Services_WebService package or the PHP 5 SOAP extensions. It is. However, it has the advantage of not requiring PHP 5 to have the SOAP extensions enabled (the Services_WebService package uses the extensions), so this package can readily be used on a server that doesn't have them enabled.

The PhonebookWebService here is a simple example class with a single method that accepts a last and first name in the lookup() method and returns a phone number. Now, that's oversimplifying things a little bit, but the point of the example is not to demonstrate a realistic phonebook class.

```php
<?php
/* Implementing a SOAP server with PEAR::SOAP */

require_once 'SOAP/Server.php';
require_once 'SOAP/Disco.php';

/**
 * A web service example class that provides a method of
```

```
 * looking up phone numbers by a person's last and first
 * names.
 */
class PhonebookWebService
{

    /**
     * A map that is used for the methods and variables.
     * @access private
     */
    var $__dispatch_map = array();

    /**
     * Constructor.
     */
    function PhonebookWebService()
    {
        $this->__dispatch_map['lookup'] = array (
                'in' => array (
                        'lastName' => 'string',
                        'firstName' => 'string',
                    ),
                'out' => array (
                        'result' => 'string'
                    )
            );
    }

    /**
     * Method exposed as a web service method to get phone
     * numbers given a last and first name.
     * @param string $lastName Last (family) name of person
     * @param string    $firstName First (given) name of person
     */
    function lookup($lastName, $firstName)
    {
        /* Here this function is just mocking up some data
         * to make sure that the call to the service is functional,
         * but of course in real life this will be replaced by a
         * call to a data store to retrieve the information.
         */
        if ($lastName == "Five" && $firstName = "Johnny") {
            return "(555) 555-5555";
        } else {
            return "(111) 111-1111";
        }
```

```
        }
    }

    /* This is the code for creating the SOAP server and
     * responding to the SOAP request.
     */

    $soapServer = new SOAP_Server();

    $webService = new PhonebookWebService();

    $soapServer->addObjectMap($webService, 'urn:PhonebookWebService');

    if (isset($_SERVER['REQUEST_METHOD']) &&
        $_SERVER['REQUEST_METHOD'] == 'POST') {

        $soapServer->service($HTTP_RAW_POST_DATA);

    } else {

        /* If the client is not posting SOAP data, then the server
         * can expose the WSDL or DISCO so the client knows how to
         * properly call the server.
         */

        $disco = new SOAP_DISCO_Server($soapServer, 'PhonebookWebService');

        header("Content-type: text/txt");
        if (isset($_SERVER['QUERY_STRING']) &&
            strcasecmp($_SERVER['QUERY_STRING'], "wsdl") == 0) {

            echo $disco->getWSDL();

        } else {

            echo $disco->getDISCO();

        }
    }

    ?>
```

In the constructor of the PhonebookWebService class, the __dispatch_map variable is populated with information about the methods included in the SOAP server. This map includes the
name of the method as the key to an element, with the value being another array that contains
information about the input and output parameters.

The service() method handles the SOAP request by calling the method on the object and
returning the results, taking care of all the nasty SOAP details for you.

Services_WebService

Services_WebService is an abstract class that you can use to turn any PHP class into a web service, simply by inheriting from Services_WebService and calling a couple methods. The Services_WebService class uses the PHP 5 SOAP extension classes, such as SoapServer, so you must have the SOAP extensions enabled before you can use this class.

Common Uses

The classes in this package have the following common use:

- Exposing existing classes as web services.

Related Packages

- SOAP

Dependencies

Services_WebService has the following dependencies.

Required Packages

- None

Optional Packages

- None

API

__construct()

Initializes the Services_WebService class.

```
Services_WebService __construct(string $namespace, string $description,
                               array $options)
```

Parameters	Type	Description
$namespace	string	The namespace for the web service.
$description	string	A description that explains what the web service does.
$options	array	An array of options for the web services.

classMethodsIntoStruct()

Parses all the methods in the concrete class into the internal structure that will be used for generating a WSDL that describes this web service. This method is protected.

```
void classMethodsIntoStruct()
```

classPropertiesIntoStruct()

Parses all the properties in the concrete class into the internal structure that will be used for generating a WSDL that describes this web service. This method is protected.

```
void classPropertiesIntoStruct(string $className)
```

Parameters	Type	Description
$className	string	The name of the class.

createWSDL_binding()

Creates the binding section in the WSDL structure. This method is protected.

```
void createWSDL_binding()
```

createWSDL_definitions()

Creates the definitions section in the WSDL structure. This method is protected.

```
void createWSDL_definitions()
```

createWSDL_messages()

Creates the message section in the WSDL structure. This method is protected.

```
void createWSDL_messages()
```

createWSDL_portType()

Creates the portType section in the WSDL structure. This method is protected.

```
void createWSDL_portType()
```

createWSDL_service()

Creates the service section in the WSDL structure. This method is protected.

```
void createWSDL_service()
```

createWSDL_types()

Creates the types section in the WSDL structure. This method is protected.

```
void createWSDL_types()
```

handle()

Handles the request to the web service, using the methods in the concrete class. This method is one of the few public methods in the Services_WebService class.

```
void handle()
```

intoStruct()

Parses the classes into the WSDL structure. This method is protected.

```
void intoStruct()
```

Examples

Exposing a Simple Web Service

The example in Listing 5 demonstrates how to extend the Services_WebService class to transform a class into a web service. Being able to expose a class as a web service simply by extending Services_WebService can be a handy way to take functionality that you have already written and expose it as a web service.

Extending Services_WebService also provides another feature—automatically generating WSDL files when wsdl is specified on the query string in the URL. If you're using a class that's capable of automatically generating a proxy based off a WSDL, such as the PHP 5 SOAP Extensions' SoapClient class, it's relatively painless to call methods on the web service class you have written.

Listing 5. *services_webservice_ex01.php*

```php
<?php

/* Exposing a simple web service */

require_once 'Services/Webservice.php';

class TimeWebService extends Services_WebService
{
```

```
    /**
     * Gets an important time in history
     *
     * @return string
     */
    public function getTime()
    {
        return 'August 29, 2029 02:14:00 EST';
    }

}

$options = array (
    'uri' => 'timeWebService',
    'encoding' => SOAP_ENCODED,
    'soap_version' => SOAP_1_2
    );

$timeWS = new TimeWebService('TimeWebService', 'My description', $options);

$timeWS->handle();

?>
```

The web service can be tested in only a few lines of code using the PHP 5 SOAP extensions, provided they're enabled on your web server.

```
<?php

/* This simple test uses the built-in PHP 5
 * SOAP extensions to automagically create a proxy and
 * call it.
 */

$client = new SoapClient('http://localhost/~user1/pear_10/➥
services_webservice_ex01.php?wsdl');

try
{
    print ($client->getTime());
}
catch (SoapFault $sf)
{
    print $sf;
}

?>
```

The URL that's provided to the constructor of the SoapClient class is the location of the PHP file with the TimeWebService class, which extends Services_WebService. The query string provided, wsdl, tells the handle() method on the class to generate the WSDL for the service and return it to the caller. The $client object, after it's created with the WSDL, becomes a proxy that you can use to call methods on the web service—treating it just as though you were using the TimeWebService class directly.

Shown here is the WSDL that's printed when wsdl is passed in the query string.

```xml
<?xml version="1.0" encoding="utf-8"?>
<definitions name="TimeWebService" targetNamespace="urn:TimeWebService"
    xmlns:typens="urn:TimeWebService"
    xmlns:xsd="http://www.w3.org/2001/XMLSchema"
    xmlns:soap="http://schemas.xmlsoap.org/wsdl/soap/"
    xmlns:soapenc="http://schemas.xmlsoap.org/soap/encoding/"
    xmlns:wsdl="http://schemas.xmlsoap.org/wsdl/"
    xmlns="http://schemas.xmlsoap.org/wsdl/">
    <types>
        <xsd:schema xmlns="http://www.w3.org/2001/XMLSchema"
            targetNamespace="urn:TimeWebService" />
    </types>
    <message name="getTime" />
    <message name="getTimeResponse">
        <part name="getTimeResponse" type="xsd:string" />
    </message>
    <portType name="TimeWebServicePort">
        <operation name="getTime">
            <documentation>
                Gets an important time in history
            </documentation>
            <input message="typens:getTime" />
            <output message="typens:getTimeResponse" />
        </operation>
    </portType>
    <binding name="TimeWebServiceBinding"
        type="typens:TimeWebServicePort">
        <soap:binding style="rpc"
            transport="http://schemas.xmlsoap.org/soap/http" />
        <operation name="getTime">
            <soap:operation soapAction="urn:TimeWebServiceAction" />
            <input>
                <soap:body use="encoded" namespace="urn:TimeWebService"
                    encodingStyle="http://schemas.xmlsoap.org/soap/encoding/" />
            </input>
            <output>
                <soap:body use="encoded" namespace="urn:TimeWebService"
                    encodingStyle="http://schemas.xmlsoap.org/soap/encoding/" />
            </output>
        </operation>
```

```
    </binding>
    <service name="TimeWebService">
        <port name="TimeWebServicePort"
            binding="typens:TimeWebServiceBinding">
            <soap:address location="http://localhost/~user1/pear_10/➥
services_webservice_ex01.php?wsdl" />
        </port>
    </service>
</definitions>
```

Creating Another Web Service

The ClosestCheeseMarket class, which is shown here, is another example of extending the Services_WebService class to expose a method as a web service. In this example, the getLocation() method requires a string parameter, called $j in this example.

Take note of the comments in this class. The Services_WebService class uses the documentation blocks to know what type of parameters are being expected and returned.

```php
<?php

/* Using web services */

require_once 'Services/Webservice.php';

/**
 * Web service class
 */
class ClosestCheeseMarket extends Services_WebService
{

    /* The doc comments here are important!  The WSDL generator
     * in the class uses the data type given here to know what
     * type of parameter is being passed to the web service method.
     */

    /**
     * Returns the location of the nearest cheese market.
     * @param string $j
     * @return string
     */
    public function getLocation($j)
    {
        $loc = '';
```

```
        switch ($j)
        {
            case '55555':
                $loc = "Rudolph's Taxidermy, Spark Plugs, and Cheese";
                break;
            case '11111':
                $loc = "Dick's U-Pull-It Car Parts and Cheddar";
                break;
            case '22222':
                $loc = "Ye Olde Cheez Shoppe und Radiators";
                break;
            default:
                $loc = "No cheese for you!";
                break;
        }

        return $loc;
    }
}

$options = array (
    'uri' => 'closestCheeseMarket',
    'encoding' => SOAP_ENCODED,
    'soap_version' => SOAP_1_2
    );

$ws = new ClosestCheeseMarket(
    'ClosestCheeseMarket',
    'Returns the name of the cheese market in your postal code',
    $options);

$ws->handle();


?>
```

The test file uses the SoapClient class to call the method on the web service:

```
<?php

/* This simple test uses the built-in PHP 5
 * SOAP extensions to automagically create a proxy and
 * call it.  This time, the WSDL is the one for calling
 * the web service we built in the "Creating Another Web Service"
 * example.
 */
```

```
$client = new SoapClient('http://localhost/~user1/pear_10/➥
services_webservice_ex02.php?wsdl');

try
{
    print ($client->getLocation('11111'));
}
catch (SoapFault $sf)
{
    print $sf;
}

?>
```

The WSDL, which is generated automatically by the handle() method on the ClosestCheeseMarket class, is used in the SoapClient's constructor to create a proxy class that can be used to call the getLocation() method on the web service. The string that's passed to getLocation() is one of the imaginary postal codes found in the method. Of course, in a real implementation of a class such as this, you would most likely look these results up in a database or some other type of data store so that the information wasn't hard-coded.

Mail

The PEAR packages in this section are all used when working with sending and handling Internet e-mail.

- The Mail package sends a mail message.

- The Mail_Mime package allows you to create and decode MIME-encoded messages.

- The Mail_mimeDecode package is used to parse MIME-encoded messages.

- The Mime_Type package contains utility functions for working with MIME types.

Mail

The Mail package provides a single method for sending mail using a number of different back-end mail servers. As the programmer, you need to set up the `Mail` object initially using the back end that you want to connect to; then you can use a standard set of functions for sending your mail.

Common Uses

The Mail package has the following common use:

- Sending a mail message

Related Packages

- None

Dependencies

Mail has the following dependencies.

Required Packages

- Net_SMTP

Optional Packages

- None

API

factory

Creates a new `Mail` instance. Because the back end is abstracted, once you've set up your `Mail` object, the sending of mail is identical, irrespective of the mail server you're using. Returns a `PEAR_Error` on failure.

```
Mail &factory(string $driver [, array $params = array()])
```

Parameter	Type	Description
$driver	string	The kind of Mail object to create. Valid options are mail, smtp, or sendmail.
$params	array	The parameters to pass to the Mail object. The parameters will change depending on the back end.

Parameters for Mail Object

Back end	Parameter	Purpose
sendmail	sendmail_path	The location of the sendmail program on the server. Defaults to /usr/bin/sendmail.
sendmail	sendmail_args	Any additional parameters to pass to sendmail.
smtp	host	The SMTP host to connect to. Default is localhost.
smtp	port	The port to connect on; default is 25.
smtp	auth	If set to true, then you need to authenticate to the SMTP server. Default is false.
smtp	username	Username for SMTP authentication.
smtp	password	Password for SMTP authentication.
smtp	persist	Used if you want the SMTP connection to remain open across multiple sends.

parseAddressList

The parseAddressList method is contained in a separate PEAR package, but is most useful when used with the Mail package. With parseAddressList, you can validate a series of e-mail addresses to determine whether they would be valid according to RFC 822 or not. parseAddressList doesn't check whether the e-mail addresses exist or not; it simply tests the validity of the string as an e-mail address.

```
array Mail_RFC822::parseAddressList(string $address
                    [, string $default_domain = null]
                    [, boolean $nest_groups = null]
                    [, boolean $validate = null]
                    [, integer $limit = null])
```

Parameter	Type	Description
$address	string	The address or addresses you want to validate.
$default_domain	string	The default domain to use for the addresses in cases where no domain is present.
$nest_groups	boolean	If this is set to true, then addresses will be returned nested into groups for easier viewing.
$validate	boolean	If this is set to true, then individual parts of the address will be validated.
$limit	integer	Sets a limit on the number of e-mail addresses to parse, after which processing stops.

Mail_mail::send

Sends a mail message using the mail server protocol specified when the Mail object was created. Returns PEAR_Error on failure.

```
mixed send(mixed $recipients, array $headers, string $body)
```

Parameter	Type	Description
$recipients	mixed	Either a comma-separated list of recipients or an array. If the recipients are sent with an array, you can include CC and BCC recipients.
$headers	array	An associative array of headers to send with the mail, where the key is the header name and the value is the header value.
$body	string	The full text of the message you want to send, including any MIME parts if needed.

Examples

Sending a Simple Mail Message

In this first example, you'll create a simple text message and send it using the Mail package. The functionality that it provides is similar to the PHP mail() function, with the added advantage that this class will build the headers for you automatically. Let's take a look at the code involved:

```php
<?php
require_once('Mail.php');
```

After you've included the required PEAR class file, you can set up the recipients of the mail message. If you simply wanted to send directly using the To: field, you could provide the recipients as a comma-separated string, but you want to use the CC field, so you have to specify the recipients as an associative array:

```
$recipients = array('To' => 'allan@atplay.biz',
                    'Cc' => 'allan_kent@gmail.com');
```

You also need to create an associative array of the headers you want to include:

```
$headers['From']    = 'allan@mediafrenzy.co.za';
$headers['To']      = 'allan@atplay.biz';
$headers['Subject'] = 'PEAR Mail send using SMTP!';

$body = 'Here is a plain text message that we ➡
are sending with the PEAR Mail class!';
```

Because you'll be sending this e-mail via SMTP, you need to specify the SMTP host and port, because you're using a nonstandard SMTP port. Our SMTP server doesn't require authentication, so we don't need to give the username and password.

```
$params['host'] = 'localhost';
$params['port'] = 2525;
```

Then, you create the new mail object, passing it as parameters the mail server type you wish to use to send the mail, as well as the parameters you need for the server type:

```
$mail_object =& Mail::factory('smtp', $params);
```

The last step is simply to send the e-mail:

```
$mail_object->send($recipients, $headers, $body);
?>
```

Mail_Mime

The Mail_Mime package allows you to send and work with MIME-encoded mail messages. MIME stands for Multipurpose Internet Mail Extensions, and is a way of encoding binary data such as images and sounds so they can be sent via e-mail.

Common Uses

The Mail_Mime package has the following common use:

- Sending a mail message with a binary attachment

Related Packages

- Mail_mimeDecode

Dependencies

Mail_Mime has the following dependencies.

Required Packages

- Mail_MimePart

Optional Packages

- None

API

Mail_mime

The `Mail_mime` constructer function creates the new `Mail_mime` object.

`Mail_mime Mail_mime([string $crlf = "\r\n"])`

Parameter	Type	Description
$crlf	string	The character codes to use as the end-of-line character.

addAttachment

Adds a file attachment to your mail message. Returns PEAR_Error on failure.

```
mixed addAttachment(string $file [, string $type = 'application/octet-stream']
                                 [, string $name = '']
                                 [, boolean $isFilename = True]
                                 [, string $encoding = 'base64'])
```

Parameter	Type	Description
$file	string	Either the filename of the file to attach or the data for the file.
$type	string	The Content-Type of the file.
$name	string	The filename for the file attachment. Only include this if $file contains data and not the filename.
$isFilename	boolean	Set this to true if the content of $file is the filename of the file. Set this to false if $file contains the data.
$encoding	string	The encoding to use. Default is base64.

addBcc

Adds a BCC (Blind Carbon Copy) recipient of the mail. Calling this multiple times adds multiple BCC recipients.

```
void addBcc(string $email)
```

Parameter	Type	Description
$email	string	The e-mail recipient to add.

addCc

Adds a CC (Carbon Copy) recipient of the mail. Calling this method multiple times adds multiple CC recipients.

```
void addCc(string $email)
```

Parameter	Type	Description
$email	string	The e-mail recipient to add.

addHTMLImage

Adds an embedded image to the mail message.

```
mixed addHTMLImage(string $file [, string $type = 'application/octet-stream']
                             [, string $name = '']
                             [, boolean $isFilename = True])
```

Parameter	Type	Description
$file	string	Either the filename of the image to attach or the data for the image.
$type	string	The Content-Type of the image.
$name	string	The filename for the image attachment. Only include this if $file contains data and not the filename.
$isFilename	boolean	Set this to true if the content of $file is the filename of the image. Set this to false if $file contains the data.

get

Builds the MIME message based on the parts that have been added, and returns a string with the MIME-encoded message in it.

```
string &get([array $build_params = null])
```

Parameter	Type	Description
$build_params	array	An associative array that determines how the mail should be built.

Parameters for the get Method

Parameter Key	Description
text_encoding	The encoding to use for plain text; defaults to 7bit.
html_encoding	The encoding the use for HTML content; default is quoted-printable.
7bit_wrap	The number of characters before 7bit-encoded text is wrapped to the next line. Default is 998 characters.
html_charset	The character set to use for HTML content. Default is iso-8859-1.
text_charset	The character set to use for plain text. Default is iso-8859-1.
head_charset	The character set to use for the mail headers. Default is iso-8859-1.

headers

Returns an associative array of the headers that will be sent with the mail.

`array &headers([array $extra_headers = null])`

Parameter	Type	Description
$extra_headers	array	Any extra headers that you want to include.

setFrom

Sets the e-mail address that the mail message will originate from.

`void setFrom(string $email)`

Parameter	Type	Description
$email	string	The originating mail address.

setHTMLBody

Sets the HTML body part of the mail message. Returns `PEAR_Error` on failure.

`mixed setHTMLBody(string $data [, boolean $isFile = false])`

Parameter	Type	Description
$data	string	Either the HTML text that forms the body of the message, or a filename that contains the HTML.
$isFile	boolean	If this is set to true, then $data will specify a filename and not the data itself.

setSubject

Sets the subject of the mail message.

`void setSubject(string $subject)`

Parameter	Type	Description
$subject	string	The subject that you want the mail message to have.

setTXTBody

Sets the text body for the mail message. Mail clients that cannot display HTML content will display the alternate text portion instead. Returns `PEAR_Error` on failure.

```
mixed setTXTBody(string $data [, boolean $isFile = false]
                              [, boolean $append = false])
```

Parameter	Type	Description
$data	string	Either the text data for the mail message or the name of a file that contains the text.
$isFile	boolean	If this is set to `true`, then $data will be evaluated as a filename and not the actual data.
$append	boolean	If this is set to `true`, then the data will be appended to the existing text body.

txtHeaders

Gets the text version of the mail headers.

```
string txtHeaders([array $extra_headers = null])
```

Parameter	Type	Description
$extra_headers	array	Any extra headers that you want to include.

Examples

Sending Mail with Inline Images

In this example, you'll use the `Mail_MIME` class to send an e-mail message that contains inline images that will display in a mail client that can display HTML content. The great thing about sending this kind of mail is that you can send an alternate text component that's displayed to people who cannot view HTML. As you'll see, the `Mail_MIME` class doesn't send the mail itself; it's only used to construct the mail message that you then send using the standard `Mail` class.

```php
<?php
require_once('Mail.php');
require_once('Mail/Mime.php');
```

The first thing to do, then, is to set up variables for both the text and the HTML versions of your e-mail. As you can see in the HTML string, you're including an `<img>` tag. The source of the image is set to the filename of the image you want to display. Later on in the code, you'll attach the image in such a way that it's displayed correctly.

```
$textMessage = 'PEAR makes sending e-mail a pleasure.  ➥
If your e-mail could view HTML, this e-mail would be a lot more interesting!';

$htmlMessage = '<html><body><p><img src="pear.gif" width="113" ➥
height="55" /></p><p><strong>PEAR</strong> makes sending e-mail a➥
pleasure.</p></body></html>';

$crlf = "\n";
```

You then create the new MIME mail object, and start setting the component parts of it—who it's from, the subject, and the message parts. The way to add the image is to use the addHTMLImage() method—this adds the image in such a way that when the MIME message is created, the src parameter of any <img> tags in your HTML message will be replaced with a unique cid of the image that was attached.

```
$mimeMail = new Mail_mime($crlf);

$mimeMail->setFrom('allan@lodestone.co.za');
$mimeMail->setSubject('PEAR Mail... MIME Style!');
$mimeMail->addHTMLImage('pear.gif','image/gif');
$mimeMail->setTXTBody($textMessage);
$mimeMail->setHTMLBody($htmlMessage);
```

Once the MIME message has been set up, you can set up the Mail object to send this message:

```
$params['host'] = 'localhost';
$params['port'] = 2525;

$mail =& Mail::factory('smtp', $params);
```

Two of the parameter of the Mail send() method are the message body and the message headers. Use the get and headers methods of the Mail_Mime object to return them to you.

Note The order in which you call the get and headers methods is very important! The get method sets up MIME boundaries in the message and headers—if you call the headers method first, you won't get those boundaries correctly set and your mail will look like a mess.

```
$body = $mimeMail->get();
$headers = $mimeMail->headers();

$mail->send('allan_kent@gmail.com', $headers, $body);
?>
```

Mail_mimeDecode

The Mail_mimeDecode package parses through an existing MIME-encoded mail message and returns the structure to you. If you have access to the native PHP `mailparse` or `imap_fetchstructure` functions, it's better to use those because they'll be faster and offer more functionality.

Common Uses

The Mail_mimeDecode package has the following common uses:

- Returning the recipients of a MIME e-mail
- Returning the structure of a MIME e-mail

Related Packages

- None

Dependencies

Mail_mimeDecode has the following dependencies.

Required Packages

- None

Optional Packages

- None

API

Mail_mimeDecode

The `Mail_mimeDecode` constructor function creates a new `Mail_mimeDecode` object based on the MIME-encoded input provided, and splits the MIME message into headers and body.

```
Mail_mimeDecode Mail_mimeDecode(string $encoded)
```

Parameter	Type	Description
$encoded	string	The MIME-encoded string to parse.

decode

The decode method begins the decoding process. If this method is called statically, it will first create the Mail_mimeDecode object and then call the decode method on it.

```
Mail_mimeDecode decode([array $params = null])
```

Parameter	Type	Description
$params	array	An associative array of parameters that control how the message is decoded.

Parameters for the decode Method

Parameter Key	Description
include_bodies	Whether to include the body in the returned object or not.
decode_bodies	Specifies whether or not the bodies should be decoded.
decode_headers	Whether to decode the headers or not.
input	If this method is called statically, then this will contain the data that is the MIME-encoded message.

getMimeNumbers

Takes the decoded structure returned by the decode method and returns an array of references to the individual MIME parts, indexed by MIME number.

```
array &getMimeNumbers(object &$structure [, boolean $no_refs = false]
                                         [, string $mime_number = '']
                                         [, string $prepend = ''])
```

Parameter	Type	Description
$structure	object	The structure returned by the decode method.
$no_refs	boolean	If this is set to true, then the MIME numbers won't be returned as keys in the array.
$mime_number	string	This parameter is for internal use only.
$prepend	string	A string to prepend to each of the MIME numbers returned.

getSendArray

Returns an array formatted correctly to be passed as the parameter for a `Mail::send()` method. Returns `PEAR_Error` on failure.

```
array getSendArray()
```

getXML

Returns a copy of the `Mail_mimeDecode` object, as returned by the `decode` method, as XML.

```
string getXML(Mail_mimeDecode $object)
```

Parameter	Type	Description
$object	Mail_mimeDecode	The output of a previous call to `Mail_mimeDecode::decode`.

uudecode

Checks the MIME-encoded message for any uuencoded files and returns an array of them. They're returned as an associative array with bodies, filenames, and permissions.

```
array uudecode(string $encoded)
```

Parameter	Type	Description
$encoded	string	The MIME-encoded message in which to search for uuencoded files.

Examples

Extracting Images from a MIME E-Mail

For this example, you'll need a MIME-encoded message. We altered the script from the previous example to send an e-mail with both an inline message (`pear.gif`) and an image attachment (`recycle.gif`). Once the message had arrived in my mail box, I saved the message source as a file on my disk called `mime_email.src`. This file is included with the code downloads if you don't feel like creating it yourself. Here, then, is the code for the script to decode the MIME message.

The function that appears at the top of the script works on the component parts of the MIME message. We'll come back to this function in just a bit.

```php
<?php
function extractBits($piece) {
        foreach($piece->parts as $part) {
                if ($part->ctype_primary == 'multipart') {
                        extractBits($part);
                } elseif ($part->ctype_primary == 'image') {
                        echo "<p>------- Found Image: " ➥
                        . $part->disposition . "------<br />";
                        $filename = $part->ctype_parameters['filename'];
                        if ($filename == '') $filename = ➥
                        $part->d_parameters['filename'];
                        if ($filename != '') {
                                $fp = fopen('export_' . $filename, 'w');
                                fwrite($fp, $part->body);
                                fclose($fp);
                                echo "Writing out export_" .$filename;
                        }
                        echo "</p>";
                }
        }
}
```

First you include the PEAR class file and set up the parameters for the decoding. You want all the parts of the message, so set all the parameters to true:

```php
require once 'Mail/mimeDecode.php';

$params['include_bodies'] = true;
$params['decode_bodies'] = true;
$params['decode_headers'] = true;
```

The MIME message is in the mime_email.src file, so you read that up into a variable $mime_message:

```php
$mime_message = file_get_contents('mime_email.src');
```

All you need to do then is create the new Mail_mimeDecode object, and run the decode method to return the message structure. You're then ready to work your way through the returned structure.

```php
$mimeDecode = new Mail_mimeDecode($mime_message);
$mimeStructure = $mimeDecode->decode($params);
extractBits($mimeStructure)
?>
```

Let's look at the code for the extractBits() function again. The function takes as an argument the returned message structure:

```
function extractBits($piece) {
```

You then loop through each of the parts that make up the message. The parts() method returns each part. Because you might be dealing with a multipart message, you need to check for that. The primary type of the part is set to multipart. If this happens, then that individual part of the message contains a number of nested parts. Typically the first part of a message will be the text part, and the second the multipart portion that contains the HTML and any file attachments. If it's multipart, then you simply pass the current part as the argument back to the extractBits function:

```
foreach($piece->parts as $part) {
    if ($part->ctype_primary == 'multipart') {
        extractBits($part);
```

Because you're only interested in images, if the primary type isn't multipart, you then test for image. If there is an image, you return what type of image (either inline or attachment), grab the filename, and write it out. The filename can appear in either the parameters or d_parameters array:

```
} elseif ($part->ctype_primary == 'image') {
    echo "<p>------- Found Image: " ➥
    . $part->disposition . "------<br />";
    $filename = ➥
    $part->ctype_parameters['filename'];
    if ($filename == '') $filename = ➥
    $part->d_parameters['filename'];
    if ($filename != '') {
        $fp = fopen('export_' . ➥
        $filename, 'w');
        fwrite($fp, $part->body);
        fclose($fp);
        echo ➥
        "Writing out export_" .$filename;
    }
    echo "</p>";
        }
    }
}
```

The output of the script is as follows:

```
------- Found Image: inline------
Writing out export_pear.gif
------- Found Image: attachment------
Writing out export_recycle.gif
```

Mime_Type

The Mime_Type package contains a number of utility functions that can be used when working with MIME types and files. With this package, you can determine the sub-parts of a MIME type or autodetect the MIME type of a file.

Common Uses

The Mime_Type package has the following common use:

- Detecting the MIME type of a file

Related Packages

- None

Dependencies

Mime_Type has the following dependencies.

Required Packages

- None

Optional Packages

- None

API

MIME_Type

The `MIME_Type` constructor function creates a new `MIME_Type` object.

```
void MIME_Type MIME_Type([string $type = false])
```

Parameter	Type	Description
$type	string	A MIME type with which to initialize the object.

addParameter

Adds a parameter to this MIME type.

```
void addParameter(string $name, string $value [, string $comment = false])
```

Parameter	Type	Description
$name	string	Parameter name that's being added.
$value	string	The value for this attribute.
$comment	string	A comment for this parameter.

autoDetect

Attempts to autodetect a file's MIME type. The MIME type is returned if found.

```
string autoDetect(string $file [, boolean $params = false])
```

Parameter	Type	Description
$file	string	The path to the file you want to detect the type of.
$params	boolean	If set to true, then the MIME parameters will be appended.

get

Returns a MIME type from the values that have been set in the Mime_Type object.

```
string get()
```

getMedia

Returns the media portion of the MIME type. The media portion is the part before the slash and currently can be one of application, audio, example, image, message, model, multipart, text, or video.

```
string getMedia(string $type)
```

Parameter	Type	Description
$type	string	The MIME type to parse for the media portion.

getParameters

Returns a MIME type's parameters. The parameters are returned as an array. For a full list of the possible parameters, take a look at http://www.iana.org/assignments/media-types-parameters.

```
array getParameters(string $type)
```

Parameter	Type	Description
$type	string	The MIME type to return the parameters for.

getSubType

Returns the subtype of the provided MIME type. The subtype is the portion after the slash.

```
string getSubType(string $type)
```

Parameter	Type	Description
$type	string	The MIME type from which to return the subtype.

hasParameters

Determines whether this MIME type has any parameters. If it does, they can be returned with the getParameters method.

```
boolean hasParameters(string $type)
```

Parameter	Type	Description
$type	string	The MIME type to check for parameters in.

isExperimental

Determines if the provided MIME type is experimental or not. Experimental types have preceding x- characters in their media or subtype portions.

```
boolean isExperimental(string $type)
```

Parameter	Type	Description
$type	string	The MIME type to test.

isVendor

Determines if the MIME type is vendor specific. Vendor MIME types have leading vnd. characters in the subtype.

```
boolean isVendor(string $type)
```

Parameter	Type	Description
$type	string	The MIME type to test.

isWildcard

Determines whether the provided MIME type is a wildcard (matches all MIME types) or not.

```
boolean isWildcard(string $type)
```

Parameter	Type	Description
$type	string	The MIME type to test.

parse

Parses a MIME type and sets the variables in the MIME_Type object.

```
void parse(string $type)
```

Parameter	Type	Description
$type	string	A MIME type to parse.

removeParameter

Removes an individual parameter from the parameters of the MIME type.

```
void removeParameter(string $name)
```

Parameter	Type	Description
$name	string	The name of the parameter to remove.

stripParameters

Strips any MIME parameters from the provided MIME type. The plain MIME type is returned.

```
string stripParameters(string $type)
```

Parameter	Type	Description
$type	string	The MIME type from which you want to remove the parameters.

wildcardMatch

Performs a wildcard match on a MIME type against a wildcard MIME type provided. Returns true if a match is found, otherwise false if no match is found.

```
boolean wildcardMatch(string $wildcard, string $type)
```

Parameter	Type	Description
$wildcard	string	The MIME wildcard type against which you're checking.
$type	string	The MIME type you're checking.

Examples

Determining If a MIME Type Is Valid

In this example, you'll use the information returned in the MIME_Type object to determine if a given MIME type is valid or not. You'll do this by comparing the media type with the list of valid media types.

```
<?php
require 'MIME/Type.php';

$mimetype = 'video/3gpp';
```

The MIME type that you'll test initially is a valid MIME type that's used for mobile video content. You create a new MIME_Type object, passing the MIME type that you want to test as the parameter for the constructor function:

```
$mimeobject = new MIME_Type($mimetype);
```

At this point the $mimeobject has the following properties:

```
object(MIME_Type)#1 (4) {
  ["media"]=>
  string(5) "video"
  ["subType"]=>
  string(4) "3gpp"
  ["parameters"]=>
  array(0) {
  }
  ["validMediaTypes"]=>
  array(7) {
    [0]=>
    string(4) "text"
    [1]=>
    string(5) "image"
    [2]=>
    string(5) "audio"
    [3]=>
    string(5) "video"
    [4]=>
    string(11) "application"
    [5]=>
    string(9) "multipart"
    [6]=>
    string(7) "message"
  }
}
```

As you can see, the media property contains the media portion of the MIME type (the bit before the /), and you also have an array of the valid MIME types. All you need to do now is compare the two:

```
if (in_array($mimeobject->media,$mimeobject->validMediaTypes)) {
        echo "media type is valid";
} else {
        echo "media type is not valid";
}
?>
```

PROJECT 1

■ ■ ■

Intranet Address Book Website

This project was a fun one to work on, because it was easy to get going and didn't require any applications other than PHP and the web server. It's a great project to start out this series, letting you use enough of the PEAR packages to see the value of not having to write all the code from scratch.

This example demonstrates how to build a web application that stores information about contacts, such as your friends, business contacts, or relatives. The information for each contact is stored in a vCard file on the file system, which is an option that allows the site to be installed on a server or a computer that doesn't have a database. However, should you decide to use a database to store the data, the Contact class allows you to load and save the contact without having to bury the details of the implementation deep in the web pages. Although creating the extra classes adds a little more work up front, it will pay off in dividends if you decide to swap out using the Contact_VCard_Build and Contact_VCard_Parse packages with DB packages.

The site demonstrates how to use authentication so you can keep the information stored in your repository private, and it also allows you to download the vCard so you can use it locally.

The site is also easily configurable, so it's up to you to decide what directory holds the vCard files, where the site's log is kept, and other options.

You'll use the following packages in this project:

- Auth

- Config

- Contact_Vcard_Build

- Contact_Vcard_Parse

- File

- File_Find

- HTML_Form

- HTTP_Download

- Log

The application is comprised of nine PHP files. Four of them contain classes that are used to support the other five scripts, which are the ones actually used in the application's user interface.

The classes are the `Contact` and `ContactAddress` classes, which are used to hide the storing and retrieving of contacts throughout the site. The other two classes are the `AddressbookUtils` and `AddressbookConfig` classes, which are used to house repeated functions and configuration, respectively.

When this site was in its earliest phases, it didn't have the classes; instead, the code was inside all the web pages directly. This certainly works and doesn't pose any problems other than making the individual pages a bit harder to read and possibly creating some maintenance headaches in the future. By splitting the site up into manageable chunks, we've hoped to add some useful layers of abstraction, without adding layers of obstruction. (I apologize for burdening you with that cliché, but I haven't used it since my team meeting last Wednesday.)

The Contact Class

The `Contact` class in Listing 1 and the `ContactAddress` class were the first parts of the website created, because creating a web page to view objects that don't exist is an interesting exercise in futility but not particularly useful for demonstrating how the pages work.

Listing 1. *Contact class*

```php
<?php

require_once 'ContactAddress.php';
require_once 'Contact_Vcard_Parse.php';
require_once 'Contact_Vcard_Build.php';
require_once 'File.php';

/**
 * The Contact holds information about a person in our
 * address book.  It has methods that hide the saving and
 * retrieving of details from the web pages so it can be later
 * swapped out with a different method, if need be, without
 * causing changes in the pages.
 *
 */
class Contact
{
    /**
     * The given (first) name of the contact
     * @var      string
     * @access       private
     */
    var $_givenName = '';

    /**
     * The family (last) name of the contact
     * @var      string
     * @access       private
```

```php
     */
    var $_familyName = '';

    /**
     * The birthday of the contact
     * @var       string
     * @access    private
     */
    var $_birthday = '';

    /**
     * The address of the contact
     * @var       ContactAddress
     * @access    private
     */
    var $_address = null;

    /**
     * The e-mail address of the contact
     * @var       string
     * @access    private
     */
    var $_emailAddress = '';

    /**
     * The telephone number for the contact
     * @var       string
     * @access    private
     */
    var $_telephoneNumber = '';

    /**
     * A note that is associated with the contact
     * @var       string
     * @access    private
     */
    var $_note = '';
    /**
     * Returns the given (first) name of the contact
     * @return    string    Given name of conact
     */
    public function getGivenName()
    {
        return $this->_givenName;
    }
```

```php
/**
 * Sets the given (first) name of the contact
 * @param    string    $given    Given (first) name of contact.
 */
public function setGivenName($given)
{
    $this->_givenName = $given;
}

/**
 * Returns the family (last) name of the contact
 * @return    string    First name of contact
 */
public function getFamilyName()
{
    return $this->_familyName;
}

/**
 * Sets the family (last) name of the contact
 * @return    string    $familyName    Family name of contact
 */
public function setFamilyName($familyName)
{
    $this->_familyName = $familyName;
}

/**
 * Returns the contact's birthday
 * @return    string    Birthday of contact.
 */
public function getBirthday()
{
    return $this->_birthday;
}

/**
 * Sets the contact's birthday
 * @param    string    $birthday    Contact's birthday
 */
public function setBirthday($birthday)
{
    $this->_birthday = $birthday;
}
```

```php
/**
 * Returns the contact's address
 * @return    ContactAddress    Address of contact.
 */
public function getAddress()
{
    return $this->_address;
}


/**
 * Sets the contact's address
 * @param    ContactAddress    $address    Address of contact.
 */
public function setAddress($address)
{
    $this->_address = $address;
}


/**
 * Returns the contact's e-mail address
 * @return    string    E-mail address of contact.
 */
public function getEmailAddress()
{
    return $this->_emailAddress;
}


/**
 * Sets the contact's e-mail address
 * @param    string    $email    E-mail address of contact.
 */
public function setEmailAddress($email)
{
    $this->_emailAddress = $email;
}


/**
 * Returns the telephone number of the contact
 * @return    string    Telephone number.
 */
public function getTelephoneNumber()
{
    return $this->_telephoneNumber;
}
```

```php
/**
 * Sets the telephone number of the contact
 * @param     string     $phoneNumber     Telephone number
 */
public function setTelephoneNumber($phoneNumber)
{
    $this->_telephoneNumber = $phoneNumber;
}

/**
 * Returns a note associated with the contact
 * @return     string     Note
 */
public function getNote()
{
    return $this->_note;
}

/**
 * Sets a note associated with the contact
 * @param     string     $note     Note text
 */
public function setNote($note)
{
    $this->_note = $note;
}

/**
 * Saves the contact using the persistence method
 */
public function save()
{
    /* The method form has been posted back to itself, so
     * build the contact card, save it, and tell the user.
     */
    $card = new Contact_Vcard_Build();

    try
    {
        $card->setFormattedName(
            AddressbookUtils::buildFormattedName(
                $this->_givenName,
                $this->_familyName)
            );
        $card->setName($this->_familyName, $this->_givenName, '', '', '');
        $card->setBirthday($this->_birthday);
        $card->addEmail($this->_emailAddress);
        $card->addParam('TYPE', 'HOME');
```

```
        if (isset($this->_address))
        {
            $card->addAddress(
                $this->_address->_address1,
                '', /* An extended address not used in this application */
                $this->_address->_address2,
                $this->_address->_city,
                $this->_address->_state,
                $this->_address->_postalCode,
                $this->_address->_country);
        }

        $card->addParam('TYPE', 'HOME');

        $card->addTelephone($this->_telephoneNumber);

        $card->addParam('TYPE', 'HOME');

        $text = $card->fetch();

        /* TODO:  See if this already exists */
        $config = AddressbookConfig::singleton();
        $fileName = $config->getDataPath() . "/" . ➥
AddressbookUtils::buildVcardName($this->_givenName, $this->_familyName);
        File::write($fileName, $text);
    }
    catch (Exception $e)
    {
        printf("An error occurred while trying to save contact:  %s",
            $e->getMessage());
    }
}
/**
 * Loads the contact associated with the given ID using the persistence
 * method
 * @param    string    $id    An identifier that uniquely identitifies the
 *                            Contact.
 *
 * @return    Contact    New Contact object that matches the given ID
 */
public static function getContact($id)
{
    $config = AddressbookConfig::singleton();
    $dataDir = $config->getDataPath();
```

```php
            $contact = new Contact();
            $fileName = $dataDir . '/' . $id;
            if (file_exists($fileName)) {

                try {

                    $card = new Contact_Vcard_Parse();
                    $content = $card->fromFile($fileName);

                    $contact->setGivenName($content[0]["N"][0]["value"][1][0]);
                    $contact->setFamilyName($content[0]["N"][0]["value"][0][0]);
                    $contact->setEmailAddress($content[0]["EMAIL"][0]["value"][0][0]);
                    $contact->setTelephoneNumber($content[0]["TEL"][0]["value"][0][0]);
                    $contact->setBirthday($content[0]["BDAY"][0]["value"][0][0]);

                    $address = new ContactAddress();
                    $address->setAddress1($content[0]["ADR"][0]["value"][0][0]);
                    $address->setAddress2($content[0]["ADR"][0]["value"][2][0]);
                    $address->setCity($content[0]["ADR"][0]["value"][3][0]);
                    $address->setState($content[0]["ADR"][0]["value"][4][0]);
                    $address->setPostalCode($content[0]["ADR"][0]["value"][5][0]);
                    $address->setCountry($content[0]["ADR"][0]["value"][6][0]);

                    $contact->setAddress($address);

                    return $contact;

                } catch (exception $e) {
                    /* Log the error message out to the log. */
                    $logger->err("An error occurred while attempting to get the ➥
                    contact data: {$e->getMessage()}");
                }

            } else {
                /* The file does not exist... */
                printError("The specified contact cannot be found!");
            }

        }
    }

?>
```

The Contact class, along with each of the accessors for the properties in the object, contains two important methods—getContact() and save(). The web pages will use these later to retrieve and save the contact information.

The Contact class makes use of Contact_Vcard_Parse to load the information and Contact_Vcard_Build to save the contact information to a vCard 3.0 file format in a configurable location.

A Class to Store the Address

The ContactAddress class holds the address information about the Contact, and is listed in Listing 2.

Listing 2. *ContactAddress.php*

```php
<?php

/**
 * ContactAddress is used by the Contact class to store the
 * address information.  The largest benefit of breaking the
 * address part out to a different class is the ability to
 * add more than one in the future with a lot less effort.
 */
class ContactAddress {

    /**
     * Type of address
     * @var string
     * @access private
     */
    var $_addressType;
    /**
     * First line of the address record
     * @var string
     * @access private
     */
    var $_address1;
    /**
     * Second line of the address record
     * @var string
     * @access private
     */
    var $_address2;
    /**
     * Name of the city in the address
     * @var string
     * @access private
     */
    var $_city;
```

```php
    /**
     * Name of the state/province in the address
     * @var string
     * @access private
     */
    var $_state;
    /**
     * Postal code
     * @var string
     * @access private
     */
    var $_postalCode;
    /**
     * Name of the country in the address
     * @var string
     * @access private
     */
    var $_country;

    /**
     * Returns the address type.  This is for future use,
     * enabling more than one address to be stored for
     * each contact (work, home, etc.)
     * @return    string    Type of adddress.  Possible values are 'home', 'work'
     */
    public function getAddressType()
    {
        return $this->_addressType;
    }

    /**
     * Sets the address type
     * @param    string    $addressType    Type of address
     */
    public function setAddressType($addressType)
    {
        $this->_addressType();
    }

    /**
     * Returns the first line of the address
     * @return    string    First line of address
     */
    public function getAddress1() {
        return $this->_address1;
    }
```

```php
/**
 * Sets the first line of the address
 * @param    string    $address1    First line of address
 */
public function setAddress1($address1) {
    $this->_address1 = $address1;
}

/**
 * Returns the second line of the address
 * @return    string    Second line
 */
public function getAddress2() {
    return $this >_address2;
}

/**
 * Sets the second line of the address
 * @param    string    $address2    Second line of address
 */
public function setAddress2($address2) {
    $this->_address2 = $address2;
}

/**
 * Returns the city
 * @return    string    Name of the city
 */
public function getCity() {
    return $this->_city;
}

/**
 * Sets the address city
 * @param    string    $city    City name
 */
public function setCity($city) {
    $this->_city = $city;
}

/**
 * Returns the state (or province) of the address
 * @return    string    Name of the city or province
 */
public function getState() {
    return $this->_state;
}
```

```php
    /**
     * Sets the state (or province part of the address)
     * @param    string    $state    Name of state or province
     */
    public function setState($state) {
        $this->_state = $state;
    }

    /**
     * Returns the postal code
     * @return    string    Postal code
     */
    public function getPostalCode() {
        return $this->_postalCode;
    }

    /**
     * Sets the postal code
     * @param    string    $postalCode    Postal code
     */
    public function setPostalCode($postalCode) {
        $this->_postalCode = $postalCode;
    }

    /**
     * Returns the name of the country
     * @return    string    Name of the country in the address
     */
    public function getCountry() {
        return $this->_country;
    }

    /**
     * Sets the name of the country
     * @param    string    $country    Name of the country in the address
     */
    public function setCountry($country) {
        $this->_country = $country;
    }
}

?>
```

There isn't anything new or interesting about the ContactAddress class; it's a simple class used to hold data and is only listed here for the sake of being thorough.

The Login Page

The login page authenticates a user by comparing his or her username and password information with that stored in a plain file (see Listing 3). This is certainly useful in making sure that no one is accessing the web page that isn't authorized.

Although the Auth package supports many different methods of authentication (see the Auth chapter for details), because the rest of the site uses file-based storage it seems silly to break that paradigm for authentication. So, you're using the File method for authentication.

Listing 3. *login.php*

```php
<?php

require_once 'Auth.php';
require_once 'AddressbookUtils.php';
require_once 'HTML/Form.php';

function showLogin() {
    /* Use the HTML_Form class to show our login form
     */
    print "<html><head></head><body>";
    $form = new HTML_Form(htmlspecialchars($_SERVER['PHP_SELF']), 'post');
    $form->addText('username', 'Username:');
    $form->addPasswordOne('password', 'Password:');
    $form->addSubmit('submit', 'Login');
    $form->display();
    print "You are not currently logged in!";
    print "</body></html>";
}

/* See the AddressbookUtils class for details */
$a = AddressbookUtils::getAuth();
$a->start();

if ($a->checkAuth()) {
    header('location:welcome.php');
}

?>
```

It's difficult—to say the least—just to make up a passwd file and have it work. You can run the little script in Listing 4 on the command line to create a passwd file for you before you visit login.php.

Listing 4. *adduser.php*

```php
<?php

require_once 'AddressbookUtils.php';

$a = AddressbookUtils::getAuth();
$a->addUser('myuser', 'secret');
$a->addUser('user', 'password');

?>
```

When it's done running, you'll have a passwd file in the same location in which the site will be looking for it. The contents of the file will look like this:

```
myuser:MTFDDfY2zwrWg
user:oLXAmibWvWWNQ
```

Listing the Contacts

Once the user is logged in successfully, he or she is directed to the welcome.php page, which lists the contacts found by looking in the data directory (see Listing 5).

Each contact in this application is stored in its own vCard in the data directory, and the name of the file is based on the name of the contact. This script uses the File_Find package to find .vcf files in the data directory. The script iterates through the names of the files that were found, and generates the name of the contact from the name of the file.

Listing 5. *welcome.php*

```html
<!DOCTYPE html PUBLIC "-//W3C//DTD XHTML 1.0 Strict//EN"
    "http://www.w3.org/TR/xhtml1/DTD/xhtml1-strict.dtd">
<html xmlns="http://www.w3.org/1999/xhtml">

<head>
<title>Address Book - Welcome!</title>
</head>
<body>
<h1>Welcome!</h1>
<p>Here is a list of your contacts.  Click on the name of
the contact to view the details</p>
<?php

/* The Welcome page is going to display the names
 * found in the data directory.
 */
require_once 'AddressbookConfig.php';
```

```php
require_once 'File/Find.php';

$config = AddressbookConfig::singleton();
$dataDir = $config->getDataPath();

/* First, make sure the data dir exists */

if (file_exists($dataDir)) {

    /* Use File:Find to get the file names from the data dir */

    $results = File_Find::glob('/^.*\.vcf/', $dataDir, 'perl');

    if ($results) {

        foreach($results as $result) {
            /* Format the result.  Because we control the upload process,
             * we know that each name is stored Lastname_Firstname.vcf.
             * We'll reformat that to display nicely on the window.
             */
            $displayString = preg_replace('/([A-Za-z]+)_([A-Za-z]+)\.vcf/',
                "\\1, \\2", $result);
            printf("<a href=\"viewcontact.php?contact=%s\">%s</a><br/>",
                $result, $displayString);
        }

    } else {
        print "<b>No contacts found!</b>";
    }

} else {
    /* The configured data directory does not exist, so nicely
     * tell the user
     */
    print "<span style=\"color:red\"> ➡
    Error:  Directory $dataDir does not exist!</span>";
}

?>
<hr/>
<table width="100%">
<tr>
<td><a href="newcontact.php">Add New Contact</a></td>
</tr>
</table>
</body>
</html>
```

Adding a New Contact

The page for adding a new contact takes advantage of the Contact class to assign and save the contact information (see Listing 6). It also uses the HTML_Form package to draw HTML form input controls easily so the user can enter the contact information.

Listing 6. *newcontact.php*

```
<!DOCTYPE html PUBLIC "-//W3C//DTD XHTML 1.0 Strict//EN"
    "http://www.w3.org/TR/xhtml1/DTD/xhtml1-strict.dtd">
<html xmlns="http://www.w3.org/1999/xhtml">

<head>
<title>Address Book - Create New Contact</title>
</head>
<body>

<?php

require_once 'AddressbookConfig.php';
require_once 'AddressbookUtils.php';
require_once 'Contact.php';
require_once 'HTML/Form.php';

if ($_SERVER['REQUEST_METHOD'] == 'POST') {

    /* The method form has been posted back to itself, so
     * we build the contact and call the save() method.
     */

    $contact = new Contact();
    $contact->setGivenName($_POST['fname']);
    $contact->setFamilyName($_POST['lname']);
    $contact->setBirthday($_POST['bday']);
    $contact->setEmailAddress($_POST['email']);
    $contact->setTelephoneNumber($_POST['phone_nbr']);

    $address = new ContactAddress();
    $address->setAddress1($_POST['address1']);
    $address->setAddress2($_POST['address2']);
    $address->setCity($_POST['city']);
    $address->setState($_POST['state']);
    $address->setPostalCode($_POST['postal_code']);
    $address->setCountry($_POST['country']);
```

```php
    $contact->setAddress($address);

    $contact->save();

    print "<span style=\"font-weight:bold;color:blue;\">Changes saved ➥
    successfully!</span></p>";


} else {


    print("<h1>New contact</h1>");
    print("<p>Enter the information about the new contact below.</p>");

    /* This returns a static array so that it doesn't need to be created each
     * time it is called.
     */
    $states = AddressbookUtils::getStatesArray();

    $form = new HTML_Form(htmlspecialchars($_SERVER['PHP_SELF']), 'post');
    $form->addText("fname", "First name:");
    $form->addText("lname", "Last name:");
    $form->addText("bday", "Birthday:");
    $form->addText("phone_nbr", "Telephone number:");
    $form->addText("email", "E-mail address:");
    $form->addText("address1", "Address 1:");
    $form->addText("address2", "Address 2:");
    $form->addText("city", "City:");
    $form->addSelect("state", "State/Province:", $states);
    $form->addText("postal_code", "Postal Code:");
    $form->addText("country", "Country:");
    $form->addSubmit("submit", "Save contact");
    $form->addReset("Reset");

    $form->display();
}
?>


<hr/>
<table width="100%">
<tr>
<td><a href="welcome.php">View All Contacts</a></td>
</tr>
</table>
</body>
</html>
```

Viewing a Contact

Now that the new contact has been saved, the address book site will need some way of displaying the contact again (see Listing 7).

Listing 7. *viewcontact.php*

```
<!DOCTYPE html PUBLIC "-//W3C//DTD XHTML 1.0 Strict//EN"
    "http://www.w3.org/TR/xhtml1/DTD/xhtml1-strict.dtd">
<html xmlns="http://www.w3.org/1999/xhtml">

<head>
<title>Address Book - View Contact</title>
<style type="text/css">
    td.label { text-align : right; font-weight: bold; }
    .error { color : red ; font-weight : bold; }
</style>
</head>
<body>
<?php

require_once 'AddressbookConfig.php';
require_once 'Contact.php';
require_once 'Log.php';

$config = AddressbookConfig::singleton();
$dataDir = $config->getDataPath();

$logger = &Log::factory('file', $config->getLogFilename(), 'AddressBook');
$mask = Log::UPTO($logger->stringToPriority($config->getLogLevel()));
$logger->setMask($mask);

function printError($errMessage)
{
    print("<span class=\"error\">$errMessage</span>");
}


/* Look for the name of the card on the query string... */
$cardName = basename($_GET["contact"]);
/* Check the name of the card for any funny business */
if (preg_match("/(\.\.|\/)/", $cardName)) {

    printError(printf("Invalid name \"%s\"", $cardName));

} else {
```

```php
/* Now load the contact up and display the contents to
 * the window.
 */
$fileName = $dataDir . '/' .$cardName;
if (file_exists($fileName)) {

    try {

        $contact =      Contact::getContact($cardName);

        printf("<h1>Details for %s %s</h1>",
            $contact->getGivenName(),
            $contact->getFamilyName());

        print("<table>");

        printf("<tr><td class=\"label\">Email address:</td><td>%s</td></tr>",
            $contact->getEmailAddress());

        printf("<tr><td class=\"label\">Telephone number:</td><td>%s</td></tr>",
            $contact->getTelephoneNumber());

        $address = $contact->getAddress();

        printf("<tr><td class=\"label\">Address 1:</td><td>%s</td></tr>",
            $address->getAddress1());

        printf("<tr><td class=\"label\">Address 2:</td><td>%s</td></tr>",
            $address->getAddress2());

        printf("<tr><td class=\"label\">City:</td><td>%s</td></tr>",
            $address->getCity());

        printf("<tr><td class=\"label\">State/Province:</td><td>%s</td></tr>",
            $address->getState());

        printf("<tr><td class=\"label\">Postal Code:</td><td>%s</td></tr>",
            $address->getPostalCode());

        printf("<tr><td class=\"label\">Country:</td><td>%s</td></tr>",
            $address->getCountry());

        print("</table>");

        /* Allow the user to download the vCard. */
```

```
        print("<br/><a href=\"downloadcontact.php?contact=$cardName\">➥
        Download contact</a>");

    } catch (exception $e) {
        /* Log the error message out to the log. */
        $logger->err("An error occurred while attempting to ➥
        get the contact data: {$e->getMessage()}");
    }

} else {
    /* The file does not exist... */
    printError("The specified contact cannot be found!");
}
}
?>
<hr/>
<table width="100%">
<tr>
<td><a href="welcome.php">View All Contacts</a></td>
<td><a href="newcontact.php">Add New Contact</a></td>
</tr>
</table>
</body>
</html>
```

The Log PEAR package is used in the viewcontact.php script to log errors, which occurred when the contact was being retrieved, out to a file. Other PEAR packages are used indirectly, because they're included in the AddressbookConfig and Contact classes.

Downloading the Contact

Using the HTTP_Download package, a PHP script gives users of your site the ability to download vCards for each contact (see Listing 8).

Listing 8. *downloadcontact.php*

```php
<?php

    require_once 'AddressbookConfig.php';
    require_once 'HTTP/Download.php';
    require_once 'Log.php';

    $config = AddressbookConfig::singleton();
    $dataDir = $config->getDataPath();

    $logger = &Log::factory('file', $config->getLogFilename(), 'AddressBook');
    $mask = Log::MIN($logger->stringToPriority($config->getLogLevel()));
    $logger->setMask($mask);
```

```php
/* Look for the name of the card on the query string... */
$cardName = basename($_GET["contact"]);
/* Check the name of the card for any funny business */
if (preg_match("/(\.\.|\/)/", $cardName)) {

    $logger->err(sprintf("Invalid name \"%s\"", $cardName));

} else {

    /* Now load the card up and display the contents to
     * the window.  Note:  $dataDir here has to be a directory
     * that your web server has access to read, otherwise this
     * won't work!
     */
    $fileName = $dataDir . '\\' .$cardName;

    $logger->info(sprintf("Trying to send file \"%s\"", $fileName));

    if (file_exists($fileName)) {

        $file = &new HTTP_Download();
        $result = $file->setFile($fileName, true);
        if (PEAR::isError($result)) {
            $logger->err(sprintf("An error occurred:  %s",
                $result->getMessage()));
        }
        $file->setContentDisposition(HTTP_DOWNLOAD_ATTACHMENT, $cardName);
        $file->guessContentType();
        $sendResult = $file->send();

        if (PEAR::isError($sendResult)) {
            $logger->err(sprintf("An error occurred while sending:  %s",
                $sendResult->getMessage()));
        } else {
            $logger->info(sprintf("Finished sending file \"%s\"", $fileName));
        }

        print "<a href=\"javascript:history.back();\">Back</a>";

    } else {
        /* The file does not exist... */
        $logger->err("The specified contact cannot be found!");
    }
}
?>
```

The AddressbookUtils Utility Class

The AddressbookUtils class contains a couple functions that are used throughout the site. As the pages were getting built, the same code was being copied and pasted into different parts, which is a good indication that the code can be improved to make it easier to maintain (see Listing 9).

For the most part, these functions simply format things such as the contact's display name—buildFormattedName()—and the name of the .vcf file—buildVcardName(). One of the methods, getStatesArray(), returns an array that's used to populate the selection box that contains states.

Listing 9. *AddressbookUtils.php*

```php
<?php

require_once 'Auth.php';

/**
 * AddressbookUtils contains a few utility functions used in the address
 * book application
 */
class AddressbookUtils
{

    /**
     * An array containing all of the states that will be displayed
     * in the list controls on the site
     * @access private
     */
    private static $states = array (
        'AK' => 'AK', 'AL' => 'AL', 'AR' => 'AR', 'AZ' => 'AZ', 'CA' => 'CA',
        'CO' => 'CO', 'CT' => 'CT', 'DC' => 'DC', 'DE' => 'DE', 'FL' => 'FL',
        'GA' => 'GA', 'IA' => 'IA', 'ID' => 'ID', 'IL' => 'IL', 'IN' => 'IN',
        'KS' => 'KS', 'KY' => 'KY', 'LA' => 'LA', 'MA' => 'MA', 'MD' => 'MD',
        'ME' => 'ME', 'MI' => 'MI', 'MN' => 'MN', 'MO' => 'MO', 'MS' => 'MS',
        'MT' => 'MT', 'NC' => 'NC', 'ND' => 'ND', 'NE' => 'NE', 'NH' => 'NH',
        'NJ' => 'NJ', 'NM' => 'NM', 'NV' => 'NV', 'NY' => 'NY', 'OH' => 'OH',
        'OK' => 'OK', 'OR' => 'OR', 'PA' => 'PA', 'RI' => 'RI', 'SC' => 'SC',
        'SD' => 'SD', 'TN' => 'TN', 'TX' => 'TX', 'UT' => 'UT', 'VA' => 'VA',
        'VT' => 'VT', 'WA' => 'WA', 'WI' => 'WI', 'WV' => 'WV', 'WY' => 'WY'
        );

    /**
     * Returns a formatted name for the contact
     * @param    string    $given    The given (first) name of the contact.
     * @param    string    $family   The family (last) name of the contact.
     */
```

```php
    public function buildFormattedName($given, $family)
    {
        return sprintf("%s %s", $given, $family);
    }


    /**
     * Returns the name of the vCard based on the name attributes
     * of the contact.  This will help ensure that the file is
     * named consistently and that each name can be forced to be
     * unique.
     * @param    string   $given    The given (first) name of the contact.
     * @param    string   $family   The family (last) name of the contact.
     */
    public function buildVcardName($given, $family)
    {
        return sprintf("%s_%s.vcf", $family, $given);
    }


    /**
     * Returns the array containing the US states for the select
     * boxes in the application.
     * @return    array    An array containing the 50 US states.
     */
    public static function getStatesArray()
    {
        return self::$states;
    }


    /**
     * Returns an Auth object that can be used for the site's
     * authentication.
     * @return    Auth    An Auth object.
     */
    public static function getAuth() {
        // TODO:  Make sure to change this to the proper directory!
        $passwdFile = "C:\\Application\\mypasswd";
        $a = new Auth("file", $passwdFile, 'showLogin');
        return $a;
    }

}

?>
```

Only the Auth package was used in this class to provide the ability to create and return an Auth object.

A Singleton Configuration Class

Configuration in this application is handled by a class that's implemented as a singleton. The main purpose behind putting the configuration inside this class is to hide the details from the rest of the website, much like the Contact and ContactAddress classes (see Listing 10).

The advantage of adding this extra layer of abstraction into the app is hiding the method of configuration further from the site. If you were to decide to implement XML or database configuration instead of using an INI file, the code would only have to be modified in the constructor of this object, and the site's pages could stay blissfully untouched.

Listing 10. *AddressbookConfig.php*

```php
<?php

require_once 'Config.php';

/**
 * AddressbookConfig is a singleton that allows the address book
 * site to get configuration from an object that loads the configuration
 * only once.
 */
class AddressbookConfig
{

    private static $instance;
    /**
     * An array that holds the settings for the configuration
     * @var array
     * @access private
     */
    var $settings;

    /**
     * Creates an instance of the AddressbookConfig class.
     * @access private
     */
    private function __construct()
    {
        /* Get the config from here */
        $config = new Config();
        /* TODO:  Update this location to the full filename of the INI file.  */
        $configRoot = $config->parseConfig('C:\\Path\\To\\Site\\site.ini',
            'IniFile');
        $this->settings = $configRoot->toArray();
    }
```

```php
/**
 * Returns the instance of the singleton.
 * @return    AddressbookConifg    Singleton instance of the class.
 */
public static function singleton()
{
    if (!isset(self::$instance)) {
        $c = __CLASS__;
        self::$instance = new $c;
    }

    return self::$instance;
}


/**
 * Returns the path where the data is stored.
 * @return    string    Path on file system where data is stored
 */
function getDataPath()
{
    return $this->settings['root']['Directories']['data_dir'];
}


/**
 * Returns the name of the file used for logging.
 * @return string    Name of log file.
 */
function getLogFilename()
{
    return $this->settings['root']['Logging']['log_file'];
}


/**
 * Returns the level of logging for the application.
 * @return    string    Logging level.
 */
function getLogLevel()
{
    return $this->settings['root']['Logging']['log_level'];
}
}
?>
```

The package used in the AddressbookConfig class is the Config package, which exposes methods for parsing a variety of different configuration files. For more about the Config class, see the Config chapter. The configuration file for this site looks a lot like the file listed in Listing 11.

Listing 11. *site.ini*

```
[Directories]
data_dir=D:\\Application\\AddressBook\\data

[Logging]
log_file=D:\\Application\\AddressBook\\logs\\logfile.txt
log_level=error
```

■**Note** Make sure to change these directories before you run the site, or you'll get errors. Also, the web server account should have access to read and write in the directories where these files are stored.

Forum

This project will work through the process of building a simple forum using the PEAR packages. The forum will provide for both guests and members to post messages, with members having the option of making their topics viewable to members only. A signup process will allow new users to register on the site. When posting, users will have the option of using plain text, BBCode, or wiki-style markup in their messages.

You'll use the following PEAR packages in achieving this:

- DB for connecting to the forum database

- DB_Pager and HTML_Table for displaying the forum topics and messages

- Config for reading and writing configuration options of the forum

- Crypt for making sure that displayed e-mail addresses aren't harvested by spam robots

- Text_CAPTCHA and Text_Password for the registration form

- Mail for sending new registration details and posting notifications

- Auth for allowing members to log in

- Auth_PrefManager for handling member preferences

- HTML_Form, HTML_BBCodeParse, and Text_Wiki for posting messages to the forum

To start the chapter off, you'll take a look at the database structure that you'll need to support the features of your forum. You'll build the database in MySQL, but because you're using the PEAR DB package to connect, you could use any supported PEAR DB database.

You'll then jump right in and start building the forum.

Data Structures

Because your forum will be a simple forum, you'll have a simple database structure to support it. The entire database is made up of three tables and an XML file.

Database Tables

The three database tables will hold the member login information, member preferences, and messages posted to the forum. Let's look at the structure of the individual tables.

Members

The member table will store all the details required for registered members to log in. This is the basic table structure that the Auth package uses for authenticating users. To add preferences that members can set for themselves, the Auth_PrefManager package provides a way of easily adding this on without changing the original member table structure.

The Member Table

Column Name	Type	Description
member_id	varchar	The e-mail address of this user.
member_password	varchar	The password that the member was given.

Preferences

Because you'll want to store more than simply the user's e-mail address and password, the preferences table allows you to store individual data for each user and associate it with the user's login name. As you'll see later, the Auth_PrefManager package uses the currently logged in username to look up the data you want from the preferences table.

The Preferences Table

Column Name	Type	Description
user_id	varchar	The e-mail address of this user.
pref_id	varchar	The name of the preference you want to set.
pref_value	varchar	The value of this specific preference.

Forum Postings

To keep things simple, both the top-level topics and the forum postings themselves will be stored in the same database table. One of the columns in your post table is a foreign key back to the primary key of the forum table. This allows you to stipulate that posts are responses to an initial posting. Posts that have a 0 for the topic will be designated as the top-level topics themselves.

The Forum Table

Column Name	Type	Description
forum_id	integer	The primary key for the forum table.
forum_topic	integer	Foreign key to the primary key of this table to denote both whether this posting is a top-level topic (in which case the value will be 0), or which forum_id this message is in response to.

The Forum Table

Column Name	Type	Description
forum_owner	varchar	Foreign key to the member table to denote which member posted this response.
forum_member	boolean	If this is set to true, then only members can view this posting.
forum_title	varchar	The title for this message.
forum_date	datetime	The timestamp for when this message was posted.
forum_format	varchar	A plain text string that specifies the format that this message was written in. Options can be plain text, BBCode, or wiki-style markup.
forum_message	text	The actual message itself.

The following code listing includes the MySQL SQL statements to create the table structure that we've just described:

```
CREATE TABLE member (
  member_id varchar(255) NOT NULL default '',
  member_password varchar(32) default NULL,
  PRIMARY KEY  (member_id)
);

CREATE TABLE preferences (
  user_id varchar(255) NOT NULL default '',
  pref_id varchar(32) NOT NULL default '',
  pref_value longtext NOT NULL,
  PRIMARY KEY  (user_id,pref_id)
);

CREATE TABLE forum (
  forum_id integer(11) NOT NULL auto_increment,
  forum_topic integer(11) default NULL,
  forum_owner varchar(255) default NULL,
  forum_member tinyint(1) default NULL,
  forum_title varchar(100) default NULL,
  forum_date timestamp NOT NULL default CURRENT_TIMESTAMP ➡
on update CURRENT_TIMESTAMP,
  forum_format varchar(10) default NULL,
  forum_message text,
  PRIMARY KEY  (forum_id)
);
```

This file can be found in the support files for this book as _support_forum.mysql.sql.

Config File

Because you need to store the connection parameters for the database somewhere central, you'll store these in an XML file. All the files that make up the forum will access the connection information from there so that you can change it in a single location. Because you're storing the connection parameters there, you'll also store the details of the forum itself there as well.

The Config package allows you to get the details from the XML file, and if you wanted to give an administrator the option of updating those details, it allows you to write new values to it easily as well.

The contents of the config file we're using look like this:

```
<?xml version="1.0" encoding="ISO-8859-1"?>
<conf>
  <DB>
    <type>mysql</type>
    <host>localhost</host>
    <user>forum</user>
    <pass>apress</pass>
            <database>forum</database>
  </DB>
  <Forum>
    <title>Apress Simple Forum</title>
    <heading>Apress Forum</heading>
  </Forum>
</conf>
```

We saved the file outside our webroot folder so that the casual browser cannot happen upon it by chance and see the details of our database connection. The file is named forum.config.xml.

The Forum

The forum itself is made up of only three pages and is supported by three other files. The power lies in the PEAR packages that you use.

You'll build the following three pages:

- An index.php page that will display the forum and contains the code for posting new messages

- A member.php page that members will use for logging in

- A register.php page that new members can use for registering on the forum

The three support files are as follows:

- A TrueType font file that's used in building the CAPTCHA image.

- A CSS style sheet that's used for styling the forum pages.

- A connect.php script that contains all the connection information that each of the pages will connect to the database with. This is the only support file that we'll look at in detail, and as you'll see, it uses the data from the XML file to make the connection to the database.

The first script you'll look at is connect.php, because it contains all the common code for the following pages. You'll then look at register.php and how a new user will register on the site. Once registered, you can look at the member.php page and see how the user can log in. Finally, you'll take a look at the index.php page and see how the forum itself is built.

connect.php

The connect.php script contains all the PHP code that's common to all your pages, and will be included in each of the pages.

```
<?php
require_once('DB.php');
require_once('Auth.php');
require_once('Auth/PrefManager.php');
require_once('Config.php');
```

Because all your pages are connecting to and using the database, you'll need the DB package to handle your database connections. The Auth package not only manages whether the person is logged in or not, but also provides the interface for the user to log in. Auth_PrefManager relates specific information about the user to his or her login name. This allows you to split data such as the user's personal name out from the table that contains the login details. You'll use the Config package to retrieve the forum configuration details from the XML file. You're not only storing the database connection details in there, but the forum name and title as well.

First, create a new Config object and then provide the full path to the config file for it to parse:

```
$config = new Config();
$root = & $config->parseConfig('c:/xampp/forum.config.xml', 'xml');
```

The $root variable now contains a Config_Container, but for your purposes it will be easier to work with an array, so the toArray method returns an associative array of the details to you.

```
$settings = $root->toArray();
```

From the root of the XML file, you have a conf item, and then within that, a DB section and a Forum section. At this time, you only want the details from the DB section to build a DSN string:

```
$dsn = $settings['root']['conf']['DB']['type'] . '://'
        . $settings['root']['conf']['DB']['user'] . ':'
        . $settings['root']['conf']['DB']['pass'] . '@'
        . $settings['root']['conf']['DB']['host']  . '/'
        . $settings['root']['conf']['DB']['database'];
```

You should have the following DSN string at this point:

```
mysql://forum:après@localhost/forum
```

You can then use this to connect to the database:

```
$DBoptions = array(
    'debug'        => 2,
    'portability' => DB_PORTABILITY_ALL,
);
$db = & DB::connect($dsn, $DBoptions);
if (PEAR::isError($db)) {
    die($db->getMessage());
}
```

You'll always want to know if a user is logged in or not, so you'll always create a new Auth object. The Auth object takes an array of options that specify which database to use to look up user details, the name of the table that contains the login info, and which fields refer to the username and password columns:

```
$Authoptions = array(
    'dsn' -> $dsn,
    'table' => 'member',
    'usernamecol' => 'member_id',
    'passwordcol' => 'member_password'
);
$auth = new Auth('DB', $Authoptions);
```

At the same time, you can create a new Auth_PrefManager object so that you can return the currently logged in user's name:

```
$Prefoptions = array('serialize' => true);
$prefmanager = new Auth_PrefManager($dsn, $Prefoptions);
?>
```

register.php

The register.php page takes care of new user registrations. In this page, you have to provide a form to capture new user details, stop spurious registrations by including a CAPTCHA element, and mail the login details to the new user.

As you might recall from the "Images and Text" section of this book, the Text_CAPTCHA package uses a session variable to store the unique phrase from one page to the next. Therefore, the first thing you need to do is start the session:

```
<?php
session_start();
```

You then include the connect.php script, as this contains all your database connections and other common packages:

```
require_once('connect.php');
```

The HTML_QuickForm package lets you quickly build a form to capture the user details, and provides you with client-side validation at the same time. You'll use the Text_Password package to generate a random password for the new user, which you'll then mail through to the user:

```
require_once 'HTML/QuickForm.php';
require_once 'Text/CAPTCHA.php';
require_once 'Text/Password.php';
require_once 'Mail.php';
require_once 'Mail/mime.php';
```

You need to create the HTML_QuickForm object right at the top of the page, because even though you'll only display it later on, it's also initialized to handle the data submitted by the form:

```
$form = new HTML_QuickForm('registerform', 'post', $_SERVER['REQUEST_URI']);
```

You can then test to see if the form has been submitted and if it's valid:

```
if ($form->isSubmitted()) {
            if ($form->validate()) {
                    $data = $form->getSubmitValues();
```

If it's all OK, you retrieve the submitted data and store it in the $data array. You then need to test that the phrase submitted as the CAPTCHA phrase matches the one stored in the session variable. The form field that contains the CAPTCHA phrase is a text input type called CAPTCHA:

```
                    if (isset($_POST['CAPTCHA']) &&
                            isset($_SESSION['secretCAPTCHA'])
                            && strlen($_POST['CAPTCHA']) > 0
                            && strlen($_SESSION['secretCAPTCHA']) > 0
                            && $_POST['CAPTCHA'] == $_SESSION['secretCAPTCHA']) {
```

At this point you can go ahead and add the new user because everything checks out. First, remove the image that was created by the CAPTCHA package when the form was displayed:

```
                    unlink('captcha_tmp/'.md5($_SESSION['secretCAPTCHA']) . '.jpg');
```

Then, use the Text_Password package to create a pronounceable password:

```
                    $password = Text_Password::create();
```

You can then add a new record to the member table in the database, using the e-mail address provided and the password generated as the member ID and password:

```
                    $sql = "INSERT INTO member (member_id, member_password)
                    VALUES ('" . $db->escapeSimple($data['email'])
                    . "', '" . md5($password) . "')";
                    $db->query($sql);
```

You also need to store the user's real name and the member level the user is at in the preferences table. In the connect.php script, you initialized the Auth_PrefManager object to always serialize data. You could do this manually and insert the data using SQL, but the Auth_PrefManager object already has the methods to do that for you. The login name for the user is used as the identifier for the preferences. Because this is the e-mail address, store that in a variable, and then use the setPref method of Auth_PrefManager to set the preferences for this user:

```
$username = htmlspecialchars($db->escapeSimple($data['email']));
$prefmanager->setPref
($username, 'name', $db->escapeSimple($data['name']));
$prefmanager->setPref($username, 'level', '1');
```

At this point, the new user has been created in the database and his or her preferences have been saved. You now need to send the user an e-mail so that the user knows what his or her password is. We'll use the Mime mail package to send an e-mail in both text and HTML formats. First, set up the text message. Remember, when using heredoc syntax and embedding complex variables, you need to surround the entire variable name with braces:

```
$text = <<<EOD
Welcome to the forums {$data['name']}
You can log in using the username {$data['email']} and
the password $password
EOD;
```

Then set up the HTML mail portion in the same way, and create the Mime_mail object:

```
$html = '<html><body><p>Welcome to the forums '.$data['name']
.'</p><p>You can log in using the username '
.$data['email'].' and the password '
.$password.'</p></body></html>';
$crlf = "\n";
$hdrs = array(
'From'    => 'admin@apressforum.com',
'Subject' => 'Your new forum username and password'
);
$mime = new Mail_mime($crlf);
$mime->setTXTBody($text);
$mime->setHTMLBody($html);
```

Retrieve the message body and the headers, create a new Mail object, and send the mail. The SMTP server we're using to test this is on the same machine as the web server, so we don't need to pass an options array to the constructor to set a specific SMTP server.

If you need to connect to a remote SMTP server, the SMTP section of this book covered the options you'll need to pass to the SMTP constructor function:

```
$body = $mime->get();
$hdrs = $mime->headers($hdrs);
$mail =& Mail::factory('smtp');
$mail->send($data['email'], $hdrs, $body);
```

Once the mail has been sent, send the user back to the login page:

```
header('Location: member.php');
} else {
```

The following message appears if the validation of the CAPTCHA image fails. You'll display it above the form later on in the page.

```
$message = "Oops, the code you entered did not ➡
            match the one in the image.  Please try again";
        }
    }
}
?>
```

This portion of the page will be displayed the first time the page loads, and if the CAPTCHA validation fails:

```
<!DOCTYPE html PUBLIC "-//W3C//DTD XHTML 1.0 Transitional//EN"
            "http://www.w3.org/TR/xhtml1/DTD/xhtml1-transitional.dtd">
<html>
<head>
```

Here's your first look at the Forum section of the XML config file. The contents of the title tag are specified by the title element in the config XML file:

```
<title><?php echo $settings['root']['conf']['Forum']['title']; ?></title>
<link rel="stylesheet" type="text/css" href="forum.css">
</head>
<body>
```

The main heading for all the forum pages also comes out of the config file:

```
<h1><a href="index.php">
<?php echo $settings['root']['conf']['Forum']|'heading']; ?></a></h1>
<h2>New member Registration</h2>
<p><a href="member.php">Return to login page</a></p>
<?php
```

If the validation of the CAPTCHA failed, $message will be set, so you can display it if it exists:

```
If (issel($message)) {
            echo "<p><strong>" . $message . "</strong></p>";
        }
```

This next section of the code simply creates a new CAPTCHA image and writes it to disk so that you can display it in the form a bit later in the page. The font file you specify in the options array must exist on the file system in the location you give. In this case, the font file is in the same directory as the PHP script. You'll need to supply and upload the font file you wish to use.

```
$options = array(
        'font_size' => 32,
    'font_path' => './',
    'font_file' => 'arial.ttf'
);
$formCAPTCHA = Text_CAPTCHA::factory('Image');
$result = $formCAPTCHA->init(300, 120, null, $options);
```

You then store the phrase that has been written in the image in a session variable so that you can check it after the form has been submitted:

```
$_SESSION['secretCAPTCHA'] = $formCAPTCHA->getPhrase();
```

The actual image data is returned and written to a temporary folder:

```
$imageCAPTCHA = $formCAPTCHA->getCAPTCHAAsJPEG();
file_put_contents
('captcha_tmp/'.md5($formCAPTCHA->getPhrase()) . '.jpg', $imageCAPTCHA);
```

The form needs elements for the new user's name, the user's e-mail address, and a field for the user to type in the code he or she can see in the CAPTCHA image:

```
$form->addElement('text','name', 'Name:');
$form->addElement('text', 'email', 'Email Address:');
$form->addElement('image', 'CAPTCHAimg',
                'captcha_tmp/'.md5($formCAPTCHA->getPhrase()).'.jpg');
$form->addElement('text', 'CAPTCHA', 'Registration code:');
$form->addElement('submit', null, 'Submit');
$form->applyFilter('name', 'trim');
$form->applyFilter('email', 'trim');
```

You want to make sure that users provide a name, a valid e-mail address, and at least something in the CAPTCHA field. You cannot test the validity of the CAPTCHA client side, as this will expose the CAPTCHA phrase in the page, which will then expose it to spam form submission scripts.

```
$form->addRule('name', 'Please provide your name', 'required', null,
            'client');
$form->addRule('email', 'Please provide an email address', 'required',
            null, 'client');
$form->addRule('email', 'Please enter a valid email address', 'email',
            null, 'client');
$form->addRule('CAPTCHA','Please enter the code in the image',
            'required', null, 'client');
?>
<p>
<?php
        $form->display();
?>
</p>
</body>
</html>
```

member.php

You use the member.php script to log the user in. It simply displays a login form and a link through to the new user registration form.

```php
<?php
require_once('connect.php');
require_once 'HTML/QuickForm.php';
```

By default, when starting the Auth object, it will display a login form if you aren't already logged in. We'd rather use our own login form, so before you start, tell it not to show the login form:

```php
$auth->setShowLogin(false);
```

The start method tests to see if this user is logged in or not, or authenticates the user if the form has been submitted:

```php
$auth->start();
```

You'll also use the same page to log the user out, so if the user has come to this page and is logged in, but hasn't submitted the login form, you simply log the user out and redirect him or her back to the main page:

```php
if ($_POST['action'] != "login" && $auth->checkAuth()) {
    $auth->logout();
            header("Location: index.php");
```

If the user has submitted the form and has managed to log in, you also redirect him or her to the main page. The else portion is if the user isn't logged in—either coming to this page directly, or after submitting the form but failing to log in:

```php
} elseif ($_POST['action'] == 'login' && $auth->checkAuth()) {
            header("Location: index.php");
} else {
?>
```

This portion simply contains the form users will use to log in:

```html
<!DOCTYPE html PUBLIC "-//W3C//DTD XHTML 1.0 Transitional//EN"
            "http://www.w3.org/TR/xhtml1/DTD/xhtml1-transitional.dtd">

<html>
<head>
<title><?php echo $settings['root']['conf']['Forum']['title']; ?></title>
<link rel="stylesheet" type="text/css" href="forum.css">
</head>
<body>
<h1><a href="index.php">
<?php echo $settings['root']['conf']['Forum']['heading']; ?></a></h1>
<h2>Member Login</h2>
<a href="index.php">Back to forum</a>
<p>
<?php
$form = new HTML_QuickForm('loginForm', 'post', $_SERVER['REQUEST_URI']);
$form->addElement('hidden', 'action', 'login');
```

When creating your own form and not using the standard Auth login form, the field that contains the login name needs to be called username, and the password field must be called password:

```
$form->addElement('text', 'username', 'Login name:');
$form->addElement('password', 'password', 'Password:');
$form->addElement('submit', null, 'Submit');
$form->applyFilter('username', 'trim');
$form->applyFilter('password', 'trim');
$form->addRule('username', 'Please enter your username', 'required', null,
    'client');
$form->display();
?>
</p>
<p>If you would like to register, <a href="register.php">click here</a></p>
</body>
</html>
<?php
}
?>
```

index.php

The bulk of the work that happens in the forum takes place in the index.php page. Because of the way that the forum database is structured, both top-level topics and the response posts all live in the same table. This makes the database queries a lot simpler and easier to manage. Let's take a look at the code, starting with the first line, which simply includes the connect.php code we created earlier:

```
<?php
require_once('connect.php');
```

Because there's a lot going on in this page, you need to include quite a few PEAR packages. To avoid having to scroll endlessly down a page, the DB_Pager package will allow you to break the longer forum threads into a number of pages. You'll use the HTML_Table package for displaying all the forum postings, and the e-mail addresses of the forum posters will be hidden using the HTML_Crypt package. The Text_Wiki and HTML_BBCodeParser packages will give users of the forum a number of different ways to mark up their forum posts.

```
require_once 'DB/Pager.php';
require_once 'HTML/QuickForm.php';
require_once 'HTML/Table.php';
require_once 'HTML/Crypt.php';
require_once 'Text/Wiki.php';
require_once 'HTML/BBCodeParser.php';
$form = new HTML_QuickForm('messageform', 'post', $_SERVER['REQUEST_URI']);
```

You'll notice that we're using the REQUEST_URI server variable for the action of the form, and not PHP_SELF. We're using REQUEST_URI because when the user starts navigating into forum topics, there will be a query string in the URL, and you'll want to retain this after the form has been submitted.

The form that we're talking about is a form to post a new forum message.

The title field will be used as the topic title, or title for any response messages. On the main page, only the topics are displayed. You need to navigate into that topic to see the message and any response messages. The message format can be either plain text, BBCode-style markup, or wiki text. If the Members Only checkbox is checked, that message will only be visible to members of the forum who are logged in. A hidden form field stores the current topic you're viewing, and therefore the ID of the topic you're replying to:

```
if ($form->isSubmitted()) {
            if ($form->validate()) {
                        $data = $form->getSubmitValues();
```

If the form has been submitted and validated, the forum posting is added to the forum table:

```
$sql = "INSERT INTO forum
            (forum_topic, forum_owner, forum_member,
            forum_title, forum_format, forum_message)
            VALUES (" . $db->escapeSimple($data['topic']) . ",'"

            . $db->escapeSimple($auth->getUsername()) . "', "
            . (($data['members']==1)?$db->escapeSimple
            ($data['members']):0)
            . "', '" . $db->escapeSimple($data['title']) . "', '"

            . $db->escapeSimple($data['format']) . "', '"
            . $db->escapeSimple($data['message']) . "')";
                        $db->query($sql);
            }
}
?>
```

The rest of the logic in the page is involved with what's displayed:

```
<!DOCTYPE html PUBLIC "-//W3C//DTD XHTML 1.0 Transitional//EN"
            "http://www.w3.org/TR/xhtml1/DTD/xhtml1-transitional.dtd">
<html>
<head>
<title><?php echo $settings['root']['conf']['Forum']['title']; ?></title>
<link rel="stylesheet" type="text/css" href="forum.css">
</head>
<body>
<h1><a href="index.php">
<?php echo $settings['root']['conf']['Forum']['heading']; ?></a></h1>
```

Right at the top of the page, you provide a link to log in, or if the user is already logged in, a link to log out. In the logout link, you include the name that the user gave at registration. In both cases, you set the user level for the current user. A guest will have a user level of 0:

```
<a href="member.php"><?php
if ($auth->getAuth()) {
        echo "Log Out " . $prefmanager->getPref($auth->getUsername(), "name");
        $member_level = $prefmanager->getPref($auth->getUsername(), "level");
} else {
        echo "Log In";
        $member_level = 0;

}
?></a>
<hr />
```

This page will be used to display two types of pages. The first type is the main page when no topic has been selected. Here you'll only display a list of topics. Once a user has navigated into a topic, you need to display the full message for the topic the user has selected, as well as any response messages. The following piece of code returns the data for the current topic. If there's no current topic (topic = 0), no records will be returned and nothing will be displayed. In the query, you also return the name of the person who posted the message:

```
<?php
$current = & $db->query('SELECT forum_id, forum_owner, forum_title, forum_date,
                         forum_format, forum_message, pref_value from forum,
                         preferences where forum_owner = user_id AND
                         pref_id="name" AND forum_id='
                         .((isset($_GET['topic']))?$_GET['topic']:0));
if (PEAR::isError($current)) {
    die($current->getMessage());
}
```

You then create a new HTML_Table object to display the topic details. We've given the table an ID of MainTopic, and the CSS file uses this to provide advanced styling to the table:

```
$tableAttrs = array("width" => "600", "id" => "MainTopic", "cellspacing" => "0");
$table = new HTML_Table($tableAttrs);
$table -> setAutoGrow(true);
$table -> setAutoFill("");
```

The $rowCount variable is used throughout the table code in this page to keep track of where you're adding new data:

```
$rowCount = 0;
```

You then display the title of the forum posting and the date and time that it was added:

```
while ($cRow = & $current->fetchRow(DB_FETCHMODE_ASSOC)) {
        $table->setCellContents($rowCount, 0, "<strong>" . $cRow['forum_title']

                                          . "</strong>");
        $table->setCellContents($rowCount, 1, strftime("%A, %d %B, %H:%M",
                                          strtotime($cRow['forum_date'])));
```

Besides the style ID that's applied to the table as a whole, specific style classes are also applied to the individual table rows depending on what kind of data they're displaying. You use the mHead class to denote the heading row of the main topic table:

```
$table->setRowAttributes($rowCount, array('class' => 'mHead'));
$rowCount++;
```

If the current user is a member, then you can include the e-mail address of the person who posted the message. The HTML_Crypt object provides encryption of the e-mail address:

```
if ($auth->getAuth()) {
            $crypt = new HTML_Crypt($cRow['forum_owner']);
            $crypt->addMailTo();
            $mail=$crypt->getScript();
            $table->setCellContents($rowCount, 0,
                unserialize($cRow['pref_value']). ' ('. $mail .')');
} else {
            $table->setCellContents($rowCount, 0,
                unserialize($cRow['pref_value']));
}
```

This second row in the table contains info about the poster, so it's given the mInfo class:

```
$table->setRowAttributes($rowCount, array('class' => 'mInfo'));
$rowCount++;
```

The last row contains the message itself. You need to check what format the users used when posting the message, so that you can convert it from its native format into XHTML. BBCode is parsed into XHTML, wiki-style markup is transformed into XHTML, and line breaks in a plain text posting are converted into HTML br tags:

```
switch($cRow['forum_format']) {
        case 'bbcode':
                $bbcode = new HTML_BBCodeParser();
                $bbcode->setText($cRow['forum_message']);
                $bbcode->parse();
                $message = $bbcode->getParsed();
                break;
        case 'wiki':
                $wiki = & Text_Wiki::factory();
                $message = $wiki->transform($cRow['forum_message']);
                break;
        case 'text':
        default:
                $message = nl2br($cRow['forum_message']);
                break;
}
```

You then set the contents of the cell, set the colspan to 2, and apply an mBody-style class to it:

```
        $table->setCellContents($rowCount, 0, $message);
        $table->setCellAttributes($rowCount, 0, array('colspan' => '2'));
        $table->setRowAttributes($rowCount, array('class' => 'mBody'));
    }
echo $table->toHTML();
?>
```

Now you can display the list of topics, and optionally their messages. To set the page up so that DB_Pager can split the results into individual pages, you need to limit the number of records returned by the query. This works with two values—an offset that specifies where to begin returning the records from, and a limit—how many records to return. The offset will be passed on the query string called from, so you can test to see if it's there, and if it's not, set it to 0. The limit of 2 is simply for demonstration purposes so that we don't have to fill up a page of meaningless posts so that you can see how it works!

```
<p>
<?php
$from = (isset($_GET['from']))?$_GET['from']:0;
$limit = 2;
```

The forum_topic will either be 0 for top-level forum topics, or have the topic ID of the parent topic. You also want to order the forum differently depending on whether you're viewing a list of only topics (latest post at the top of the page) or the responses to a specific topic (latest post last). You use the ternary operator to include the relevant SQL for each of these parts of the query:

```
$sql = 'SELECT forum_id, forum_owner, forum_title, forum_date, forum_format,
            forum_message, pref_value from forum, preferences
            where forum_owner = user_id AND pref_id="name"
            AND forum_topic='.((isset($_GET['topic']))?$_GET['topic']:0).'
            AND forum_member <= ' . $member_level . '
            ORDER BY forum_date '.((isset($_GET['topic']))?'ASC':'DESC');
```

DB_Pager needs to know how many rows would have been returned if no limit was placed on the query, so first you pass the SQL to a normal query and save the number of rows returned:

```
$cRes = & $db->query($sql);
$nRows = $cRes->numRows();
```

You can then use the limitQuery method to return only the number of rows you want to display on the page:

```
$res = & $db->limitQuery($sql, $from, $limit);
if (PEAR::isError($res)) {
    die($res->getMessage());
}
```

You then build a table to display the results:

```
$tableAttrs = array("width" => "600", "id" => "topics", "cellspacing" => "0");
$table = new HTML_Table($tableAttrs);
$table -> setAutoGrow(true);
$table -> setAutoFill("");
$rowCount = 0;
while ($row = & $res->fetchRow(DB_FETCHMODE_ASSOC)) {
```

When displaying this table, you're constantly going to have to check if you're displaying a list of topics or the responses to a topic, as you'll display things differently depending on the situation. Here you're displaying the topic of the posting, but if you're viewing a topic, you won't link anywhere, and if you're viewing a list of topics, you'll need to link to that topic to view the messages within it:

```
if (isset($_GET['topic'])) {
        $table->setCellContents($rowCount, 0, $row['forum_title']);
} else {
        $table->setCellContents($rowCount, 0, "<a href='index.php?topic="
                    . $row['forum_id'] . "'>" . $row['forum_title'] . "</a>");
}
$table->setCellContents($rowCount, 1, strftime
                    ("%A, %d %B, %H:%M",strtotime($row['forum_date'])));
$table->setRowAttributes($rowCount, array('class' => 'sHead'));
$rowCount++;
```

Just as you did with the main topic table earlier, you only want to display e-mail addresses to logged in members, and even then you want to encrypt them:

```
if ($auth->getAuth()) {
        $crypt = new HTML_Crypt($row['forum_owner']);
        $crypt->addMailTo();
        $mail=$crypt->getScript();
        $table->setCellContents
            ($rowCount, 0, unserialize($row['pref_value'])
                                            . ' ('. $mail .')');
} else {
        $table->setCellContents
            ($rowCount, 0, unserialize($row['pref_value']));
}
```

If there's no topic, you're viewing a list of topics, and you should display how many responses you have to that topic:

```
if (!isset($_GET['topic'])) {
        $countResult = $db->query
            ('SELECT * FROM forum WHERE forum_topic = ' . $row['forum_id']);
        $table->setCellContents($rowCount, 1, $countResult->numRows()
                    . ' replies');
}
$table->setRowAttributes($rowCount, array('class' => 'sInfo'));
$rowCount++;
```

This next row displays the message itself, and you only want this to display if you're viewing an actual topic:

```
if (isset($_GET['topic'])) {
        switch($row['forum_format']) {
                case 'bbcode':
                        $bbcode = new HTML_BBCodeParser();
                        $bbcode->setText($row['forum_message']);
                        $bbcode->parse();
                        $message = $bbcode->getParsed();
                        break;
                case 'wiki':
                        $wiki = & Text_Wiki::factory();
                        $message = $wiki->transform($row['forum_message']);
                        break;
                case 'text':
                default:
                        $message = nl2br($row['forum_message']);
                        break;
        }
        $table->setCellContents($rowCount, 0, $message);
        $table->setCellAttributes($rowCount, 0, array('colspan' => '2'));
        $table->setRowAttributes($rowCount, array('class' => 'sBody'));
        $rowCount++;
    }
}
echo $table->toHTML();
?>
```

Now that all the topics and messages have been displayed, you need to include some navigation to be able to view the additional pages of messages. The limited data was displayed by using the limitQuery method. All that DB_Pager does is build an array of data that you can use to build the navigation around the specific limits you placed on the query:

```
<?php
$data = DB_Pager::getData($from, $limit, $nRows);
$tableAttrs = array("width" => "600", "id" => "navigation", "cellspacing" => "0");
$table = new HTML_Table($tableAttrs);
$table -> setAutoGrow(true);
$table -> setAutoFill("");
```

The $data array contains a pages key that contains an array itself of page numbers and offsets for each of those pages. With your settings of a limit of 2, you'd expect the offset for page 1 to be 0, page 2 to be 2, and for page 3 to be 4. This gives you two records per page, as per our limit. You can simply loop through this array and display a link to each of the individual pages:

```
foreach ($data['pages'] as $key => $value) {
```

Because you might or might not have a topic value in the query string, you need to pull apart the query string and re-create it so that you have a well-formed query string for each of your links.

First you grab the current query string parameters from the $_GET array:

```
$qArray = $_GET;
```

You then replace the current from parameter with the one for this current page:

```
$qArray['from'] = $value;
$qArrayTemp = array();
```

You then create a new indexed array and loop through the copy of the $_GET array, adding key–value pairs to it as a single string separated by an = sign:

```
foreach($qArray as $qKey => $qValue) {
            $qArrayTemp[] = $qKey . '=' . $qValue;
}
```

You then concatenate the array back together using the implode function, and join the individual elements with the & symbol. You can then tack this onto the end of a URL with a ? symbol, and you'll have a well-formed query string, no matter how many parameters there were before and how many you added now:

```
$qString = implode('&', $qArrayTemp);
```

You then test to see if you're on the current page, in which case you don't link to yourself. Otherwise, link to the page:

```
if ($_GET['from'] == $value) {
            $table->setCellContents(0, intval($key), "Page " . $key );
} else {
            $table->setCellContents(0, intval($key), "<a href='"
                    . $_SERVER['PHP_SELF'] . "?"
                    . $qString . "'>Page " . $key . "</a>");
}
}
```

Then, display the navigation table:

```
echo $table->toHTML();
?>
</p>
<hr />
```

Because you only want to allow logged in members to post, you check to see if the member is authorized, and if so, display a form to add a new posting:

```php
<?php
if ($auth->getAuth()) {
?>
<h2>Post new</h2>
<?php
        $form->addElement('text', 'title', 'Title:');
        $form->addElement
                ('hidden', 'topic', (isset($_GET['topic'])?$_GET['topic']:0));
        $form->addElement('select', 'format', 'Message Format', array
                ('text' => 'Plain Text', 'bbcode' => 'BBCode', 'wiki' => 'Wiki'));
        $form->addElement('checkbox', 'members', 'Members Only:');
        $form->addElement('textarea', 'message', 'Message:');
        $form->addElement('submit', null, 'Submit');
        $form->applyFilter('title', 'trim');
        $form->applyFilter('email', 'trim');
        $form->addRule
                ('title', 'Please provide a title', 'required', null, 'client');
        $form->addRule
                ('message', 'Please enter a message', 'required', null, 'client');
        $form->display();?>
<?php
}
?>
</body>
</html>
```

The SQL that makes up the query for returning the messages uses the current member level to decide whether to include the record or not. Because new members are set with a member level of 1, this gives you the opportunity to create new levels of members that can post messages that only members of their level or higher can view.

You also had some code that transformed the code depending on the format that you added it in:

```php
switch($row['forum_format']) {
        case 'bbcode':
                $bbcode = new HTML_BBCodeParser();
                $bbcode->setText($row['forum_message']);
                $bbcode->parse();
                $message = $bbcode->getParsed();
                break;
        case 'wiki':
                $wiki = & Text_Wiki::factory();
                $message = $wiki->transform($row['forum_message']);
                break;
        case 'text':
        default:
                $message = nl2br($row['forum_message']);
                break;
}
```

Web Calendar

This application allows users to register, log in, and create personal appointments that can be displayed on a web-enabled calendar that also displays holidays. Users can see free and busy information while they're creating the appointments so they don't double-book themselves. All-day appointments can be created that allow users to easily block off an entire day for an appointment.

You'll use the following packages in this project:

- Auth

- DB

- DB_DataObject

- Date

- Date_Holidays

- HTML_Form

- HTML_AJAX

Because this is a database-driven site, it's composed of database scripts to build the database and tables, as well as PHP files. The site contains seven PHP files written from scratch, and uses one file that's automatically generated for dealing with data objects.

Because this application relies on the data, it's best to start out looking at how to build the database and its tables. MySQL was used in the making of this application, but the application will also work with any database that the PEAR DB package supports.

Building the Database

The data for the calendar application is stored in a MySQL database. There are only two tables. One of them contains user information and the other contains the appointments. The database in this project is called calendar and can be created with the following SQL:

```
CREATE DATABASE calendar;
```

The first table contains the user information. The Auth package will read user information out of this table using the DB data container, which uses the PEAR DB package. The Auth DB container has a default schema that it will use. However, it also allows the name of the table and columns containing the username and password, which allows a custom table to be used for user information. The following SQL creates the users table used in the calendar application:

```
CREATE TABLE users (
  user_id varchar(255) NOT NULL default '',
  password varchar(1024) NOT NULL default '',
  PRIMARY KEY (user_id)
);
```

The user_id column contains the login name for the user and will be used to identify the user uniquely, because no two users can share the same login. Unless you absolutely need to use *surrogate* keys (that is, arbitrary indexes) for performance reasons, use the *natural* keys (keys based on data) to keep your data in integrity. The database used by the calendar application is an example of one where performance won't be an issue unless it's running on modest hardware. The surrogate key versus the natural key debate is a hotly discussed one in data circles, so now after voicing our preference we'll move on to the appointments table.

The second table contains the information about the appointments for each user. It keeps track of the start and end dates and times, as well as a description about the event, the ID of the user that owns the event, and a flag that tells us if it's an all-day event. The SQL used to create the table that contains the appointments is listed here:

```
CREATE TABLE appointments (
  appointmentid int(10) unsigned NOT NULL auto_increment,
  start_date datetime NOT NULL default '0000-00-00 00:00:00',
  end_date datetime NOT NULL default '0000-00-00 00:00:00',
  description text NOT NULL,
  user_id varchar(255) NOT NULL default '',
  is_allday tinyint(1) NOT NULL default '0',
  PRIMARY KEY  (appointmentid)
) ;
```

After running these two SQL statements, two new tables will be created in the database and are ready to be accessed. In this application, the code to add new entries and get information from these tables is nearly eliminated by the PEAR packages. As you'll see later, the Auth package is used to add users into the users table, and also to verify that a user exists. The DB_DataObject package is used to add new entries into the appointments table.

Building the Data Objects

The DB_DataObject package allows developers to add data container objects quickly to simplify CRUD (create, read, update, delete) operations without having to write the cumbersome and boring code that actually runs SQL statements. The creation of these objects is a huge time saver when building data-dependent applications, and was one of the reasons that this application was built so quickly.

If you're the type of person who likes to skip reading documentation and prefers to go straight to hacking away at INI files or PHP scripts, it's important that you *restrain yourself* when dealing with the DB_DataObject package. The documentation tells you of a script that's included with the package that will generate your objects and INI files for you based off a simple starting configuration. If you skip that step and go straight to building the objects, you'll end up spending more time working with the objects than you would have if you'd written all the CRUD code yourself. One of the authors of this book is speaking from experience in this matter. Eh, hem.

The script included with DB_DataObject is called `createTables.php` and is located in the package's directory, which is `DB/DataObject` (or `DB\DataObject` in Windows), relative to the PEAR directory where the packages are placed. As discussed in the DB_DataObject chapter, all you have to do is supply the name of the application's base INI file to the script and it will create the data objects and schema INI files for you. This base INI file contains information about your database and locations of files. The INI file for the calendar application is shown in Listing 1.

Listing 1. *site.ini*

```
[DB_DataObject]

database      = mysql://calendar:secret@localhost/calendar
schema_location = /path/to/DataObjects
class_location  = /path/to/DataObjects
require_prefix  = DataObjects/
class_prefix    = DataObjects_
```

The database key is set to the URI of the database, as understood by the PEAR DB package. The `schema_location` key defines where the schema files (INI files that describe the tables in the database) are located, and the `class_location` key defines where the new classes will be located. Lastly, `require_prefix` and `class_prefix` specify the directory location used before the class names in `require_once` statements and the name prepended to the name of the class.

The script creates data objects for the `users` table, but it really doesn't matter. The data objects to access users won't be used in the application, because the Auth package is used to do all the user management. The class was left in the project, though, in case it would be used in the future.

The class you'll use is the newly created `DataObjects_Appointments` class, which is shown in its entirety in Listing 2.

Listing 2. *Appointments.php*

```php
<?php
/**
 * Table Definition for appointments
 */
require_once 'DB/DataObject.php';

class DataObjects_Appointments extends DB_DataObject
{
    ###START_AUTOCODE
    /* the code below is auto generated - do not remove the above tag */
```

```
    public $__table = 'appointments';                    // table name
    public $appointmentid;                    // int(10)  not_null primary_key ➡
    unsigned auto_increment
    public $start_date;                       // datetime(19)  not_null binary
    public $end_date;                         // datetime(19)  not_null binary
    public $description;                      // blob(65535)  not_null blob
    public $user_id;                          // string(255)  not_null
    public $is_allday;                        // int(1)  not_null

    /* Static get */
    function staticGet($k,$v=NULL) { return ➡
    DB_DataObject::staticGet('DataObjects_Appointments',$k,$v); }

    /* the code above is auto generated - do not remove the tag below */
    ###END_AUTOCODE
}
```

The calendar.ini file that's created (the schema INI file has the same name as the database) looks like the one in Listing 3.

Listing 3. *calendar.ini*

```
[appointments]
appointmentid = 129
start_date = 142
end_date = 142
description = 194
user_id = 130
is_allday = 145

[appointments__keys]
appointmentid = N

[preferences]
user_id = 130
pref_id = 130
pref_value = 194

[preferences__keys]
user_id = K
pref_id = K

[users]
user_id = 130
password = 130

[users__keys]
user_id = K
```

Now the data objects are ready for their use.

Allowing Users to Register

A register page allows users to be added easily to the site (see Listing 4). The register page uses the Auth package, attached to the database with the DB container, to add a new user. Although you have data objects that can be used to insert new users, the Auth package has some nice features that make it a better choice for adding users. Namely, when the password is stored it will be encrypted automatically, whereas if the data objects were used instead, the password would have to be encrypted first.

Listing 4. *register.php*

```php
<?php

require_once 'Auth.php';
require_once 'HTML/Form.php';

/**
 * Validates the form's data.
 */
function validate()
{
    /* Do some sort of validation here, like on the e-mail
     * address...
     */
    return true;
}


/**
 * Processes the data in the form.
 */
function process($a)
{
    /* We first validate it to see if it is a valid e-mail address */

    $result = $a->addUser($_POST['username'], $_POST['password']);

    if (PEAR::isError($result)) {
        // $errs = array('Error!');
        return false;
    } else {
        // $errs = array('User added successfully!');
        return true;
    }
}
```

```php
/**
 * Displays the form to the user
 */
function display()
{
    print <<<END
<!DOCTYPE html PUBLIC "-//W3C//DTD XHTML 1.0 Strict//EN"
"http://www.w3.org/TR/xhtml1/DTD/xhtml1-strict.dtd">
<html xmlns="http://www.w3.org/1999/xhtml">
<head>
<title>Web Calendar Application - Login</title>
<style type="text/css">
    body { font-family:sans-serif;font-size:small; }
</style>
</head>
<body bgcolor="#FFFFFF" text="#000000">
END;

    /* Set up custom options here, as we are not using the default
     * schema for database authentication.  Create script for our
     * table is:
     *
     * CREATE TABLE users (
     *     user_id VARCHAR(255) NOT NULL,
     *     password VARCHAR(1024) NOT NULL
     *     );
     */
    $form = new HTML_Form(htmlspecialchars($_SERVER['PHP_SELF']), 'post');
    $form->addText('username', "Login (email address):");
    $form->addPasswordOne('password', 'Password:');
    $form->addSubmit('submit', 'Register');
    $form->display();

    print <<<END
</body>
</html>
END;
}

/* Alternatively, use a class that returns the auth statically
 * or a class that returns the Auth options.  See the Addressbook
 * project for an example.
 *
 * TODO:  Make sure to change your DSN here to be the
 * appropriate one for your database.  See the DB chapter for more
 * information about DSNs.
 *
```

```
    */

$authOptions = array (
    'dsn' => 'mysql://calendar:secret@localhost/calendar',
    'table' => 'users',
    'usernamecol' => 'user_id',
    'passwordcol' => 'password',
    'crypttype' => 'md5'
);

$a = new Auth('DB', $authOptions);

if ($_SERVER['REQUEST_METHOD'] == 'POST') {
    if (validate()) {
        if (process($a))
        {
            print 'The user has been added!';
        } else {
            print 'An error occured while processing the form!';
        }
        display();
    } else {
        print 'The form is invalid!';
        display();
    }
} else {
    display();
}

?>
```

Creating a Login Form

The login form is a typical username and password entry form (see Listing 5). It uses the Auth
and HTML_Form packages to log the user in to the application and to display the login form if
the user isn't already authenticated. The user, once logged in, is forwarded to the calendar.php
page.

Listing 5. *login.php*

```
<?php

require_once 'Auth.php';
require_once 'HTML/Form.php';
```

```
function showLogin() {
    /* Use the HTML_Form class to show our login form
     */
    print "<html><head></head><body>";
    $form = new HTML_Form(htmlspecialchars($_SERVER['PHP_SELF']), 'post');
    $form->addText('username', 'Username:');
    $form->addPasswordOne('password', 'Password:');
    $form->addSubmit('submit', 'Login');
    $form->display();
    print "You are not currently logged in!";
    print "</body></html>";
}

/* Set up custom options here, as we are not using the default
 * schema for database authentication.  Create script for our
 * table is:
 *
 * CREATE TABLE users (
 *     user_id VARCHAR(255) NOT NULL,
 *     password VARCHAR(1024) NOT NULL
 *     );
 *
 * TODO:  Make sure to update the DSN to be the correct one for your
 * environment...
 *
 */

$authOptions = array (
    'dsn' => 'mysql://calendar:secret@localhost/calendar',
    'table' => 'users',
    'usernamecol' => 'user_id',
    'passwordcol' => 'password',
    'crypttype' => 'md5'
);

$a = new Auth("DB", $authOptions, 'showLogin');
$a->start();

if ($a->checkAuth()) {
    header('location:calendar.php');
}

?>
```

If the user isn't logged in, the Auth class calls the login callback, which is the showLogin() method. The showLogin() method uses HTML_Form to display the input boxes for the username and password, as well as a submit button. The login.php page will take you to the calendar.php page, which is covered last in this chapter. The following sections show you how to expose free and busy information, and then show you how to make a page that allows you to create new appointments and use Ajax to get free and busy information.

Exposing Free Information with Ajax

To use the HTML_AJAX package in the site to expose free and busy information, you first make a server page that will be used to generate the JavaScript that will be included as source in other pages. The newappointment.php page that was created in the last section includes a <script> tag that points to this file:

```
<script language="javascript" type="text/javascript"
    src="ajax_server.php?client=all"></script>
```

The page is simple, only having a few lines in it, which is kind of the point—using this package frees you from having to write all the code yourself (see Listing 6).

Listing 6. *ajax_server.php*

```php
<?php

require_once 'HTML/AJAX/Server.php';

$server = new HTML_AJAX_Server();
$server->handleRequest();

?>
```

The newappointment.php page must specify a URL from which to get free and busy information, and that URL will point to this file and pass along variables that specify the start and end dates (see Listing 7).

Listing 7. *freebusyinfo.php*

```php
<?php

require_once 'DB.php';

if (isset($_GET['start']) && isset($_GET['end'])) {

    /* This script checks to see if a given time spot for a given user is
     * already taken.  It exposes the results as a web service that can
     * be consumed by other applications.
     *
     * TODO:  Make sure to update your DSN
     *
     */
    $db =& DB::connect('mysql://calendar:secret@localhost/calendar');
```

```php
        if (PEAR::isError($db)) {
            die($db->getMessage());
        }

        try {

            $start_date = $_GET['start'];
            $end_date = $_GET['end'];

            // Once you have a valid DB object named $db...
            $statement = $db->prepare('select count(appointmentid) from appointments ' .
                    'where (? <= start_date AND ? >= end_date) ' .
                     ' OR (? >= start_date AND ? < end_date AND ? >= end_date) ' .
                      ' OR (? < start_date AND ? > start_date AND ? <= end_date)');

            $data = array($start_date, $end_date,
                $start_date, $start_date, $end_date,
                $start_date, $end_date, $end_date);

            $result = $db->execute($statement, $data);

            if (PEAR::isError($result)) {
                die($result->getMessage());
            }

            /* Check the result to see what we have now */

            $result->fetchInto($row);

            if ($row[0] > 0) {
                print "<span style=\"color:red\">You are <b>busy</b> ➥
                during this time!</span>";
            } else {
                print "You are <b>free</b> during this time!";
            }

            $db->freePrepared($statement);

        } catch (Exception $e) {
            /* TODO:  Print the error out here */
        }

        $db->disconnect();
    }

?>
```

This page doesn't use the appointments data object, mainly because the query is fairly complex and just as straightforward shown here in normal, everyday vanilla SQL. Also, for performance reasons, this page is just getting a count of the matching rows—it doesn't care about the detailed data. The page returns one of two different messages: You are busy during this time! if there are any appointments found given the timeframe, and You are free during this time! if there are zero appointments in the given timeframe. For simple free and busy information that will allow the newappointment.php form to check if the slot is already taken before allowing the user to submit the form, this page does just the trick.

Adding Appointments

Now that users can be added to the system and logged in, it would be useful to be able to create new appointments. The newappointment.php script does that function, using the Auth, DB_DataObject, and HTML_Form packages (see Listing 8). As in the other forms in this application, the HTML_Form package is used to display the input fields to the user.

Listing 8. *newappointment.php*

```php
<?php

include 'dataobjects.inc.php';

require_once 'Auth.php';
require_once 'DataObjects/Appointments.php';
require_once 'DB/DataObject.php';
/* require_once 'DB.php'; */
require_once 'HTML/Form.php';

function displayLoginMessage()
{
    print "You need to log in!  You can do that <a href=\"login.php\">here</a>.";
}

/**
 * Validates the form's data.
 */
function validate()
{
    /* Validate the date format and the date information here */

    return true;
}

/**
 * Processes the data in the form.
 */
```

```php
function process($a)
{

    /* Save the data to the database */
    try {

        $appt = DB_DataObject::Factory('appointments');

            if (PEAR::isError($appt)) {
             die($appt->getMessage());
        }

        if (isset($_POST['allday']) && $_POST['allday'] == 'on') {
            $appt->start_date = $_POST['date'] . ' 00:00:00';
            $appt->end_date = $_POST['date'] . ' 23:59:59';
            $appt->is_allday = 1;
        } else {
            $appt->start_date = $_POST['date'] . ' '. $_POST['start_time'];
            $appt->end_date = $_POST['date'] . ' '. $_POST['end_time'];
            $appt >is_allday = 0;
        }

        $appt->description = $_POST['description'];
        $appt->user_id = $a->getUsername();

        /* Now that the object is populated, this will actually put
         * it into the database. */
        $id = $appt->insert();

        /* Not doing anything with the ID here, but it could be logged.  See
         * the Addressbook project for examples of logging!
         */

    } catch (Exception $e) {
        print $e->getMessage();
    }

    header('location:calendar.php');
}

/**
 * Displays the form to the user
 */
function display()
{

    print <<<END
```

```
<!DOCTYPE html PUBLIC "-//W3C//DTD XHTML 1.0 Strict//EN"
    "http://www.w3.org/TR/xhtml1/DTD/xhtml1-strict.dtd">
<html xmlns="http://www.w3.org/1999/xhtml">
<head>
<title>Web Calendar Application - Create/Edit Appointment</title>
<style type="text/css">
    body { font-family:sans-serif;font-size:small; }
</style>
<script language="javascript" type="text/javascript"
    src="ajax_server.php?client=all"></script>
<script language="javascript" type="text/javascript">
function updateSels(chk) {
    if (chk.checked) {
        document.getElementById('selStartTime').selectedIndex = 0;
        document.getElementById('selEndTime').selectedIndex = 0;
        document.getElementById('selStartTime').disabled = true;
        document.getElementById('selEndTime').disabled = true;
        updateFreeBusy();
    } else {
        document.getElementById('selStartTime').disabled = false;
        document.getElementById('selEndTime').disabled = false;
    }
}
function updateFreeBusy() {
    /* Get the values of the dates and send them along on the URL */
    var d = document.getElementById('txtDate').value;
    var st = document.getElementById('selStartTime').value;
    var et = document.getElementById('selEndTime').value;
    var fb = document.getElementById('chkAllDay').checked;
    if (fb) {
        var qry = encodeURI("?start=" + d + " 00:00:00&end=" + d + " 23:59:59");
    } else {
        var qry = encodeURI("?start=" + d + " " + st + "&end=" + d + " " + et);
    }

    HTML_AJAX.replace('status', 'freebusyinfo.php' + qry);
    /* alert('freebusyinfo.php' + qry); */
    /* Check the result */
    var s = document.getElementById('status').innerHTML;

}
</script>
</head>
<body bgcolor="#FFFFFF" text="#000000"
    onload="updateSels(document.getElementById('chkAllDay'))">
END;
```

```
$times = array (
    '' => '', '24:00:00' => '12:00 AM', '00:30:00' => '12:30 AM',
    '01:00:00' => '1:00 AM', '01:30:00' => '1:30 AM',
    '02:00:00' => '2:00 AM', '02:30:00' => '2:30 AM',
    '03:00:00' => '3:00 AM', '03:30:00' => '3:30 AM',
    '04:00:00' => '4:00 AM', '04:30:00' => '4:30 AM',
    '05:00:00' => '5:00 AM', '05:30:00' => '5:30 AM',
    '06:00:00' => '6:00 AM', '06:30:00' => '6:30 AM',
    '07:00:00' => '7:00 AM', '07:30:00' => '7:30 AM',
    '08:00:00' => '8:00 AM', '08:30:00' => '8:30 AM',
    '09:00:00' => '9:00 AM', '09:30:00' => '9:30 AM',
    '10:00:00' => '10:00 AM', '10:30:00' => '10:30 AM',
    '11:00:00' => '11:00 AM', '11:30:00' => '11:30 AM',
    '12:00:00' => '12:00 PM', '12:30:00' => '12:30 PM',
    '13:00:00' => '1:00 PM', '13:30:00' => '1:30 PM',
    '14:00:00' => '2:00 PM', '14:30:00' => '2:30 PM',
    '15:00:00' => '3:00 PM', '15:30:00' => '3:30 PM',
    '16:00:00' => '4:00 PM', '16:30:00' => '4:30 PM',
    '17:00:00' => '5:00 PM', '17:30:00' => '5:30 PM',
    '18:00:00' => '6:00 PM', '18:30:00' => '6:30 PM',
    '19:00:00' => '7:00 PM', '19:30:00' => '7:30 PM',
    '20:00:00' => '8:00 PM', '20:30:00' => '8:30 PM',
    '21:00:00' => '9:00 PM', '21:30:00' => '9:30 PM',
    '22:00:00' => '10:00 PM', '22:30:00' => '10:30 PM',
    '23:00:00' => '11:00 PM', '23:30:00' => '11:30 PM'
    );

$form = new HTML_Form(htmlspecialchars($_SERVER['PHP_SELF']), 'post');
$form->addText('date', 'Appointment date:', null, 0, 0, "id=\"txtDate\"");
$form->addCheckbox('allday', 'All day event:', false, "id=\"chkAllDay\" " .
    "onclick=\"javascript:updateSels(this)\"");
$form->addSelect('start_time', 'Start time:', $times, null, 1, '',
    false, "id=\"selStartTime\"");
$form->addSelect('end_time', 'End time:', $times, null, 1, '',
    false, "id=\"selEndTime\" onchange=\"updateFreeBusy();\"");
$form->addText('description', 'Description:');
$form->addSubmit('submit', 'Save appointment', "id=\"btnSubmit\"");
$form->addReset('Reset');

$form->display();

    print <<<END
<span style="font-style:italic;font-size:small;">Make sure to
format the date like 'YYYY-MM-DD' so your database recognizes it.
You could always use the Date package to get the date
and format it in the way that your database understands!</span><br/>
<div id="status"></div>
```

```
</body>
</html>
END;

}

/* Authenticate the user
 *
 * TODO:  Make sure to update your DSN!
 */

$authOptions = array (
    'dsn' -> 'mysql://calendar:secret@localhost/calendar',
    'table' => 'users',
    'usernamecol' => 'user_id',
    'passwordcol' => 'password',
    'crypttype' => 'md5'
);

$a = new Auth("DB", $authOptions, 'displayLoginMessage');
$a->start();

if ($a->checkAuth()) {
    if ($_SERVER['REQUEST_METHOD'] == 'POST') {
        if (validate()) {
            process($a);
        } else {
            display();
        }
    } else {
        display();
    }
]

?>
```

The actual page is displayed to the user with code in the display() method. The validate() method contains any validation code that you should impose on the user, and the process() method does the actual work of using the objects to save the appointment information.

In the process() method, the DB_DataObject Factory() method is used to get a new instance of the DataObjects_Appointments class that's assigned to the variable $appt. After checking to make sure $appt isn't an error, the data from the form is put into the correct properties on the object. Finally, once the object has been fully populated, the insert() method is called to insert a new row into the appointments table. Because of the ease of use of the automagically generated data objects, the bulk of the code in this page is responsible for displaying the page instead of doing the processing.

A feature included on this page is the ability to get free and busy information concerning the appointment without the form being posted back to the server. This is because the form uses Ajax to call the freebusyinfo.php page in your application and get that information.

You'll notice the page includes another PHP file, dataobjects.inc.php. That page contains some setup that needs to be done any time you're using the DataObject classes, and because the code is the same it's easy to put into a single page and include it where it needs to be. The dataobjects.inc.php file is shown in Listing 9.

Listing 9. *dataobjects.inc.php*

```php
<?php
require_once 'PEAR.php';

// this  the code used to load and store DataObjects Configuration.
$options = &PEAR::getStaticProperty('DB_DataObject','options');

// the simple examples use parse_ini_file, which is fast and efficient.
// however you could as easily use wddx, xml or your own configuration array.

$config = parse_ini_file ➥
('C:\winnt\profiles\ngood\workspace\PEAR\project4\site.ini,TRUE);

// because PEAR::getstaticProperty was called with and & (get by reference)
// this will actually set the variable inside that method (a quasi-static variable)
$options = $config['DB_DataObject'];
?>
```

Drawing the Calendar

The most complex single page in the calendar is calendar.php, the PHP script that draws a calendar for the current user. Using PEAR packages such as Date and Date_Holidays, the page can be pretty smart when it comes to drawing each date on the correct weekday, just as the user would expect from a normal calendar (see Listing 10).

Listing 10. *calendar.php*

```
<!DOCTYPE html PUBLIC "-//W3C//DTD XHTML 1.0 Strict//EN"
    "http://www.w3.org/TR/xhtml1/DTD/xhtml1-strict.dtd">
<html xmlns="http://www.w3.org/1999/xhtml">
<head>
<title>Web Calendar Application - Main Calendar</title>
<style type="text/css">
    .holiday { color:gray;font-size:smaller }
    td.day { height:100px;vertical-align:top;padding-left:0.5em; }
    td.head { font-weight:bold; }
```

```
    td.weekend { width:10%; background-color:lightyellow; }
    td.weekday { width:14%; }
    td.weekend,td.weekday,td.appt,td.allday
        { border-style:solid;border-width:1px;border-color:gray; }
    td.appt { font-size:smaller; background-color:lightblue;padding-left:0.5em; }
    td.allday { font-size:smaller;background-color:lightgreen;
        padding-left:0.5em;height:4em; }
    body { font-family:sans-serif;font-size:small; }
</style>
</head>
<body bgcolor="#FFFFFF" text="#000000">
<?php

require_once 'Auth.php';
require_once 'DB.php';
require_once 'Date.php';
require_once 'Date/Holidays.php';
require_once 'HTML/Form.php';

function displayLoginMessage()
{
    print "To see your appointments you need to log in!  " .
            "You can do that <a href=\"login.php\">here</a>.";
}


function drawAppointment($row)
{
    if (! $row['is_allday']) {
        print("<td class=\"appt\">");
        $sd = new Date($row['start_date']);
        $ed = new Date($row['end_date']);
        print "<b>" . $sd->format("%I:%M %p") . " - " .
            $ed->format("%I:%M %p") . "</b> " . $row['description'];
    } else {
        print("<td class=\"allday\">");
        print $row['description'] . " <b>(All day)</b>";
    }

}


/* Check to see if the users are authenticated.  If they are not, draw
 * a nice link so they can go get themselves logged in.
 *
 * TODO:  Make sure to update the DSN!
 *
 */
```

```
$authOptions = array (
    'dsn' => 'mysql://calendar:secret@localhost/calendar',
    'table' => 'users',
    'usernamecol' => 'user_id',
    'passwordcol' => 'password',
    'crypttype' => 'md5'
);

$a = new Auth("DB", $authOptions, 'displayLoginMessage');
$a->start();

// if ($a->checkAuth()) {
if (true) {

    /* If the form has been posted back on itself, grab the dates
     * out of the drop-down boxes.  Otherwise, just use the current
     * month.
     */

    if ($_SERVER['REQUEST_METHOD'] == 'POST') {
        $date = new Date();
        $date->setDay('1');
        $date->setMonth($_POST['month']);
        $date->setYear($_POST['year']);
    } else {
        $date = new Date();
        $date->setDay('1');
    }

    print "<h1>" . $date->format("%B %Y") . " Calendar</h1>";

    $form = new HTML_Form(htmlspecialchars($_SERVER['PHP_SELF']), 'post');
    print $form->returnStart();
    $months = array (
        '01' => 'January',
        '02' => 'February',
        '03' => 'March',
        '04' => 'April',
        '05' => 'May',
        '06' => 'June',
        '07' => 'July',
        '08' => 'August',
        '09' => 'September',
        '10' => 'October',
        '11' => 'November',
        '12' => 'December'
    );
```

```php
$years = array (
    '2006' => '2006',
    '2007' => '2007',
    '2008' => '2008',
    '2009' => '2009',
    '2010' => '2010'
);
print "Go to:  ";
print $form->returnSelect('month', $months, $date->format('%m'), 1, '',
    false, "onchange=\"document.forms[0].submit();\"");
print $form->returnSelect('year', $years, $date->format('%Y'), 1, '',
    false, "onchange=\"document.forms[0].submit();\"");
print $form->returnEnd();
print "<br/>";
print "<table id=\"calendar\" summary=\"calendar\" " .
        "style=\"width:100%;border-style:solid;border-width:1px\">";
print "<tr>";
print "<td class=\"weekend head\">Sunday</td>";
print "<td class=\"weekday head\">Monday</td>";
print "<td class=\"weekday head\">Tuesday</td>";
print "<td class=\"weekday head\">Wednesday</td>";
print "<td class=\"weekday head\">Thursday</td>";
print "<td class=\"weekday head\">Friday</td>";
print "<td class=\"weekend head\">Saturday</td>";
print "</tr>";
print "";

$holidays = &Date_Holidays::factory('USA', $date->format('%Y'), 'en_EN');

$numWeeks = $date->getWeeksInMonth();
$startDow = $date->getDayOfWeek();

/* TODO:  Update the DSN */
$db =& DB::connect('mysql://calendar:secret@localhost/calendar');
if (PEAR::isError($db)) {
    die($db->getMessage());
}

try {

    $statement =
        $db->prepare('SELECT DAYOFMONTH(start_date) AS day, ' .
                'start_date, end_date, description, user_id, ' .
                'is_allday FROM appointments WHERE user_id = ? ' .
                'AND MONTH(start_date) = ? AND YEAR(start_date) = ? ' .
                'ORDER BY start_date ASC');
```

```php
$db->setFetchMode(DB_FETCHMODE_ASSOC);

$data = array($a->getUsername(), $date->getMonth(), $date->getYear());
/* Now we have a list of all of our appointments */
$appointments = $db->execute($statement, $data);

$appointments->fetchInto($row);

for ($pad = 0; $pad < $startDow; $pad++) {
    if ($pad == 0 || $pad == 6) {
        if ($pad == 0 ) {
            print '<tr><td class="weekend day"> </td>';
        } else {
            print '<td class="weekend day"> </td>';
        }
    }
    else
    {
        print '<td class="weekday day"> </td>';
    }
}

/* Now we should be at the first day */

$daysInMonth = $date->getDaysInMonth();
for ($day = 0; $day < $daysInMonth; $day++) {
    printf("<td class=\"%s\">",
        ($date->getDayOfWeek() == 6 || $date->getDayOfWeek() == 0) ?
            "weekend day" : "weekday day");
    print $date->format("%e");
    /* Is it a holiday? */
    if ($holidays->isHoliday($date)) {
        $holiday = $holidays->getHolidayForDate($date);
        print "<span class=\"holiday\">  (" .
            $holiday->getTitle() . ")</span>";
    }
    print "<br/>";

    /* Is there anything for this day in the appointment database? */
    if ($row['day'] == $date->getDay()) {
        print "<table width=\"95%\"><tr>";
        /* If there is something that matches, display it and
         * keep going until something doesn't match anymore
         */
        drawAppointment($row);
```

```
                    /* Now get the next one to make sure that it may match */
                    while (($appointments->fetchInto($row)) && ($row['day'] == ➥
                    $date->getDay()))
                    {
                        print "</td></tr><tr>";
                        drawAppointment($row);
                    }
                    print "</td></tr></table>";
                }

                /* Close out the day's cell */
                print("</td>");
                if ($date->getDayOfWeek() == 6) print "</tr><tr>";
                $date = $date->getNextDay();
            }

            for ($day = $date->getDayOfWeek(); $day < 7; $day++) {
                if ($day == 0 || $day == 6) {
                    print '<td class="weekend day"> </td>';
                } else {
                    print '<td class="weekday day"> </td>';
                }
            }

        print "</table>";

        } catch (Exception $e) {
            /* Print the details of the exception out to the screen for now */
            print $e->getMessage();
        }
        $db->freePrepared($statement);
        $db->disconnect();
    }

?>


</body>
</html>
```

To start drawing the calendar, the first day of the month is always retrieved at the beginning. This is easily accomplished by getting a new Date object and setting the day to 1 using the setDay() method.

After doing some display work, such as preselecting the current month and year from the select boxes and displaying them in the heading, the next task is to get the list of holidays so the page can check each day as it's drawn to see if it's a holiday. The holidays here are the US holidays for the en_EN locale, which can be something that's easily taken out of the script and stored in user preferences with relatively little effort by using another PEAR package (see the Auth_PrefManager chapter).

The script gets the appointment information for the currently logged-in user for the current month only, just to cut down on how much information is retrieved and to make it easier to draw the appointments on the calendar. As each page is being drawn, the isHoliday() method is called to see if the day is a holiday. If it is, more information about the holiday is retrieved so the name can be displayed on the day. Then the results from the database are checked to see if there are any appointments for the current day.

Because the page is reading forward through the list of appointments, it's important that they are sorted by start_time. If they aren't, the page will step right over appointments as the days are drawn but won't go back to pick any earlier appointments up.

The calendar has two drop-down boxes supplied by HTML_Form, but they're drawn differently than the other forms in this application. Here, the methods simply return the input tags as strings so they can be printed by your code instead of inserted into a table. With this finer-grained control, the two select boxes for month and year are drawn in a fashion that's a little more presentable on the page.

Using just a few PEAR packages, this calendar application became functional to the point of adding new appointments and displaying them, per user, including the ability to get free and busy information with Ajax. The use of PEAR packages has great time and stability advantages over writing all the code from scratch.

Index

Find it faster at http://superindex.apress.com

You Need the Companion eBook

Your purchase of this book entitles you to buy the companion PDF-version eBook for only $10. Take the weightless companion with you anywhere.

We believe this Apress title will prove so indispensable that you'll want to carry it with you everywhere, which is why we are offering the companion eBook (in PDF format) for $10 to customers who purchase this book now. Convenient and fully searchable, the PDF version of any content-rich, page-heavy Apress book makes a valuable addition to your programming library. You can easily find and copy code—or perform examples by quickly toggling between instructions and the application. Even simultaneously tackling a donut, diet soda, and complex code becomes simplified with hands-free eBooks!

Once you purchase your book, getting the $10 companion eBook is simple:

❶ Visit **www.apress.com/promo/tendollars/**.

❷ Complete a basic registration form to receive a randomly generated question about this title.

❸ Answer the question correctly in 60 seconds, and you will receive a promotional code to redeem for the $10.00 eBook.

2560 Ninth Street • Suite 219 • Berkeley, CA 94710

eBookshop

THE EXPERT'S VOICE™

Offer valid through 5/07.